Criminals, Nazis, and Islamists

Criminals, Nazis, and Islamists

Competition for Power in Former Soviet Union Prisons

VERA MIRONOVA

OXFORD
UNIVERSITY PRESS

Oxford University Press is a department of the University of Oxford. It furthers the University's objective of excellence in research, scholarship, and education by publishing worldwide. Oxford is a registered trade mark of Oxford University Press in the UK and certain other countries.

Published in the United States of America by Oxford University Press
198 Madison Avenue, New York, NY 10016, United States of America.

Library of Congress Cataloging-in-Publication Data
Names: Mironova, V. G. (Vera Grigor'evna), author.
Title: Criminals, Nazis, and Islamists : competition for power in former
Soviet Union prisons / Vera Mironova.
Description: New York, NY : Oxford University Press, [2023] |
Includes bibliographical references and index.
Identifiers: LCCN 2023003790 (print) | LCCN 2023003791 (ebook) |
ISBN 9780197645666 (paperback) | ISBN 9780197645659 (hardback) |
ISBN 9780197645680 (epub) | ISBN 9780197645697
Subjects: LCSH: Prisoners—Former Soviet republics—Social conditions. |
Prisons—Former Soviet republics. | Prison gangs—Former Soviet republics.
Classification: LCC HV9712 .M57 2023 (print) | LCC HV9712 (ebook) |
DDC 365/.91717—dc23/eng/20230302
LC record available at https://lccn.loc.gov/2023003790
LC ebook record available at https://lccn.loc.gov/2023003791

DOI: 10.1093/oso/9780197645659.001.0001

Paperback printed by Marquis Book Printing, Canada
Hardback printed by Bridgeport National Bindery, Inc., United States of America

Contents

Preface xi

Introduction: Prison's Closed Society 1
- Why Study Prisons in the Former Soviet Union? 2
- Contribution to the Literature 3
- Argument 5
- Book Plan 6
- Gathering Evidence 7
- Scope of the Book 9

1. Theory 11
- Prison Criminal Leadership 11
- Prison Caste System 13
  - Lower-Caste Purpose 15
- Infrastructure 16
  - Use of Money and Goods 17
  - Communication 18
- Relations with Prison Authorities 19
  - Why Inmates Work with Authorities 19
  - Working Against Authorities 20
- Replacing Criminal Leadership 22
  - Step One: Neutralize Leadership 22
  - Step Two: Show of Power 22
  - Step Three: New Rules 23
- Prison Criminal Leadership Challenges 24
  - Prison Reform Policies Cause Challenges 24
  - Corruption of Criminal Leadership 25
- Competition for Power 25
  - Why Inmates Join *Jamaats* 27
- Gaining and Losing Power 28
- Conclusion 30

2. History of the *Vory* Criminal Organization 31
- Gulag 35
  - Relations with Prison Authorities 36
  - Relations with Inmates 37
- World War II 40
- Post–World War II 42

Prison State-Building 45
Vory Criminal Ideology 47
Conclusion 48

3. Prison Criminal Leadership 50
Criminal Family Leadership 50
Criminal Family Government 52
Caste System 55
Upper Castes 56
Subcastes 60

4. Lower Class of Inmates 64
Purpose 64
Sherst' Caste 66
Types of *Sherst'* 66
Degraded Caste 68
Evolution of Ideological Rules 71
Different Approaches to *Ponyatiya* 75
Minimum-Security Prisons 76
Medium-Security Prisons 77
Maximum-Security Prisons 77
Right to Justice 79
Conclusion 81

5. Prison Criminal Law Enforcement 83
Crime Prevention 84
Punishment 85
New Inmates 87
Ignorant Inmates 87
Trials 88
Evidence 89
Philosophy behind Law Enforcement 92
Problems with Law Enforcement 94
Conclusion 96

6. Prison Criminal Economy 98
Criminal Budget 98
Donations 99
Exports and Imports 101
Exports 101
Imports 101
Trade 102
Gambling 104
Debt Collection 108

Prison Criminal Government Expenses 109
Basic Necessities 109
Bribes 109
Prison Repair and Construction Work 109
Welfare 110
Celebrations 110
Rewards for Inmates 110
Conclusion 111

7. Everyday Life Behind Bars 112
Communication 112
Ropes 112
Plumbing and Ventilation 113
Holes in Walls 113
Purposes for Communication 115
Information from a *Vor* 115
Culture 117
Religion 117
Views on Women 118
Language 118
Names 120
Music 121
Tattoos 122
Traditions 124
Conclusion 126

8. Conflict with Prison Authorities: Getting Power 127
From Red 128
Prison Administration and Guards 129
Activisty 131
To Black 133
Dealing with Guards and *Activisty* 134
Defrosting a Prison 138
Conclusion 143

9. Conflict with Prison Authorities: Losing Power 145
From Black 145
Informants 147
To Red 149
Step One: Neutralize Leaders 149
Step Two: Intimidate General Population 152
Step Three: The Final Freeze 153
Gray Prisons 158
Conclusion 160

10. Problems within the *Vory* Criminal Organization 162
Fall of the Soviet Union 162
More Benefits 164
Self- versus Inmate-Interest 165
Infighting 166
Conflicts between Generations 166
Conflicts between *Vory* 167
Ethnic Conflicts 169
Prison Regulation Changes 170
Better Treatment of Inmates 170
Parole 172
Separation of First-Timers 172
Longer Sentences 174
Relative Trust of Judicial System 174
Oversight of Prisons 174
Corruption of Courts 175
Changes within the *Vory* Prison System 175
Commercialization 175
Mixing Castes 176
Punishment 176
Cooperation with Prison Authorities 177
Outdated Criminal Traditions 177
Quality of Prison Criminal Leadership 178
Security 180
Fixing the Problem 181
Machnovshina 182
Conclusion 184

11. Prison Islamist *Jamaats* 185
Original Leadership 185
Internal Organization 189
Designations 189
Jamaat Rules 190
Interactions with the Enemy 191
Ideological Rules 193
Economy 196
Culture 197
Islamist Family 198
Language 198
Names 199
Appearance 199
Heroes 200
Music 200

Activities 201
Celebrations 201
Competition 202
Official Islam 202
Official Imams 202
Traditional Islam 203
Other Islamist Groups 203
Conclusion 205

12. Islamist *Jamaat* Rise to Power 206
Phase One: A Silent Insurgency 206
Islamist Perspective 206
Criminal World Perspective 211
Outside Perspectives 213
Phase Two: A Parallel Structure 213
Islamist Perspective 213
Personal Benefits 214
New Norms and Customs 215
Reputation 215
Protection 216
Criminal World Perspective 219
Outside Perspectives 220
Conclusion 222

13. *Jamaat* Conflict with the Criminal Organization 223
Phase Three: A Shift of Power 223
Islamist Perspective 223
Criminal World Perspective 227
Outside Perspectives 229
Phase Four: War 230
Jamaat Inmate Perspective 231
Criminal Inmate Perspective 232
The Clash 232
Conclusion 237

14. *Vory* Criminal Organization Resurgence 239
Rise to Power 239
Jamaat Membership 241
Relations with the Criminal Hierarchy 244
Corruption in the *Jamaat* 246
Running a *Jamaat* from a Distance 248
New Leadership 251
De-*jamaat*ization 252
Coexistence 256

15. Neo-Nazis behind Bars 262
Culture 263
Language 263
Music 263
Dress Code 264
Emphasis on the Non-Material 264
Religion 264
Gender 265
Broader Community 265
Whites in Prison 265
Upper Caste 266
Lower Caste 266
Personal Indicators 267
Building a (White) Parallel Structure 273
Obstacles 274
Changing Perception 277
Advancement in *Vory* Criminal Family 277
Education 277
Alliances 278
Conclusion 279

Conclusion 280
Deradicalizing Prisons 281

Notes 287
Bibliography 307
Index 311

Preface

In a small town in Central Asia, a major hub for drug traffic and jihadist activities, two cars leave the main market. One car is a very expensive SUV with tinted windows. Inside, it is filled with huge quantities of dry goods and produce—dozens of boxes of spaghetti, twenty-five pounds of tea and coffee, numerous sacks of potatoes, and every cigarette the market had to sell. The driver, Rustem, is a well-known member of the underground criminal world in the region, and many locals are afraid to even speak to him. I sit in the passenger's seat. Behind the SUV is the second car, a beat-up old Soviet-times taxi. It has a sheep in the trunk. Not happy with her fate, the sheep bleats nonstop and attracts a lot of attention at traffic lights. The destination of this strange convoy is a local jail.

The two vehicles park in allocated spaces, next to the police cars and those of the prison guards in front of the prison gate. There, people in uniform smoke and chat and relax on benches. In front of them stands a long line of poverty-stricken females with crying kids, nervously repackaging bread and sweets they have brought for their loved ones behind bars. From time to time as the women pass through, arguments between females and prison guards erupt about what is and is not allowed inside. But because females have absolutely no say in it, they eventually give up and agree with the guards, although they keep complaining about it. The young guys in uniforms visibly enjoy using their power in this way.

Rustem (and me with him) cut in line and enter the prison guards' office. Such behavior does not raise protest from either of the women, who had already spent hours standing there in the hot sun, nor the guards inside. Those in line are too afraid to say anything, and those behind the metal door are used to it. Rustem notifies prison guards that we have boxes that need to be moved from the car into the prison.

Guard: Can you bring it here to the room please?
Rustem: Sure, but we also have a sheep, and it will not pass through your revolving metal doors.
Guard: What do you mean, *a sheep*? Like a live animal?
Rustem: Yes. It's waiting in the taxi.

The prison guards are confused, but instead of asking us if we had lost our minds and maybe even arresting us (which is the reaction I would expect), they very politely ask us to go to the butcher, kill the sheep, and return with meat.

This answer does not satisfy Rustem, who clearly does not want to waste more time dealing with the issue. He goes outside and calls the person in charge of the prison. Soon, the prison guards come looking for us and say everything was sorted out and that our cars were welcome inside, and they show us the gates.

As we sit in the car ready to move in, we notice the gates are blocked by an expensive (but less expensive than ours) parked vehicle. Before we could begin thinking of how to proceed, we see someone running from the internal security building towards us, holding car keys in his hands. It is the director of the jail.

Rustem lowers his window slightly, and the jail director greets him. "I heard you brought a sheep. I guess there will be a party tonight," he smiles, visibly trying to be nice. Rustem nods in response. The director moves out of the way, the gates open and we enter.

Once inside, we are met by a very well-dressed inmate holding not one, but three smartphones in his hands. He is accompanied by four inmates: two who act as bodyguards and two inmates who are something like servants.

"This is the person in charge of the prison I talked to on the phone," says Rustem, and he introduces him to me.

It takes a quarter of an hour for the two servant inmates to unload the boxes and the sheep, which is still bleating so loudly that it was definitely heard in all law-enforcement offices around. Our vehicles were not searched. Neither were we or the boxes, and there was not a prison guard in sight.

For a person like me who lives in the United States, the whole situation is confusing. How could security be so lax in a place that, by definition, is supposed to be one of the most secured places in the country? Is anyone controlling this place, and if yes, who?

We had not even left the parking area when Rustem got a phone call from an inmate who served as the accountant for the mafia-like organization in prison. The inmate asks him to list the quantities and prices of everything we have just delivered, along with other details. After everything is recorded, the person thanks Rustem for the goods, but instead of the regular Russian reply "It is my pleasure," Rustem replies with a strange expression that I, a native Russian speaker, have never heard before and that could be translated as "From the heart to the heart."

Right after that, another person calls and asks the exact same questions about quantities and amounts, and it followed by the same expression of gratitude and uncommon reply. Rustem explains, "Since it was a big delivery, it had to be recorded by the criminal leadership inside the prison, then double-checked by the criminal leadership of the whole town. They need to make sure that everything is accounted for, and exactly who contributed what because everyone's help is appreciated."

It seems like this organization has not only its own language and culture, but also a very effective bureaucracy. I even catch myself wishing that the country where the prison was located was as careful with its budget as this mafia was with theirs.

But running an organization effectively and having everything under such tight control are not easy tasks. While we are driving, Rustem's phone rings non-stop. From time to time, he turns to me and complains, "Why are people so dumb that they are not able to figure out things themselves?"

Then a call about an issue comes that is important enough for Rustem to take care of personally. While still on the phone, he turns the car around and, because leaving me on the highway is not an option, takes me along. We arrive at a restaurant often frequented by the mafia in town. Two people are already waiting for him. One of them is an ex-director of the prison we had just been to, while the other is a regional criminal leader. Although the three speak in their native language, from time to time—when the topic is not so sensitive—they switch to Russian out of politeness for me.

It seems a mutual friend had just been arrested and imprisoned in another town, and they—representing both law enforcement and the mafia—were trying to figure out how to help him. The more I listen, the more and more it seems to me, at least in relations to prison matters, the two are, in fact, on one side.

I was glad most of the discussion was carried on in a language I did not understand since its legality was questionable at best. But I did want to take the opportunity to ask them about someone I had interviewed in the past, but who had since been arrested and imprisoned in the country.

Criminal leader: Was he an ex-ISIS foreign fighter? And which prison is he in now, do you think?

Me: Yes, he fought in Iraq and Syria, and I think he is in prison #N. I just want to check if he's doing okay.

My two interlocutors pause for a minute, trying to remember details about this particular prison. Then the mafia guy continues.

Criminal leader: I don't know the contacts in this prison off top of my head since it is not our prison. Those are Islamists. We have to find the phone number of their person in charge—an amir. But I would not worry about him. He is an ISIS foreign fighter with a good fighting track record, so if he is also good at talking to people, I would not be surprised if he himself is an amir of the prison by now.

*Amir*s in prison? Suddenly, prison politics had just gotten more complicated. So, it was not just prison authorities and mafia anymore potentially controlling prisons, but also Islamists, and I wondered how it all worked between the three sides in a closed territory surrounded by high prison walls.

Introduction

Prison's Closed Society

One of the most significant works of Soviet literature is *Gulag Archipelago*, by Nobel Laureate Alexander Solzhenitsyn. It is an autobiography of his experience as a political prisoner in Stalin's infamous Gulag. The title of this landmark work refers to prison camps as islands separated from the mainland society. And as on an island, or in any other closed society, inhabitants develop relationships, establish rules and norms, and even adhere to unique culture and traditions. These prison societies have become a fusion of inmate ideologies that affect life both inside and outside of prison walls.

On the other side, as in any society, conflicts inside prison are unavoidable and occur on different levels including conflicts between individual inmates, conflicts between groups of inmates, and conflicts between inmates and prison authorities.

These dynamics give us an opportunity to study social and political processes in the closed environment of prisons. In particular in this book, I look at the conflicts and cooperation between inmates in male prisons in the former Soviet Union. I chose these prisons to illustrate my theory for several reasons.

Since the 1920s, one criminal gang known as *Vory v zakone* (Thieves in Law) has retained total control within most post-Soviet prisons. This expansive, ninety-year timeframe makes it possible to trace the origins and development of the internal organization, rules, norms, and unique criminal ideology of this prison-born system. Their longevity has spanned major governmental upheavals (including the death of Stalin and the dissolution of USSR), which allows a comprehensive view of internal changes adopted because of the outside pressure of shifting government and penal system policies. Finally, beginning in the 1990s, members of radical ideological groups such as Islamists and neo-Nazis began to challenge *vory* norms behind bars with their own goals and systems of ideas. This more recent change has become a serious threat to the monopoly of one of the world's oldest prison criminal organizations. And this clash of different ideologies on one side and mundane conflict for power on the other is still ongoing, reflecting on life even outside of prison.

For ordinary people, this secret world is hard to understand and even harder to get a glimpse of. So in this book, I want to not only shed light on the

Criminals, Nazis, and Islamists. Vera Mironova, Oxford University Press. © Oxford University Press 2023.
DOI: 10.1093/oso/9780197645659.003.0001

clandestine life behind bars, but also use it to illustrate the social and political processes in closed societies by studying the dynamic relations between inmates' self-organization and outside pressure of prison authorities, and the competition for scarce resources and political leadership among the incarcerated population.

Why Study Prisons in the Former Soviet Union?

In addition to prisons being interesting societies with their own internal processes and dynamics, understanding what is going on behind prison gates is crucial for policy makers.

From organized crime to radical extremism, almost all illegal activities pass through prison systems like light through a prism, and it colors the entirety of the criminal underworld. Prison gives inmates time to rest in a relatively safe place, develop new connections, and study and plan for the future. As a result, it is virtually impossible to design effective policies to combat crime or extremism without understanding the internal dynamics of the prisons.

And former Soviet Union prisons are central to most global criminal activities, partially because of the total number of people incarcerated there. According to the Institute for Criminal Policy Research, there are currently 10.35 million incarcerated people around the world. Russia alone is in third place for their number of inmates, and all of the former Soviet Union countries combined could be second only to the United States. The global influence of these prisons is also because they are the least government-controlled (as opposed to inmate-controlled) among the top five countries with the highest prison populations, making post-Soviet states fertile ground for development and export of illegal activities.

In terms of the geographic reach, although these prisons are in former Soviet Union countries, issues originating there already currently reach much further. For example, such ex-USSR countries as Latvia, Lithuania, and Estonia are themselves members of the European Union, and prisons in former Soviet Central Asia often house inmates from Afghanistan and Pakistan. Even prisons in distant Middle Eastern Israel and Mediterranean Greece have a disproportionally large number of inmates from former Soviet Union who brought their traditions with them.

Also, for a long time, the *vory*, a product of Russian prisons, has been a major headache for European law enforcement, and in 2017, a dozen ex-USSR *vory* leaders were even placed on the US sanctions list. According to the US Department of Treasury, the *vory* organization has grown into a vast criminal network that has spread throughout the former Soviet Union, Europe, and the

United States, and engages in a variety of crimes such as money laundering, extortion, bribery, and robbery.

Many Russian-speaking ISIS foreign fighters (who made up the second largest contingent of ISIS foreign fighters after Arabic speakers) also had prison experience previous to going to Syria and Iraq. Even Umar al-Shishani, top Islamic State's military leader, was radicalized in a Georgian prison where he was doing time for illegal weapons possession. And some Russian-language Islamic State recruitment videos used such heavy prison slang that they were difficult for a person with no prison background to even understand.

Now the fall of ISIS has only increased the number of Islamists behind bars in post-Soviet Union countries where they have sanctioned time to spread propaganda, coordinate future plans, orchestrate operations in other countries, and even develop technical equipment. But their activities among themselves are only a small part of the problem. While in prison, these inmates may also recruit others who are serving sentences for non-ideological crimes. And if what happened in the prisons before ISIS's rise is any guide, the consequences will be significant.

Contribution to the Literature

With this book, my academic goal is threefold. First, I want to contribute to the literature on the internal politics of prisons.

Organized crime has always been of interest to criminologists studying ways to predict and deter crime, but it is only recently that crime's underbelly has attracted the attention of economists and political scientists. Their work shed light on the Mafia's internal organization in different countries including Italy (Gambetta 1993), Russia (Varese 2001), Brazil (Arias 200), China (Wang 2017), and transnational criminal organizations (Varese 2011). But despite prisons being an integral, if not crucial, part of the Mafia's overall structure (basically all of its members are incarcerated at some point), the scholarly understanding of the organization's processes going on behind bars is still limited.

Recent literature on this topic has been mostly focused on internal inmates' self-governance (Sykes 1958; Skarbek 2010, 2011, 2016), looking at individual cases of prisons and gangs through an ethnographic lens (Varella 1999; Owen 1998; Kaminski 2004; Pickenpaugh 2013; Biondi 2016; Darke 2018), and a comparative prospective of prisons (Skarbek 2012, 2014, 2019). These are important fundamental insights, but they are largely missing a time dimension. So in this book, I plan to apply how the historical development of rules and norms govern an inmate's everyday life.

Also other aspects of prison life, beyond self-governance, attract much less scholarly attention (see Lessing and Denyer Willis [2019] on business behind bars; Trammell [2012] on internal law enforcement; Crewe [2009] on social life and Gambetta [2009] on criminal communication). So to have a complete picture of the workings of prison society, I plan to move this line of research further and study other aspects of life in prison, from internal illegal economy through public goods provision behind bars to prison culture (including music and art).

Finally, because the majority of previous studies look at a static picture of prisons in a particular time frame, the relationship dynamics between inmates and prison guards and between different groups of inmates over a period of time need to be explored. So in this project, I plan to look at those dynamics through the lens of conflict research. That will allow me to understand under what conditions peaceful coexistence turns into open hostility (that often results in real causalities). It will also help me trace conflict processes and study how conflicts are resolved either through peaceful negotiations or the decisive victory of one group over the other.

Second, I speak to terrorism research. On one side, while there is an expanding literature on the recruitment of particular demographics such as females and children (Cook 2018; Vale 2019; Bloom 2019) and migrants (Bove and Bohmelt 2020), I will look at the recruitment of prison inmates. And on the other side, while scholars of terrorism are looking at fighters' motivation for joining and their behavior on the battlefield (Hegghammer 2010; Malet 2013; Bakke 2014; Mironova 2019), their behavior after they are forcefully demobilized and imprisoned is still understudied. This is also a gap I plan to fill with my book.

And finally, I want to contribute to a broader debate on ideologies (Kramer 1999; Blaydes and Rubin 2008; Sanin and Wood 2014) and the lifespan of ideological movements and societies (Kuran 2004; Kuran 2011; Davenport 2015). Using the closed environment of prisons, where inmate behavior is, by definition, highly visible and constantly monitored, I address individual movement from one ideological organization to another. Radicalization and de-radicalization studies are interested in how people active in one ideological organization turn to another one, but often the nature of data used does not allow for a clear observation. Prisons, on the other side, offer such opportunity, providing microcosm conditions. So by looking at inmates shifting between communism, *vory* criminal ideology, Islamism, and neo-Nazism inside former Soviet Union prisons, I am able to see when and under what conditions individuals voluntarily make the choice to change the ideological organization they belong to and when and why some ideological movements increase in popularity while others decrease.[1]

Argument

To ensure their own survival, prison internal leadership's goal is to make inmate life behind bars as comfortable as possible taking into account restrictions imposed on them by their inmate status. To be able to achieve that, first and foremost, an inmate body has to be united. As a result, their incarcerated life is governed by a very strict set of rules enforced by their own internal leadership. That allows leaders to not only reduce conflicts inside the prison population, but to also have bargaining power vis-a-vis prison authorities (similar to that of labor unions in relation to business owners).

But to do their job effectively, prison internal leadership has to have enforcement tools for inmates who violate those rules. And compared to conventional societies, they have much fewer tools at their disposal. For example, they could not imprison anyone like regular law enforcement could.

So to increase the set of punishment tools prison leadership can use, in addition to regular beatings and killings, they established a caste system. Having low-level castes allows them to separate those who are causing trouble to the rest of the prison population (and leadership) and to have people who do the dirtiest jobs, like cleaning toilets. It also works as a deterrent—no one wants to end up in the lowest caste, especially because it is impossible for an inmate to rise up from there.

Since a caste system is something not widely used, an explanation for such government structure had to be provided by prison leadership. And the necessity of the caste system, along with some other internal prison rules, was explained using an artificial *vory* criminal philosophy. And having such ideological explanations to rules also allowed criminal leadership to legitimize some rules that are in place solely to increase their own authority and power.

But when the group governance becomes less effective, and inmates are not satisfied with its qualities, they start looking for alternatives. As in any other society, some inmates want to change that system and themselves take a leadership position. But because there is no way for them to change it within that current social system, they turn to what is called a radical solution and try to change the whole social order. And to legitimately declare that their proposed social order is better than the one currently in place, they choose a different ideology to base their claims on.

In the case of prisons in the former Soviet Union, the opposition group that went against *vory* criminal organization leadership in prisons based their legitimacy on Islamist ideology. In particular they claimed that internal prison rules should be based on their interpretation of Islam instead of criminal rules, and that those in charge should be religious instead of criminal. In substance, Islamist leadership proposed a set of rules that were only a little different from those of *vory*, but they had different names and ideological explanations for their necessity.

To increase in manpower, the Islamists started recruiting, mainly targeting those who feel underprivileged and discriminated against, like members of the low caste. And it is not important if those recruited are in an underprivileged position rightfully or not, as long as they are dissatisfied. Such status gives them the desire to disregard rules that currently guide the society, and joining a different group offers them exactly this.

And such competition for manpower between two groups not only caused internal conflicts that sometimes resulted in real casualties, but it also made the prison population much weaker in front of prison authorities.

Book Plan

Following the introduction and theory, in the first part of the project, I talk about the *vory* criminal organization. In Chapter 2, I start with the history of the Soviet Union prison society with its unique rules and norms. I trace the development of the inmates' self-organization behind bars, starting with the October Revolution of 1917 through Stalin's Gulag system and WWI to present. In particular, I show how the *vory* criminal organization managed to secure a monopoly in governing the Soviet Union criminal world both in and outside of prisons and how their own ideology helped them achieve that.

In Chapters 3 and 4, I talk about the *vory* criminal organization enforced prison caste system, which helps group leadership both stay in power and govern more effectively. Not only does this divide-and-conquer strategy prevent inmates from organizing against *vory* leadership, having different castes with different social statuses doing different jobs allows leadership to keep their biggest support group happy because they are on top of the social hierarchy. I also show how, with time, the group's ideologization changed the caste system and made the group vulnerable to inside and outside enemies.

Since the *vory* criminal organization oversees most of the former Soviet states' inmate population, they have to govern. So first, in Chapter 5, I explain how they ensure law and order for their territory and talk about a special set of rules and norms called *ponyatiya* (understandings), which guide life in prison. These rules dictate inmate relations with prison authorities, ensure peaceful coexistence and conflict resolution mechanisms, and also deter potential challengers to *vory* rule.

Then, like the government of any legitimate country, the *vory* criminal organization is in charge of running the prison's economy and providing social security and public goods for their citizens. So in Chapter 6, I discuss the *vory* prison budget and tax system, and in Chapter 7, the provision of crucial prison-wide public services like communication and even entertainment.

In prison, like everywhere else, rules are defined by those in charge. So in the second part of the book, I discuss the struggle for self-governance of inmates (headed by the *vory* criminal organization) against prison authorities, and what role *vory* criminal ideology plays in this battle. I explore the circumstances under which prisons become either *black* and are controlled by the *vory* criminal organization (Chapter 8), or *red* and inmates live under prison guards' dictatorship (Chapter 9). I will show that while strict *vory* criminal ideology helps the group take power away from prison authorities, when the group is in an established position, its ideology becomes its weakness and a weapon in the hands of prison guards.

In the third part of the book, I talk about the *vory* criminal organization's struggle with internal challengers and what role their rules play in it. In particular, I discuss how the *vory* criminal organization, after losing its main enemy after the fall of Soviet Union, became weaker and its monopoly on the internal government of the prisons was challenged by those in the lower class of the prison criminal society.

I start with recent internal problems within the *vory* criminal organization (Chapter 10). Then, to answer the question of who challenged their rule behind bars, I turn the conversation to their competitors—Islamist *jamaats*. In particular in Chapter 11, I talk about the jamaats' internal organization, rules and norms that guide their behavior, and the ideology they employ to legitimize their actions. Then, in Chapter 12, I discuss their rise to power and the tactics they use to exploit the *vory* criminal organization internal problems. In Chapter 13, I look at prisons where Islamist jamaats were experiencing internal problems, and in Chapter 14, how the *vory* criminal organization was able to exploit this situation to regain power.

Since Islamists are not the only inmates behind bars that have their own ideology and desire for power, Chapter 15 will explore the position of neo-Nazis among the general prison population and explain why they, when compared to Islamists, are not able to establish their own rule inside prisons, and, in some cases, even have to turn to Islamist jamaats for protection from the *vory* criminal organization.

I conclude with policy implications for prisons in the former Soviet Union and other regions.

Gathering Evidence

I start with looking at prisons in Czarist Russia times. Many famous Russian writers like Dostoyevsky, who had done time in the prisons, and Chekhov, who had visited those prisons, wrote about their observations, which provided me with detailed descriptions of those remote places.

Then, to understand the history of the Soviet Union prison system and its internal governance, I relied on Gulag Museum documents, and law enforcement and international historical society "memorial" archives. Also, many prominent residents of the Soviet Union went through those prison camps, including poets Osip Mandelstam, Vladimir Mayakovsky, and Joseph Brodsky; and writers Daniil Kharms, Alexander Solzhenitsyn, and Varlam Shalamov, among numerous others. Many of these men wrote memoirs describing their life behind bars, which provided a historical prospective on the development of the internal organization and culture within those prisons. Many other, less famous former Gulag inmates also left us first-hand accounts of their experiences.

To obtain data on the more current status of prison life, I added witness interviews to my archival work. In particular, using snowball sampling, I conducted hundreds of interviews with current and former inmates of prisons in every post-Soviet country, except Turkmenistan.[2] Since I am looking only on internal organization of male prisons, all my respondents are men who served their sentences in adult prisons. Also trying to capture different time periods, I interviewed people who were serving their sentences in different times. My oldest respondent was an eighty-three-year-old former inmate who served his first sentence in the 1950s, and my youngest respondents are still behind bars.

In an effort to obtain as representative a selection as possible, in addition to regular regional prisons I interviewed former inmates of notorious prisons like Jaslik in Uzbekistan—which, until it was closed in 2019, was off limits to human rights organizations and the press—and prisons in Tajikistan that have recently experienced bloody riots led by members of ISIS. Also, although it is a very narrow group, I also interviewed former inmates who served their sentences in special prisons for former members of law enforcement.[3]

Finally I developed rapport with several inmates on the frontline of the internal war between the *vory* criminal organization and Islamists, and followed developments in their prisons in real time for more than a year to minimize the known biases associated with retrospective interviews. By construction, serving prison sentence is a very boring time, so many inmates were happy to be able to talk to a researcher about their everyday life.

The cumulative prison time of my respondents exceeds several hundred years, and their charges include anti-government opposition, financial crimes, robbery and theft, forgery, drug trafficking, murder, assassination, arson, terrorism, extremism, rape, and child molestation. And while some of them are regular inmates, others occupy high positions within *vory*, Islamist, or neo-Nazi groups. The inmates also vary on their approach to prison life. Many try to quietly serve their sentences in hopes of early release while others lead hunger strikes and riots and are proud to spend the majority of their life behind bars.[4] For this book I was also able to interview a famous Russian *Vor* Alexandr Sever, a rare luck for the researcher since according their rules it is not allowed for *Vor* to talk to journalists or researchers.

Because prison is such a diverse place, my respondents were also of different social backgrounds. For example, I interviewed two former prison mates. One had been sentenced for bombing a church and a train before he had even finished high school and who now lives with his mother in a one-bedroom rented apartment in a small city near Moscow. The other was formerly the richest person in Russia, Mikhail Khodorkovsky, whom I interviewed in his office in the center of London. Having such a broad spectrum of respondents allows me to also look at prison from the prospective of different actors.

With many respondents I developed long relations and talked to them for dozens of hours in total to make it as comfortable as possible for them to discuss particular topics, especially those related to the male sex and rape so widespread in prisons. It was probably the hardest part of the fieldwork for me as a young female from an academic background talking with sometimes much older males who often belong to the lowest class of society. Not to make them feel uncultured and vulgar talking about such issues, long before raising this topic in the course of our interviews, I tried to show to them, through stories and jokes, that I am absolutely comfortable with those discussions. In particular my goal was to show them that I do not see those topics as inappropriate and do not shame and look down on people who live in that society, neither as a woman nor as a member of what they consider a higher class. But even after my best efforts, some respondents were still not entirely comfortable talking to me about it in person and, for example, preferred to discuss it by writing in text messages.

Finally, to understand the other side of the complicated inmate-versus-prison-authority relations, I interviewed several prison guards who spent the most time working with inmates and authorities in charge of developing prison policies. Included are authorities in Georgia, where, in 2010, there was the biggest prison reform in former Soviet Union with a major goal to unroot the *vory* criminal organization from prisons.

Scope of the Book

As a scholar, my first ambition is to contribute to academic literature on internal prison governance. But as a member of society, there are also several policy goals I hope to achieve with this book.

First, I want to help policy makers understand what is going on behind high prison walls. Unfortunately, many policy makers think that when a particular criminal or member of a terrorist organization is arrested and locked up, their job is done. In the best-case scenario, they think that the threat is neutralized and not dangerous to society anymore, and in the worst case, they forget about the inmates, as if those criminals no longer exist.

Second, while conducting interviews with members of law enforcement, it became clear to me that many of them have very little understanding of the politics among the inmate population. Basically, most law enforcement officers I interviewed fall into one of two opposite camps of thought. Either they are not interested in understanding prison inmate society and believe force is the only way to control them, or they accept inmate society and, as a result, are sometimes even manipulated by them.

Third, I want to help the family members of inmates understand the different society their loved ones become a part of once they pass through prison gates. Also, the vast difference between without and within is often what makes it harder for ex-inmates to reintegrate back into society once they are released.

Fourth, the book will also be interesting to a broader audience of people—those who want to understand societies in the countries of former Soviet Union. Due to the reality of the law enforcement and judicial system there, a substantial number of males in Russia (around 15–20%) at some point in their lives spend time inside prison walls.[5] As a popular saying goes, "In the Soviet Union, half of the population are inmates, and the other half guard them." And being part of that prison society leaves unavoidable traces of the culture on an individual's opinions and behavior outside of the prison for the rest of his life.

Finally, looking at the example of prisons in the former Soviet Union and the *vory* criminal ideology that is in power there, I hope readers will be able to look at the ideology from a different perspective. For the majority of readers, and myself when I started this project, the *vory* criminal ideology was something strange, and the prison settings of the distant, former Soviet Union completely alien. So using it as an example makes it easier for readers to look, soberly and without bias, at the instrumental role of ideology as used by those in power, something that would be harder to do with examples of legitimate countries with conventional government systems.

1
Theory

Major criminal groups know that basically all their members, including leadership themselves, will at some point end up in prison. So if they cannot avoid that, they at least have to assure that they will be serving their time the most comfortable way possible. Otherwise their criminal group would be less desirable for potential recruits and could even lose members already in its ranks.

So if a criminal group cannot dominate a prison by brute force, it has to drastically change its tactics from openly oppressing other inmates to claiming to work for their benefit. But as a consequence, they now became responsible for providing inmates with public goods, settling internal conflicts, and representing and defending all inmates in front of prison authorities. So once just a group of criminalized rebels, the criminal organization has now to perform the duties a regular government would perform for its citizens. Just inside prison walls.

In addition, to further cement their legitimacy inside and outside of prison, they have to make sure that their ideology or code of conduct is also being carefully followed behind bars.

It is a complicated and expensive job for criminal groups that they would prefer not to take on themselves, but since they have no other options, that expense is permanently written in the criminal group budget and those duties are assigned to particular group members.

Prison Criminal Leadership

Governing any society is not an easy task, and prison conditions and type of people behind bars make it even harder. Because one person could not do it, prison governance structure is rather big but is very similar to that of a country. It consists of the prison criminal leader,[1] who is helped by people similar to governors who are in charge of different geographic areas inside prisons (such as barracks and cells) and people similar to ministers in the sense that they have a particular portfolio they are in charge of. That included medical (who controls of the medicines), economy (and warehouse), gambling (a main source of internal income in prisons), prison factory, kitchen, ideology, and communication (his job is to make sure that all inmates could be reached and there is a contact with criminal leadership outside of prison).

Criminals, Nazis, and Islamists. Vera Mironova, Oxford University Press. © Oxford University Press 2023.
DOI: 10.1093/oso/9780197645659.003.0002

Their main job is to make sure inmates are as comfortable as they could be taking into consideration their inmate status. To achieve that general population should be united, which minimizes internal conflicts and makes their position the strongest in resistance to prison authorities—which in turn allows them to be in a stronger position vis-à-vis prison guards to negotiate for more benefits and freedoms. And because the situation in prisons is important for criminal organizations, those in prison internal leadership all have an incentive to perform their tasks to the best of their abilities because it would be taking into account when they would be rising in ranks within the criminal family.

So the criminal leader of the prison resolves conflicts among the inmate population and keeps relations with prison authorities friendly. On one side, he is a judge and jury for the inmate population, and on the other, he is like the leader of a labor union negotiating with authorities for better conditions for his members. So the first thing criminal organization in prison does is make sure everyone is following a set of internal rules that are being communicated to all new inmates once they cross prison gates. The key rules include:

First, supporting in-group: (1) contribute to the internal criminal mutual fund, (2) do not hit a criminal leader (unless he defects to the government; then he could be killed), (3) do not accuse someone without solid proof, (4) do not offend anyone, (5) do not steal from your own kind, and (6) follow criminal organization decisions.

Second, opposing out-groups: (1) no spying, (2) do not work with government institutions, and (3) do not respect government law.

And finally, a particular group that is currently in charge of prison governance installs their own ideology-inspired rules. That could be religious rules or codes acquired from a particular philosophy like communism. It could also be an absolutely artificial set of rules, such as those of *vory* criminal organization, currently the main criminal group controlling prisons in former Soviet Union.

Also, to help keep peace within a very diverse inmate population some individual freedoms also should be ensured among them: freedom of religion, freedom of lifestyle (individual sexual preferences), and no discrimination based on race and nationality.

Prison internal rules also extend into everyday civilities. Everyone has to be extremely polite. No matter how many times a day an inmate leaves the cell, every time he returns, he has to greet those inside. And inmates have to thank each other for every favor.

Also, a lot of attention is paid to mutual respect. Inmates living by the code are not allowed to hit others, and swearing is strongly discouraged if not prohibited. An inmate always has to be clean and wear clean clothes so as not to bother the other inmates with his body odor. Additionally, since the epidemic and the absence of sanitation are widespread, basic cleanliness rules are also institutionalized and enforced.

Spies and dishonest inmates are a threat to the criminal organization, but inmates who lack restraint are also potentially dangerous. As a result, if any inmate runs off at the mouth and threatens someone else, he has to execute his threat because in prison, words equal deeds.

Without the stability and unity of the internal system in front of government authorities and prison administration, the criminal system does not stand a chance of survival, so criminal leadership takes enforcing those rules very seriously.

Making sure that those rules are followed is also a job of prison criminal administration, which is in charge of providing courts on different level. For example, a particular problem could be solved on a lowest level—level of a cell (by a person in charge of the cell)—or by a criminal leader of the prison if dispute is important enough. In case a defendant does not agree with those decisions, he could appeal to the higher prison criminal leader. The final word would be made by a member of the leadership of a criminal family (located inside or outside of prison).

It is mandatory for the inmate population to observe those trials, and because the goal of the criminal family justice system is to keep peace, in some cases, the fate of the person who was found guilty is chosen by the victim. But in choosing a punishment, the victim has an incentive to be fair because the treatment he chooses for his offender will reflect on his own reputation. There is also no expiration for a serious punishment. Any violator of the criminal rules can be sure he will be punished sooner or later.

So that those criminal court judgments are taken seriously, prison criminal leadership should make sure that punishment would follow any wrongdoing. And compared to societies outside of prison, their punishment options are more limited and basically only include beating or killing (the most popular punishment option such as imprisonment, for example, by default is off limits to prison criminal leadership). So they had to be creative and institutionalize a caste system.

Prison Caste System

In addition to the upper caste of people who have not violated a major prison rule, there are two lower castes with specific rules of interaction. The most crucial aspect of this prison caste system is the relative ease with which an inmate can fall from an upper caste to a lower caste, but the absolute impossibility of an inmate rising up from a lower caste, even to a previously held status. Also, when an inmate is moved between prisons, his status travels with him (with some exceptions for juvenile prison), and he has to announce it immediately upon arrival at the new prison. If he does not tell the truth, when the truth becomes known (and it will because of communication between prisons), he will be severely punished—possibly killed. Even if inmates are released and later rearrested, their original caste status remains with them. As a result, the possibility of being downgraded is terrifying for inmates and works as a deterrence mechanism.

One low-level caste is for those who violated rules related to in-group and out-group interactions, such as those who steal from other inmates or work as informers. Compared to prison general population who work, for example, in prison factories, inmates in that caste work in prison maintenance, the medical unit, the kitchen, construction, or landscaping, and generally help prison authorities.

Because members of that caste are considered supporters of the enemy (prison authorities), there are several restrictions on their interaction with members of the upper caste. They are not allowed to just walk around upper caste barracks. If they need to enter, they first have to wait outside while the inmate they came to see is notified. Then they have to loudly announce they are entering the room. While they are in the barrack, they are not allowed to sit down. A member of this caste is also considered to have lost his honor or credibility—the most important inmate characteristics in the criminal world, so he cannot testify in prison trials.

Being a member of that caste is hard, but it is not the worst. If a person violated criminal group ideological rules, which means he basically disrespected the group and its members, he is downgraded to the lowest caste. And life there is, by definition, almost unbearable. Members of that caste do the dirtiest jobs like cleaning bathrooms and trashcans, and the most dishonorable jobs like clearing the strip of land near the prison fence so prison authorities can easily see any footprints left by inmates trying to escape. Some of them also prostitute themselves and are used for sex.

It is a very small caste, but the rules for interacting with its members are very complicated. Members of this caste are basically untouchables. Inmates from other castes are not allowed to touch them (except during sex), take anything from their hands (although one could give them something), or eat and drink from the same tableware as they do. And any inmate who oversteps these boundaries for any reason is degraded and also becomes a member of the caste.

Their segregation is also as thorough as possible. In a prison camp, the degraded usually live in a separate barrack. In some prisons, they have a special table assigned to them in the canteen. There, they usually eat from special tableware marked with a drilled hole or other identifiable mark. In some prisons, the degraded have their own gym, sit in a dedicated row in the cinema room, and only use a particular washstand and electric sockets.

Sometimes they have to lean against the wall when anyone from the higher caste is walking down the same hallway, and they are never allowed to stand physically higher than upper-caste inmates. If a member of an upper caste is standing, a member of the lowest caste has to sit, and if an upper caste inmate is sitting, the member of the lowest caste has to lie down. Sometimes, these inmates are not even allowed to look at members of the higher caste as they pass by. Finally, because of their untouchable status, they cannot even be beaten with hands or feet, only with objects.

Lower-Caste Purpose

The existence of the lower castes is based on need and designed to solve the following problems:

Doing the dirty jobs. To make the majority of inmates happy, someone has to do jobs no one else wants to do. The remedy is to appoint a small group of constantly oppressed and unhappy inmates who are forced to perform those unpleasant tasks. This solution works best as opposed to either making all inmates do the work (and making everyone unhappy) or leaving those tasks undone (which also makes everyone unhappy).

Punishment. Inmate leadership has few options to punish those who misbehave, and thus less of a mechanism to scare inmates into complying with their rules. Basically they can either kill someone (and be punished for it by prison authorities) or beat him. And since they are already imprisoned, the only way to isolate those they want to punish is with a lower caste.

Security. In the outside world, a dangerous person can be isolated in prison, but again, within the prison, the only recourse is a lower caste. This is especially true of informants or the psychologically unstable who pose a threat to the general inmate population. Relegating such inmates to lower castes makes it clear who they are and what can be expected from them, and, as a result, what the norms of interaction with those inmates should be.

Emotional well-being. Inmates with long sentences are trapped in an intimate environment with people of different practices and personalities for years, making it necessary to have a system where they can at least tolerate each other.

Show of power. Because criminal leadership can make the decision to degrade any inmate to the lowest caste, the caste system operates as a powerful tool to control the masses and to project the groups' power to potential outside enemies, such as prison authorities.

And although from the outside, criminal rules may look like unnecessary and excessive cruelty, criminal leadership constantly struggles to make sure punishments are not *too* harsh. Reaching this balance proves to be an exceptionally hard task, but a necessary one. On one side, if an inmate is terrorized and terrified by the criminal world, he will go to the prison administration and start cooperating with them. But on the other side, prison criminal leadership still has to ensure law and order.

Infrastructure

In addition to three main components of any legitimate government—executive, legislative, and judicial—there are several other provisional functions a prison government has to perform. A prison government is in charge of the economy, goods import and export, social security, and the provision of public goods, all of which ensure the comfort of its citizens.

It is not a simple task, but since they claim to work on behalf of the general inmate population, these tasks become their main responsibilities, and their success or failure in governing has a direct effect on their legitimacy and the loyalty of the inmate population.

Prison criminal leadership is usually doing their best to raise money inside prison. For example, some inmates are able to produce quality manufactured goods. Their skills are applied at factories inside prison, and it is a job of criminal leadership to find clients for those products outside of prison.

Also if an inmate family member wishes to help their loved ones behind bars with regular goods (food and basic necessities), it also falls into prison criminal responsibility to negotiate with prison authorities to make sure those goods are let across the prison gates.

Inside the prison, criminal prison leadership also runs a shop that accommodates quick, small purchases. Although the shopkeeper is always from a low caste, it is the prison criminal leadership who facilitates his supply and controls his prices. This ensures that goods are affordable to the majority of the inmates. Also because the prison criminal leadership controls it, one could buy goods on credit. But compared to delivery services, retail is not considered a public good. The shopkeeper earns money from his job, but any profit goes to the prison criminal mutual fund.

Although the funding sources mentioned above are important for the prison economy, the main source of income for the prison criminal government is the taxes on gambling (around 15–20%), which has always been a big part of prison life. But despite the money involved, it is strictly prohibited for members of the upper caste to play with members of the lower caste, and the gambling tax is not collected from members of the lower caste playing among themselves.

In addition to tax collection, a member of prison criminal leadership in charge of gambling judges games and ensures that no one is cheating. It is also up to him to enforce public safety rules during the game. Despite the desire of prison criminal leadership to maximize the profits from gambling, as a government, they also have to make restrictions that keep inmates safe. For example, in some prisons there is a monetary roof for the games, and sometimes new inmates are not allowed to participate in card games.

But money earned inside prison walls is often not enough to balance the prison budget, so every month, members of the criminal family of a town or region where a particular prison camp is located use their money to bail criminal prison leadership out. They are collecting goods from businesses and private individuals and then take them into the local prisons.

Use of Money and Goods

Money and goods collected by prison criminal leadership of the mutual fund inside prison are usually used for:

Basic necessities. Mutual funds usually pay for everything—food, cigarettes, tea, and clothes (socks and underwear). Cells have a box or a dresser drawer where a criminal organization places these goods and where inmates can get what they need.

Bribes. Mutual funds are often used to bribe administration for any number of privileges: a longer walk in the yard, scissors in a cell, and so on.

Prison repair and construction work. Although, theoretically, the governments give money to prisons for such work, it is often stolen by prison authorities instead of used for its purpose.

Welfare. While those who do not contribute to prison mutual fund cannot benefit from it, exceptions are often made for new inmates, inmates in the prison hospital, and inmates in a special security ward.

Celebrations. For major holidays, criminal prison leadership organizes celebrations for the upper caste with expensive food, alcohol, and often drugs.

Rewards for inmates. Not only is there a short list of ways to punish inmates, there are also few rewards. But one way for an inmate to earn one-time rewards is by doing something beneficial for either the prison population or criminal leadership.

Communication

As for any society, communication is also one of the most important public goods a government has to offer its citizens. So one of the prison criminal government jobs is to develop a functional system of communication services within the prison and make sure that inmates are connected not only to each other but also to the outside criminal world and their loved ones.

Although communication is now modernized, it does not solve all of the problems. For example, sending goods (usually cigarettes, tea, drugs, and cell phones) between cells and prison camp buildings is still done as it was a hundred years ago—through physical "road" systems.

One form of communication happens through ropes. Ropes are attached between cells and through windows conduct pieces of paper or small goods in a sock. This is the easiest to operate and the most popular method of cross-cell communication. Other forms of communication include through plumbing and ventilation and holes in walls, in case of old prison buildings.

Despite that, sometimes members of the lowest caste are the only means of moving messages to the most isolated locations, and only inmates from the upper castes are allowed to benefit from using the "roads." This avenue of communication excludes the low caste because they are not trusted and could read messages, steal goods, or bring sensitive information to the attention of prison authorities, and the lowest caste because they are believed to contaminate whatever they touch.

Also, since now almost all prison camps have cell phones inside and although they are in the hands of prison criminal leadership and richer inmates, they are considered public goods. By prison criminal code of conduct, any upper-caste inmate has a right to ask another one for a cell phone and cannot be refused.

A special member of prison criminal leadership is in charge of communication. This is a crucial and difficult job. It is up to him to maintain a road map of the whole prison and know who sleeps where, which is basically an inmate's postal address.

Inmates in charge of roads on a cell level are also responsible for always keeping their cell connected to the prison road system. If something happens in a particular cell, and they are not able to connect to the road system, that inmate would have to answer for it by explaining to the prison criminal leader what happened and what he did to fix the situation. Also, if the road system is compromised by prison guards, or there is an unexpected search, it is this person who must hide or destroy messages passing through their cell at that time.

Relations with Prison Authorities

The most comfortable life inmates have is if the criminal family is running the prison, but that is not always the case. Sometimes prison authorities have a tight grip on prison, and then prison roles are reversed. Inmates that are in leadership positions in the criminal family are at the bottom, and members of the lower caste (people cooperating with the administration) have the leadership positions.

Relations between prison authorities and criminal leadership in those prisons are like those of a dictator and his opposition. When prison administration enjoys unlimited power, they can exercise it in many different ways: extracting money from inmates, extracting false confessions to get rewarded for successful investigations, or using them for forced labor and SWAT trainings. And of course, there is no safety net such as the criminal mutual fund to help with goods that make prison life bearable—things like food, cigarettes, other basics, and communication between cells.

And because the administration does not want a regime change, their main enemy is any organized opposition, which means members of the criminal family. So the administration has two strategies. First, to keep them out of such prisons altogether. But when that is not possible, then the plan is to break such inmates before they join the general population. In particular, these inmates are forced to publicly violate criminal prison rules that would automatically put them into the low caste in a criminal-controlled prison.

Why Inmates Work with Authorities

And in case the authorities do not want to get their own hands dirty by beating and torturing inmates, they use groups of inmates from the low caste to do it for them, a practice very similar to using pro-government militias for human rights violations in non-democratic regimes. Such delegation of inhumane actions also gives administration scapegoats later if needed. And those members of the low caste agree to do those jobs for several reasons:

They want power. In some prisons, they even participate in searches along with prison guards.

They want an easy life. Not only are they able to dress in more comfortable clothes, go unshaven, and own cell phones, they also enjoy benefits that range from extra packages from the outside, extra visitation rights, restaurant deliveries, and access to gyms, saunas, and swimming pools.

They depend on administration. Because they have to be in prison for long sentences, they are very dependent on good relations with the administration.

They had problems with criminal leadership. Often these are inmates who had a problem with the criminal world and had to ask prison authorities for protection. Once that is done, they not only have to depend on prison administration for survival, but they often want revenge against the criminal family.

And the last category is the most dangerous for members of the criminal family. Because these inmates know how the criminal world works from the inside, they are very effective in manipulating it. They usually chose this path if they are accused of violation of criminal rules, but do not want to lose their power and move to the lower social castes. They are also very loyal to the prison authorities. They do not have any other option but to fully comply with their orders because, again, prison authorities become their only protection against the criminal world they betrayed.

Working Against Authorities

It is a very hard and dangerous job for the criminal family to try and retake control of such prisons, but their efforts are still sometimes successful. It takes the right combination of personnel to make it happen.

First, inmates need a strong person—or better, a group of people—who are willing to take risks and even sacrifice themselves for the goal. Potential leaders in a "defrosting" are inmates who want to rise in the criminal world hierarchy, inmates who are willing to go against prison leadership and rules. So their goal is to start an opposition movement inside the prison, and even, if needed, be punished for such actions by the prison authorities. Although the punishment will be severe, it will help promote them in the criminal family.

In addition to a strong leader, successful resistance also requires communication between cells, or "roads," so that inmates can coordinate their efforts. And successful defrost also requires support from the outside so usually criminal-family-controlled prisons are located in or near big cities, where the criminal world is strong.[2]

Second, inmates need to draw as much public attention to the prison as possible. They could start with following the rules and writing complaints to the highest authority. But since it is not clear whether complaints will be effective, inmates need to reach the general public by engaging media and human rights activists. If the unlawful actions of prison guards are not enough to draw publicity to a prison, inmates may take action to draw the public's eye. These actions are limited to the tools they have at their disposal:

Self-Harm

The most accessible option is hurting themselves en masse. These tactics might include a group of inmates holding hunger strikes, slitting their wrists, and stabbing themselves in the stomach with construction nails or sharpened toothbrushes. Since the main idea of mass self-harm is to draw attention to the prison and support from outside, it helps to make the event coincide with a prison inspection or family visiting day, so that when it happens, there are many concerned family members near the prison gates.

Rioting

Prison administration might be able to hide self-harm from headquarters, but not prison riots. Not only can riots not be hidden from the media and government, when inmates take control of a prison, they have the tools to make the riot even more public.

In general, conducting a revolution inside the prison to change its regime is possible but, as in a country, very difficult. And to bring it about, extreme measures are often required. And if they fail, it leads to terrible consequences for participating inmates, so inmates riot only as the last possible resort.

If it is possible to change a prison regime from an imposed dictatorial prison guard one to more liberal and democratic criminal family controlled, it is also possible to move in the opposite direction. Prison administration could tighten the screws and bring a criminal-controlled prison under their total control. And in that case, criminal prison leadership is in a defensive position.

Prison authorities might try to gain control of the prison by replacing internal criminal leadership with an inmate they have more control of. Sometimes prison authorities make a deal with a new high-level member of the criminal family who is moved into a prison to push the old one out from this position. Basically, when he comes in, he solves problems for the inmate population that previous criminal leadership could not. One example might be making an illegal channel to bring prohibited items inside the prison. Of course, the new leader does this with the help of the administration, but inmates do not understand this and support the new criminal leader.

Replacing Criminal Leadership

Although slowly replacing criminal leadership this way is the quietest way to solve the problem, it is complicated and time-consuming. So prison authorities often apply quicker and more violent techniques. The majority of regime changes in prison follow the same scenario:

Step One: Neutralize Leadership

First, prison administration has to neutralize the existing criminal leadership. In the past, prison authorities used extermination, but now these inmates are usually either locked in prison inside the prison or transferred to another prison.

Then, prison authorities discredit the criminal leadership among the inmates. This could be done with any small action, like a guard making a slight expression of appreciation to a criminal leader in front of the other inmates. By doing so, the administration plants a seed of suspicion that a criminal leader is somehow working with administration.

Step Two: Show of Power

While leadership is confined, the prison authorities need to show their power over the general population inmates to deter them from any action. Often, this starts with police SWAT teams doing searches. These searches are usually highly theatrical and often involve shooting, screaming, beating, and confiscation of inmates' personal property.

Then prison guards chip away at communication both inside prisons ("roads" are cut) and with the outside world. Free movement inside prisons is also stopped, usually by metal fences between prison camp buildings. Finally, everyone who violates even the tiniest regulation (such as smoking in a non-smoking area) is placed in the inner prison.

Since by that time, prison authorities have decapitated the criminal administration, they use that window of opportunity to replace leadership with someone under their total control. So prison authorities prepare members of the low caste to take control of the prison.

The process is simple. Prison guards meet with low-caste inmates and tell them that, if they want to make parole, they need to provide prison authorities with the names of two or three inmates a day who are violating prison rules. Usually those inmates are afraid to do so, but prison administration assures them they will be protected. And since many of members of low caste already do not like upper caste inmates, they are happy to get revenge (when protected by prison authorities). But if low-caste inmates still refuse to go against criminal leadership and members of upper caste (because they had good relations in the past), prison authorities will transfer low-caste members from another prison to do the job.

Step Three: New Rules

When general population inmates are left without strong leadership and low caste members agree to work in a more violent capacity, inmates can do little to stand up against prison authorities. So prison guards start replacing prison criminal rules with new rules, and their main goal is its cornerstone—the caste system.

They start by prohibiting inmates from using the names of the criminal caste. They then work on making all inmates of the same caste, of the lowest one. To do so, prison authorities make everyone use the tableware that is used by those in a lower caste.

Inmates consider being made to do actions like this the worst thing prison guards can do, and with good reason. According to criminal prison rules, eating from the same tableware as a member of the lowest (untouchable) caste immediately degrades one into that caste, so it is often much more dangerous than any torture or beating inmates might receive. While a beating hurts for a short period of time, violating prison criminal rules will hurt every day of an inmate's sentence and any subsequent ones. But stakes are high, and if prison guards are successful in doing so, inmates will no longer be interested in supporting a prison criminal leadership that will regulate them to the lowest possible caste.

When authorities regain control of a prison in this way, it is referred to in prison slang as a *freeze*. A freeze is a very hard time for inmates from the criminal family, and not everyone survives. Such inmates could try to live on outside food sent by their relatives and criminal family members, so they can eat without touching official prison-provided tableware, but prison guards might not accept packages from outside. Basically those inmates take only bread and drink tap water. And if they are lucky, they are able to boil this water in their cell with a self-made heater made from razors attached to the electric outlet by wires. After living like that for a long period of time, some members of criminal family give up and leave criminal family altogether.

Although gaining control of the prison is possible for the prison administration, it is not sustainable. It is very time consuming with no clear benefits, so not many prison directors are interested in doing so. As a result, the majority of prisons are considered something in between prison-guard-imposed dictatorship and criminal-family stronghold, where governance is done in negotiations between prison administration and prison criminal leadership.

Prison Criminal Leadership Challenges

Just as the criminal family is the most effective under pressure from law enforcement, criminal prison governance works best in response to the pressure from prison authorities and correction authorities. But when this pressure is reduced, it leads to internal problems inside the organization.

Originally, the main purpose of prison criminal leadership was to suffer for its members, and taking a leadership position was associated more with dangers and responsibility than with benefits. But when the benefits associated with being in a leadership position in the criminal family increased, while costs and risks associated with the position decreased, less qualified people started to join and rise in ranks. So some judicial and prison-system reforms negatively affect criminal organizations in general and in prison in particular.

Prison Reform Policies Cause Challenges

Relative trust of judicial system. When people, including members of the criminal family, increase in their trust of the system (or in their ability to bribe it to get decisions in their favor), they have less reason to turn to the criminal family for justice.

Oversight of prisons. If information about any kind of abuse or torture becomes public knowledge, directors of prison camps can be fired for mistreating inmates, which makes them less free to do whatever they want with inmates.

Better treatment of inmates. One of the biggest problems the criminal organization had to solve was ensuring that only the best people were promoted to leadership positions. And promotion in the criminal family was closely related to an individuals' behavior in prison. So prison brutality was a good screening mechanism and helped identify the strongest candidates for promotion to criminal leadership.

Parole. Since it is possible for an inmate to be released earlier for good behavior, he is more likely to side with prison administration and not defend criminal family with his health or even life.

Separation of first timers. Being separated, experienced criminal inmates could no longer educate the next generation or choose the most qualified among new inmates for promotion.

Longer sentences for prison crimes. With a prison sentence extended to ten years for killing in prison, fewer people are willing to sacrifice their freedom by executing a criminal family order to kill someone.

Corruption of Criminal Leadership

Such major changes in governmental policies, and as a result the criminal world, also have major negative effects on the prison criminal government, and it becomes less trusted by the inmate population. In the absence of existential threat, money and power started playing a bigger role in the criminal organization, eventually corrupting it. In particular, looking for profit, prison criminal leadership becomes more commercialized, and it shapes the new prison criminal organization on many dimensions.

First, cooperation with prison authorities. In many prisons, on the issue of commerce, criminal leadership started working in conjunction with the prison administration.

Second, there is widespread financial punishment for inmates, which makes inmates more likely to violate prison internal rules.

Third, it leads to commercial relations between castes, which makes them less segregated, the main purpose of the caste system to start with.

And with the decrease in the quality of the criminal organization prison governance, inmates openly voice their dissatisfaction and even challenge its power. And the most powerful group that is able to challenge the criminal family power monopoly in prisons is Islamists.

Competition for Power

Imprisoned radical Muslim inmates, unlike everyone else in a criminal-controlled prison, refuse to follow prison criminal rules or operate under the criminal family leadership. Instead they form their own groups called *jamaats* and establish a parallel structure with the long-term goal of taking total control of prisons.

Originally, the founders of the prison *jamaats* had been veterans of wars, imprisoned for extremism and terrorism. These fighters were not only very respected among the criminal inmates, they also had many qualities and goals that easily overshadowed those of the new prison criminal leaders.

In the beginning, the goal of the criminal organization was to present strong opposition to the government. However, many inmates see criminal family leadership now as coconspirators with, rather than opposition to, the prison authorities. These are criminal leaders who can easily be bought with money of favors from prison administration.

At the same time, based on the Russian law, inmates on terrorism and extremism charges are never eligible for early release, so they have no incentive for good behavior and nothing to lose by standing up against prison authorities' injustice. And even if they wanted to increase cooperation with prison authorities to improve their own life in prison, it is not possible because prison guards are often biased against them. This led *jamaats* (Islamist organizations) to quickly rise to power among prison inmates.

First, it is common knowledge that inmates locked within the four walls of a prison cell have a deep need for hope and are very keen to get involved in something superstitious as one way of getting it. And in the case of Islam, inmates who want to turn to it (such as ethnic Muslims) are hijacked by Islamist veterans and their interpretation of the religion.

On the other side, there is a big difference between practicing religion and joining an Islamist organization and eventually standing up against prison criminal leadership. So in their early attempts to exert influence, when jamaats are still weak, Islamists are very careful. In particular they show inmates that their interpretation of Sharia law is, for the most part, in line with criminal rules. This keeps criminal family leadership from feeling threatened by an internal fifth column. Basically, Islamist veteran inmates carefully follow criminal rules, pay attention to what is allowed and what is not, and try to fit their proliferation into the small space they are given.

At this point in an Islamist takeover, members of the criminal family have little understanding of a *jamaat*'s ultimate goal. As a result, they have no real means or desire of deterring them. Especially since, according to prison criminal rules, everyone is allowed to practice his religion and express his opinion.

At this stage, not having had previous experience with Islamists, criminal leadership makes a fatal mistake in assuming the main goal of Islamists is more religious freedom, when it is, in fact, power. Their assumption is that by giving Islamists more concessions to their ideological demands, they will remain under criminal leadership, and prison criminal leadership is willing to do everything possible to keep them there. *Vory* leadership also try to incorporate them into prison decision-making, so they will be more engaged with prison criminal values.

At the second phase, the *jamaat* officially announces it existence, leadership, and rules. In some prisons, the *jamaat* physically segregates, for example, onto one floor or in one barrack. And all incoming inmates have to decide with whom they want to live and, as a consequence, whose command they will be under.

In addition to physical separation between Islamists and criminal leadership, separate jurisdictions also result. While *jamaat* leadership solves conflicts related to jamaat members (according to their interpretation of Sharia law), criminal leadership solves problems arising among the rest of the inmates.

Although at this point a jamaat has independent governance, in terms of economy, they are freeloaders on the criminal family system. They withdraw from contributing to the mutual fund (claiming that it is against their religion), but still use the public goods provided by prison criminal leadership. This loophole allows jamaats to rapidly increase their own savings while depleting criminal organization finances.

Why Inmates Join *Jamaats*

Also, because the majority of inmates do not realize that provision and main governance is still the responsibility of criminal leadership, they begin to think the jamaat is a better option. After all, inmates do not experience the constant conflicts they associate with criminal leadership fundraising efforts with jamaat leadership, and they attribute that to jamaats being a superior system. At that point, new members start to join jamaats for the following reasons:

Personal benefits. Because *jamaats* freeload on the public goods provided by prison criminal leadership, they are in a position to offer more benefits to *jamaat* members.

New norms and customs. Again, because *jamaats* are freeloading on what the criminal organization provides, they do not need to raise money among inmates—an activity that the general inmate population does not like.

Reputation. Because *jamaats* are respected, many incoming inmates want to join simply to increase their status in front of peers (inside and outside of prison).

Protection. Because of their separate standing and a respected position, *jamaats* start offering protection to inmates from the upper caste who are not satisfied with their treatment in the criminal family.

Separate jurisdiction. *Jamaats* also target other inmates who do not agree with their position in the criminal caste system. But because this system is a cornerstone of criminal prison ideology, *jamaat* leadership still proceed with great caution.

By this point in phase two, the criminal family leadership clearly understands that they are rapidly losing power, and that the shift is getting dangerous for them.

First, they realize they are being used by the *jamaats*. *Jamaat* inmates do not contribute to the prison mutual fund like the other inmates do, yet they are still benefiting from the public-goods provision. They also do not work criminal jobs, like on the roads, yet they still use them. Second, because of the different jurisdictions, the prison criminal leader finds he is losing control of what is going on with all the inmates, yet he is still responsible for all of them before the prison authorities. Third, the inmates who have remained under the authority of the criminal leadership become extremely dissatisfied with the situation.

Gaining and Losing Power

By this point, the *jamaats* already have a strong position in relation to the prison criminal leadership and can now enforce their own rules in prisons. And this has been their goal from the beginning: to increase their own well-being, to decrease the well-being of the competitors—the criminal-family community—and to become the only real force in the prison. This is done two different ways, either peacefully or by force.

In Muslim-majority regions, *jamaats* very quietly enforce their Islamized rules on the rest of the inmate society, and basically push the criminal world to be ideologically closer to *jamaats*. Their end goal is to slowly raise the level of Islamization in the criminal world. The other option is to keep an Islamized version of criminal ideology but distance their prison from the rest of the criminal world.

Prisons in non-Muslim-majority regions, however, have a very different situation. In those regions, Islamists take power by force. Their plan then is to subdue the prison criminal leadership by fear. So in these regions, their strategy is to simply make the criminal leadership as weak as possible and dependent on the *jamaats* for all rules and decisions.

And this is reached by maximizing *jamaat* size by both lowering their recruitment standards and breaking the cornerstone of the criminal caste system at the same time. Because everyone who was willing to join the *jamaat* from upper castes has already done so, the *jamaat* begins to accept inmates from the lower caste. Even though *jamaat* leadership understands that many of those people were moved to a lower caste for a reason, they are willing to take a chance and admit them. This swell in ranks leads to a laundry list of problems for the *jamaat*'s internal operations.

First, the quality of *jamaat* members becomes lower than that of the criminal organization, because, by definition, it accepts those who were on the lowest rung of the criminal ladder.

Second, because *jamaats* recruit inmates who were kicked out from the upper level of the criminal hierarchy, those inmates have an increasing grievance against the criminal leadership. If originally, *jamaat* leadership mostly wanted to take the power inside the prison, now *jamaats* members also want revenge on criminal leadership.

Third, the overall situation for all inmates in the prison rapidly deteriorates. The quality of the goods provision decreases for the whole prison. Even if *jamaats* themselves are not capable of governing the prison and providing public goods, they will not help criminal leadership do it. Not only that, they actively sabotage the system.

In those prisons, the discontent among inmates in the criminal hierarchy is extremely high. As a result, criminal leadership tries to keep the peace by stabilizing relationships with their remaining inmates and not reacting to provocations from the side of Islamists. But as situation becomes more complicated, tension between the inmate groups runs very high.

Many inmates join the *jamaat* because of the discrimination they experienced under criminal leadership. As a result, members of the *jamaat* (from the lowest member to leadership) feel extreme animosity toward the criminal family.

Jamaat members start threatening members of the criminal family and are also willing to act on their grievances. But that is only half of their motivation. The other half is fear. These inmates fear being kicked out of the *jamaat*—which would leave them defenseless against the criminal hierarchy and their retribution—so they are very loyal to *jamaat* leadership and will follow any orders just to remain a part. Leadership then often uses this loyalty to further their power. For example, they rely on these inmates to provoke conflict with criminal family members.

Regular inmates on the criminal side are extremely disappointed with the parallel structure's double standard and their leadership's waning authority. In particular, they are irate about those once in the lowest caste now demanding to be treated equally and often using their *jamaat* status to settle old scores.

By this point, both groups understand the volatility of the situation and have no illusions about how long the thinning veneer of a peaceful coexistence will last. Both groups prepare for the possibility of a big confrontation. This preparation includes making homemade knives and other weapons that might be needed for mass fighting.

And it takes only a spark to start an inter-prison war with real causalities and unknown outcomes. While some prisons remain under Islamist rule, others turn back to criminal prison leadership, and in some prisons, prison authorities use such a window of opportunity take full control of the prison, turning it into dictatorship.

Conclusion

Since it is basically inevitable for members of criminal family to end up in prison, they have to make sure conditions there are the most comfortable for them. This can be done by brutal oppression of other inmates or by taking control of prisons and governing it. In that case, members of the criminal family have to become leaders of the inmate population. They not only have to ensure peaceful coexistence of inmates but also become negotiators on their behalf with prison authorities. And to have better control of the prison population, they install a caste system where members who violated different prison rules are downgraded to lower castes.

Governing prisons is not an easy task for a criminal family, but they have to dedicate manpower and resources to it. It is especially the case in times when law enforcement is particularly tough on crime, so the chances of leaders of the criminal family ending up behind bars is high and so is pressure from prison guards on those already inside.

On the other side, when such pressure is reduced, meaning that fewer members of criminal family are arrested, their sentences are shorter, and conditions in prison are better; criminal family leadership loses incentive to ensure the prison criminal leadership is doing their best governing behind bars. That leads to a reduction in the quality of governance inside, which in turn leads to an increase in dissatisfaction of a prison's general population with criminal prison leadership and inmates looking for alternatives.

In particular in the case of former Soviet Union, the only alternative is Islamists, who by the nature of their crimes are in opposition to prison administration (they have long sentences, cannot be released on parole, and are discriminated against by prison guards). At the same time, they manage to successfully use a loophole in criminal prison rules that ensures freedom of religion to increase in power in prisons (something that, e.g., Nazi groups behind bars were not able to do). At the early stages of their rise to power, they claim that their religion does not allow them to follow prison criminal rules. As a result, they first manage to start a parallel governance structure inside the prison and then significantly increase their ranks by accepting members of low caste who were against the prison criminal family that degraded them. Those new *jamaat* members want revenge against the criminal family and, once outside of their control, start provoking them.

In many prisons, this leads to internal conflicts with real casualties and uncertain results. Sometimes Islamists are able to hold to power, sometimes prison criminal leadership is able to get power back, and sometimes prison authorities take full control of prisons, making the life of inmates very difficult.

2

History of the *Vory* Criminal Organization

It is not clear when and how the *vory* criminal organization started. On one side, Gurov in his book said that pre-revolutionary criminologists (such as B. S. Utevskii, S. N. Krenev, and I. N. Iakimov) did not mention either the phenomenon or the term, Thieves in Law. He comes to the conclusion that the Thieves in Law did not exist in tsarist Russia and emerged only after the revolution.[1] At the same time, a former inmate, Maximilen Santerre, in his book expressed an opinion that "the *vory* existed in Russia long before the revolution." But despite that, he also adds "the Soviet reality, and especially its social and economic system, created the specific conditions, in which a criminal world with its completely peculiar features was born and flourished."[2] As Federico Varese has shown, what is known is that, since 1930, the *vory* criminal organization is already widely mentioned in law enforcement documents and Gurov, drawing on classified Ministry of Internal Affairs (MVD) material, in his book concludes that "the *vory v zakone* were firmly established by the beginning of the 1930s."[3]

Taking power, the Bolsheviks irreversibly changed the lives of everyone, law-abiding citizens and criminal underworld members alike. Basically, life was flipped upside down.

On one side, many ex-criminals who were behind bars in czarist prisons joined the Bolsheviks, starting with its leadership, Josef Stalin, who had previously spent a significant amount of time behind bars. Hero of the Russian Civil War, Georgy Kotovsky, who used to participate in criminal activities in his hometown of Odessa, and the commander of the Red Army in Ukraine, Moisey Vinnitsky, more known by his criminal world name Mishka Yaponchik (or Mikey the Jap) had also been incarcerated before rising to power.

The same was true for lowest-ranked group members. For example, as mentioned in M. Gernet's book, *Moscow Criminal World*, published in 1924, "Legend of the criminal world, killer Petrov Komarov, who, for profit, had killed twenty-nine people in two years, voluntary joined the Red Army in 1917. He then learned how to read and write, became a brigade commander, and took part in battles."[4] That should not be surprising since even one of the official slogans of the Bolshevik government was "rob the robbers,"[5] directly targeting such demographics. And many of those criminals later ended up working as police.

After taking power, the new regime also fired all of the previous Czar-regime-affiliated police officers and investigators—considering them members of the

Criminals, Nazis, and Islamists. Vera Mironova, Oxford University Press. © Oxford University Press 2023.
DOI: 10.1093/oso/9780197645659.003.0003

enemy class—and replaced them with ideological communists who had no experience and, as mentioned before, often had criminal records. Such low-quality law enforcement did not bother the Bolsheviks, however. In general, they did not even consider fighting crime a priority at that point. They believed crime would naturally disappear with the development of socialism. According to their ideology, there were criminals in the past because there was inequality that made poor people (criminals) hate rich people. But because in communism there would be neither rich nor poor, and everyone would be equal, there would be no crime.

On the other side, some members of society, particularly those affiliated with Czarist Russia, lost everything they had and had no choice but to go underground. After the White Movement was defeated in the Russian Civil War, while some defected and joined the Red Army, other members of the force either joined the ranks of the criminal underground or left the Soviet states. But even those who left soon returned, either because the Soviets declared amnesty, the situation in the refugee camps had become difficult, or they had become a burden to the countries hosting them. Upon arrival back home, they also joined their former brothers-in-arms in the underground.

In the secret report of VChK (All-Russian Extraordinary Commission) in 1920, former White officers and other former bureaucrats were mentioned as second major group of criminal-world members, right after career criminals.[6] In Russia's far east, on the border with China, those White-officers-turned-criminals were so widespread that members of law enforcement in their internal reports used terms like "White-banditism" and "White gangs" referring to criminal groups headed by former White Army officers.[7] Local newspapers then were also writing about how the "Russian counterrevolution turned to criminal."[8]

At that time, these criminal leaders became known as the *vory*. Although in English, *vory* is translated as *thieves*—and this is also how present-day Russian speakers would understand this word—at that time, a *thief* was anyone doing something illegal, not just stealing, and so the word could more closely be translated *criminal*.

Compared to career criminals, these *vory* lacked professional criminal experience. For example, they did not know how to open locks or enter an apartment without being noticed. But their knowledge of weapons and their experience in operation planning far outstripped that of other criminals.[9] So they found their niche in gang robberies. From a police report dated January 10, 1919: "On the road near Avtov, a gang under the leadership of ex-czar officer Zidkovskim-Maksimivim attacked the car of a railroad cashier. The driver and cashier were killed, and a bodyguard wounded."[10] And on November 21, 1920, a newspaper on another side of Russia—in Habarovsk—reported that law enforcement uncovered and liquidated a criminal group headed by a former White Army officer Polosin, who had been terrorizing Habarovsk for a long time.[11]

Also, according to the book by a historian and an employee of Russian Correction Authority, Alexander Sidorov, because of their leadership experience and organizational skills, these *vory* soon began taking control of the chaotic criminal world.[12] According to him, they were different from the criminals before them in several aspects that later changed the whole structure of the Soviet's crime:

First, the ex-officers brought their military background with them into the underground. If previously criminals were mostly disorganized, the *vory* installed their own leadership structure[13] and adopted a strict, military-inspired code of conduct, including establishing courts of honor.[14]

Dmitry Likhachev who met *vory* in 1931–1932 when he was a convict working on the Belomorsko-Baltiiskii canal construction site wrote, "Despite thieves' apparent lack of discipline, their lives are governed by a network of strict regulations that extend to the most minute matters and ultimately by a system of 'collective beliefs' that is remarkably uniform among criminals with different ethnic roots."[15] For example, spilling blood was allowed only under special circumstances. And like the military in times of war, members were strictly punished for disobedience. Adherents were also permitted to quit and leave whenever they wanted.

Second, if the previous generation of criminals were only interested in immediate monetary benefits, these newcomers had different goals. Not only had they lost everything they owned, but they had witnessed the atrocities committed by the Red Army. Because of this, they had extreme grievances against the Soviets and wanted to defeat them, and they adopted a strict ideology that prohibited, among other things, any interaction with the regime.[16]

In addition to prohibiting official government interaction such as with courts and police, they also prohibited taking part in official events such as celebrations of communist holidays, birthdays of communist leaders, or communist-organized parades and elections. Their hate for the Bolshevik regime was so strong that, according to their teaching, *vory* were not allowed to be interested in politics or even read the newspapers.[17] They also prohibited taking part in any legal trade or commerce. So the organization's main sources of income became money stolen from the government and those who became rich working for the government, while their code prohibited stealing from the poor and those who earned a living by manual labor.[18]

Inside the organization, they enforced equality in its top ranks and took special pride in highlighting that all *vory* are equal. And because, compared to previous generation of criminals, *vory* followed a strict code of conduct, or a law of sorts, they soon were called *Vory v Zakone* (Thieves in Law).

The Bolshevik's disastrous economic and social policies (such as a class system) soon provided the underground world with numerous potential recruits. Vast pools of residents of the Soviet Union became the lowest class and had two things in common: nowhere else to turn to survive, and a robust hatred for the ruling regime.[19]

First, there were the intelligentsia. After the October Revolution, roughly three million people—mostly middle class (traders, clergy, landlords, and police officers)—lost not only their property, but also their rights. They were not allowed to vote, join organizations (because all of them were politically affiliated), or work for the government and in factories. Even their children were not allowed to attend universities or join the Red Army. And the worst thing was they were not eligible for food-ration cards (when there was shortages of food) or government-provided healthcare. These policies put the intelligentsia on the borderline of survival. And after selling everything of value they had been able to hold onto (jewelry, gold, and Christian Orthodox icons), they turned to crime to avoid starvation.

Second were the villagers. In 1921, when starvation in the villages began, agricultural workers moved to the towns. But many were not able to find work, so they turned to criminal activities. Then, in 1928, Stalin was faced with two problems—to ensure the food supply for its citizens and the export of grain, and to neutralize the countryside as a potential base for future revolt. And the Bolshevik solution for the first problem—forcefully confiscating peasant grain—only increased the risk of the second.

So the government first seized all farmland, machinery, and livestock for the state. Then they deported, imprisoned, or shot all smallholders and middle-ranked peasants in a campaign known as dekulakization. Finally, they transferred the remaining poorer peasantry onto newly established, state-owned collective farms. As a result, villagers once again ran away to towns, but since they did not have proper documents, they were not able to officially register, so the only way for them to survive was also through illegal activities.

A third group were the orphans. As a result of a civil war (1917–1922) that killed at least seven million people, many children were left parentless, and because the leadership on collective farms was not interested in extra mouths to feed during mass starvation, many orphans ended up in towns where they earned money by begging, singing in train stations and on trains, and robbing. They often lived in big groups in empty buildings, cemeteries, and old train cars.

All of these outcast people became part of the *vory*-led Soviet criminal world. Often, adults and orphan children worked together. For example, while older criminals stole food-ration cards, it was the children who cashed them in, a job they were paid for with a slice of bread.

Because so many people joined the criminal organization so quickly, modifications to its internal organization were made to ensure its survival. First, the organization became more selective about who could be called *vor* (singular from *vory*). Now someone had to be nominated by the original respectful *vory*, and if someone knew something bad about a *vor* nominee but did not say anything, he and the nominee would be punished when the truth was discovered.

More rules restricting in-group behavior and punishment were also articulated. If a *vor* made a mistake, he would be slapped publicly; if he did something dishonorable, he would lose his title; and if he betrayed the organization or its members, he would be killed. There were even special meetings called *pravilki* (roughly translated as *corrections*) where behavior and conduct were discussed, while all other business was discussed in meetings called *shodka* (translated *getting together*). These *vory* were the leaders of the organization.

Soon the Bolshevik government realized that the lowest class was not only growing quickly, but it also was becoming a dangerous opposition to the regime. If the regime was to survive, they needed to take action. But instead of treating the source of the problem, they chose to treat the symptoms and turned to imprisoning those members of the lowest class they were so afraid of.

Thus, in 1921, prison sentences for those involved in organized crime were significantly increased. One well-known statute—article 58 of the Soviet criminal code for counter-revolutionary political activities—also had a so-called sister article: number 59. And just as 58 was used to sentence those who opposed the Bolshevik Revolution, 59 was used to sentence those who took part in "organized crimes against the government" and targeted those who participated in organized robberies of stores or offices (both of which were government property at the time).

Technically, those conducting crimes against regular people were still sentenced to short sentences. But it is important to mention that while one who robbed a villager, no matter how much he took, would qualify for a short prison sentence of one to three years, one who robbed a member of *komsomol* (political youth organization) or a prominent factory worker would be considered a counter-revolutionary, and be accused under article 58 and get a long prison sentence of twenty-five years or even a death sentence.

Also, to starve the criminal organization of new young members, the government decided to radically solve the problem with orphans. At first, the Soviets made an attempt at integrating them into civilian life.[20] When that did not work, they simply arrested and imprisoned any street children older than twelve.

Gulag

When the Bolsheviks took power, they organized many corrective prison camps under the control of different law enforcement organizations, including

NKVD (People's Commissariat for Internal Affairs) and VChK (All-Russian Extraordinary Commission). But with time and ideologization, the governmental attitude and behavior toward members of the enemy class were getting worse and worse. And in 1934, when the Soviet Union started the industrialization process, they relied on the free labor of inmates, and all the prison camps were united under the Gulag (Main Administration of Camps) umbrella. Even the word *correction* once used in the name of the prison camp system was replaced with the word *labor*, leaving no room for confusion about the true purpose of those camps.

As the Bolsheviks continued to jail people, labor-camp populations swelled. Between the Aprils of 1929 and 1930, the main Solovetsky prison camp grew from 19,876 inmates to 57,325. When the main influx (19,720) occurred between November and January, it prompted the construction of several new camps. By August of 1930, the total number of inmates in the camps was about 170,000. Eight years later, the number of prisoners had reached 2,000,000.[21]

The labor camps were located in remote areas and inmates lived in barracks or canvas tents. They worked in the two most dangerous industries—mining and logging. Conditions in the camps were often beyond terrible. Inmates endured Siberian winters without proper clothes and were made to work up to nine hours a day while being fed a little more than a pound (600 g) of bread in that time.

Because *vory* and other members of the criminal organization were not able to avoid Gulag, they had to adjust to the prison-camp environment, and a new chapter in the organization's development began.

Relations with Prison Authorities

It was well known that to survive Gulag, an inmate should work to take the best positions in camps—official positions like foreman or cook. That was exactly how the inmates of the previous generation had survived the czarist prisons. However, this idea was in direct opposition to *vory* ideology. Taking these positions would mean cooperating with the government, which was a cornerstone prohibition of the *vory* rules and had an organizational logic behind it. *Vory* used to say that to maintain their authority in the criminal organization, they could not, for example, work in the kitchen and be accused of such mundane things as not giving enough bread to others.

So *vory* decided they could increase their well-being by placing their most trusted members, often called *blatnyje*[22] or *brodyagi*, in those positions. By doing so, the *vory* received the benefits related to cooperation with prison authorities but did not violate their ideological rules themselves.

Prison guards often had no option but to allow it. According to article 58, the intelligentsia—who were actually more qualified to do the work—were not allowed to take those positions because of their supposed counter-revolutionary political activity. However, article 59—which the *vory* were sentenced under—had no such restriction.

According to Petr Yakubovic, who spent eighteen years in a prison camp and wrote a book, *In the World of Outcasts: Notes of an ex-Katorzanin* [inmate of Katorga],[23] the brodyagi were truly privileged:

> *Brodyagi*: kings in the prison world. They do what they want because they are cohesive. They take all the good jobs—prison inmate leadership, their deputies, cooks, bakers, medical assistants. They are everywhere. In those positions, prison inmate leaders sell good jobs; cooks steal food and give it to their friends (while others are fed leftovers that even the pigs won't eat); and those who work in hospitals are starving their patients and even kill them if it benefits them.

In his book, *Archipelago Gulag*, Aleksandr Solzhenitsyn also clearly says that White Army officers turned *vory* were basically running the prison camps:

> Taking all administrative positions in Solovki [prison camp] under control, White Movement officers started fighting with *chekists* [prison authorities]. [White officers would say] "Your prison camp is outside, and our prison camp is inside. And it is our job to decide who will work where and who will be sent where. We are not intervening in your business outside, and you should not intrude on our business inside."[24]

Relations with Inmates

In addition to benefiting from the *blatnyje*'s positions, *vory* easily took maximum advantage of other inmates through parasitic relationships. "*Vor* would not give other inmates even a cigarette butt, but would prefer to throw it instead," remembered former inmate Yuri Taushkanov.[25]

As former soldiers and noblemen, *vory* were much stronger than the other inmates and did not avoid violence, including with weapons.[26] And such abusive behavior to other inmates lined up with *vory* ideology because the majority of other inmates were still dedicated to the communist regime (and considered their arrest a mistake[27]), so parasitizing them was absolutely in line with the *vory* ideology of robbing those related to the Bolshevik regime. In her memoirs, a former inmate, Stefanskaia, recalls her arrival at Karlag: "First I saw the criminals, the *blatnyje* as they were called here. . . . Seeing us coming in *etap* [a prisoner transport] dressed decently with suitcases, they shouted: 'Counterrevolutionaries, they are bringing the counterrevolutionaries . . . now we will smoke!' "[28]

The *blatnyje* robbed the other inmates mercilessly. They took of all their belongings (especially warm clothes), which led to many other inmates freezing to death in the cold Siberian forest. They also took the best food from the prison kitchen while other inmates starved to death. They forced other inmates to do all the labor and then confiscated from 50 to 75 percent of any money inmates might have earned. In gender-mixed camps, they would often rape females and, in male camps, male inmates.

There were no limits on their behavior, and they were known to even kill for fun. In one of his books, *Kolyma Tales*, Varlan Shalamov mentioned how one *blatnoj* lost a card game and wanted to pay his debt with a nice sweater he saw on an inmate. The inmate obviously did not want to give his sweater to *blatnoj* (it had been a present from his wife), so the *blatnoj* just killed him.

Since the main purpose of prison camps was labor, *vory* had to find a way around it. Because prison guards were only interested in filling the quota and reporting back to Gulag headquarters that the job was done, they were not particularly interested in *who* was doing the work. So *blatnyje*, working in the leadership positions in units, would count what others had produced as the work of *vory*. This meant that the other inmates had to double their own work quota. One political prisoner, Olga Sliozberg, remembers in her book:[29]

> You could not get anything by working hard. We were always fooled, and unit leader *blatnyje* recorded our results as results of their friends. We were getting the heaviest equipment and the hardest tasks. . . . Labor was the last thing that differentiated us from demoralized and cynical *blatnyje*.

Behaving in such a way toward other inmates was not that hard to do since, for example, members of the intelligentsia who were in prison on political charges[30] could not stand against them or reason with them without being killed. Inmates who tried to argue with *vory* that they were all basically in the same boat in the prison camp were answered with what later even became idioms in the Russian language: "You die today, I die tomorrow," and "Greed kills, *fraer* [regular inmate]." According to Solzhenitsyn, "The psychology of the *urki*[31] [meaning *vory* and *blatnyje*] was exceedingly simple and very easy to acquire: 1) I want to live and enjoy myself, and I do not care about the rest; 2) Whoever is the strongest is right; and 3) As long as we're beating up someone else, don't stick up for the ones being beaten. Wait for your own turn."[32]

And the guards, who clearly understood what was happening, did not want to intervene. According to one prison guard's memoirs, the "most hard-boiled group of criminals and gangsters in the camps obeyed only their own rule, which was, 'We do not work.' Following this rule, the only thing these prisoners were allowed to do was to work 'for themselves.' In other words, they could fix food, prepare wood, light the stove, and clean shoes, but nothing else. In preserving their own existence, the criminals had subordinated some of the inexperienced, simple, and healthy prisoners, by using threats and intimidation. These new guys were forced to work 'for two,' that is, for themselves, and in order to defend themselves, for their 'godfathers.'"[33]

But inmates not associated with the *vory* believed that prison guards were actually helping *vory* and *blatnyje* in their abuse. According to Solzhenitsyn memoirs, prison guards told incoming *vory* to "clean up our camp," which meant "stealing and parasitizing to split the prison general population" of political prisoners. Solzhenitsyn also noted "Prison guards smiled at the *vory*, like they only do to *vory*, when *vory* heard there was a female prison camp nearby and already started demanding, 'Show us the women, boss.'"[34]

Vory and *blatnyje* also often lived separately from other inmates, in the most comfortable barracks or tents. These dwellings were called Abyssinia (present-day Ethiopia) or India because they were always warm and crowded, admirable qualities in a Siberian Forest. Sliozberg remembers in her book:

> [It was a] different picture in the "fun" [*blatnyje* occupied] tent. There, seven wooden beds were covered with colorful blankets (pink and blue), and the pillows had embroidered pillowcases. On them were pictures of girls with big eyes, birds, flowers, and the words "Come to me in my dreams, my dear, I love you" or "I cannot be without you day and night." Above the beds were wall hangings made of sacks with embroidered pictures of cats, birds, and flowers. And on the table, they had what we were all most jealous about—a glass kerosene lamp. In this tent, there were night parties, sounds of music and drunk voices of girls and heavy voices of men.[35]

In other prison camps, prison authorities were themselves bringing women to *blatnyje* and *vory* for sex.[36]

And there was no one other inmates could turn to for protection because, as mentioned previously, members of the criminal family had taken all the prison government positions—for example, according to memories of one Gulag inmate, when a prison doctor appointed him to the position of food tester. The inmate was to write an evaluation of the food and the performance of the cooks in a special book, but the doctor warned him that "the cooks were *urkas*, so I had to choose my words carefully."[37]

Even non-criminal inmates who managed to get appointed to camp administration positions could do nothing against them and were even more terrified than others. According to an inmate who used to work in the prison camp hospital:[38]

> Two *urkas* demanded drugs and a work release. Both had been patients in ophthalmology, and I knew them fairly well. They appeared when I was closing the clinic for a day.
>
> "We're sick," Scorpion [nickname of one of *urkas*] said. "We need codeine and a week off work."
>
> I said I'd give them one day off, but that a week was impossible.
>
> "What do you mean, a day?" Scorpion snarled. He parted his tunic to reveal the blade of an ax. We settled on ten packages of codeine apiece and three days off. The decision cost me many sleepless nights. Giving out drugs to *urkas* was a major camp infraction for which I could be rearrested. I was in great danger of being blackmailed. . . . The *urkas* made more frequent visits. They liked opium, alcohol, and codeine. The ax tucked in the tunic accompanied every visit, and I complied with every request.

World War II

Another major event in Russian history, WWII, also brought major changes to the Gulag and the lives of inmates. The setting became even less bearable, and the chances of any inmate surviving the term of his sentence significantly decreased.

Prison camps, particularly those in the north of Russia, were under extreme pressure to increase production when their product was essential for the frontline (e.g., many prison camps in Siberia were producing gunpowder). To achieve that, workdays were increased to ten hours and weekends were canceled. At the same time, because the frontline became the main priority for the country, food rations for the inmates were reduced even further. As a result, starving inmates were unable to work and were dying en masse. The only small chance at survival was admittance to the prison camp hospital, and many turned to self-harm to get a bed. Inmates would cut their fingers off, inject kerosene beneath their skin, and put pencil lead in their eyes. More complicated ploys included eating large amounts of salt, soda, and soap to simulate heart disease, burning the penis with a cigarette to simulate syphilis, and injecting soap or kerosene into the urinary tract to simulate gonorrheal urethritis.

Such Gulag policy changes also changed the life of *vory* and *blatnyje* behind bars. In some camps, prison administration tried forcing *vory* and *blatnyje* to work, and special punishment units for those refusing to work were organized. *Vory* and *blatnyje* were relocated to the worst tents and given minimal food rations. The logic behind it was that if a prisoner does not work, he will die. But if he starts working, he will be moved to a regular unit where his chances of survival increased—albeit marginally. As a result, many top members of the criminal organization gave up their ideology and started working. Basically, they resigned from their positions in the organization, which led to the decrease in the overall number of *vory*.

In other prisons, prison authorities and *vory* made an agreement, with guards basically offering *vory* even more power if they could make the other inmates work harder. So again, *vory* increased their well-being while further decreasing that of other inmates.

The following excerpt from a prison guard's memoir illustrates not only the attitude of *vory* toward these new work-related rules at that time, but also the position young prison guards were in. They often had to cooperate with *vory* in order to not be punished themselves:

> Then I asked an elderly prisoner who was lying on a wooden plank, "Why aren't you at work?" In answer, I heard, "I have been sitting for twenty-five years in the Gulag, and I have never worked for anyone. And you think I'm going to work for you, you little snot-nose? Fuck . . . your mother!" All at once, the whole barracks broke into guffaws.
>
> . . . When we left the barracks, the labor assistant said, "We won't get anywhere until we find the leader."
>
> I asked to see this leader, and we spoke for a long time. . . .
>
> I continued speaking, "If you refuse to get out there and help build these railways tracks, then I will have no choice but to send you and your friends to the Punishment Unit. If you agree to work with me, then you may form your own brigade and organize it however you see fit; I will not interfere. I will have nothing to do with who is in it and who is not."[39]

This guard also offered the *vor* several other preferences like being able to get back to the barracks from the worksite earlier and having their own representative in the kitchen to control food. *Vory* still did not work, but technically their brigade was not only fulfilling the norm but also doing a third more.

At the same time, to fill the place of the huge number of soldiers dying on the frontlines, on July 12, 1941, the Soviet government issued an order allowing inmates to join the Red Army and leave the prison camp. At first, it excluded those sentenced based on the article 58 (who were the most willing to volunteer for the frontline) and criminal leadership, the *vory* and *blatnyje* (who were the least interested in this opportunity).[40] Despite that, around 420,000 inmates (mostly low-level criminals) did exchange a prison uniform for a military one.

As frontline causalities continued to mount, the Soviet government turned again toward Gulag, and this time, they targeted *vory* and *blatnyje* for recruitment.[41] And many of them agreed to volunteer and take up weapons, even though it was counter to one of the *vory* organization's cornerstone rules. Why would they choose to do so?

They did it for several reasons, with patriotism being the last. They were afraid of Stalin's mass executions taking place in Gulag, afraid to starve to death in Gulag as the food supply had become completely inadequate; promised freedom after military service, and lured by the possibility of looting during the war. In fact, *vory* and *blatnyje* became especially interested in joining after the breakthrough battles of Stalingrad and Kursk, when the Soviet Army went from defense to offense and were soon entering Germany, a rich country that looked like a promising looting opportunity.

On the frontline, *vory* and *blatnyje* filled the ranks of the special-penal battalions that were stationed in the most dangerous parts of the frontline.[42] And only after major achievements there, which usually meant being wounded, was one able to move to a regular unit, which was much safer. Desertion was also the highest in those battalions.

Because of the specificity of the membership of these units, they were often run as the prison criminal organization had been. Its members were often involved in stealing from and killing their own brothers-in-arms, and forging documents (e.g., to get food in villages they were passing by). They also brought some of the criminal prison customs with them. One notable example was often bringing the severed heads of Nazis back to their commanding officer, which was the way prison guards in Gulag would prove the death of runaway inmates. The young officers who had to work with the population were often afraid of the criminals and tried not to give them orders they would not like to follow. And when those units finally got to Germany, they were almost totally out of military command, and were involved in massive looting, raping, and killing of local civilians.

Despite their lack of submission, many of those ex-inmates were indeed good fighters. Their fearlessness and general love of adventurism and risk-taking helped achieve the victory against Nazi Germany. Although they were usually used for the most dangerous and almost suicidal operations, some not only survived but won the highest military awards, including five people who won the highest honor: the Hero of Soviet Union award.

Post–World War II

Since Stalin's dictatorial regime was still strong, war medals did nothing to save ex-*vory* war veterans from being reincarcerated in Gulag after their military service had ended. The Soviet government was afraid of any Red Army veterans with combat experience, and often imprisoned them right after they returned from the battlefield.[43]

Understandably, those ex-criminal-leaders-turned-war-veterans expected to move right back into the same class in the *vory* criminal prison system they had enjoyed before they left for the frontline—living work-free and parasitizing other inmates. However, they were met with resistance from the criminal leadership that had spent WWII behind bars because they did not violate a major group rule about relations with the enemy, a rule that *vory* criminal organization could not let pass while struggling for power. This led to a major split in the group that significantly reduced the organization's power, basically putting it on the brink of survival.

The legitimate *vory* considered these veterans weak cowards, assuming they had gone to fight the war in order to avoid going through Gulag hardships. *Vory* also considered joining the Red Army a major violation of criminal rule, and so veterans were labeled as *suki*. This name was chosen because it was basically the most offensive word in the criminal slang at that time. *Suka* not only is a female term (which signals qualities opposite from masculinity), but also literally means a female dog.[44]

According to Shalamov, "You were in war? You carried a rifle? It means that you are *suka*, a real *suka* and have to be punished according to the 'law.' Also you are a coward! You did not have guts to refuse to join an army. Serve your sentence or maybe even die, but don't carry a rifle!"[45]

However, the *suki* did not understand why they had been singled out. Because of WWII, other concessions to the criminal rules had been made, so why was the issue of fighting in the Soviet Army so crucial? For example, although criminal rules also prohibited work in prison and *vory* still did not work inside the prison (as cooks or in the hospital), to survive, the *vory* worked outside of the prison camp logging and mining. *Suki* claimed not further modifying the criminal rules to allow for their military service was hypocrisy.

In addition to these ideological disagreements, legitimate *vory* had no intention of sharing their power with returned *suki* because there was still a shortage of resources in Gulag at that time. In those hungry post-war years, not only was there even less food available in prison camps, the end of the war amnesty on July 1945 released many regular inmates, so there were fewer people for the leadership to parasitize. This *suki-vory* conflict is illustrated in an autobiographic book by Michail Demin called *Blatnoj*:[46]

> "You are not *blatnoj* anymore," I said. "You are no one! So live quietly in the corner. You will be better off that way!"
>
> "Quietly? In the corner?" he said gloomily. "No way . . . I am not stupid . . . So you are like aristocrats, but I should do hard work? Eat empty soup that regular

working inmates eat? No way! I want to live like you . . . What life do you have? A comfortable one."

This conflict was not solved peacefully, and in 1949, a full-scale war between *vory* and *suki* began in prison camps all over the country. And from the beginning, *suki* had the upper hand. First, being ex-military themselves, they had no prejudices against people in uniform and, as a result, were willing to cooperate with prison camp authorities, which garnered them support from prison guards. Second, *suki* had extensive combat experience and were not afraid of blood. And third, they often served as prison guard assistants, which gave them access to weapons.

This internal war was exceptionally bloody, and on any given night, five to ten people might end up dead in one prison camp. That is how Demin describes one such event:

> With the help of one of the prison guards, a *suka* managed to get an automatic rifle. It happened around midnight. He hid the automatic rifle under his coat, carefully left the headquarters barrack, entered the *blatnyje* barrack and, from the door, opened fired. At that time, *blatnyje* were not sleeping, a major card game was ongoing. Players (there were several couples) were on the floor near the stove. They were surrounded by viewers. . . . They all died from bullets. Only the ones who were on the other side of the stove managed to survive. . . . Thirty dead bodies in one night was too much! And although everyone in prison camps had gotten used to blood over the years, such a big number alarmed everyone."[47]

The main goal of *suki* was to coerce legitimate *vory* to join their side, and for that they used brutal beatings and death threats. For example, often a group of *suki*, armed with knives and sharp metal objects, would enter a cell, separate regular inmates from criminal leadership, and offer *blatnyje* and *vory* to publicly reject the *vory* criminal law and follow their rules instead. If a *vor* agreed to join *suki*, he had to perform a public act of kissing the knife or ringing a bell. In prison camp, ringing a bell signaled an official prison activity such as work or dinner, so by doing so, a *vor* signaled that he was ready to cooperate with prison authorities.

But if he did not agree, he was killed. Usually, he would be killed slowly and painfully to terrify the others. According to the book *Black Candle*, about those times in Gulag,[48] "They [*suki*] put a metal sheet on top of a *vor* laying on the floor and two people were hitting it with a hammer." Despite the terror, many *vory* chose death over becoming *suki*.

Bloodshed was on such a massive scale that the remaining *vory* even had to make exceptions to their code of conduct to stay alive. In particular, they agreed that in prison, *vory* were allowed to become hairdressers to have access to sharp objects, such as razors and scissors, so they could defend themselves.

Being supported by the administration, that were also interested in getting rid of the *vory* criminal organization within their prison camps, *suki* were often moved from camp to camp. In particular, one such traveling group of *suki* is often mentioned by inmates who had been in the prison camps around Karaganda (present-day Kazakhstan). The group was headed by Pivovarov, who had once been a respected *vor* but had some kind of problems with other *vory* and was sentenced to death in absentia.[49] He was supported by two Chechens who served as his bodyguards, and they did all the dirty work for him. The Chechens were in prison for a murder they had committed in deportation.[50]

But at some point, prison authorities started losing control, so they decided to stop it by dividing the *vory* and *suki* within the prison camps. This stabilized the camps while still giving prison guards the option of eliminating troublesome members of either group; all they had to do was move an offensive *vory* or *suki* to the other side of a camp.

Because both *vory* and *suki* knew such a move meant certain death, they found ways to avoid it. One way was getting into the hospital after declaring a hunger strike or doing other self-harm. Another more dramatic way would be by earning a new sentence, especially one based on article 58. There have been cases where *vory* or *suki*, after learning they would be moved to a camp controlled by the other gang, went to the center of their prison camp and yelled something like "Death to the Soviet Union."[51]They were then immediately accused of counter-revolutionary political activity, and were given a new, longer prison sentence, but at least they stayed alive to serve it.

Despite the conflict being bloody, it was comparatively short and ended in 1953, as fast as it had begun, with the death of Stalin. General amnesty was given to the *suki*, and they were released from Gulag. And while legitimate *vory* remained imprisoned, their numbers had significantly decreased to no more than a few dozen.[52]

Prison State-Building

Although the *Suki* War was over, the *vory* criminal organization learned crucial lessons from it. First, to prevent such a war from happening again in the future, it became even more difficult to get the title of *vor* and to prove one's dedication and loyalty to the criminal organization.

Second, *vory* realized they also needed support from other inmates. Prison guards had supported the *suki* in the prison leadership struggle because they saw them as fellow WWII veterans who would be easier to work with. So who could the ideological *vory* turn to for support? Only their fellow inmates, whom, in fact, they had been terrorizing for many years. This was the first signal for *vory* to become less oppressive toward other inmates because now they understood very well that in times of need, other inmates were their only chance for survival.

To be fair, choosing between the two evils, other inmates had preferred *vory* to *suki* because they respected *vory* for standing up for what they believed in—opposition to the government—and did not agree with *suki* cooperating with prison authorities. According to an ex-Soviet Army soldier, Janusz Bardach, in a memoir of his Gulag times, "The *urkas* ignored all things political, and in some ways, I admired them for it. Through arrogant and vulgar, they displayed a sense of honesty and dignity I had rarely seen in the Soviet military."

Bardach particularly highlighted inmate respect for *vory* for taking revenge on members of Soviet law enforcement who themselves ended up behind bars: "You didn't have to be an *urka* to get revenge . . . all you had to do was point out your former interrogator to them. I saw one former interrogator stabbed in the heart with a pickax, another smothered with a coat, another kicked and beaten to death in the barracks. In every case, the prisoners collaborated and claimed not to have seen a thing."[53]

Also, the profile of those other inmates had changed.[54] Before WWII, the inmate population was mainly weak intelligentsia who were terrified of their prison surroundings, but the war had changed the population immensely. Now inmates included WWII Soviet veterans (including those who had already survived Nazi military prisons), Soviet veterans who were prisoners of war in Finland during the Russia-Finland war, Russian nationals who had fought on the Nazi Germany side (including Russian prisoners of war who had voluntarily joined Nazi forces), Kazaks who served in the German Nazi Army in Yugoslavia, and members of a national separatist insurgency from Ukraine and the Baltic region.

These people not only had combat experience, they were willing to apply it in prison against potential oppressors, making them a serious threat to *vory*. In addition, there were also regular villagers who were physically strong that had no interest in following *vory* orders. Starting in the 1950s, memoirs recorded more and more stories of regular inmates standing up against the *vory* criminal organization. For example, *blatnyje* who used to go through the luggage of newcomers and take anything of value with little objection now were often beaten (if not killed) by the new inmates.

Since *vory* were not able to rule the new inmates with fear and terror, they tried to build coalitions. At first, the *vory* decided to gather new groups of inmates, particularly the strongest and most segregated. They started by targeting those who served on the Nazi Germany side of the war because they were strong but also segregated. They hated everyone else in the camp and they were hated. Then, the *vory* tried to gain support of Red Army veterans, even respectfully addressing them by their ranks. But neither venture was successful. It did not take the *vory* long to realize they needed to find other ways of ensuring their leadership.

According to historian Alexander Sidorov, not being able to make small coalitions, the *vory* decided to incorporate all inmates into their own prison structure and start a wholesale state-building exercise.[55] But with such a strong constituency, the *vory* had to move from being dictatorial to something more aligned to liberal democracy—something that would make all those different prison citizens happy and, as a result, loyal.

As a government, the *vory* ran all aspects of a prison's internal life (government, budget, public goods provision, and relations with prison authorities) and were held accountable by the prison population. Also, to cement their position as the only legitimate prison leadership, *vory* validated their rule with their code of conduct, very similar to ideology. This neo-code soon became something between a constitution and a religion in prisons all over the Soviet Union. It remains as such even now.

Vory Criminal Ideology

Based on its official ideology since the 1960s, *vory*-run organized crime claims to operate by what is known as A.U.E. This abbreviation, transcribed from Russian, comes from the Russian phrase, which can be translated as the Unified Prisoner's Code.[56] This ideology portrays the *vory* as a Robin Hood–type family—a group of honest people who rob dishonest rich people and give the money to the poor. Additional honorable attributes include avoiding violence, the prohibition of killings (because no one should suffer death for their actions), and respect for the elderly.

The *vory* are also considered to be a brotherhood in a sense that, according to interviewed members of the group, their ideology is more important than any individual member's life. The importance of this family identity is emphasized in sayings like, "One by one we will fall, but together we will survive."

In this same vein, a *vor* is a like a father of the family, meaning it is his responsibility to take care of his sons—lower members of the criminal organization—and to be strict but fair with them. One of the most well-known *vory* tattoos is one that says, "Will not forget mother," where mother refers not to a criminal's birth mother, but to the criminal family itself.

For members of this criminal organization, A.U.E. is more than just an ideology. For many, it is a way of life, and when someone makes a mistake and is kicked out of the organization, he is told, "You do not live the same life as we do."

Some members go even further and see A.U.E. more like a religion, the only right and fair one. And many view *vory* as something close to saints, crystal-clean human beings who cannot be criticized or questioned. Their orders are immediately implemented, their birthdays are celebrated, and their deaths are commemorated every month with a special tradition. Even the official motto of the group testifies of their importance. Dozens of times a day in Russian prisons, this motto rings out: "Life to *vory*, and death to police."

Members of the criminal organization also take particular pride in suffering for the family, much like a martyr might. For example, some members will intentionally provoke prison guards to take stronger actions against them—like placing them in solitary confinement—to show their allegiance to the group. And those places inside the prison where such members are locked up are considered to be something like holy places of suffering. And when these members return from confinement to the general population, they are warmly welcomed by other criminal family members.

So ingrained is incarceration within the A.U.E. brotherhood that prison is considered the family's home, which is something they express in their language. For example, during Soviet Union times, one of the most popular tattoos for members of the *vory* criminal family were the three letters K.O.T., which in Russian stands for *Native Inhabitant of Prisons*. Also, if an inmate is satisfied with conditions in a particular prison, he characterizes them as *homey*, and criminals who spend most of their lives behind bars, with only short periods outside, say, "We may go for walks, but we always return *home*."

This is most likely because prison is where they feel most comfortable. While some of them would be lost, irrelevant, and miserable outside of prison, within its walls, they are very important and powerful; it may even be in their hands to destroy someone's life. As a result, while many regular inmates do not want to return to prison, many members of the *vory* criminal organization are nostalgic about their time there, and never mind going back to the place they call home.

Conclusion

With the radical change in government after the Bolsheviks took power, Russia's criminal world also changed. Bolsheviks empowered those who had been in the lower social class during the previous regime, while those who had lost the most had to turn to the criminal world to survive. As a result, unqualified but dedicated communists got government leadership positions while ex-officers—using their organizational experience, military cohesiveness, strict internal rules, and code of conduct—were able to take control of the chaotic criminal world and organize an ideological *vory* criminal group. The group was later joined by others who found themselves in the lowest class of the communist social order.

As a result, Soviets soon had to turn to mass imprisonment to save their regime, and leaders of the criminal world found themselves behind prison bars. And there, as they had in the criminal underworld, *vory* had the advantage and were able to parasitize on other inmates, who were mostly political prisoners.

So before the end of WWII, the *vory* criminal organization was able to cement its power in prisons by brutal force. But with the mass incarceration of combat-hardened veterans, that was no longer the case, and their monopoly was challenged. On one side, they had competition from ex-colleagues who violated a major *vory* rule in relation to cooperation with the enemy and had fought against Nazi Germany during the war and were now back behind bars. On the other side, the opposition against *vory* members among the regular inmate population had also dangerously increased. Instead of members of intelligentsia accused of counter-revolutionary political activities, now other inmates were battle-hardened WWII veterans, often with Nazi prison camp experience. So to survive, the organization had to drastically change its tactics from openly oppressing other inmates to claiming to work for their benefit.

Although it worked and they were able to maintain their power, the *vory* became responsible for providing inmates with public goods, settling internal conflicts, and representing and defending all inmates in front of prison authorities. Once just a group of criminalized rebels, the *vory* criminal organization now performs the duties a regular government would perform for its citizens.

Also, to cement their position as the only legitimate prison leadership even further, *vory* validated their rule with an ideology based on the original White Movement honor code of conduct that helped them achieve power in the first place.

3
Prison Criminal Leadership

After the bloody *Suki* Wars in the early 1950s, to stay in power, *vory* had to change their tactics from parasitizing other inmates to governing them. But this was not an easy task because they had to build the government structure, develop institutions, and create social structure, all from scratch. They did this with two key objectives. One was to ensure continued *vory* governance and the other was to make the society unified in front of its main enemy—prison authorities.

Criminal Family Leadership

The home for angels is heaven, and the home for a vor is prison.
—A popular saying in the criminal world

On the top level are the *vory* who serve as generals and are the face of the organization. In the beginning of the criminal organization, they were from the middle or even top class who lost everything after the October Revolution in 1917. But since Soviet times, *vory* are mostly from poor families in villages and small towns who took this path because they did not see any way to express themselves and achieve success in regular society.

The *vory* motto is, "Do not believe [anyone], do not be afraid [of anything], do not ask [for anything], and do not kill," and according to a set of general official (but unwritten) rules, *vory* are also supposed to actively support in-groups who (1) live by and support criminal laws and customs, (2) are fair in dealings with each other, (3) work to recruit new young people into the criminal world, (4) help the criminal world control prisons and jails, and do everything possible to oppose the out-groups (not cooperate with the law enforcement and not get involved in politics).

Criminals who obtain this rank are only initiated after demonstrating an "ideal" criminal biography, which might include being in prison on the right charges, and while there, defending other inmates from the prison authorities.

Becoming a *vor* is no easy task as the requirements are fairly rigorous. At least theoretically, *vory* should have no interaction with the official government, which in some interpretation even includes public education. Originally, because *vory*

Criminals, Nazis, and Islamists. Vera Mironova, Oxford University Press. © Oxford University Press 2023.
DOI: 10.1093/oso/9780197645659.003.0004

could not express feelings, they were not allowed to have families (marriage was prohibited, and they had to distance themselves from their parents). They were also not allowed to own homes. These last two requirements were also necessary for security purposes because family and property could be used by the government to exert pressure on the *vory*, something they could not risk.

In addition, a candidate must also have recommendations from two other *vory*[1] and be fluent in criminal rules and norms, which is tested during the ceremonial meeting, an event that usually conveniently coincides with other *vory* birthday celebrations (and sometimes funerals).[2]

Before the decision to crown a *vor* is made, the organization circulates a message about the candidate throughout prisons. This is done to, first, inform inmates about the potential *vor* and, second, to collect information about him. If no information comes back that identifies potential problems with the candidate, he could then be "crowned" at a semi-official ceremony.

Once a *vor* receives his status, he takes an oath to uphold the code, which includes living exclusively off of their criminal profits and supporting other *vory*:

> I am dead. I do not have family and relatives. For me, only the community of criminals and criminal law exists. I lived, live, and will live only according to criminal law. I promise to follow criminal law, be proud of my criminal caste, and work for the benefit of other criminals.

The elevation to *vory* is also marked by specific tattoos, usually two eight-pointed silver stars with eyes in the middle.[3] These are tattooed on the *vor*'s shoulders. Another bestowed tattoo is of a heart with a sword through it. This is to remind a new *vor* what will happen to him if he does not follow the criminal code. These *vory* tattoos allow all other members of the criminal world to instantly recognize them. It also makes it impossible for him to hide his position. Because the punishment for a person who either proclaims himself a *vor* or a *vor* who tries to hide his status is death, these tattoos are taken very seriously.

Being crowned *vor* is not only an honor and a position of power, it is also a big responsibility and a very dangerous job. *Vory* are in charge of enforcing criminal rules on a controlled territory, raising money for the criminal budget, settling all kinds of disputes between both individuals and gangs, and controlling prisons and ensuring the well-being of its inmates.

When a *vor* is imprisoned, it is considered big luck for the inmates of that institution. Because *vory* have connections with high-level people in business and politics, not only can they increase the supply of goods (like food, cigarettes, and even drugs) to the prison from outside, but they can also make sure friendly prison guards get promoted, or at least bribed.[4] According to interviewed inmates, "When a *vor* is in the house [in prison], we have enough of everything and no problems with prison authorities. Everyone wishes to have a *vor* [in their prison]."

Often even prison authorities are happy to have a *vor* because it means more money for them and less trouble with inmates. According to another interviewed inmate, "Our prison was attached to the juvenile prison, and when prison guards could not calm the teenagers down, they would come and ask our *vor* to go talk to the juveniles with them. The *vor* was the only person who was able to control them. They respected him and were terrified of him at the same time."

In prison, a *vor* has a veto power over everything related to the inmate population.[5] When asked to describe the status of a *vor* in prison, many inmates compare it to that of the Queen of England in her country. *Vory* lead a privileged life behind bars, are the ultimate authority, and serve as a very visible projection of the organization's good will by supporting poor inmates and sending presents to the prison hospital. On major holidays, *vory* use their own money to buy food, alcohol, and drugs, and then organize celebrations for the inmates—something that makes *vory* very popular. On these occasions, there are always toasts to the *vor* and his well-being. "You should have seen the high-level of pride *vor* usually walked around the prison yard with, and how everyone greeted him and gave him room," highlighted one ex-inmate behind bars in the 1980s.

Some *vory* take their cult of personality even further and want to be considered a messiah (and elevate A.U.E. from the rank of ideology to the rank of religion). According to one interviewed inmate, one *vor* even went as far as boasting of special powers and some even believed him:

> We had a *vor* who would often say in the morning that he saw in a dream that so and so would happen that day. Then the same day, exactly what he said happened. I am sure that he just knew in advance that these things would happen, but the way he played it made all those devout criminals around him shocked with his "clairvoyant" abilities and put him on an even higher pedestal. Basically, they almost considered him a saint.

Criminal Family Government

Even when a *vor* is behind bars, he is not involved in the day-to-day operations of the prison. Those tasks are considered too menial for his status. Instead, he is usually solving organizational problems on a regional or countrywide scale and running a business outside of the prison, all by phone. Often a *vor* will arrange for a private prison space, complete with office furniture, television, and computer, and use it to hold meetings (including with prison authorities) and make important phone calls.

A *vor* appoints a chief operating officer (COO) of sorts to govern a prison. This inmate is called *polojenets*, which literally means "in the position of [a *vor*]." Since there are many *vory*, which particular *vor* the prison will be looking to depends on inmates. For example, if in a particular prison the majority of inmates are from one region, they will be oriented towards a *vor* from that region.

Sometimes, due to inmate transfers, a prison could be temporarily without a *polojenets*. In that case, inmates elect their leader (but he is not called *polojenets*) until they are able to reestablish contact with a *vor* who will appoint another *polojenets*.

A *polojenets* is usually a *vor* candidate, and the position proves whether or not he deserves promotion.[6] According to inmates, this position is not about power as much as it is responsibilities, if it is done well. A *polojenets*'s main job is to keep things running smoothly. He resolves conflicts among the inmate population and keeps relations with prison authorities friendly. On one side, he is a judge and jury for the inmate population, and on the other, he is like the leader of a labor union negotiating with authorities for better conditions for his members. And his is not a simple job, and in his position, he is very busy all the time. He basically works from the time he stands up from his bed in the morning until he comes back late at night and falls asleep.

While others are watching TV and chatting on their cell phones and just chilling, he solves all kinds of everyday problems. They are small problems, but they are many, and they occur every day. He has to arrange the schedule of family visitations and resolve problems with the prison authorities, like if someone sends something into prison that is not allowed. If an inmate wants to get married, *polojenets* has to arrange it with prison administration. If someone got drunk and stabbed someone, *polojenets* also has to solve this problem, both with prison administration and within the inmate population.

And under prison conditions, solving these issues takes a long time. For example, one inmate's relatives brought him more than the officially allowed 20 kg of food, so the prison guards did not allow the extra food in. The *polojenets* has to solve the issue by first looking for an inmate who did not have relatives to help him (by sending food) and make a deal with him to write this extra weight under his name. Then the *polojenets* has to make a deal with a friendly prison guard so he will close his eyes to such an arrangement. This could take time and effort because the particular prison guard might be busy, and the *polojenets* has to wait for him. Then they have to make a deal and so on. Also, hold-ups could happen on the inmate side. If an inmate writes a complaint about a prison guard, the prison authorities ask *polojenets* to have the inmate withdraw the complaint before any deals can be made.

By hierarchy, a *polojenets* is accountable to a *vor*, and if he does not do his job well, not only will he not get promoted, but he could also be punished. At least in theory, for problems in his prison, a *polojenets* could answer for it with his own life. For example, he might be simply told, "What is going on under your watch? It is your job to make it work, so go suffer yourself [referring to starting a hunger strike or cutting veins], but fix it," according to an interviewed inmate.

One interviewed inmate remembered an event that happened in 1990s in one of the prisons in Russia: "A *vor* arrived at the prison and to welcome him, the *polojenets* put out a table filled with food. But before eating, the *vor* stood up and went to the other inmates living quarters. He opened their dresser drawers, and there was only the basic minimum [of clothing]. It was a big scandal because the *vor* accused the prison criminal leadership of 'eating all that good food while the rest of the inmates have nothing.' " Most likely it was a PR move, but it worked and left a strong impression on inmates.

Since one person cannot solve all the arising problems in prisons, the *polojenets* is helped by a group of lower-level leadership known as *smotryashchiye* (watchers).[7] Some *smotryashchiye* are similar to ministers in the sense that they have a particular portfolio they are in charge of. For example, the right-hand men of a *polojenets* are the *smotryasçiy* of the *obshyak* (mutual fund)[8] and the *smotryasçiy* of the gambling, because both are similar to the ministers of finance and economy, respectively. The next most important level of *smotryashchiye* is those in charge of "the road," which is the communication lines between inmates. According to interviewed inmates, these *smotryashchiye* should be very trusted and have been in a criminal family for a long time. Also, they have to be qualified for their positions. A "*smotryasçiy* of the game" should know gambling and card game rules and be a good accountant. A *smotryasçiy* of the *obshyak* also must be a good accountant because, in addition to working with money, he is also overseeing a warehouse with all kinds of goods.

In addition, there is often a *smotryasçiy* for ideology, whose job is to ensure that *vory* traditions are followed. For example, his portfolio includes gathering all inmates together every month to celebrate the birthdays or deaths of important *vory*. During this ceremony, he also often tells stories about those *vory*, making sure inmates are familiar with their contributions to the *vory* criminal organization.

Then, there are *smotryashchiye* over geographic locations within the prison, and their job is similar to that of a *polojenets*, but on a smaller scale; a *polojenets* is in charge of a prison, while a geographic *smotryasçiy* would be in charge of one of several barracks (in prison camps) or one of several building cells (in prisons). Usually, a *smotryasçiy* is also appointed to manage the stricter prison-inside-prison[9] as well as the quarantine cell (the place where incoming inmates stay for fifteen days before mixing with the general population to ensure they do not have contagious diseases). There are also several other *smotryashchiye* listed in the chart below.

President	*Polojenets*	• Operates prison government • Negotiates with prison authorities
Governors	*Smotryashchiye* of buildings (prison camp)/cells (prisons)	• Oversee locations • Maintain order • Solve minor conflicts between their inmates
	Smotryasçiy of quarantine	
Ministers	***Smotryasçiy*** of the gambling	• Keeps order during games • Acts as a referee • Collects gambling taxes
	Smotryasçiy of the mutual fund (*obshyak*)	• Controls income and spending
	Smotryasçiy of communication	• Maintains connections between cells • Ensures safe passage of goods and messages
	Smotryasçiy of inmate movement	• Gathers information about incoming inmates • Provides necessities to incoming inmates: food, cigarettes, underwear, soap, and toothbrush • Provides civilian clothes for inmates being released
	Smotryasçiy of ideology	Ensures that *vory* criminal organization traditions are followed
	Smotryasçiy of the medical kit	Maintains prison's medical supply
	Smotryasçiy of prison factory	controls the work of the prison factory (supplies and working equipment) Performs HR duties
	Smotryasçiy of the kitchen	Controls food in the kitchen

Figure 3.1 System of criminal governance in prisons

Not only is the *vory* government very similar to that of a country's government, there is even a special room where leaders gather to discuss prison-related issues. This room is called *Kremlin*, after the official residence of the president of Russia.

How is an inmate appointed to one of the *Smotryasçiy* positions? There are three ways. First, a prison's *polojenets* could appoint him. Second, a *smotryasçiy* who is released or moved to another prison could appoint him as a successor. Third, inmates in his cell could appoint him if he shows leadership qualities and is trusted and respected.

When there are several candidates for a *smotryasçiy* position, elections could be held. When no one wants the work and responsibility of a *smotryasçiy*, as is the case sometimes, the *polojenets* will ask an inmate he trusts to take it.

Caste System

Below the top tiers of the *vory* prison criminal hierarchy, the prison population is divided into castes, which are referred to as "colors" or "suits" (like card suits) in criminal slang. One's status in this caste system is based on *vory* criminal family rules and is a purely prison construct. Theoretically, a person's social or economic status outside of prison has absolutely no bearing on his caste status inside of the prison. It is not uncommon for a person who comes to prison with a higher education and an upper-middle class background to belong to the lowest caste, while an alcoholic who can barely read and write and has spent half of his life behind bars will rank much higher in the prison hierarchy.

The most crucial aspect of this prison caste system is the relative ease with which an inmate can fall from an upper caste to a lower caste, but the absolute impossibility of an inmate rising up from a lower caste, even to a previously held status. Also, when an inmate is moved between prisons, his status travels with him (with some exceptions for the juvenile prison), and he has to announce it immediately upon arrival at the new prison. If he does not tell the truth, when the truth becomes known (and it will because of communication between prisons), he will be severely punished—possibly killed. Even if inmates are released and later rearrested, their original caste status remains with them. In dealing with inmates, prison authorities also adhere to this criminal hierarchy and segregate inmates by caste not only inside the prison, but also when transferring them. This makes the prison caste system central to the prison's internal organization, the *vory* criminal ideology, and the life of every inmate.

Upper Castes

Members of this caste follow an unwritten set of rules (or even the customary law or code of honor) called *ponyatiya*, which is translated "the understandings." All other rules are based on *ponyatiya* as well. They are divided into subgroups depending on their purpose:

The first purpose is supporting in-groups: (1) Contribute to the internal criminal mutual fund; (2) Do not hit a *vor* (unless he defects to the government; then he could be killed); (3) Do not accuse someone without solid proof; (4) Do not offend anyone; (5) Do not steal from your own kind; and 6) Follow criminal organization decisions.

The second, opposing out-groups: (1) No spying; (2) Do not work with government institutions; and (3) Do not respect government law.

Finally, honor: (1) Respect seniors; (2) Respect parents (especially mother);[10] and (3) Support those with families.

Behavior with the Enemy

Since the first purpose for the prison rules is resistance against the government (and causing it as much harm as possible), criminal prison leadership follows rules governing the relationship with the enemy:

First set of rules prohibit any help to the enemy including (1) No contact with the law enforcement; (2) No cooperation with any government entities; (3) Never give a witness statement; (4) Never give a confession; and (5) Never be an informer.

A second set of norms call for sabotage of the enemy institutions, including (1) Never work, particularly in prison;[11] (2) Never give allegiance to or follow orders of a government entity (e.g., in relation to military service); (3) Outside of prison, one is not allowed to register where he lives;[12] and (4) Never participate in official events (celebrations and commemorations).

Those rules outline criminal relations with the government and in general distancing itself. Basically everything that a normal person would do in the Soviet society, like officially working, being a member of various communist groups, and participating in communist meetings and parades, was not allowed.

Also, particularly important in the criminal code of conduct is relations with law enforcement and the judicial system, the two main government institutions opposing the criminal world. But as with any ideology, there are different ways and degrees of strictness in interpreting those rules, from the extremely radical to moderate.

Basically, for people following the original *ponyatiya*, any interaction with these enemy institutions is prohibited. In particular, any member of the organized crime system must not seek any help, involvement, or cooperation with the government, even if it would benefit him. He cannot ask police for protection or look for justice in official government courts.[13] And even if someone sued a member of the criminal family or was a witness in a case where he was convicted, he is not allowed to retaliate in kind.

Another consequence of this rule is the prohibition of inmate complaints about prison guards to higher prison authorities. According to the original *ponyatiya* logic, if a particular prison guard is doing something bad, the right course of action is not reporting him; it is killing him.

And in prison, the rules about cooperating with authorities affect even the smallest details of an inmate's everyday life. For example, according to criminal rules, an inmate cannot deal with official prison documents. It used to be that when an inmate received mail, even if a prison guard asked him to sign a receipt for mail he had received, the inmate had to refuse.

Following the same logic, according to the original *ponyatiya*, it is also not acceptable for an inmate to leave prison early on a conditional release, because that would have required him to apply to the court and sign official court documents.

Another forbidden interaction is one inmate turning to prison administration to solve his problem with another inmate. Being afraid of other inmates, asking to be moved to solitary confinement, or even letting prison authorities know about the existence of any conflict is considered major wrongdoing. If an inmate thinks he was punished unlawfully by the criminal leadership, he has to appeal to a higher person in the prison criminal hierarchy. He can never ask the guards for protection. And if an inmate does turn to prison guards and they do not protect him, he will be very likely degraded to the lowest caste.

These rules are so important that even wearing a symbol that signifies cooperation with law enforcement is absolutely prohibited. For example, people who officially work for prison administration historically wear a red band on their arm. So, according to criminal rules, even just wearing the armband for several minutes will qualify an inmate for the lower caste. In fact, a *vor* is not even allowed to introduce himself in prison if he is asked to do so by the prison guards because, according to the logic of *ponyatiya*, by doing so he would be following prison authority orders, which is prohibited.

Not all the members of criminal family agree with such a strict interpretation of those rules, though. For example, many think that if he is called upon to be a witness in a lawsuit, while he cannot contribute in any way to another person's conviction in an official court, he can be a witness for the defense side.

Behavior within the Criminal Family

The second purpose for prison rules comes from the logic of never harming your own kind (other inmates), but instead trying your best to help them. Those rules are crucial to organize a society, and to ensure a peaceful coexistence and cohesive atmosphere. And if peace is not easy to ensure in any normal society, it is particularly hard in overcrowded cells with the worst criminals because, according to an interviewed inmate, "In jail everyone experiences a so-called 'cell-sickness.' It is when you are with the same people 24/7, and in very short time, you start hating everything about them. For example, the way your cellmate washes dishes. And there is nothing particular about him doing so, but still it drives you nuts and you are willing to kill him for it."

Also, without the stability and unity of the internal system in front of government authorities and prison administration, the criminal system does not stand a chance of survival. According to an interviewed *blatnoj* ex-convict, "The main goal of a *polojenets* is to maintain cohesion and respect among the inmates [for each other], because if there are conflicts, it makes the inmate population weak in front of prison authorities, and that means that he [*polojenets*] is not doing his job well." And that is the main difference between *ponyatiya* and traditional laws, according to interviewed inmates. "The purpose of the regular, government justice system is to punish a wrongdoer; the purpose of our system of justice is to restore peace," commented an inmate high in the criminal hierarchy.

This basic philosophy prohibits an inmate from physically or psychologically hurting another inmate or doing something that could hurt the criminal family, and many minor rules and norms of behavior stem from this premise. First of all, several basic personal freedoms and rights are guaranteed by *ponyatiya*:

Freedom of religion. As a general rule, an inmate is judged by his deeds and not his thoughts. So all inmates have to respect each other's religious and political opinions as long as those opinions do not affect other inmates. Opinions that do affect others, however, are dealt with. If inmates had popular WWII and Soviet Union tattoos saying, "Kill Jews, save Russia," they were made to erase them.

Freedom of lifestyle. By prison criminal rules, inmates are guaranteed freedom to live the lifestyle they want, as long as it does not bother others. This is the case even for homosexuals.[14]

Race and nationality. Any discrimination based on ethnicity and national background is absolutely prohibited and punished.

Inmates living by the code are also not allowed to hit others, and swearing is strongly discouraged if not prohibited. For the same reason, often inmates speak in a very monotonous voice—they do not want to be accused of raising their voices at someone. In addition, inmates are not allowed to buy food from the prison kitchen workers because it is considered stealing from other inmates.

A lot of attention is also paid to mutual respect. An inmate always has to be clean and wear clean clothes so as not to bother the other inmates with his body odor. Also since the epidemics and absence of sanitation are widespread, basic cleanliness rules are also institutionalized and enforced by *ponyatiya*. For example, an inmate cannot eat or use anything that falls on the floor if it cannot be washed. For example, it is okay to pick up an apple, but not a cigarette or a piece of bread.

These rules also extend into everyday civilities. Everyone has to be extremely polite. No matter how many times a day an inmate leaves the cell, every time he returns, he has to greet those inside. Also inmates have to thank each other for every favor. In addition, inmates should not spread rumors about each other. It is prohibited and considered intrigue, a punishable norms violation.

In the prison norms, it is also required to respect an individual's feelings and offer support during psychological hardship. For example, it would not be considered polite to ask a person for a favor the day after he had a family visit because family visits are considered to be emotionally difficult. And when an inmate returns from the inner prison (for violation of prison rules), his cellmates will cook him food, boil water for his tea, offer him cigarettes, and often even bake a cake for him.[15]

On the other side, since the most enduring concerns are always the group's safety and resistance to prison authorities, sometimes politeness is compromised to maintain secrecy, and criminal rules reflect that. For example, when one or two inmates are hiding contraband in the cell, everyone in the cell (or even on a floor) will have to leave and wait outside so they will not know where the contraband is hidden. Even if only two people are hiding something, their fifty or more cellmates may have to remain outside of the barrack for several hours, even in winter. Inmates are also not allowed to approach each other in the middle of a conversation without an invitation because the conversation could be about something secret. And asking questions about an individual's lawsuit and trial is strictly forbidden. Without secret knowledge, inmates are less likely to later use that information for their own purposes by sharing it with prison authorities.

Spies and dishonest inmates are a threat to the criminal organization, but inmates who lack restraint are also potentially dangerous. As a result, if any inmate runs off at the mouth and threatens someone else, he has to execute his threat because in prison, words equal deeds. According to an inmate, "Prison rules do not recognize something being said or done by accident. If you said something by accident, it means that you did not think about the consequences of what you said, which in turn means that you are not reliable. And this is not acceptable. Everyone has to be reliable. This way no one has to worry that the person next to him will make a mistake that will cause harm to everyone." Another inmate explained it this way: "Try to be a restrained and reliable person. The most dangerous person in the criminal world is a spontaneous and unpredictable person."

Subcastes

Until the 1980s, the *vory* organization was one class living by *vory* rules. But with the increase in benefits associated with membership, the situation changed. The organization underwent increasing ideologization, and in order to rise in the ranks, more people tried to claim they were as ideologically dedicated to the group as *brodyagi* (*vory* candidates) and even *vory* themselves. As a result, the upper caste split between those who aspire to become *vory* (*blatnyje*) and those who do not (*muzhiki*, men).

To signal their dedication, members of *blatnyje* voluntarily took on more responsibilities inside the group and applied stricter rules to themselves. For example, in times of Gulag, they were not only allowed to work in prison. But it was their main contribution to the criminal organization, by taking official prison positions, to help *vory* and other group members. But with time, they started claiming that working any official prison job was not acceptable for them, as it was not acceptable for *vory*. They also voluntary took additional ideological obligations, and now *blatnyje* cannot have ever worked for the government (in the army, police, or any other government job).

Muzhiki, on the other side, do not have *vory* aspirations and, as a result, do not take additional ideological rules on themselves and, for example, continue working in prison factories (but not in prison maintenance or for administration).

Blatnyje

In prison, *blatnyje* are inmates who usually surrender to a *vor* and follow everything he says. When the *vor* shares his experience with them, they bring symbolic presents (usually food and cigarettes) and are willing to enact any advice he offers. And for them, being constantly near a *vor* is like an apprenticeship.[16] One interviewed ex-inmate—who, out of his twenty-nine years on the planet, has spent ten behind bars—explained it this way: "Relations between us and a *vor* are something like that of a teacher and his students. We could talk to him about anything and ask him whatever we wanted. I am particularly close to one *vor*. I could stay at his house after I am released; he will share his food with me. But I also feel that it is right that whenever I make money, I will share it with him. It is a sign of respect."

Usually *blatnyje* are career criminals in prison for one or more of the following charges: (1) theft, (2) robbery, (3) fraud, (4) extortion, or (5) organized crime. And at least theoretically, a *blatnoj* can never have been imprisoned for a violent crime.

To get into this caste, an inmate should be very involved in the criminal life of the prison and volunteer to do tasks that benefit all inmates. According to interviewed inmates, for that, one needs to be strong with good communication skills that enable him to negotiate with prison authorities.

In prison they usually take leadership positions. If one is not qualified to do so but is physically strong, he could be a so-called *bull* and be used to apply violence (to beat someone) on criminal leadership orders.[17]

Often people in this group come from troubled and underprivileged backgrounds (deep poverty, alcoholic parents, and so on) and have never experienced fairness on any level. Because of this, they have deep-rooted grievances against society. One ex-inmate who had served more than a decade behind bars in 1980s said that *blatnyje* "live by animal instinct based on survival. They divide the world into black and white and the in-group and the out-group. They have a very tribal mentality. For example, [they believe] if someone steals from another tribe, it is good and honorable; but if he steals from his own tribe, then it is bad and dishonorable."

Because opposition to authority, and particularly law enforcement, is highly valued, to increase one's status as a *blatnyje* (and potentially become *brodyaga*), an inmate needs to prove his defiance and does so by refusing to follow any rules given by police or prison guards. This disobedience can take on a range of forms from mild—ripping prison numbers off of his clothing or not closing the top button of his uniform (to extreme) organizing riots, hunger strikes, and mass self-harm. Of course, the more risk an inmate takes in opposing prison authorities, the more respect he earns.

For example, one *blatnoj* inmate garnered immediate recognition when he refused all interaction with the prison administration. Prison guards had appointed him an official cell leader, and as such, one of his duties was saying the number of inmates in the cell every time prison guards asked for it. Not only did he refuse to do so, but every time guards entered the cell, he pretended not to notice them. Each such incident of disobedience earned him fifteen days in solitary confinement, but that did not stop him. He was only interested in increasing his status in the eyes of his peers.

On the other side, with increasing ideologization and members of this caste competing for most dedicated status, it sometimes takes extreme forms. For example, one inmate claimed that he did not recognize his prison uniform or his bunk bed, so he wore only his underwear year-round and slept sitting on the floor.

Muzhiki

The biggest group of inmates falls into this category. These are inmates who only want to peacefully and comfortably serve their sentence and return to normal life. Although *muzhiki* are very respectful of common inmate interests, and help when possible, they are different from *blatnyje* in that they are not expected to put their personal interests lower than those of the criminal organization. They take a neutral position in prison authorities versus prison criminal leadership power struggle. They do not challenge criminal leadership, and they do not cooperate with prison authorities or work in jobs that help maintain prison operations (e.g., working in the kitchen).

In prison criminal bureaucracy, *muzhiki* usually take low-level, nonmanagement positions such as watching hallways for passing prison guards[18] or being in charge of the book of inmates—a ledger with the basic demographic information of everyone in the prison population.

Inside the *muzhiki* caste, there is also a group of inmates who do not work for the benefit of the general prison community, but for the personal benefit of the top criminal leadership. They are called *sniri*. They are also not an original subcaste but appeared with time. As more people who wanted to reach leadership roles in the *vory* organization for benefits associated with it did so, they wanted to enjoy those roles. One such benefit was having a *snir*.

Sniri are usually tasked with doing what one interviewed inmate called "female jobs." They wash dishes and clothes and clean the cell (except for toilets). Usually only members of the upper castes, such as *blatnyje* and *vory*, have *sniri*. They pay *sniri* with money, food, cigarettes, and favors. For example, as *sniri* for the criminal leadership, these inmates are also allowed some of the same small privileges prison administration allow the criminal leadership. They are sometimes allowed to sit on the bed (which is prohibited during the day) or have colored bed sheets. Inmates become *sniri* for several reasons:

1) They volunteer. These are inmates who are not getting any help from outside the prison, so they work to support themselves. For example, if they cook for criminal leadership, they can also eat their food.
2) A psychologically stronger inmate coerces a weaker one into becoming his *snir*. This can only be done verbally because it is prohibited to make anyone a *snir* by force. According to an interviewed inmate, "A *blatnyje* would choose a weak, quiet guy and start doing a carrot and stick exercise to him. He would press him, saying things like, 'What is the use of you in this room? What are you doing? How are you contributing to everyone's well-being?' At the same time, the *blatnyje* would also tell him that if he agrees to work as a *snir*, the *blatnyje* will take care of him."
3) Sometimes a person could become a *snir* because he owed someone money and was unable to return it on time and is repaying his debt by working for the person.

According to an interviewed inmate, "*Sniri* are often not bad people that did something wrong. They are simply stupid and very useless people." And once a person agrees to be a *snir*, it becomes very complicated (but still possible) for him to leave this job.[19]

4
Lower Class of Inmates

> *In prison you are alone. If you start looking for friends there, you will fail. Before prison I was fighting in war. War is a terrible place. But prison is worse. In war, you have a friend next to you and feel his support. In prison you do not.*
>
> —An interviewed former inmate

As in any ideological organization, the *vory* have a very strict divide between group members (upper caste in prisons) and non-group members (lower caste).

To distinguish themselves, members of the higher criminal class call themselves "people" or "decent inmates," while members of lower classes are referred to as "not people," "not decent inmates." And when someone is moved from the upper caste to the lower caste, it is often officially explained with the literal translation, "He does not live the same life as we do." That means a downgraded person does not have the same moral values or has violated prison criminal rules. As a result, he has lost his honor or credibility—the most important inmate characteristics in the criminal world.

Purpose

The existence of these lower castes is based on need and designed to solve the following problems:

Doing the Dirty Jobs

To make the majority of inmates happy, someone has to do jobs no one else wants to do. The remedy is to appoint a small group of constantly oppressed and unhappy inmates who are forced to perform those unpleasant tasks. This solution works best as opposed to either making all inmates do the work (and making everyone unhappy) or leaving those tasks undone (which also makes everyone unhappy).

Criminals, Nazis, and Islamists. Vera Mironova, Oxford University Press. © Oxford University Press 2023.
DOI: 10.1093/oso/9780197645659.003.0005

People	Leadership	Have to follow all the rules	*Vory*	Top Criminal Leaders
			Polojenets	Top Prison Criminal Leader
			Blatnyje	Prison Criminal Leadership
	Decent Inmates	Have to follow majority of rules	*Muzhiki*	Ordinary inmates
			Sniri	Servants to the leadership
Not People	Not Decent Inmates	Violated in-group or out-group rules	*Sherst*	Those who cooperate with authorities (and work in prison maintenance)
		Violated ideological rules	*Petukhi*	Passive Homosexuals and those equal to them

Figure 4.1 Prison caste system

Punishment

Inmate leadership has few options to punish those who misbehave, and thus less of a mechanism to scare inmates into complying with their rules. Basically they can either kill someone (and be punished for it by prison authorities) or beat him. And since they are already imprisoned, the only way to isolate those they want to punish is with a lower caste. And the system works. According to one inmate, "Guys are so afraid of being moved to the lowest caste, it stops them from doing a lot of things. It even works with drug addicts. They stop taking hallucinogens because they are afraid that, in an uncontrollable state, they will do something punishable and be downgraded in the caste system."

Security

In the outside world, a dangerous person can be isolated in prison, but again, within the prison, the only recourse is a lower caste. This is especially true of informants or the psychologically unstable who pose a threat to the general inmate population. Relegating such inmates to lower castes makes it clear who they are and what can be expected from them, and, as a result, what the norms of interaction with those inmates should be.

Emotional Well-being

Inmates with long sentences are trapped in an intimate environment with people of different practices and personalities for years, making it necessary to have a system where they can at least tolerate each other. Since inmates do not have the option of kicking others out of their prison *home*, they need to reduce interaction with some inmates just to make the situation bearable. For example, since the majority of inmates do not want to be anywhere close to a child molester, separating him into a lower caste affords separation, which reduces conflict. Other inmates may just cause too much trouble and conflict, so interaction with them can also be reduced by making them members of a lower caste.

Show of Power

Because criminal leadership can make the decision to degrade any inmate to the lowest caste, the caste system operates as a powerful tool to control the masses and to project the groups' power to potential outside enemies, such as prison authorities.

Since, as any ideological organization, the *vory* organization has three sets of rules, this lower caste of the prison criminal society is divided into subcastes according that coordinate with the particular criminal rules its members violated:

Sherst' Caste

Any inmate who violates rules related to relations with the enemy (prison authorities) or in-group relations' rules become members of the *sherst'* caste (individual members are called *koza*, goat[1]), and they officially work in prison under the guidance of prison authorities. Compared to the *muzhiki*'s subcaste (of the upper caste) who work in prison factories, members of *sherst'* caste work in the prison maintenance, the medical unit, the kitchen, construction, or landscaping, and generally help prison authorities.[2]

Because members of *sherst'* caste are considered supporters of the enemy, there are several restrictions on *sherst'* interaction with members of the upper caste. They are not allowed to just walk around upper-caste barracks. If they need to enter—say to bring prison laundry or to talk to criminal leadership—they first have to wait outside while the inmate they came to see is notified. Then they have to loudly announce they are entering the room. While they are in the barrack, they are not allowed to sit down.

Types of *Sherst'*

There are many different ways for inmates to end up in this caste, and divisions within the caste are very hard to classify. Even the Russian word for this caste—which translates *wool*—comes from the Russian word *raznošerstnyj*, which means *patchy*, implying that this caste is made up of all different kinds (patches) of people.[3] Here are the main identifiable divisions, all of which are based on an inmate's actions:

Suki (or *Bitches*)

These are inmates who, at some point, had cooperated with law enforcement or informed on someone. As discussed in Chapter 1, in the early days of the organization, these inmates would have been killed. But now they are just moved to this caste.

Krysy (Rats)

Inmates become rats if they have stolen from other inmates. In the past, those people also would have been killed, but now they are only badly beaten[4]—set in a chair and struck on his back with a wet, knotted towel by everyone—before being demoted to *sherst'*.[5]

Fuflyzhnik

An inmate who owed money he could not return on time and, as a result, violated in-group relations rules. A *fuflyzhnik* is moved to the *sherst'* barrack.

Troublemakers

Inmates may also send people who constantly stir up trouble to *sherst'*. For example, a *muzhiki* inmate was constantly lying, being rude, and occasionally showing aggression toward fellow prisoners. When the other inmates had enough of him, they told the troublesome inmate to take his mattress and move to the *sherst'* barracks.

Lomonuvshiesya

If an inmate is unable to solve his conflicts with other inmates or criminal leadership, and he goes to the prison authorities for intervention or protection, he becomes *lomonuvshiesya*. An example might be one inmate about to be punished for violating criminal rules asking prison guards to remove him from his cell and put him in a safer place like another cell, solitary confinement, or the inner prison.

Often, this tactic is employed by an inmate about to be released on parole and other inmates do not know it.[6] In these cases, an inmate would take advantage of the other inmates' ignorance by first borrowing money or breaking criminal rules, and then asking prison guards to move him to a safe place until his release date.

Although this works temporarily, the offending inmate is eventually found out, and his misdeed will not go unpunished. Even if prison guards drive a released inmate to a bus or train to avoid him being beaten outside the prison gates (by members of the prison family outside), there is a good chance the offender will be imprisoned again at a later time. Whenever (and wherever) that happens, his *lomonuvshiesya* status will be waiting for him, along with a severe beating.

Dishonorable People

This catch-all status is for everyone else whose actions vary from what is considered normal in-group relations by other inmates and is therefore arbitrary. For example, an inmate lent his cell phone to a friend. The friend used the phone to call his sister. When the friend returned the phone, his sister's phone number was in the recently dialed log. When the first inmate got his phone back, he began calling his friend's sister and asking her inappropriate questions (like her bra size). When she complained to her brother, the first inmate was beaten and moved to *sherst'*.

Such an absence of defined qualifications leads to a softening in the once well-defined border between *muzhiki* and *sherst'* caste, and as a result, *blatnyje* have to apply extra effort to reinforce it. One interviewed inmate who had spent ten years behind bars in the *blatnyje* caste explained:

> *Muzhiki* often sympathize with the *sherst'* and communicate with them. The two groups are socially close, and *muzhiki* understand they could easily end up in *sherst'*. So we always have to limit their communication. *Blatnyje* often ask *muzhik*, "Why are those people [*sherst'*] hanging out near your bed? Are you friends with him? Why are you blurring the lines?" They need to be constantly reminded that *sherst'* should not be near *muzhiki*.

As a result, so that *muzhiki* are not overly friendly with members of this caste, upper caste inmates are not allowed to enter *sherst'* barracks for any reason. If they need to talk to a *sherst'*, they ask at the door for the *sherst'* to step out of the barrack and talk to him there.

Degraded Caste

Members of this lowest and the most complicated caste have many names including *petukhi* (roosters), *obizhenyye* (that could be roughly translated as "offended" and comes from the slang expression "offended by life"), and P.I.N.C.H.—a Russian-language abbreviation of *Pust' Idet Nizhe Cheloveka*, meaning "let him walk lower than a man." And officially, prison authorities call them people with low social status.

Basically, the inmates in this caste are passive homosexuals, ones who are acted upon, and other inmates believed to be equal to them. Active homosexuals are usually from higher castes because being an active homosexual is not prohibited. Currently an inmate can end up in this caste a number of different ways:

First, some passive homosexuals either voluntarily inform other inmates about their homosexuality, have a reputation that has followed them into the prison, or are seen performing this homosexual act within the prison.

Second, an inmate raped by another inmate—who is looking for sex (and found a particular inmate handsome) or showing his power—becomes a member of this caste. Even though, according to criminal rules, rape is unacceptable and punishable, the victim was still involved in passive homosexuality and so is degraded.

Third, an inmate who enters the prison on criminal charges like rape and pedophilia are immediately put in that caste for so-called immoral crimes.[7] One person in the degraded caste was in prison because of some kind of psychological problem: he hated children. He would beat them on the streets, pee in the strollers, and put banners near the maternity ward of hospitals saying, "Give birth to a dead child."[8]

Fourth, this subcaste also contains people who touched or were touched by excrement, even by accident (known as *forshmanutsy*),[9] and those who touched or were touched by a penis (or by something that was touched by penis). This is known as *zakontacheniye*. But this is not a cleanliness issue. There are so-called *cherti* (devils), who do not take care of themselves—do not shower regularly and do not wash their clothes—yet they are not violating prison ideological rules and are still part of the upper caste. They live in the farthest corner of a prison barrack, but they are still in the *muzhiki* caste. The official reasoning here is that usually the attitude of these inmates is associated with the stress of being in prison, and with time they change their behavior and become no different from other members of *muzhiki* caste. At that point, they move out from the barrack corner.

Finally, people end up in this caste because of stupidity. Some inmates find themselves in this caste for reasons that could not fall under any other rational category. For example, in one prison there were two inmates who got drunk and had an argument that turned into a fight. Then one of them decided to degrade the other by raping him. He got undressed and started the process but was not successful, and because they were both drunk, they passed out. When their prison mates found them naked on the floor, they immediately moved both to the degraded caste.

Also once an inmate decided to pretend to have a psychological disorder so he could serve his sentence in the hospital instead of the prison camp. In trying to simulate psychological problems, he would regularly cover himself with excrement. Experienced doctors immediately uncovered his simulation and, instead of at the mental hospital, he served his sentence in the lowest caste of the prison general population.

According to interviewed inmates, inmates who grew up in state orphanages are disproportionally overrepresented in the lower and, particularly, the *petukhi* caste because (1) they often consider snitching an acceptable practice; (2) they have socialization problems and often run into conflicts with other inmates; (3) they do not have outside family support and have to earn money by prostituting themselves; (4) homosexuality and rape are widespread in the orphanages, and those inmates cannot hide being raped because many orphans from the same institution end up in the same prison;[10] and (5) many of them spent time in juvenile prison where rape and being degraded are also widespread.

In prisons, *petukhi* do the dirtiest jobs, like cleaning bathrooms and trashcans; and the most dishonorable jobs, like clearing the strip of land near the prison fence so prison authorities can easily see any footprints left by inmates trying to escape.[11] Some of them also prostitute themselves and are used for sex.

It is a very small caste (around 5% of inmates), but the rules for interacting with its members are very complicated. Members of this caste are basically untouchables. Inmates from other castes are not allowed to touch them (except during sex), take anything from their hands (although one could give them something), or eat and drink from the same tableware as they do. And any inmate who oversteps these boundaries for any reason is degraded and also becomes a member of the caste.[12]

In a prison camp, the degraded usually live in a separate barrack. In some prisons, they have a special table assigned to them in the canteen. There, they usually eat from special tableware marked with a drilled hole or other identifiable mark. In other prisons, however, they are not allowed to enter the canteen, and food is delivered to their barrack by inmates from the *sherst'* caste. If there is an inspection by correction authorities and everyone has to attend the canteen, degraded inmates will sit separately and not touch anything, not even a plate.

Their segregation is as thorough as possible. In some prisons, the degraded have their own gym, sit in a dedicated row in the cinema room, and only use a particular washstand[13] and electric sockets. They are also not allowed to put their food in communal refrigerators or enter the cooking area. When the unit is moving between buildings in formation, the degraded have to be at the end of the row. Sometimes, there are also special door handles for them (usually just a nail in the door), so that they do not even touch the door handles used by others.

In prisons like those in Central Asia, *petukhi* have to lean against the wall when anyone from the higher caste is walking down the same hallway, and they are never allowed to stand physically higher than *muzhiki* inmates. If a *muzhik* is standing, a member of the *petukhi* caste has to sit, and if a *muzhik* is sitting, the *petukh* has to lie down. Sometimes, in prisons in Georgia, these inmates are not even allowed to look at members of the higher caste as they pass by. Finally, because of their untouchable status, they cannot even be beaten with hands or feet, only with objects.

Not only is being in this caste extremely difficult—almost unbearable for inmates—once degraded, there is no way for an inmate to change his status. As a result, although *petukhi* are a very small group of the inmate population, they commit almost half of all prison suicides. The emotional damage is also evident. Previous to becoming infamous serial killers in the post-Soviet Union, several had once been members of this caste.[14]

Evolution of Ideological Rules

Rules in relation to the lowest caste described above are how they work right now, but the rules were not always like that. In his memoirs, former Gulag inmate Janusz Bardach describes the following scene he witnessed in a prison camp shower in 1943:

> Through the stream I saw two young men, both *urkas*, standing together. They held each other at the waist and brushed their erect penises over each other's bodies. Sitting on a bench, another skinny fellow masturbated a friend, who held him in return. I glanced around to see if anyone else had noticed and became aware of several other couples in intimate positions. A middle-aged man lay on a bench masturbating in front of everyone. He ejaculated and smeared semen all over his body. No one reacted.[15]

Such situations seem absolutely unimaginable to anyone familiar with prisons today. So how did the *vory* organization move from such openness in homosexual relations among even its top leadership to now even throwing away a table once touched by someone who had touched a toilet a decade before (degraded)? It is a result of the organization's ideologization.

Events described in memoirs above took place before the *Suki* War when the *vory* criminal organization was fighting for its survival and was focused only on rules regulating in-group interaction and relations with the enemy. But when in 1954, the *vory* got involved in state-building inside prisons, to legitimize their leadership they basically invented an ideology and, as a consequence, ideologically inspired rules to serve their purposes. Those ideology-based rules gave prison criminal leadership a lowest class to do dirty jobs, a punishment mechanism, and the ability to signal their control and power by enforcing those rules. And they chose to base the ideology on individual sexuality.

One could think that because so many sex-deprived males live in a closed, intimate environment, it is understandable that many customs could have come up around disassociating with the homosexual population and that it would be considered safer for the entire group to separate a person the minute there is a slight suspicion he is a homosexual. But if that were the case, it is the active homosexuals who should be shunned, not just the passive ones like is done by *ponyatiya*. In reality, not only are active homosexuals not punished, they even are proud of their active homosexuality.

First, it should be taken into account that those rules were introduced in times when top criminal leadership had the longest prison sentences, and many had been in prison most of their life and have never even had sex with the female. So the ideology basically institutionalized and legitimized what they already did anyway, whether it be raping a fellow inmate or having consensual sex with him.

And second, since one of the main goals of these ideological rules is to show that the organization could enforce even the worst and most unpopular rules, those acts are often done publicly. According to an interviewed inmate, *petukhi* are often used sexually to show domination. An upper-caste inmate will parade through the cell with the *petukh* and then do the act while everyone is awake in a highly visible area near the toilet.

On the other side, prison criminal leadership tried to make sure that ideological rules related to the caste system did not negatively affect members of the upper castes. So despite strict separation rules that do not allow touching anything a *petukh* touched, there is one exception: contraband items. Often cell phones, drugs, or other prohibited objects are hidden with *petukhi*. *Petukh* might even smuggle contraband into a prison in their underwear or anus, and those items are allowed to be touched by others.

And in the beginning of the *vory* criminal organization, running prisons with those rules and a caste system served its purpose. But the problem was that, with time, those ideologically inspired rules and their enforcement took an unexpected turn—they disproportionally increased in strictness of enforcement.

First, ideological rules came to be enforced almost religiously, and much more strictly than crucial out-group rules, which lead to one being degraded to the *sherst'* caste. So when inmates want to show their dedication to the criminal family, they do so by showing how strictly they can enforce its ideological rules. Also those caste aspects of *ponyatiya* are the easiest to follow and the least costly for a person to enforce. It is much easier to prove one's loyalty by enforcing the rules on someone weaker than to uphold oneself. For example, it is much easier for one to make *petukh* clean toilets than it is to abstain from talking to prison authorities.

Second, as a result, inmates who want to rise within the organization often overdo the rules involved with the lower caste. Over time, these overblown regulations have evolved into something hard to rationalize, but still, these rules are very carefully observed. Even the criminal leaders whose job is to enforce *ponyatiya* say the fear of violating the rules, in some cases, goes way too far. But despite that, not many people in leadership will dare say or do anything to lessen those rules. They are afraid to be accused of not supporting the organization (and its ideology) enough. And because there is a constant competition within the prison criminal leadership, being too lenient is an easy rule to accuse someone of violating.

For example, in the beginning of the *vory* criminal power, while members of this caste were segregated and untouchable, other inmates were still allowed to talk to them and even play cards with them. They even lived in the same barrack as other inmates, just in the corner. But now the lower-caste rules have increased in intensity. One prison had a major problem with tuberculosis, and once a medical unit from the nearest hospital came to do crucial, early diagnosis chest x-rays. They were not familiar with the prison caste system and started doing x-rays based on everyone's last name in alphabetical order. When inmates from the *muzhiki* caste noticed that inmates from the lower castes did x-rays before them and had touched the x-ray machine, they refused to do it themselves and demanded a new x-ray machine.

Despite these caste rules, it is still important to show that criminal leadership does not force anyone to do anything other than comply with official *vory* prison organization rules. So if an inmate from the *muzhiki* caste has sex with *petukh*, there has to be payment involved.[16] This payment signifies two things: that *petukh* was not forced into having sex, and the *muzhik* who had sex with *petukh* had no feelings for *petukh*. If it appeared there were any feelings between the two individuals, the *muzhik* would also be degraded to the *petukhi* caste.

Another such disproportionate rule is that one cannot touch a penis or excrement or anything that was touched by a penis or excrement. Though the original reasons for these rules most likely had in root in some practicality, due to extreme enforcement over time, these rules were forced into illogical dimensions.

One issue is taking the rules too literally. For example, those who worked as plumbers outside of prison end up in the lowest caste (touching excrement). Also, there is currently a lawsuit in the European Court of Human Rights from an inmate who was degraded because he slipped while in the out-house toilet and touched what was inside and is now accusing Russia of tolerating caste systems in prisons.[17] And due to the strictness of such rules, terrified inmates go to great lengths and through serious inconveniences not to violate those rules.

For example, old traditional *vory* used to smoke using a mouthpiece. This was done in case the cigarette had either fallen to the ground by accident or been touched by a member of a *petukhi* caste. In rare cases, inmates might go as far as doing something that could seriously hurt themselves so as to not violate *ponyatiya*. For example, an inmate was diagnosed with prostate cancer but refused treatment because, according to *ponyatiya*, the penis is a sacred organ and cannot be touched by someone else.

Second, having no leeway for rules that contradict each other or require common sense. For example, if passive homosexuality is punishable, another action that directly contradicts a suspicion that a person is a passive homosexual is also punishable.

In particular, the most dangerous, unexpected, and common way for many newcomers to be degraded to the *petukhi* caste is by divulging a history of oral sex with a female. By *ponyatiyá*, oral sex with a female is, in fact, a prohibited action. The logic is, that by having oral sex, an inmate has touched something that was before touched by the penis (even his own). So doing it (or having done it) immediately puts an inmate in the lowest caste.

Of course, engagement in oral sex with a female is impossible to check especially if it happened outside of prison, but experienced inmates who want to degrade a newcomer will start an open conversation about sexual practices in hopes that the new inmate will confess. According to an interviewed inmate, "We even had a guy fresh from juvenile prison who had definitely never had any kind of sex. But he wanted to show off in front of others and talked about having oral sex with his girlfriend. Of course, we felt bad for this stupid kid, but there is nothing that could be done about him. He is a *petukh* now."

And like the majority of other *ponyatiya*, there are no exceptions to the rule. There was a foreign inmate with poor Russian skills and very little understanding of prisons in general, not to mention the strange concept of *ponyatiya*. Some of his cellmates decided to degrade him, and since it was the easiest way to do so, they started a discussion about sex. Not expecting any problem, he admitted to kissing a girl after she had given him a blowjob. As a result, he was immediately degraded, even though he had no idea what that meant. In this particular case, because he was a foreign national, the prison authorities eventually intervened and transferred him to a special prison under total control of prison authorities and not the criminal world where the caste system was irrelevant.

In another case, an inmate was showing photos of his girlfriend on the phone and mentioned that she had given him a blowjob. In the next picture, they were kissing. There was nothing he could do at that point to remain in the *muzhiki* caste, and he peacefully moved to the *petukhi* barrack.

This particular rule was also officially used during a criminal family gathering in 1956, and it prohibited females from ever becoming *vor*. This position followed the particular case of the female *vor*, Aglaya Demidova. When she was imprisoned (ten-year sentence), she decided to escape to be with her lover, another *vor*. To accomplish this, Aglaya began a romantic relationship with the prison doctor so he would write her a tuberculosis diagnosis and procure her an early release.

But what she was doing became known in the criminal circles. Because she technically violated two criminal rules—cooperation with prison authorities and having sex with males (being-penetrated-by-a-penis rule)—the decision was made to kill her. Her cellmate in prison tried to execute this verdict and strangle her, but she was not successful. Aglaya instead killed her by smashing in her skull. As a result, she had to attend a new criminal trial. During transport to the court, Aglaya escaped and found her *vor* lover. It was he who had to execute the *vory* verdict. He ended up stabbing her to death with a knife.

Third, there are no exceptions to a rule even if it is counterproductive and makes the organization weaker. Sometimes prison authorities use the caste system to punish, exact revenge on, or extract information from an inmate. And even when it is the prison authorities who do the degrading, there are still no exceptions. For example, in the Caucasus, one person was imprisoned for killing the director of one of the prisons (who had tortured his brother). Immediately after the police caught him, to avenge the director, in addition to torture, they degraded him. And although inmates respected the killer for what he did, he is still serving his sentence in the lowest caste. According to an interviewed *blatnoj* inmate who served his sentence in the same prison: "Everyone is respectful to this guy. They make jokes with him, give him things [for example food or sweets] and he is allowed to watch TV with *muzhiki*. But at the same time, no one will drink tea with him or have any physical contact with him. Of course, we felt very sorry for him, but that does not change anything."

And according to a respondent who was in prison in 1960s and is now also in the same prison with this person, "Back then, *vory* could not have even imagined that it could be the case [prison guards could degrade]. They would roll over in their graves. Not only would no one even think of putting this person to the lowest caste, but he would have been very respected by all *vory* for what he did and most likely been promoted in the criminal family." But in the current situation, there is nothing to be done, and even the old respondent has to follow those new rules.

Different Approaches to *Ponyatiya*

Since those ideologically inspired rules serve particular purposes, the attitude toward them and, as a consequence, their enforcement may vary, depending on the need and status of those applying it in the criminal family. And that allows reasons for ideologization to be traced not only looking at how enforcement varies over time, but how it varies in space—between different prisons and with different types of inmates. And in prisons, the context depends on a prison's security levels. In former Soviet countries, prisons are divided into *Obsiy*, or common (minimum security); *Strogiy*, or strict (medium security); and *Osobiy*, or special (maximum security).[18]

The level of prison security an inmate is assigned to not only has to do with the seriousness of his original crime, but also his behavior within the prison. For example, if an inmate in a medium-security prison follows A.U.E. ideology and *ponyatiya* and, as a result, refuses to even tell his name to the prison guard during the mandatory formation, he would first be placed in the inner prison for some time. Then, if the inmate does not change his behavior, with an order of a special committee, he would be sent to a maximum-security prison.[19] Also, while there is a division in prisons for first-time offenders and repeat offenders in minimum and medium-security prisons, they are mixed together in maximum-security prisons. As a consequence, the attitudes and adherence to *ponyatiya* in those prisons also varies.

Minimum-Security Prisons

At the lowest level of security, inmates are obsessed with the visible symbols of *ponyatiya* but not interested in the logic behind them. Prison criminal leadership mostly use *ponyatiya* to show off and increase their standing among their peers. As a result, they often overdo it. According to an interviewed high-level member of the criminal organization, "Competing for power, young guys would accuse each other of all kinds of *ponyatiya* violations, and as a result we ended up with a lot of degraded." Also, since the inmates in these prisons usually have short sentences, they do not care about the long-term consequences of their actions for the prison society.

The situation is even worse among first-time offenders. Many of them have never interacted with *ponyatiya* before, and so they have no real understanding of its rules and its logic. Not only that: there is no one to explain it to them. As a result, fights among inmates and conflicts with administration are frequent.

As one interviewed inmate mentioned, "Here, inmates are obsessed with the form of *ponyatiya*, but have little understanding of its substance." These inexperienced inmates are concerned with the rules so much that new inmates are often advised to do strange things, like not to use any bird or bird-related words. This is in order to avoid making reference to anything related to *petukhi* by mistake. And in facilities that allow colorful clothes, inmates will avoid wearing red because it is considered the color of *petukhi*.

More experienced inmates make jokes about how minimum-security inmates interpret *ponyatiya*. One goes like this:

> A very old, experienced, and respected criminal is being transferred by prison train to a camp where he will serve his sentence. Some new inmates are on the train with him. They are cup stealers and are eagerly waiting for the older criminal to drink his tea so they can take his cup.
>
> When the older criminal takes his cup from his luggage, the new inmates are shocked and puzzled. The cup is decorated all over with bright red *petukhi*. The older criminal smiled. "This is the only way I can protect my cup from you first timers," he explained, and he calmly drank his tea.

As can be expected, the general ignorance of minimum-security inmates means life for the lowest caste, the *petukhi*, is the worst in these facilities. Not only are inmates degraded for almost no reason, once there, they are constantly offended and abused. Everyone wants to exercise their power over them. *Petukhi* also have no recourse because the criminal leadership in these prisons is also inexperienced. As a result of not understanding *ponyatiya* well themselves, the leader has problems enforcing law and order on the prison population.

Medium-Security Prisons

Here, inmates understand the *ponyatiya* are in place for the sole purpose of making life for all inmates easier, and so they are focused on the aspects of it that ensure peaceful coexistence. As a result—and especially in medium-security prisons for repeat offenders—the rules are applied logically and conflicts are very rare. Life for *petukhi* in these prisons are also much better. Other inmates are not allowed to offend them, further humiliate them, or remind *petukhi* about their status. And if such an offense were to occur, a *petukh* could complain to the *polojenets*, who would deal with the situation effectively.

Maximum-Security Prisons

First-time offenders and recidivists are housed in these facilities, so they are the most radical A.U.E. inmates, those who refuse to follow prison guard orders. These inmates usually have long sentences, and they not only follow *ponyatiya* explicitly, they are obsessed with its logic and philosophy, paying much less attention to the ideologically inspired rules.

The following joke is popular about maximum-security prison inmates:

> An inmate on a prison train is eating a sausage. An inmate from a minimum-security prison comes in and asks the first inmate to share his sausage. "Of course, no problem. But I am a degraded" replies the first inmate. The minimum-security inmate gets afraid and leaves immediately. Then an inmate from a medium-security prison comes in and asks the first inmate to share his sausage. "Of course, no problem. But I am a degraded," replies the first inmate. The medium-security declines the offered sausage and moves on. Then a person from a maximum-security prison comes in and asks the first inmate to share his sausage. "Of course, no problem. But I am a degraded," replies the first inmate. "You should not slander yourself," replies the maximum-security inmate. "That you are degraded should be proven first," and then he takes the sausage.

Interestingly, although inmates in maximum-security prisons are in for more violent crimes and are serving longer sentences, there are never any major conflicts among them. The atmosphere is actually more relaxed, inmates are more likely to forgive each other, and punishment is only meted out as a very last resort. Or as inmates say, "In a minimum-security prison, they beat you and then explain rules; in a maximum-security prison, they explain the rules five times, and only then do they consider physical punishment."

This is especially true among old and respected criminal leaders serving long sentences. They are no longer concerned with increasing their reputation and have no desire to enforce a stringent and twisted version of *ponyatiya.* So these leaders tend to be more lax on issues that are not as crucial to the prison population, such as ideological rules, and they are more interested in the parts of *ponyatiya* that pertain to relations with the enemy. In one known case, a former death-row inmate (whose sentence was later reduced to ten years) who was having sex with *petukh* kissed him on the back at some point, something considered to be a show of affection. *Petukh* told everyone about it, and the caste status of the offending inmate was brought into question. However, the *vor* who judged the case ruled in favor of the inmate, and he remained in the *muzhiki* caste. This is an absolutely unimaginable ruling in any other prison.

For *petukhi*, maximum-security facilities are the most pleasant. Although their status is a factor, other inmates still consider them as part of their society. Some upper-caste inmates often even have their own *petukhi* whom they treat like wives. According to an interviewed inmate from such a facility, "[*Petukhi*] work for the well-being of the prison community [like cleaning and even sex] is important, and, in exchange for that, we give him cigarettes and food. Yes, he is a *petukhi*, so there are some rules to follow. But he is like that, and it is his lifestyle. We do not judge and hold that against him."

Right to Justice

Vory leadership is aware that by having a caste system, especially such a strict one, they are playing with fire and are doing their best to keep the balance between having those lowest castes and not pushing them too far.

According to *ponyatiya*, every inmate in the criminal organization has a right to justice. Even inmates in the lowest caste—*petukhi*—have rights and social guarantees. A *Smotryasçiy* for a prison building explained, "Inmates are free to decide how they want to interact with *petukhi*, but they cannot offend them or even mention hurting them. They always have to be respectful to them."

In one prison in 2003, there was an old *petukh*. One *muzhiki* inmate called him *suka*, a word for a dishonorable person who cooperates with the government. The degraded man complained to the *polojenets* saying, "I may be a *petukh*, but I am not a *suka*," meaning that he was indeed equal to gays but had never turned to law enforcement and betrayed other inmates. And this difference is indeed very important. So the *polojenets* talked to the *muzhik* who had offended *petukh*, explained to him the difference between the two names, and strictly advised him not to say such things in the future.

When questioned about rights for the lower caste, one inmate said, "In prisons where organized criminals have all the power, members of the degraded caste live okay. They have rights, and everyone deals with them fairly. The only way they are different from others is that they have to work, like clean toilets."

In regard to sex work, all *petukhi* voluntarily choose whether to engage, and no one can force a *petukh* (or any other inmate) to have sex. For example, in 2003, In Butirka jail, there was a leader of one of the most famous and dangerous gangs in Russia whose father was a *vor*. He was a built, athletic-type guy, and there were so many crimes in his file that he was in jail for eight years still waiting for a trial. Although the cell was crowded, he had his own corner where he had a plasma TV and was drinking alcohol with friends nonstop. The prison guards did everything for him. They brought alcohol and drugs and removed people he did not like from his cell.

Once while he was drunk, he raped his cellmate near the toilet. The next day after the mandatory formation, the raped inmate was moved to a different cell, and he told inmates there what happened. The cell *smotryasçiy* immediately called the *polojenets* and told him the story. At that time, there were two *vory* in the jail, so they discussed the situation.

When this gang leader got sober and realized what he had done, he got very scared. He cut all communication ropes on the windows between his and other cells (the road) and stopped answering his phone because the criminal leadership was trying to reach him.

Several days later, jail inmates got a message from the *vory* and *polojenets* that the gang leader was punished for what he had done. It is not clear exactly what they did, but according to interviewed inmates who were in that jail at that time, most likely he was almost beaten to death and moved to the *sherst'* caste.

Currently, sex in prisons is done only by mutual consent, and there are particular rules pertaining to *petukh*-client relations. Another interviewed inmate explained how those rules came about in one particular prison:

> There is a person in charge of *petukhi* called the "main *petukh*."[20] He went to talk with the prison criminal leadership, and they agreed on the total prohibition of rape (sex without consent) with members of *petukhi* caste and the approximate price for services, which was two packs of cigarettes and a pack of tea. This price could slightly vary depending on the qualities [look and experience] of the particular *petukh*.
>
> They also agreed that—because most likely all the *petukhi* have HIV and AIDS—the use of condoms should be mandatory. It was obvious to the criminal leadership that *muzhiki* would not want to pay for condoms, so it was agreed that the price of a condom was included in the bill. Also, any disputes between *petukhi* and clients about the services performed (e.g. if a *petukh* was accused of biting a *muzhik* while performing a blowjob, and the *muzhik* hit him) are solved between the members of the criminal leadership and main *petukh*.

These rules for respectful interaction with *petukhi* are not done out of respect or kindness, but as a strategic way to maintain a unified body. Members of *petukhi* caste are still part of the prison population, and prison criminal leadership needs it to maintain their rule.

First, they need *petukhi* to snitch if someone from the upper caste violates ideological rules. For example, it often happens that an active homosexual asks a *petukh* to change sex roles. Not only does *petukh* have to report that to the prison criminal leadership, but he also needs to cooperate in proving it. Often *petukh* puts drops of iodine (or another similar medicine popular in Russia of a bright, staining green color) on his penis, and then after the penetration, the involved *muzhik* is checked.

Second, prison criminal leadership needs *petukhi* to not share information about any inmate's sex life with prison administration. It would be particularly dangerous if prison administration learned of an active *muzhik* inmate asking *petukh* to change sex roles. If they did, they would blackmail the *muzhik* and use him as a spy.

And finally, without *petukhi*, it would be hard to stand against the prison authorities. According to one interviewed *blatnyje*, "We don't even allow prison guards to do anything bad to our *petukh*. Maybe he is *petukh*, but he is *our petukh*, and if he does something wrong, we will deal with him ourselves."

Also, it is prohibited by *ponyaitya* to tell anyone outside of prison and the *vory* criminal family if someone is *petukh*. For example, in several instances a member of the upper caste was punished for telling a girlfriend of *petukh* that her loved one is a member of the lowest caste. According to an interviewed member of the prison criminal leadership, "Once I was driving and saw *petukh* from my prison looking for a taxi. He was with his wife and a small child. I picked them up and made sure that his wife did not notice I did not shake his hand. He also sat in the back with the child instead of in front next to me." That is done not because of kindness, but for security reasons. The *vory* organization is much less powerful outside of prison, so if a member would try to enforce or even mention such prison rules in a regular society, they would be punished, or could be even destroyed.

It is a similar situation with members of the *sherst'* caste. Their cooperation is also necessary for a unified prison population. They also serve an important service, and often only they can enter the inner prison and possibly smuggle items in.

According to an inmate from the *blatnyje* caste, "When I am sitting in solitary confinement in the inner prison [for refusing to follow prison guard orders], there is a small hole in the door through which something can be passed to my cell. While a prison guard is monitoring the hallway, only a member of the *sherst'* caste who is cleaning the hall could pass me something like food or construction tools [to make holes in the wall for communication] through this door hole. Of course, I am in good relations with them. From time to time, I give them things like cigarettes, and no one could ever force me to do something bad to them."

In addition, if someone violates any of these rules in front of a third inmate, and that third inmate does not either stop the offender from breaking the rules or punish him afterward, that third inmate will also be punished for aiding in the crime.

Conclusion

A caste system, and in particular the existence of a lowest caste, is a cornerstone of the *vory* prison criminal society. Not only are members of the lowest caste the ones doing the dirty jobs no one else wants to do—and, as a result, it keeps other prison inmates happy—but having those castes allows the group to demonstrate its power and deter potential challengers to *vory* leadership. It is particularly the case with ideologically inspired rules that shows an organization's strength in its ability to enforce such bizarre rules.

On the other side, the organization should always be very careful not to fall into a situation where modification and enforcement of rules are no longer manageable. For example, it is the case when group members, aspiring to be promoted to the group's leadership, are competing among themselves in dedication to the group's ideology and, as a consequence, in strictness of ideological rule enforcement. In that case, enforcement becomes religiously strict and the rules themselves counterproductive to the organization. As a result, the whole caste system and ideology becomes the group's weakness.

In the case of this century-old *vory* criminal organization, this is exactly what happened. Those ideologically inspired rules got out of control, dragging the group deeper and deeper into internal problems.

5
Prison Criminal Law Enforcement

A heavy metal door closes behind a new inmate. It is his first time in prison, and he is visibly scared as he stands in front of dozens of eyes, all looking at him. He holds an old plastic bag with basic necessities—whatever he was allowed to keep from his own belongings—and a dirty, rolled up, paper-thin mattress given to him by prison authorities. Immediately he is asked to go to the furthest corner of the cell to talk to the person in charge, a man not wearing a dark prison uniform like the others but an expensive training suit. This man is sitting on a big king-size mattress that spans the first level of two bunk beds pushed together. Bed sheets on it are also not white like on all other beds, but colorful. Despite the cell being full, the second level of his bed is empty.

The leader conducts a basic interview about the new inmate's background including age, family situation, employment, and criminal charges. It is clear the leader has done this a million times. He's bored, yet it's clear that he is the kind of a person who knows when someone is lying and who is probably dangerous. The new inmate tells the truth.

Once a leader has a basic idea about the new inmate, he makes the new inmate aware of the rules, so he will not cause any trouble.

Leader: The prison inmate population is one body, and there are people who are privileged and people who are not, so you have to share with others. You also have to be polite to others. How do you feel about vory and their ideology?

New Inmate: Unfortunately, I am not familiar with it, so cannot answer this question.

Leader: Have you interacted with people in prison before?

New Inmate: Unfortunately not.

Leader: OK, fine. Honesty is valued here. Don't be afraid to ask if you are not sure what to do. There is no punishment for questions. It is the other way around—questions are appreciated. Spend time talking to people and learning how things are done here.

Then the criminal leader asks a person sitting on the bed next to him to show the newcomer around and explain not only how the cell

Criminals, Nazis, and Islamists. Vera Mironova, Oxford University Press. © Oxford University Press 2023.
DOI: 10.1093/oso/9780197645659.003.0006

> *functions physically (where toilet is, how to boil water and so on), but what the rules and norms are that run its life.*
>
> —From an interview with the inmate

The job of the criminal leadership in prison is to maintain law and order. On one side, they have to ensure peace among the prison population. And on the other side, it is also their job to make sure that agreements with prison authorities (in exchange for inmate privileges) are honored on the side of inmates. So they have to manage control of inmates who could decrease their bargaining power vis-à-vis prison authorities.

In this chapter, I will talk about how prison leadership tries to minimize conflicts inside the inmate population and deal with agreement violations. I will also talk about what punishment tools *vory* leadership has at its disposal to deter future violations.

Crime Prevention

As in any country, law enforcement in prison starts with conflict prevention. "We had a very good regime in our prison camp. Basically everyone could do anything they wanted," said one member of the prison criminal leadership. "But then new inmates robbed the prison store. Of course, the inmates were beaten, but that doesn't even really matter. The only thing that mattered is it all became a huge problem for us. The prison authorities were not happy."

So what methods do crime leadership use to prevent criminals from doing anything that could hurt the prison population? Although *vory* leadership believes its system is different from (and superior to) that of official law enforcement in regular society, the methods they use are not that different.

Their first crime prevention tool is persuasion. A major aspect of a criminal leader's job is explaining the importance and logic of the rules to all inmates—a sometimes fruitless endeavor. One *blatnoj* explained, "We [leadership] are sick and tired of explaining to inmates why they should not bring drugs into the prison through food parcels. We have other methods. But then they still do it, and get caught, and it again becomes our problem."

The second tool is prohibition. Many violations in prison occur when inmates are under the influence of hallucinogenic drugs. As a result of not being able to control the behavior of these inmates, hallucinogenic drugs are prohibited by prison criminal leadership in almost all prisons in the former Soviet Union. Drugs like heroin, methadone, and marijuana, however, are still allowed.

A third tool is policing. While it is necessary to prohibit some types of drugs, it is not possible to prohibit all substances that change one's perception of reality. When I asked a member of the criminal leadership why they did not just ban all drugs and alcohol, he replied, "Prison is a place where people rest and want to spend time in the most comfortable and fun way. An overwhelming majority of inmates were taking drugs before coming here. And I am not even talking about alcohol. So they expect to continue doing it here, which makes it absolutely unimaginable for us to prohibit it."

Inmates who use sedatives are not a danger to public safely and so are not a problem for the criminal leadership. The same could not be said, however, about those drinking prison-produced alcohol, which has little resemblance to the regular alcohol people drink outside of prison.

Like any alcohol, it is made with sugar and yeast. But because there are no special filters in prisons like those used in factories, the alcohol is not refined and contains dangerous chemicals. As a result, drinking this alcohol causes inmates to hallucinate and makes their behavior unpredictable. And because *blatnyje* cannot control the inmates drinking, he must instead control their behavior to reduce the danger of negative consequences.

As a result, if an inmate plans to drink with some friends, he has to let the *smotryasçiy* of his barrack know. *Smotryasçiy* will then designate someone to chaperone the party and make sure there is no fighting and no one commits suicide. Although in general this policy works, it is not a guaranteed success, and prison criminal leadership is not always able to control the behavior of inebriated inmates. "One time we had a very serious correction authorities inspection coming," remembered one middle-level criminal leader, "and [we] banned all alcohol and drugs for a month. But after the inspection, it was like a zombie apocalypse here. Everyone was wasted, and we absolutely lost control of what was happening. Unfortunately, several people died."

Punishment

When conflict prevention measures are not successful and *ponyatiya* and prison criminal leadership orders are not followed, those who violate them have to be punished. How criminal family members are punished also depends on their caste and whether or not they are still incarcerated.

If a *vor* violates the rules, there are three acceptable ways to punish him. First, he could be publicly slapped (but only by a person of the same rank) for a light violation of the criminal code, such as offending someone. The *vor* being punished is not allowed to hit back or even move. Second, he could lose his status. That could happen for several reasons including misappropriation of funds, lying, being a witness in court, not maintaining control of his territory, being a witness in a case for the prosecution, killing someone without permission, or becoming a *vor* unlawfully in the first place.[1]

Third, in rare cases, a *vor* might also be killed,[2] the punishment for an act of betrayal. This would be the case for a *vor* found cooperating with law enforcement, stealing money from the criminal family, or killing someone without permission. Sentencing a *vor* to death can only happen in a regional meeting of *vory*, while recalling status could happen in a smaller circle. Since *vory* do not know the topic of the meeting until they attend, if the *vor* sentenced to death arrives, he could be asked to commit suicide (usually leaving the note saying "Do not blame anyone in my death"). But if the *vor* could guess that the meeting is called to sentence him to death, and does not show up and goes into hiding, a killer is appointed. Here, there are also two types of death—with and without honor. A dishonorable death requires the *vor* to be shot in the stomach while an honorable death entails being shot in the head or heart.

If an offending inmate is not *vor*, but a member of the *blatnyje* or *muzhiki* caste, there are many more types of punishment for violations of the criminal rules: (1) death (this, however, is rarely applied and can only be sanctioned by a *vor*), (2) beatings, (3) broken limbs (for violations like stealing), (4) reduction in the caste (for violation of core in-group interactions or out-group relations rules), and (5) being degraded and moved to the *lowest* caste for violation of ideological rules. This could be done by:

a. rape (very rarely used now)[3]
b. symbolically touching the offender's lips with a penis
c. peeing on the offender
d. putting the offender's head in the toilet

For minor *ponyatiya* violations, an inmate should be punished inside the barrack/cell by a *smotryasçiy*. There are three main options for such punishment: (1) punching the offender in the chest, (2) hitting the offender with a metal cup on the forehead, or (3) slapping the offender on the neck with a hand.

Because, according to interviewed inmates, the goal of the criminal-family justice system is to keep peace, in some cases, the fate of the person who was found guilty is chosen by the victim. But in choosing a punishment, the victim has an incentive to be fair because the treatment he chooses for his offender will reflect on his own reputation.

There are two groups of inmates who can break some *ponyatiya* without punishment.

New Inmates

For new inmates, punishments can only be applied after their cellmates have explained all the rules and prison norms in detail. Inmates are not held accountable for violating the rules, other than ideological ones, until they have a clear understanding of them.

In a case where an inmate does not understand the rules and commits a minor violation, the prison criminal leadership will first politely talk to him. But if the inmate repeats the same violation again, the *vor* or *polojenets* (or one of the *smotryashchiye*) will beat him. If the inmate commits the same violation a third time, he will be accused of ignoring words of the people, and he will be beaten again and moved to the *sherst'* caste. According to an interviewed inmate, the logic behind it is as following: "If you are not listening, you are ignoring us. If you are ignoring us, you do not live the same life as we do. And in this case, go to your people—*sherst'*."

Ignorant Inmates

This applies to an inmate who did not realize he was violating the rules. But it is important to specify that, similar to regular jurisprudence, not knowing the rules and not knowing that you are *violating* the rules is very different. For example, once a *polojenets* had a *snir* who was preparing him food. While the *polojenets* was on a long three-day visit with his wife, his *snir* was raped (degraded). When the *polojenets* returned, no one told him about it for several days, and he continued to eat the food his *snir* prepared for him. In that case, the *polojenets* did not violate *ponyatiya* for touching what the degraded *snir* had touched because he did not know. That is different than taking things from *petukh* not knowing that it is prohibited to do so.

Not only are punishments an important issue, but so is who will execute the punishments. Theoretically, according to classic *ponyatiya*, only a crystal-clean member of the criminal family—one who never served in the army or violated *ponyatiya*—could carry out punishment. Today, this is often ignored, but a defendant has a right to request this. In one prison, there was a minor *ponyatiya* violation that inmates in one barrack did not want to be known to the whole prison. The *smotryasçiy* of the barrack decided on a punishment, and the defendant agreed with it. However, there was no crystal-clean inmate to deliver the punishment, on which a defendant insisted. So because they were not able to administer punishment inside the barrack, and they did not want the problem to be known to a higher level of prison criminal authority, the punishment was commuted to a box of cigarettes and a contribution to the barrack mutual fund instead.

Punishment also cannot be administered in the prison hospital. According to the original (Gulag times) *ponyatiya*, if an offender is in the hospital, his punishment has to be postponed until he is recovered, discharged from the hospital, and back in the general population.

If a punishment is something that should be executed by a group of people, such as a beating, everyone in the cell or barrack has to participate by punching the offender at least one time.

In general, punishment in the prison criminal world is very strict and severe. If an inmate is beaten, he is nearly beaten to death (definitely until he loses consciousness), and if an inmate is degraded to a lower caste, there is no way for him to move back up. So theoretically, an inmate who steals one cigarette from a cellmate could be cleaning toilets for the rest of his ten-year sentence and the next time he is arrested.

There is also no expiration for a serious punishment. Any violator of the criminal rules can be sure he will be punished sooner or later. Once, in the 1980s, a *vor* got very sick while in prison. His cellmate decided to seize the opportunity to beat him in his weakened state. The violator then used all his connections to be relocated to a different cell, but the *vor* could not leave such an offense unpunished. When the *vor* learned that his offender was working in a prison factory, despite the strict prohibition in the criminal world against working in prison, he asked to be appointed to a job in the same factory, claiming a desperate need for money. As expected, on the *vor*'s very first day, he found his attacker and stabbed him with a sharp object. Despite all odds, the violator survived and finished his sentence. But after his release, he disappeared immediately, most likely assassinated on the orders of the *vor* he had beaten.

Trials

> *Those ponyatiya sometimes are so complicated that it is time to open a ponyatiya law school to educate ponyatiya lawyers!*
>
> —A prison guard

Whether one is guilty or not of violating the criminal rules is up to the criminal leadership to decide. That leadership could either be a *vor*, *polojenets*, or a group of *blatnyje*, and they might be judge and juror for any of the following issues:

(1) Personal conflicts between inmates. Leadership will only get involved in settling a personal dispute if asked by either of the two parties.
(2) Common problems. Issues related to everyday prison issues that affect the general population.
(3) Crucial questions. Important decisions like degrading someone.

It is important to note that the prison criminal leadership understands the jurisdiction of their justice system is the prison. So it is prohibited for them to rule on any conflicts that took place before inmates were incarcerated.

Lower castes also have similar conflict resolution mechanisms but are judged by their caste mates. But if a mundane conflict occurs between members of different castes, the member of the upper caste is considered right and the member of the lower caste guilty by default. In the case of a more serious conflict—one that could have potentially long-term consequences—the dispute is solved by the leadership of the higher caste, usually in negotiation with the leader of the lower caste, such as the main *petukh*.

Evidence

During a so-called trial, any inmate with a legitimate complaint must provide proof, which the defendant is allowed to dispute. Those considered above the decent line of the caste (*muzhiki* and *blatnyje*) can participate as witnesses, while those of the lower castes cannot. In rare circumstances, it is possible that the court will listen to a testimony from a member of a *sherst'* caste out of politeness or to get a better understanding of the situation. However, no ruling can be made based on his testimony.

Theoretically, in very rare cases, the testimony of a respectful (not decent) member of the *sherst'* caste who had proven himself a reliable and faithful member of the organization might really be considered. But in reality, none of the interviewed inmates were able to recall such an instance. According to a middle-rank criminal, "We do not listen to the *sherst'*. They do not have a word. They lost it. In fact, that is exactly why they became *sherst'* in the first place." Another inmate continued, "Let's assume someone based their decision on the testimony of *sherst'*. The defendant would appeal to a *vor*, and not only would the decision be overturned, but the original decision maker would be beaten."

Any information from an inmate's official prison file or court charge also cannot be consulted because, according to *ponyatiya*, nothing produced by the government is credible. In cases where a problem involves a defendant's criminal history, the defendant is given time to communicate with people in other prisons where he was formerly incarcerated before the trial takes place. And while a case is in process, two inmates cannot continue their conflict.

If the issue is degrading a person, the inmate is considered suspect and is separated during the trial (which might last for years). This means that he is moved to *petukhi* section, others in the upper caste will not talk or drink tea with him, and no one can touch him or the things he touched. However, since he has not officially been degraded to *petukhi* caste, no one can make him do things *petukhi* do, such as clean toilets.

While some questions can be decided by the middle-level criminal leadership, crucial questions can only be decided by a *vor*. And if one *vor* settles a dispute, his verdict is final. Neither party involved can appeal to another *vor* in hopes of a different outcome.

If there is no *vor* or he cannot be reached, one or a group of respected *blatnyje* could decide on it. They would, however, be prepared to explain any decision to the *vor*. As a result, the *blatnyje* only take on straightforward cases where their verdict is easily justifiable.

In one Russian prison in 2016, a *vor* prohibited inmates to ask people to send drugs into the prison in the food packages, but someone did it anyway and got caught. So did the person who put the drugs in the package (his girlfriend), and she was sentenced and put in prison. According to *ponyatiya*, this was a major problem for several reasons. First, it was done against a *vor* order; second, the actions of the inmate caused an innocent person to suffer—his girlfriend; and third, it also brought suffering on the whole prison population. After that event, prison guards searched every package more carefully and became very strict about prohibited items. Basically an agreement with prison authorities had been broken from the side of inmates, and someone had to answer for that.

Such an issue could be judged only by a *vor* or a *polojenets* because it falls under the category of crucial questions—the inmate could be beaten and degraded to *sherst'*. It could also be that the inmate had a rather complicated explanation for his actions. For example, what if the defendant says that he was bringing drugs in, not for himself, but for a member of criminal leadership with his knowledge and permission. Or he could say that he had no idea there were drugs in the package, that it was a gift. According to middle-level criminal leader from that prison, "To make a decision on a case like that, you need a person who knows *ponyatiya* and the psychology of people, and that is a *vor*. It is not a technical decision anymore."

While there are no lawyers in the prison criminal court, a person who is smart and well versed in *ponyatiya* (who has spent significant time behind bars among decent inmates) could successfully defend himself or his friend using mitigating factors that only experienced inmates know about.

In 2013, an inmate "under question," meaning that the decision on which caste he belonged to had yet not been made, arrived at one Russian prison and was put on quarantine. Although a decision had not been made, there was a possibility he would be in the degraded caste. This was because when he was in juvenile prison, he was accused of drinking beer from the same bottle a prostitute had (it is assumed prostitutes do blowjobs, and drinking from the same bottle would fall under the category of prohibited actions). In juvenile prison, he was put "under question" until the senior members of the criminal family in the new prison could decide on him.

By *ponyatiya*, while a person is under question, he is still separated from the rest of the prison population, and while he was separated, he kind of gave up on his status. He started comfortably hanging out with the degraded, eating with them, washing dishes with them, and so on. Soon he was seen as one of them.

After fifteen days in quarantine, he was moved to the general population and there, eight to ten people from the *blatnoj* committee (a group of respected *blatnyje*) came together to decide on him. Usually such a decision is made by a person in charge such as the *polojenets*, but at that time, the prison did not have one, so the issue had to be decided by the majority.

The defendant was invited in for questioning. In particular he was asked whether he was drinking from the same bottle with a girl; whether he understood that it was not allowed; and whether while, being under question, he lived with the degraded, shaved with them, washed with them and so on, instead of living like others with questionable status and so on. And on all those questions, he was silently nodded his head.

According to a *blatnyje* inmate close to prison criminal leadership (who had been in prison for ten years and was on the *blatnoj* committee deciding on that particular matter): "It would have been so easy for this guy to say that he simply did not know that the girl he shared the bottle with was a prostitute, and that he was drinking with her like she was a regular girl, and then he would have been okay. We care about getting good people inside our ranks [into the upper caste]. There is a shortage of human resources. But he did not. He gave up and did not even try to defend himself. So we had no option other than placing him in the degraded caste. He now lives with them, [and] cleans floors and toilets."

Sometimes, decisions about which caste inmates should be in cannot be easily reached. For example, it is the case if there are no witnesses and it is the words of one inmate against the other. In those cases, there are two ways of moving forward. First, the inmates could shake hands and move on, or second, criminal leadership could put them both under question (almost degraded caste). In the majority of such instances, according to interviewed inmates, decision-makers just get tired of those cases and drop them, sending both inmates away with no penalty.

Sometimes an issue is minor and does not need to be brought before criminal leadership. These cases can be solved at the cell or barrack level. For example, one inmate was talking on the phone with his wife about what she was doing and why she was not home. Another inmate who overheard the conversation mentioned that his wife was probably cheating on him. Soon an argument started. The *smotryasçiy* of the barrack overheard it and, since the conflict was getting close to a fight, had to get involved. He sat them at the table surrounded by the other inmates in the cell (all inmates have to listen to make sure they understand the trial was fair). It was noon, and he told the inmate who had made the comment, "By 6:00 pm, I will call the *polojenets* unless you tell me that you were wrong. If you do, I will punish you and this problem will not leave this room." Defendant agreed that he should be punished inside the cell. Then *smotryasçiy* had three options of punishment for such an offense: punching him in the chest, hitting him with a metal cup on the forehead, or slapping on the neck with his hand. "The defendant agreed to the third option," commented a *smotryasçiy*. "So then I hit him as hard as I could where everyone could see it to make sure that such problems never happened again in my cell."

Like in civilian courts, there is basically a chain of courts a defendant could appeal to. During a trial for a minor *ponyatiya* violation, everyone is sitting in a circle (if the defendant is *petukh*, he squats on the floor). If the decision was that the defendant is guilty and he should be physically punished, the *smotryasçiy* says, "Stand up and take it [punishment] as a decent [inmate]." The defendant standing up is a very symbolic act of punishment because it has serious reputational costs.[4]

If the defendant does not agree with a decision, he says, "I disagree," and then the case goes to a higher level, from the cell *smotryasçiy* to the building *smotryasçiy*. If the defendant again does not agree with the decision of the building *smotryasçiy*, the case can then go to the *polojenets*. If the defendant is found guilty and appeals again, then a high-level criminal leader outside of the prison—ideally a *vor*—is called. His decision is final.

If the defendant appeals the decision of the first and second courts, but agrees to submit to punishment before the *polojenets*, he will also be punished (beaten) at the previous levels as well. The *smotryashchiye* will question the defendant's credibility and his motives for appealing their decisions, and even accuse him of instigating intrigue (also a punishable offense), all of which will affect the defendant's reputation from there on out.

Philosophy behind Law Enforcement

Although from the outside, criminal rules and *ponyatiya* may look like unnecessary and excessive cruelty, criminal leadership constantly struggles to make sure *ponyatiya* punishments are not *too* harsh. Reaching this balance proves to be an exceptionally hard task, but a necessary one. On one side, "If an inmate is terrorized and terrified by the criminal world," one inmate explained, "he will go to the prison administration and start cooperating with them. So under no circumstances should we back people into a corner so they think going to the administration is their only way out." This is a particularly serious problem when the inmates cooperating with administration were once in the criminal hierarchy and are now seeking revenge for some perceived wrong. Their intricate knowledge of how the criminal organization functions from inside would make them a very dangerous tool in the hands of the prison administration.

Excessively harsh punishments also reflect poorly on a prison's *polojenets* and may affect any future promotions. One inmate talked about the delicate touch *polojenets* needs when dealing with degrading:

> If there are many people being moved to non-decent castes in a prison, how does that look for the *polojenets*? It will look like he cannot control his territory. So *polojenets* will do anything possible to avoid it [degrading]. For example, someone who stole something from other inmates is a rat. Although technically he has to be sent to *sherst'*, if he is a first-time thief, or he stole something small, or if he was hungry [or any other mitigating factors], he may be beaten a little, but he is then allowed to stay with *muzhiki*. Or maybe moved to *sniri*. But very rarely is he moved to *sherst'*. We should not be producing *sherst'*.

Downgraded inmates could also become a problem for the criminal family once they are released from prison. Since they are of the lower caste, the *vory* criminal family will not accept them once they are on the outside, which leads them to form their own gangs, which could then become competition within the criminal underworld.

Although leaders avoid extremely harsh rulings, strict punishment for those who violate the rules is still the only way to stabilize prison life. One inmate believes the strict rules serve two purposes. First, it keeps the ranks of inmates strong against prison authorities inside. Second, it keeps order in small cells where ten to twenty people are together all day every day. "It would be very hard," the inmate said, "to have any order or peaceful coexistence with all those different criminals in such a miserable, psychologically hard environment without such draconian rules."

Regardless of whether the punishments are too harsh, the system works. Not only has it allowed the criminal organization to survive—it has caused it to be generally successful. For example, any time an inmate is suspected of working for the prison authorities, he is moved to *sherst'* so that does not participate in the lives of decent inmates in any capacity. And because there is no second chance given, it decreases the chances of having a spy among the ranks. This significantly increases the overall trust among the higher caste members of the criminal organization.

One inmate illustrated why separating certain inmates into *sherst'* was safer for everyone. In his prison, members of *sherst'* often come to *muzhiki* and *blatnyje* to use their illegal phones to call home. Why do they have to do so? Because their *sherst'* do not have any illegal phones in their caste. It is not because they cannot get their own phones, but because they all snitched on each other, and, as a result, all their phones were confiscated by prison authorities.

Also, the severity of punishment terminates the majority of conflicts before they even occur by promoting proactive measures. For example, because the punishment for stealing is so harsh, customs have developed to avoid the risk of even being accused. If an inmate wants to borrow something, he not only asks permission, but also only takes it directly from the owner's hands. Even with an owner's permission, a borrowing inmate would not dare take something from another person's bed or drawer, simply to avoid absolutely any possibilities of being suspected of stealing. This risk aversion also translates to never talking to a prison guard alone, no matter what the circumstance. Doing so would make the inmate suspect because he could be passing information on about other inmates.

So extreme are the precautions taken, that even the language reflects a sort of political correctness in an effort to not offend anyone. Usually, any open conflict would begin with an exchange of disrespectful words. But according to one respondent, "One wrong word could lead to a long-lasting resentment between two people that, based on my experience, will flare up in the most dangerous moment." So to avoid even the appearance of hostility, inmates almost always speak to each other with extreme politeness, something that shocks newcomers. An inmate conversation might sound like they are "drinking tea with the Queen of England and not sitting in prison with criminals and killers," commented one of the interviewed inmates.

Problems with Law Enforcement

Although in general, the majority of interviewed ex-inmates are satisfied with such a criminal justice system, like any justice system, *ponyatiya* and its enforcement are not immune to problems.

One issue is that inmates who know the often-complicated *ponyatiya*—generally those in the criminal family and prison the longest—have a great advantage over those who do not.

Once in Butirka jail in 2012, a *smotryasçiy* of the part of the prison, who was also in charge of the criminal mutual fund, lived in a same cell with an Azeri inmate who got heroin every day from his friends in another cell. He did not talk to anyone about it, but everyone would see him get it and then go to the bathroom to inject it. Technically, even by *ponyatiya*, it is his right to do so, and he does not need to share. But the *smotryasçiy* was not happy that he was not sharing with others or contributing some of it to the prison mutual fund.

One day, prison guards took the *smotryasçiy* outside to meet a lawyer, and while he was gone, another inmate stopped by to give cigarettes to the mutual fund located in the cell. This inmate saw that the *smotryasçiy* was not there and so he asked those inside where to leave cigarettes for the mutual fund and personally for the *vor*. The Azeri inmate casually told him to put everything in the mutual fund box so that when the *smotryasçiy* came back, he could deal with it.

When the *smotryasçiy* came back and learned about it, he used the opportunity to start a conflict with the Azeri inmate, accusing him of giving orders to inmates about contributing to the mutual fund. "Why did you tell the guy to put cigarettes for the *vor* into the mutual fund box? The mutual fund cigarettes were already distributed to those who need them, so the *vory* cigarettes are gone."

"So from basically nothing, the *smotryasçiy* raised the problem to the level that technically this Azeri inmate should be punished by *ponyatiya*," commented their former cellmate in an interview. "It was absolutely a non-event. The *smotryasçiy* was simply pissed that the Azeri inmate did not share his heroin."

So even when an inmate wants to quietly serve his sentence and stay away from prison criminal politics, if an experienced inmate wants to get to him, he will do so. Not only will *ponyatiya* not protect him, it will be used against him as a weapon.

Second, not all *vory* (or those appointed by them) are right and fair, or always rule according to *ponyatiya*. And even when *vory* are fair, not everyone is satisfied with their decisions. Some prison criminal leadership decisions may not be popular even with the majority of inmates. When an unpopular decision is made, the inmates could refuse to follow it, protest it, and even eventually overthrow it. For example, in one maximum-security prison, a new inmate with several rape charges moved in. Because rape charges can often be false accusations for political purposes, inmates do not trust such a verdict and do their own investigation. For this particular inmate, the prison criminal leadership decided that he was not guilty of the charges and should be in the *muzhiki* caste. However, the majority of inmates disagreed with that ruling and thought he should join the ranks of the degraded. So, despite the leadership decision, the inmates agreed to ignore the person. No one was willing to sit next to him. Even *sniri* would not take cigarettes from him. Soon this inmate, who could not handle being ostracized, started misbehaving and was soon moved by prison guards into solitary confinement.

Third, with time, the *vory* criminal organization has undergone ideologization and because it is not always possible to balance power, sometimes criminal leadership is not able to do so. As a result, the position of those in the lowest caste becomes so bad, they are willing to do anything to hurt those whom they see as responsible for their situation. According to one degraded ex-inmate, "I was terrified to be in this caste [*petukhi*] that I would be severely beaten and would almost have a heart attack if I heard my name mentioned by my cellmates. I dreamt of revenge day and night and could clearly see myself getting revenge on those who degraded me." And since there is no way for a degraded person to move higher in the caste system, a degraded person can often be very dangerous. The objects of his revenge then are usually those who made them *petukhi*—criminal leadership.

As a result, even knowing it will cost him his life, degraded members have been known to jump on a person they hate the most in the middle of the night—even those in criminal leadership—and start touching and kissing him. Yes, the offender is killed immediately, but the inmate he touches also becomes dirty and will have to become *petukh* himself.

There have also been instances when *petukh* just released from prison immediately finds and kills the [outside] *vor* who made the decision to degrade him. And in the past, gangs that had problems with the *vory* crime syndicate intentionally hired degraded ex-inmates because their hate toward the whole system was stronger than any fear they might have, which made them fearless in dealing with *vory*.

Conclusion

Although those criminal rules and punishments look brutal, violent, and sometimes absolutely illogical, all interviewed former inmates agreed they serve three particular purposes. First, they ensure peaceful coexistence of the inmate population, a population that, by definition, consists of people who are not good at following rules and orders.

Second, such enforced cohesion among inmates is basically the only way for them to have at least some rights against the total dictatorship of prison authorities. Only when prison criminal leadership has control over the inmate population are they able to make legitimate agreements with prison authorities that would benefit the whole prison population.

And this is supported by the situation in special prisons for members of law enforcement, such as police, judges, and prisons guards who have themselves broken the law. Although those prisons are obviously not under the *vory* leadership, inside them, inmates also live according to the *ponyatiya* and have a similar caste system.

And finally, success in ensuring law and order increases loyalty to the *vory* criminal leadership by the inmate population and further enforces their power inside prisons.

6
Prison Criminal Economy

In addition to three main components of any legitimate government—executive, legislative, and judicial—there are several other provisional functions a government has to perform. A government is in charge of the economy, goods import and export, social security, and the provision of public goods, all of which ensure the comfort of its citizens.

Prison criminal leadership is no different in that they also perform these tasks on a smaller scale. But smaller does not necessarily mean easier. Prison leadership operates from behind bars, which makes a difficult job even harder. So in this chapter, I will talk about the prison criminal budget and its main income sources and expenses.

Criminal Budget

In the 1959 book *Kolyma Tales*, Varlam Shalamov wrote about the "committee of the poor" (*Komitet Bednoty* or *Kombed*) in Butirka prison and said it was the simplest way for inmates to help each other. Every inmate had to give 10 percent of what money they had to spend in the prison store to people who did not have any. According to him, in a cell of seventy to eighty people, there were often seven to eight such inmates. Once those poor inmates got money from other sources, they tried to pay it back, but were instead encouraged to also donate 10 percent of what they got to the committee of the poor (mutual fund). Those payouts were not considered donations but the right of those inmates who needed assistance.

Donations to the fund were technically voluntary, but not donating subjected the cheapskate to humiliation. For example, when food was distributed, the person in charge of a cell (in the 1930s, he was called "the elder") was in charge of who ate first. This was very important because the best, most nutritious part of soup was given out in the beginning.[1] So the elder would instruct whoever was handing the meals out to serve the person who had not contributed to the mutual fund last. Such a shameful reminder would be made four times a day, whenever food was distributed.

If that did not coerce someone to contribute, an elder could ask prison guards to transfer that inmate out of the cell, and he would be, immediately and with no need for explanation.[2] The offending inmate's life in the new cell would also be

Criminals, Nazis, and Islamists. Vera Mironova, Oxford University Press. © Oxford University Press 2023.
DOI: 10.1093/oso/9780197645659.003.0007

problematic. First, he would be questioned about why he was transferred and might be suspected as an informant. And second, the new cell would also have the same system of mutual fund, and the inmate would be expected, again, to contribute.

Although this mutual fund was invented by members of intelligentsia imprisoned in Gulag, *vory* and *blatnyje* would often rob it. In the 1950s, when *vory* began governing prisons and claiming to work for inmate benefits, they themselves adopted this mutual help system. And with time, this simple concept also developed into a complicated prison economy, and the person in charge of it is the *smotryasçiy* of the mutual fund (or *obshyak*). The *smotryasçiy* is the bookkeeper who keeps track of contributions and expenses in a notebook called a *tychkovka*. Every month, he sends this notebook around the prison for everyone to see. Also, according to *ponyatiya*, at any time, an inmate could ask to see this budget report, and he could not be refused. This made the leadership financially accountable to the other inmates.

But this notebook is considered crucially important to the prison criminal organization. If there is a chance at any time that a prison guard might find and read its contents, the person in possession of it has to destroy it. Losing it could cost not only the *smotryasçiy* but also his *polojenets* their lives.

In addition to a prison-level *obshyak*, there are usually also smaller mutual funds on the cell level and, if a cell is big, on a family level (a group of two to four inmates united by ideological views, religion, ethnicity, or geographic origins who share their possessions). But these smaller funds are continually intertwined; funds and goods from the prison *obshyak* could be sent to a particular cell, yet the cell contributes to the prison *obshyak*.

Originally, everywhere (but currently only in maximum-security prisons) mutual funds consisted of everything any inmate had. No one owned personal property, and everything sent from the outside became property of the cell. Now the situation is different, and such shared property exists mostly on the family level of inmate society. Also, while during the Soviet times mutual funds of medium and minimum prisons contributed to the mutual funds of the maximum-security prisons, with time, the need to do so decreased and then completely disappeared.

Donations

When Russia began deporting people en masse to mandatory labor camps in Siberia, civilians—relatives and friends—began collecting money to help the forced laborers. Fyodor Dostoevsky's autobiographic book, *Memoirs from the*

House of the Dead, gives an account of the generous donations he remembered from his prison days (1849–1854):

> Donations from the townspeople were coming almost every minute in enormous quantities. I think there were no women left in town who did not bring bread to congratulate "miserable" inmates. There were rich donations—bread from first class flour—and there were very poor ones—once-cent loaves of bread slightly glazed with sour cream. It was a donation from a poor person to a poor person. Everything was accepted with the same gratitude, with no differentiation to what was given. Inmates took off their hats, bowed, wished them good holidays, and took the donations to the kitchen.[3]

Those contributions became the first outside contributions to the prison *obshyak*. Now, according to an interviewed inmate, when someone gets something from outside, he gives 10 to 15 percent to the mutual fund, and then usually shares the rest with everyone in the cell (small cell) or with a group of inmates close to him (in big cell or barrack).

Not all inmates, however, can contribute to the mutual fund. Only inmates from upper castes are allowed. And, although by original *ponyatiya* contributions to the *obshyak* are voluntary, it is not always the case in reality.

Also not everyone who supports those behind bars does so out of good will. Some do so strategically. Free people involved in illegal activities clearly understand that, at some point, they will end up on the other side of prison wall, so they are willing to donate to the prison mutual fund. Also by giving to the fund while they are free, a person helps secure good standing with criminal leadership if and when they ever need it.

The mechanisms for providing such support are also well functioning. At the beginning of the month, goods are collected from businesses and private individuals and then taken into the local prisons. In regions where A.U.E. ideology is strong or where the criminal organization is active, there is usually no shortage of donations. According to one interviewed, mid-level criminal from the south of Russia, "In our area, there are no problems with goods collection. And young people are happy to participate. You do not have to ask them twice."[4]

Also if needed, additional goods and funding could come from the criminal *obshyak* of the region where a prison is located, the region where the majority of the inmate population is from, and from wherever a prison's outside *vor* is based.

And although prison authorities are well-aware of the illegal origins of some donations, they gladly accept them and officially register such as humanitarian aid.

Exports and Imports

It is also the criminal government's job to ensure their prison produces something in demand outside of prison for export and facilitate the import of goods not available inside.

Exports

Some inmates are skilled and able to produce quality manufactured goods. And any money raised from selling such items outside of the prison are also contributed to the *obshyak*.

Many prison factories were built during Soviet times and are no longer working. This is usually because of corruption or a lack of interest among the prison authorities. In these cases, it becomes the job of the criminal leadership to reboot the factories and make them both operational and profitable. This may require, among other things, finding a demand for the manufactured product, coordinating the delivery of supplies, and even training the labor force. And their efforts are often successful. In one prison, an experienced criminal leader turned a profit in just two years by starting metal works in the prison factory and developing an agricultural business (raising chickens and growing mushrooms).

Imports

Because inmates are only allowed to receive care packages once every several months, and because prison meals are so bad only the poorest inmates eat them, there is a high demand for food and other items. So prison criminal leadership organizes and manages the import of regular goods (food and basic necessities).

Inmates or their families will send money either online or via cell phones, and the *blatnyje* will collect this money. Then they will connect with members of the criminal organization on the outside and transfer the money along with a list of needed goods. They will also negotiate with prison authorities to make sure those goods are let inside the prison. Local criminal family members will then buy the food and bring it into the prison. Usually this type of service is considered public goods, and criminal leadership does not charge a fee for its services.

On the other side, ensuring supply of drugs and non-prison made alcohol in prisons is not only part of public goods provision, but also a money-making business. There are several ways of getting drugs and alcohol inside the prisons. The most commonly used one is through prison guards who will bring in the substances for a fee. Another way—though prohibited by prison leadership—is through food packages. And in some cases, these substances are dropped inside prison via a drone or are being shot inside with an arbalest or RPG type of a system.[5]

In the past, drug dealers contributed to the prison *obshyak* with a supply of drugs. Now it works differently. For example, if there is a group of ten to fifteen inmates who want drugs, they collect money and give it to the *polojenets* or other leadership. The leader then gets those drugs inside the prison, but they take half of the drugs to the *obshyak* as a commission. There are several reasons for such a policy change:

Power. Monopolizing the delivery of drugs within the prison increases both the income and power of prison criminal leadership.

Price control. To make sure prison guards do not increase the smuggling price, the prison leadership maintains a monopoly on buying drugs from them.

Inventory control. Since criminal leadership controls all the drugs in prison, if they see an inmate under the influence and it is not clear where he got his drugs, it is assumed he got them in a food package. Since this is prohibited, the inmate is punished.

Ensuring the quality of drugs. Drugs inside the prison are less expensive and of better quality than those on the streets. The way they can ensure better drugs is by finding and punishing anyone on the outside that sends in laced or cut product. In the criminal family, it is considered a sacred duty to take care of those behind bars.[6]

Trade

Before the 1920s, trade between inmates was widespread and many inmates earned their living by selling something they produced, smuggling in goods and reselling them, or doing some service (like fixing clothes) for other inmates, Petr Yakubovic, who spent eighteen years in a prison camp in Czar times, writes,

> We have a lot of profitable businesses [in prison], and everyone can find something for himself. Some people are playing card games for money, at the same time one is guarding them and earns money from that. Some sell vodka. Those with families sell bread and milk [at that time, families were allowed to follow their imprisoned husband or father to prison]. Some earn money by hiding card decks. There are so many ways a smart inmate could earn money! One could wash my things, and I would pay him. You could simulate an illness, get admitted to the hospital, and sell the extra milk and meat you got there and earn yourself cigarette money.[7]

But when *vory* took control of the prison, the situation changed. The original *ponatiya* prohibited any monetary relations between inmates of an upper caste, including selling something, even if the item was a personal belonging one inmate no longer needed. And any trade could only be done through the prison criminal leadership. According to an interviewed member of the leadership, "Our ideology encourages inmates to be brothers who help each other in times of despair, and they should not look at each other thinking how they could make money by ripping each other off. If someone needs something basic, he could get it from the *obshyak*, and if someone does *not* need something, he should give it as a present—like you would do with a brother."

In every prison, there is a *baryga* inmate who is in charge of an unofficial shop that accommodates quick, small purchases. This shop is separate from the official shop run by prison administration, which usually does not have much to offer customers. When an inmate runs out of soap, for example, he can buy it from the *baryga*, who also accepts online payments. A different *baryga* produces and trades alcohol.

Although a *baryga* is always from the *sherst'* caste, it is a *blatnyje* who facilitates his supply and controls his prices. This ensures that goods are affordable to the majority of the inmates. Also because the prison criminal leadership controls it, one could buy goods on credit. But compared to delivery services, retail is not considered a public good. The *baryga* earns money from his job, but any profit goes to the criminal *obshyak*. Such a monopoly on trade increases not only income but also the power of the criminal organization.

This rule worked well until expensive items, such as cell phones, started appearing in prisons. An inmate could not usually afford to give higher-priced items as a gift. That led to a major reconsideration of this rule. Now, there is an exception for cell phones. If someone wants to sell his cell phone to another inmate, he is now allowed.

But in some prisons this process is complicated. First the seller needs to go to the *smotryasçiy* of his barrack and ask him if it is okay to sell his item. If the *smotryasçiy* says yes, the seller then goes to the *baryga* and gives the cell phone to him. The *baryga* usually already knows who is looking to buy it and will facilitate the transaction, record it, and collect a tax for the prison criminal government budget.

When I asked an inmate how such a system was enforced, one inmate explained, "Not only is it philosophically and morally right, but no one would dare not obey this rule. Inmates know that spies are everywhere, and sooner or later, the criminal leadership will know if you violated it." Inmates also obey trade rules because if one party cheated in a trade transaction, the other party would have no recourse for justice. Who could he complain to, knowing he was also guilty of violating *ponyatiya*?

Some prisons, however, already allow one inmate to sell his cellphone or sim card directly to another inmate. But the seller would still have to let the *baryga* know that a transaction took place, and then pay a tax—10 percent of the item price—to the *obshyak*.

Gambling

Although the funding sources mentioned above are important for the prison economy, the main source of income for the prison criminal government is the taxes on gambling, which has always been a big part of prison life.

A famous Russian writer, Anton Chekhov, who visited prisons in a remote Russian region in 1890, wrote the following about card playing, the biggest form of prison gambling, in his travel notes:

> Cards is an epidemic that has already taken over all prisons; prisons now look like casinos, and areas around it [halfway houses] are their branch. Business is so widespread, that there are rumors that its organizers, who have hundreds and thousands of rubles found during [the prison] search, have business relations with other prisons where, as inmates say, "the real game" takes place. Card games fog your head like drugs, and an inmate who loses food and clothes in a game does not feel hunger and cold, and when he is leashed, he does not feel pain. And even during hard labor on a boat with coal, with waves are all around and people seasick, the card games are going on.[8]

And paying gambling debts was a matter of honor, so it was not uncommon that someone who was unable to pay his debt committed suicide by shooting himself. So even now, to be respectable, a *vor* has to be an excellent card player.[9] And it is still not uncommon that inmates would rather commit suicide than be known as one who did not pay a gambling debt. To them, it is a matter of honor. Once a *blatnoj* lost a large sum of money in a card game. He was able to collect the money from outside sources, but prison authorities prevented it from reaching the prison in time, so rather than bearing the shame of his condition, he killed himself.

This card playing tradition is still supported not only among leadership, but also among other inmates for several reasons. First, it helps kill time, something inmates have in abundance. Second, according to interviewed inmates, "Playing card games gives you adrenalin. It makes you feel human, compared to your everyday almost vegetable-like state. And it helps time move faster."

A third reason is, according to several interviewed inmates, card games indicate an individual's risk aversion, which helps members of the criminal family understand each other. At the card table, an inmate can lose anything from his money to his honor, and even his life.

Famous Russian philologist Dmitry Lichachev says that the 1920s and 1930s, so many inmates lost their bread rations for a month that prison authorities proposed losers stopped paying their debt, so they did not starve. Losers were allowed to vote on the matter, and they voted to continue paying their debt. These inmates ended up being force fed and "searched after mealtimes to make sure they were not hiding the bread."[10]

In Gulag times, inmates went even further and used to play for females and even body parts. Lifelong humiliation might also be imposed on the loser like being tattooed on his face with an enormous penis pointing towards his mouth. A loser might also become like a deaf-mute by forfeiting the use of his voice and voluntarily not speaking again.

Finally, and most importantly, the criminal leadership encourages gambling because facilitating card games is a major source of income for the criminal prison leadership.

According to Dostoyevsky, in the 1850s, gambling facilitation was a business run by individual inmates:

> In almost all barracks, there was an inmate who owned a small old rug, a candle and very used and dirty cards. All that together was called *maydan*. The owner collected money from those who played, around fifteen cents for the night . . . The game usually lasted till late night or even sunrise, when prison guards opened barracks . . . Every *maydan* had a person who was hired by players for the night and was paid five cents. His main job was to watch for prison guards and alert players if they were approaching.[11]

When the *vory* criminal organization engaged in state building in prisons, they monopolized the gambling industry, and now those from the *blatnyje* caste are the ones who govern the games. There is also a *smotryasçiy* of the game, and, after the *polojenets*, his job is the most important in the prison criminal government.

This *smotryasçiy* has several responsibilities. First, collecting taxes from the game. In the 1970s, the amount of this tax depended on the type of game being played and began at 25 percent of winnings. Now it is around 15 to 20 percent. And since, in some prisons, the amount of money changing hands in one game night could reach several hundred dollars, it makes a significant contribution to the mutual fund. According to an interviewed ex-inmate high in the prison criminal leadership, "In 2019, in my prison camp there were around 800 people. Let's say 200 of them were playing regularly . . . so it would give around 1,500–2,000 dollars to the *obshyak* in an average month."

Inmates can also bet items, and there is an up-to-date, official price list of items that can be played for and their prices. Sometimes inmates even play for cars and apartments they have left outside of prison. In that case, they have to notify the *blatnyje* in advance, who in turn will have to notify the *vor* in charge of the prison and region. Then they will get in contact with members of criminal family in the town where the car is parked or apartment is located, check that it exists, and approximate its price.

Why would someone bet such costly items? One former inmate, who had spent a total of ten years behind bars, explained that if an inmate who has a long sentence inherits an apartment or car when a family member dies, he does not really care about it. "It will be a pile of trash when he gets out," he said, "so why not have fun with it at least."

This inmate also remembered that in his ten years in prison, such bets have been made several times. Once a guy who was an orphan had an apartment in some small town. The *polojenets* notified the *vor* that the orphan wanted to gamble with it. Members of the criminal family went to this apartment, approximated its value, sold it, and sent the majority of the money to him to prison to play with, and with the rest, they bought another, much cheaper and smaller apartment, so that he still had a place when he got out of prison. It was the *vor*'s decision.

The deadlines for tax payments are usually scheduled for the first and fifteenth of the month,[12] and if an inmate cannot pay his tax on time, he either is sent to the *sherst'* caste or becomes a *snir* for the inmate he owns money to.[13]

Sometimes inmates will do anything possible to avoid punishment for their debts. For example, once an inmate (in prison for forgery) paid his card game debt ($200) and criminal tax with fake money that his friends had brought to him from outside. Prison criminal leadership did not notice it and accepted the payment. When much later it was found that the money was fake, the prison criminal leadership asked their *vor* what should be done. To everyone's surprise, the *vor* said that, since the money was already officially accepted, nothing should be done with the inmate.

It is also important to mention that tax on gambling is the only tax in prison that is not exclusively for the *obshyak* or inmates' mutual fund. It also feeds a special fund dedicated solely to the criminal leadership's personal use. This is also a legacy passed down from Gulag times. According to original *ponyatiya*, card playing is the only way a *vory* can earn money in prison.

According to an interviewed inmate, "From the money you win in the card game, you pay a tax. You could either transfer money to a special *obshyak* bank account, or you could buy stuff (usually cigarettes) in the prison store and donate them. Usually cheap cigarettes are given to the *obshyak* and good (expensive) cigarettes are given to the fund for criminal leadership."

Second, a *smotryasçiy* is responsible for facilitating the gambling. That includes judging games and ensuring that no one is cheating. For example, discussion about the game is absolutely prohibited while playing, and a person who is heard talking could be forced to pay the money lost on the card table. Also, the *blatnyje* usually provides a gambling box—which house teas, cigarettes, and food—during the game. And like in the best casinos in Las Vegas, there are often waiters, special *sniri* whose job is to prepare tea for those who play. The issue with drugs and alcohol during the game is more complicated, and though, in some prisons, they are part of the gambling box, in other prisons it is prohibited so that players can think clearly during the game. There, players are offered drugs only when the game is over.

It is also up to the *smotryasçiy* to enforce public safety rules. Despite the desire of prison criminal leadership to maximize the profits from gambling, as a government, they also have to make restrictions that keep inmates safe.

(1) In some prisons, the *blatnyje* sets the roof for the games at around fifty dollars. Anything higher than that requires special permission from prison criminal leadership. This is done because huge losses often lead to suicide, which in turn leads to problems with prison authorities.
(2) To avoid old inmates ripping off inexperienced newcomers, in some prisons it is prohibited to play for money with an inmate who has been in prison for less than a year.
(3) In the inner prison, inmates are only allowed to play with what they have available on hand. It is hard to move money and goods in the inner prison, so this rule limits the chances of an inmate not getting what he is owed.
(4) Making sure that all players know the stakes. Because by default all games are played for money, if inmates plan to play cards just for fun, this is loudly announced to the whole cell or barrack before the game starts. That is done because sometimes experienced players will play a new inmate without announcing they are playing for money, but when the new inmate loses, he is expected to pay.
(5) Finally, this *smotryasçiy* last responsibility is to encourage gambling. And to do so, he relies on usual marketing methods. One is word of mouth. Those in charge of the game (*smotryashchiye* for game on prison and barrack levels) walk around the barracks encouraging people to play. Others organize competitions with significant prizes, like drugs and cell phones.

Despite a clear monetary interest in increasing the number of games being played, the caste division always remains intact. It is strictly prohibited for members of the upper caste to play with members of the lower caste, and the gambling tax is not collected from members of the lower caste playing among themselves.

Like any government has to adopt to the rapid changes in technology, prison criminal leadership is now faced with an unexpected problem of competition from online casinos. And although they are trying hard to prohibit betting online and using spies to enforce this prohibition, they are still losing "clients" to it. As a result, they are also losing tax revenue.

Officially, prison authorities fight against such widespread gambling. In some prisons, guards try to enforce it, but simple prohibition and confiscation of cards do not deter inmates. Now inmates just get a new deck, and, in the past, they would fashion one from newspaper and glue (made of soaked bread). And only very rarely do prison guards try to find other, more efficient ways to stop the gambling industry. For example, those who were caught playing may be forced to report to prison authorities every two hours during the day. This would mean the inmate could not sleep during the day and, as a result, would not be awake enough to play at night, the usual time for card playing.

In other prisons, guards not only close their eyes to card games but allow rolling tables to be moved in. Sometimes they even take part in those games themselves when they get bored during shifts.[14]

Debt Collection

Like everywhere, it could be the case that an inmate needs to borrow money. Prison criminal leadership does not offer credit because, according to an interviewed inmate, "No one would dare to use *obshyak* money for that," again referring to mutual fund money being sacred and prison criminal not willing to risk it for such non-essential spending.

On the other side, an inmate is allowed to borrow from another inmate interest free, and ideally this transaction should be done with a witness and both sides signing a paper confirming a transaction.

What criminal prison leadership will do in such cases is ensure that the money would be returned. Theoretically there is no mandatory fee for this service and no set amount one contributes to *obshyak* after his money is returned, but, according to inmates, it is usually around 20 percent.

And in cases where a lender does not expect his money to be returned, he can donate this debt to *obshyak*. In that case, the borrower owes the *obshyak* money, and not paying it back would be a dangerous violation of the criminal family rules. One interviewed inmate commented, "You can be sure the borrower will return the whole amount of money." Basically, such debt collection for a fee is a major business for the criminal family outside of prison, so they are professionals at making sure a person pays his money to the *obshyak*, even if it is after he is released from prison.

On the other side, a person who does not return money he borrowed on time is not equal to a person who did not pay his card game debt. It is a much lesser *ponyatiya* violation, and one will not be moved to the *sherst'* caste for it.

Prison Criminal Government Expenses

Basic Necessities

Mutual funds usually pay for everything—food, cigarettes, tea, and clothes (socks and underwear). Cells have a box or a dresser drawer where a *smotryasçiy* places these goods and where inmates can get what they need.

Also, since drugs are also officially in the *obshyak*, according to *ponyatiya*, anyone could ask for them. But that is not the norm. However, if a respected member of an upper caste asks the *smotryasçiy* or *polojenets* for drugs, that inmate will, most likely, not be denied.[15]

Bribes

Mutual funds are often used to bribe administration for any number of privileges: a longer walk in the yard, scissors in a cell, and so on. For example, the *obshyak* of one jail in Ukraine is about $500,000, and it is used for getting illegal things inside the jail like drugs, alcohol, and prostitutes, and also to bribe the prison leadership. For example, the director of the jail receives $30,000 a month from this fund.

Prison Repair and Construction Work

Although, theoretically, the governments give money to prisons for such work, it is often stolen by prison authorities instead of used for its purpose. As a result, inmates have to pay for those projects themselves. For example, if the Department of Corrections allocates money for the prison camp building repair, that money would be stolen by the prison administration, who would then ask inmates to contribute to the building repairs so that prison authorities could still report that the job was done.

Welfare

While those who do not contribute to *obshyak* cannot benefit from it, exceptions are often made for new inmates, inmates in the prison hospital, and inmates in a special security ward. Sometimes in the hospital and special security wards, goods are even given to members of the lowest caste. Often, when an inmate is locked in solitary confinement or in the prison hospital, he does not have access to the outside world, and the only way for him to survive is through what other inmates provide. The mutual fund can provide them with relief.

Celebrations

For major holidays, criminal prison leadership organizes celebrations for the upper caste with expensive food, alcohol, and often drugs. In one prison, all members of the upper caste received some kind of drugs as New Year's presents from the criminal leadership. Also, individual birthdays are celebrated from the *obshyak*. A special person is in charge of keeping track of all birthdays in prison, and in the morning, a birthday boy gets a present (usually cigarettes, tea, or sweets) and a card from the prison criminal leadership. In the evening, he is invited for tea in the prison leadership corner of his barrack. These kinds of gifts and celebrations serve a dual purpose. One leader confided, "We do it to please inmates and buy their loyalty."

Rewards for Inmates

Not only is there a short list of ways to punish inmates, but there are also few rewards. But one way for an inmate to earn one-time rewards is by doing something beneficial for either the prison population or the criminal leadership.

If prison authorities need inmates to manufacture something extra in the prison factory, they would go to the *polojenets* to bargain. For example, in exchange for the service, authorities might promise to allow a package through that is much bigger than the limit. When they agree, the *polojenets* goes to members of the *muzhiki* caste who work in the factory and ask them to fulfill the order, and then reward them for their work with something from the mutual fund.

In some cases, the reward is alcohol, but in most cases, it is drugs. When asked what the reward might be for an inmate who does not drink or do drugs, an interviewed member of the criminal leadership paused for a second, probably to recall if he had ever met such an inmate. He then replied, "If they do not do drugs themselves, they could give it as a present to someone. But if one really does not want the drugs, I guess he could get tea, cigarettes, candy, or some benefits in relations to visitation."

Conclusion

Running the economy, facilitating the import of goods, and providing social assistance to the indigent is not a simple task for any government, and for *vory* prison governments in particular. But since they claim to work on behalf of the general inmate population, this becomes their main responsibility and their success or failure in this area has a direct effect on their legitimacy and the loyalty of the inmate population.

As a result, particular attention is paid to those in charge of prison economics—*smotryashchiye* of *obshyak* and *smotryashchiye* of the game are the second most important people in prison after the *polojenets* himself.

Criminal leaders budget operating costs and collect taxes (on people, trade, and import), but a major source of income is from the tax on gambling. And that is similar to US states that operate state lotteries and some US cities that are homes for casinos. Those taxes are used not only for the needs of the leadership, but also for services that benefit all prison inmates. These services range from bribing prison administration to relax official prison rules to providing social security for inmates who have no outside support.

Of course, criminal leadership is doing their best to be sustainable and balance the budget inside the prison, but if they are not able to do so, the *vory* criminal organization of the town or region where a particular prison camp is located could use money from their own *obshyak* to bail them out. They have an interest in the sustainability of their leadership behind bars.

7
Everyday Life Behind Bars

What other services does a government have to provide its citizens to increase the quality of their lives and, as a result, legitimize its rules? One such service is communication. Inmates want to communicate with each other and preferably with the outside world. And to supply this demand is the job of prison criminal leadership. In fact, they also crucially need such communication to ensure security inside the prison camp and be connected to the criminal world outside.

Also, since prison, by definition, should be a boring place, it also becomes the job of *vory* leadership to make it less so. Not only do they entertain inmates, but they use culture and entertainment that increases the legitimacy of their A.U.E. ideology. So in this chapter, I will talk about public goods the prison criminal leadership provides to inmates, and how their use serves as propaganda for their ideology.

Communication

In general, communication between inmates not only functions well, but also is in step with modern standards of technology. During the times of Soviet Gulags, when inmates were prohibited from any type of communication, conversations consisted of Morse code tapped on the walls between cells. Then, when the first radiophone became available, criminal leadership would make a deal with residents of a nearby house, install a radiophone there, and bring a handset inside the prison. Now cell phones and smartphones are widespread behind bars.

Although communication is now modernized, it does not handle all of the communication problems. For example, transactions that require moving goods (usually cigarettes, tea, drugs, and cell phones) between cells and prison camp buildings is still done as it was a hundred years ago—through physical "road" systems.

Ropes

One form of communication happens through ropes. Ropes attached between cells and through windows conduct pieces of paper or small goods in socks. This

Criminals, Nazis, and Islamists. Vera Mironova, Oxford University Press. © Oxford University Press 2023.
DOI: 10.1093/oso/9780197645659.003.0008

is the easiest to operate and the most popular method of cross-cell communication. One interviewed inmate explains, "When drugs get into prison, you can hear the sound of dozens of toothbrush cases with syringes inside hitting the metal bars on the *blatnyje* window—clang clang clang—and then, in twenty minutes, the same sound on the window bars in different cells."

However, the rope system can be hard to install and often requires a certain degree of creativity. In Butirka in 2015, there was a new building seventy meters from the closest building. It was a big problem to connect to it. So to establish the first connection, inmates made a crossbow and then shot an arrow with burning cotton from a mattress (so it is visible) toward that building, and then inmates from there were able to pull it up with a hook.

Also, because ropes are so hard to install—and prison guards often cut them—in addition to regular ropes, there is usually a tiny nylon "control string" very high in the air that allows inmates to reconstruct a damaged rope system relatively quickly.

Plumbing and Ventilation

Every cell houses part of sophisticated plumbing and ventilation systems. Something sent down the pipe in one cell could be caught in another cell. This is a more complicated type of a road and is used less often.

Holes in Walls

Some prison buildings in the former Soviet Union are very old, and inmates have made holes between cells that most prison authorities have no interest or funding to repair. At least in one prison, a hole was big enough for smaller inmates to crawl through.

Because not all places in prison can be connected, messages are also exchanged by writing them on walls in common places like the bathroom or yard or writing them on paper and throwing them over walls between barrack yards. And because the inner prison or solitary confinement buildings are more isolated, messages and goods are usually passed by *balanderi*, members of the *sherst'* caste who distribute food between cells.[1] Sometimes members of the *sherst'* caste are the only means of moving messages to the most isolated locations.

Only inmates from the upper castes are allowed to benefit from using the "roads." This avenue of communication excludes *petukhi* because they are believed to contaminate whatever they touch, and *sherst'* because they are not trusted and could read messages, steal goods, or bring sensitive information to the attention of prison authorities.

A special *smotryasçiy* is in charge of the prison roads. This is a crucial and difficult job. It is up to him to maintain a road map of the whole prison and know who sleeps where, which is basically an inmate's postal address.

Under this *smotryasçiy* leadership, there is a person in every cell responsible for working those roads. They usually sleep on the upper level of the bunk beds near the windows because that is where the rope roads are, and the roads only operate at night.[2] They are also responsible for always keeping their cell connected to the prison road system. If something happens in a particular cell, and they are not able to connect to the road system, that inmate would have to answer for it by explaining to the *polojenets* what happened and what he did to fix the situation. Also, if the road system is compromised by prison guards, or there is an unexpected search, it is this person who must hide or destroy messages passing through their cell at that time.

The confidentially of messages is treated very seriously. According to interviewed inmates, "Such an old-fashioned road system is very reliable, and messages are always delivered safely, which cannot be said about sending messages by phone where everything is intercepted." And if a message arrives for someone who has moved out of the cell (or prison), it is returned to the sender. If that is not possible, the message is destroyed.

If a message is particularly sensitive (perhaps accomplices coordinating their witness statements), it could be encrypted and wrapped in plastic from a pack of cigarettes and sealed with heat. In addition, the time at which that message passed through each cell is also recorded on a separate piece of paper attached to the message. This ensures there is no delay that would allow someone to open, read, and then reseal the message.

It is also up to the inmate in charge of the road to remember all the secret signals inmates use to communicate. For example, several knocks on the heater could mean that there is a search going on, and if the person responsible for the roads does not hear it on time and pass it on, there could be serious problem for other inmates, and for him as a consequence.

It is also important to note now that almost all prison camps have cell phones inside, and although they are in the hands of prison criminal leadership and richer inmates, they are considered public goods. By *ponyatiya*, any inmate has a right to ask another one for a cell phone and cannot be refused.

Communication with other prisons or free members of the criminal family is also a well-oiled machine. In Gulag times, communication between prisons was done through inmates as they moved between them. Inmates would write messages on a handkerchief or piece of fabric that was then sewn to the clothes. If the message was particularly sensitive, it might be written with invisible ink that becomes visible only when a special chemical is applied to the text.

Inmates might also move messages inside their own body. A small piece of paper sealed in plastic could be attached by a string to a tooth and swallowed or put inside an anus.[3] Now, since cell phones are widespread, this method is used only to move goods.

Purposes for Communication

Communication with other prisons or those on the outside is important for several purposes:

Information from a *Vor*

This is called a *progon*. In the past, it came with incoming inmates but now it comes by phone. This message includes general information in relation to the life of the criminal family:

Vory arrests
Vory deaths
Newly crowned *vory*
Demoted *vory*
Vory authorization to kill someone (e.g., "*Vor* Y decided that *Vor* X is *gad* [did something bad for the criminal family] and has to be killed")
Vory dates of birth and death[4]

Second, *progons* also contain messages about new rules *vory* have instituted and that need to be implemented. A *progon* could be signed by one or a group of *vory*.[5] However, according to interviewed inmates, because rules do not change often, such messages are rare.

It is important to highlight that when new rules are circulated, members of upper castes are not allowed to discuss them, or any *vory* messages, especially the ones about conflicts between *vory*. According to an interviewed inmate,

> If someone is discussing a conflict between two *vory*, he could easily say something by accident that could lead to a serious problem. For example, someone might accidently defend one *vor* by saying that the second one did something wrong. So then, technically, that person has insinuated that the second *vor* did something indecent. So those *progon*, an inmate can hear or read and accept as

a fact, but he cannot discuss it. How could *muzhik* give his opinion about a *vor*? It is not acceptable.

And at least once (in Central Asia), an inmate was degraded for questioning the character of a *vor*.

In prison, there is usually a specific person in charge of writing those *progons* down to pass on to inmates. This job is done be someone respected and trusted by the criminal leadership, and because the formal nature of *progon* is complicated (more about that later in this chapter), the transcriber must have good writing skills. According to an interviewed person in charge of writing *progons* in his prison, "It is a very important task, and I cannot afford to make a mistake. That is why I always ask an experienced *blatnoj* [who has spent a long time in prison] to look through what I wrote before sending it out." On the other side, the actual language of the *progon* is always in conventional Russian and never prison slang so it can be understood by everyone.

It is the responsibility of a *polojenets* to make sure that all inmates in his prison receive and follow the message. If he is not able to do so, he will be punished. As a result, after the *progon* message, there is a list of cells written on the piece of paper. In each cell, someone is responsible for reading the *progon* out loud and making sure all inmates hear it. Then that inmate writes his name and the words, "Read out loud and everyone got it" next to his cell number. It could take the whole night for a *progon* to go around the entire prison. When this paper returns to the main cell, they check which cells saw it. Because there could be cells that are not connected to the road, the *progon* may have to be read to some separately.

Consultations with *Vory*

If there are no *vory* in a particular prison, but there is an important issue to solve that the *polojenets* does not feel comfortable solving himself (e.g., potentially degrading someone for violation of *ponyatiya*), he needs to reach his *vor*. The *polojenets* would explain all the details to him, and the *vor* makes the final decision.

Checking New Inmates

Often, information about a new inmate reaches a particular prison way before the inmate does, being passed from either a jail or an inmate's old prison. In particular, the most important piece of information will proceed any inmate to his new destination, and that is his caste. And if it does not proceed him, finding out is the first order of business.

When a new inmate arrives to prison, a message is sent to everyone mentioning the name of the person, where he is from, and what he has been charged with. This way, if someone knows him, he will inform the others. And if in the past that new inmate had done something not according to *ponyatiya*, it would become known.

It is also important to mention that it is in the criminal leadership's jurisdiction to not only ensure communication between cells and prisons, but also to censor or prohibit it if necessary.

For example, a cell could be cut off from the prison road system if necessary. Or now, when many inmates have access to not only cell phones but also smartphones, prison criminal leadership might prohibit particular inmates from using them if it might affect the general population's well-being. For example, to not put pressure on prison authorities who allow prison violations, there is a *progon* that prohibits posting pictures on social media. Not only would doing so show that inmates have access to prohibited items such as cell phones, but also pictures would reveal that inmates often live in better conditions than they are supposed to (according to prison regulations).

So if an inmate is not careful and reveals what is going on behind prison bars to the outside world, a *blatnyje* may take his phone and allow him to use it only with someone else present. And in one prison, prison criminal leadership required all smartphone cameras to be broken, except for those used by leadership.

Culture

Around any regime that is in power long enough, a specific culture develops. This culture is strongly associated not only with the rules of the regime, but also with reinforcing its legitimacy. And the criminal world is no exception. A.U.E. ideology and culture set the criminal world up as its own community. And since opposition to the current government and law enforcement—and the idea of suffering for a just cause is central—prison culture has evolved around this center.

Criminal prison culture includes several distinctive attributes.

Religion

In Gulag times, criminal culture had a strong emphasis on religion. This is not because inmates had a deep belief in God or had repented of their crimes, but because it served as a visible opposition to the regime. First, inmates enjoyed reminding prison authorities that everyone is equal in front of God. And second, A.U.E. ideology started in Soviet times, when the official religion of the Stalin regime was communism, and the government was enforcing secularization by turning churches into cinemas and arresting and imprisoning priests. As a result, in the flurry of opposition to the government, criminal culture embraced everything associated with religion.

A cross tattoo was the first symbol that served as a costly signaling of opposition to prison authorities. Usually on arrival to prison, prison guards would take crosses off of the necks of inmates, but it was impossible to do the same with tattoo, so those inmates were often beaten.

Also, during the WWII, *vory* called themselves "guardians of the true Christian religion" and adopted an initiation process that closely resembled baptism. There, a new *vor* was given either a tin cross to wear on his neck or a cross was tattooed on his chest. Of course, any religious traditions were laced with criminal values, and so tattooed crosses were usually decorated with images of cards and even naked females.

Views on Women

A specific attitude toward females has developed in these all-male prisons. Talking between themselves, inmates often elevate the roles of their mothers and the mothers of their children, but downgrade other females by considering them useful only for pleasure.[6] Despite that, there is also a community of females who "meet" inmates (by phone or through letters), get into relationships with them, support them while they are behind bars, and wait for them to be released. They are called *zhduli*, which is a disrespectful form of the phrase, "someone waiting." One inmate described the process of finding a zhduli:

> Inmates are good at bullshitting, so they find a girl who often has some kind of problem with relationships with normal guys. . . . Inmates have tons of free time, so they are nonstop on the phone with those girls. They constantly participate in their lives. Girls love it because such people do not exist in a normal society—guys are busy with other things and can't be that engaged. So those girls often come for visitations and send money to their "loved ones" behind bars. It makes it kind of a beneficial coexistence despite it's for the wrong reasons.

Language

Over time, a special slang called *fenya* has developed in prison that is difficult for an outsider to understand. Because the environment is very tense in prison, and words equal deeds (with the same consequences), one cannot afford to be misunderstood. It could be very dangerous. Therefore, one of the distinctive characteristics of the prison slang is that it is very simple and direct.

Some slang words are from regular Russian words shortened for convenience. For example, the word for "inmate," which originally was the abbreviation Z/K (*zaklyuchennyy kanaloarmeyets* or in English it is translated as *inmate canal builder*[7]), has become the word *ZeK*. Other words come from religious vocabulary. Insults like *kozly* (goats) or *cherti* (demons) in relation to prison guards are from Christian writings in the Old Slavic language.

Card games, as an important aspect of prison culture, also contribute to the criminal slang. For example, even the most often used word in Russian for "castes" is *masti*, which means card suit. The verb for causing a problem or being offensive is *ramsit* and comes from the Russian word *rams*, the name of a card game. In this game, the inmate running the *rams* game chooses which card suit will trump, and mixing it up is considered cheating or making problems.

Other words come from other languages, especially Yiddish and Hebrew. This is a byproduct of the number of Jews imprisoned under Stalin. The word *fenya*, their name for the prison slang, comes from the Hebrew word *Ofhem*, which means expression. Another example is the word for young children who are already in the criminal family—*patzani*. This word comes from the Yiddish word *potz*, meaning penis, and in particular its diminutive form, *potzen*.

Some words also come from the Chechen language, another group of people also imprisoned by the thousands. And since, in Gulag times, many prison guards were from the Ukraine, Ukrainian words are also heavily incorporated into prison slang, especially in relation to prison guards. The word for the prison guard himself if *vertuhay* from a Ukrainian word that means to spin around, and the word for prison cell is *hata*, the Ukrainian word for house.[8]

Also, when words are associated with the *vory* justice system, keywords are intentionally replaced to distance themselves from the official government system. This is yet just another way to highlight their opposition to the current government.

In addition to slang, the criminals' concentration on politeness and mutual respect is profuse in their everyday language and at every level. A *vor* will not say, "I prohibit something" (which would make what he's saying resemble an order from official authorities). Instead, when correcting an inmate, he might say, "I strongly advise you to abstain from that action."

Language, both spoken and physical, is also what makes one member of the criminal world immediately recognizable to another, particularly when it comes to greetings. First, prison inmates would never shake hands with a new inmate because they are not initially sure of his caste status. Second, an inmate entering a cell would never say a general greeting, like hello or good evening, because he also might be greeting people from the lowest caste who are present, which, again, is not acceptable. But because it is not prohibited to wish peace to people of different castes, he might say something like, "Peace and prosperity to the cell, health to the inmates, and greetings to the respectful [upper caste] inmates."

Another greeting might be "Life to *vory*," to which other inmates would reply, "Death to police" or simply "A.U.E." These greetings might be used when someone in a small cell needs to figure out what caste an inmate in the next cell is. If the reply to his yell, "Life to *vory*" is "Death to police," an inmate knows his neighbor is from the upper caste. An inmate from lower caste will not answer. At night, before the road starts to operate, inmates often yell "A.U.E." to signal that they are ready to run the road. These phrases also serve as slogans, and inmates may yell them back and forth to each other as a show of unity to intimidate prison guards.

Since those words are basically signals of belonging to the criminal family, they could be updated if needed. In particular, after the 1950s, it was necessary to distinguish legitimate *vory* from *suki*, so the meaning of many slang words were changed. For example, the word *krasnishnic*, which before WWII meant a train robber, after the *Suki* Wars, referred to a jewel thief. It was assumed that *suki* would not be able to follow changes in the slang and as a result would out themselves when speaking.

Because a lot of communication between inmates is still done in writing, even the written language is replete with special treatment of certain words. When an inmate is writing a message to other inmates, such as a *progon*, he has to follow certain rules. Names of prisons and the words *cell* and *prison* are underscored with one line; names and nicknames of *vory* and the word *vor* itself are underscored with two lines; everything related to religion, including the word *God*, is underscored with three lines; and the word *policeman* is underscored with a broken line.[9]

Names

Usually after getting to prison, an inmate gets a nickname, and for a *vor*, it used to be even considered offensive to be called by his legal name once he was crowned.

In the past, the naming process was taken very seriously. A special interview was required, and other inmates also asked about any old nicknames a new inmate might have had (even in school). Then the other inmates closely watch his behavior for a while until they came up with two name options and let the new inmate choose between them.

Later, that particular ritual for newcomers changed. A newcomer would go to his cell window and yell, "Prison, give me a nickname," and the respondents would ask what he was in prison for. Once the newcomer answered, respondents would start yelling proposed nicknames back. Of course, at first, most of the names were offensive, so a newcomer had to yell back, "Not going to work!" Eventually, the options being proposed became more appropriate, and a newcomer would choose from among them. After that, the other inmates could request the new inmate sing a song as a symbolic payback for their help.[10] Now, most often inmates choose their own nicknames.

Some inmates, and especially *vory*, have longer nicknames awarded during the crowning. These nicknames more closely resemble regular Russian names, except the surname often refers to an inmate's old profession, some physical distinctions, the inmate's hometown or region, or his nationality or ethnicity. In a name like Dato Tashkensky, the surname refers to the town of Tashkent.

Members of *petukhi* caste who offer sex services usually have female nicknames given to them when they are degraded. Among the popular names are those from soap operas that were popular at the time they were degraded.

Music

Over the years, a particular style of music has developed whose main theme is the A.U.E ideology or the injustice and suffering of inmates. These are called *blatnaya pesnya*, or "Russian Chanson." While the style of music has changed to reflect general changes in the style of popular music, the main theme of its lyrics continue to depict prison life and government injustice, and celebrate the thieves' code of honor. The first famous Russian Chanson is "Murka," and was written in 1920s:

A gang arrived from Odessa in Amur	*Pribyla v Odessu banda iz Amura*
There were gamblers and urki.	*V bande byli urki, shulera.*
The gang was doing its criminal business	*Banda zanimalas' tomnymi delami,*
And law enforcement was watching.	*I za ney sledila Gubcheka.*
A woman gave a speech, and her name was Murka.	*Rech' derzhala baba, zvali yeyo Murka*
She was sneaky and smart.	*Khitraya i smelaya byla.*
Even angry notorious criminals Were afraid of her.	*Dazhe zlyye urki i te boyalis' Murki,*
She was living the life of a criminal.	*Vorovskuyu zhizn' ona vela.*

Many of these songs are dedicated to a particular *vor*. Probably the most famous of those is "Vladimir's Central Prison" (one of the most infamous prisons in ex-USSR), written in 1998. It was dedicated to *vor* Sasha "*sever*," which means north. (He later asked the artist not to mention his name in the song). The words illustrate the suffering associated with the prisons:

Vladimir's Central Prison, northerly wind	*Vladimirskiy tsentral, veter severnyy,*
On a prison train out of Tver, evil immeasurable.	*Etapom iz Tveri, zla nemereno,*
A heavy weight rests on my heart.	*Lezhit na serdtse tyazhkiy gruz.*
No matter that I betted, life is decided	*Kogda ya bankoval, zhizn' razmenyana,*
It's not a game of chance that brings wreck and ruin,	*No ne "ochko" obychno gubit,*
But an ace to an eleven.	*A k odinnadtsati tuz.*

Tattoos

An inmate's body—particularly one who has done time during the Soviet years—is often covered with specific criminal-family tattoos. They serve as a resume of sorts and signal their status to others in the criminal world. Their symbolic importance mixed with the increase in enforced prohibition during Soviet times increased the value of having them. The more inmates were punished for having them, the more important it was for *vory* inmates to be tattooed.

One popular tattoo is that of a spider in a web, which indicates that an inmate is living according to criminal rules.[11] Usually the spider is climbing up the web, but if he is depicted climbing down, it means the inmate left the criminal family.

Some of the tattoos simply indicate that an individual has done time. Five dots (four in a rectangle and one in the middle) symbolizes being alone surrounded by four walls. This tattoo is usually placed between the index and middle finger, so that it will be very visible during a handshake (outside of prison). Everyone who has been in prison is allowed to have this tattoo, from *blatnyje* to *petukhi.*

The number of domes on a tattoo of a Russian Orthodox Church represents how many sentences a person has had (if an inmate is not a Christian, he might have a tattoo of a boat with a different number of girders). A tattoo of the Virgin Mary means the inmate wearing it started his incarcerated life in the juvenile prison.

Other tattoos, such as of rings (on fingers), could signal the caste a person belongs to or which prisons he had been in. Stars, badges, and epaulets[12] are like medals, given for bravery in opposing government and prison officials.[13] They can signal that an inmate was punished for upholding the criminal ideology by being imprisoned in solitary confinement or a special security ward for not following orders. Participating in prison riots might also earn an inmate the right to wear one of these tattooed "medals."

Tattoos could signal not only a radical opposition to the prison authorities—so-called *rejector's stars* tattooed on the chest—but also opposition to another prison group. For example, during the *suki* wars, a tattoo of the butterfly was popular among legitimate *vory* and members of their criminal family. It signaled that its owner would never turn to *suki*.

A tattoo of a grinning predator such as a wolf, lion, or bear generally indicates strong and forceful opposition to the current government. The eight-pointed stars have a similar meaning: opposition to prison authorities who, for inmates, symbolize the oppressive government.

Other tattoos signal an individual's philosophy in mottos, although usually in the form of an acronym. Examples include phrases like "Was sentenced by a USSR court," "I will take revenge on the police," or "My children will take revenge on police."

Also, some tattoos speak to a different audience, not government or law enforcement, but fellow inmates. For example, open eyes tattooed on the chest mean, "I can see everything" and that their owner was a *smotryasçiy* in the prison criminal government.

Also, *obizhenyye* used to be marked with tattoos of flowers, *petukhi*, or explicit words in visible places such as on the hands or face. Of course, after serving his sentence, an inmate could try to get rid of those tattoos, but there was little point in doing so. The scar would still be visible, and it would be clear to people in the criminal world what tattoo had been there.

Criminal tattoos are done in prison with the permission of that prison's highest criminal authority, whether that be a *vor* or *polojenets*. If an inmate is caught getting unauthorized tattoos, he is beaten and forced to remove them, which is very dangerous and an extremely painful experience. In the past, this was done either with some kind of a chemical acid or scraped from beneath the skin with a brick.

In the past, tattoos were crucial in the criminal world because they would immediately tell anyone who was able to read them the whole criminal history of a particular person. Now, with the development of advanced communication, the need for them has decreased tremendously, and classic prison tattoos are becoming less and less popular.

Traditions

Like any other established ideology, a lot of symbolic tradition permeates the A.U.E culture and reinforce its customs. Many of these traditions stem from honoring those who have gone before.

Heroes

Every ideology has its heroes—those who model the strengths of a people and their beliefs. In A.U.E ideology, the most famous such hero is a *vor* named Vasya Diamond. In sum, he was sentenced to more than ninety years in prison, thirty-five of which he actually spent behind bars before dying at the age of fifty-seven. His heroic deeds included not joining the *suki* during the *suki* wars, serving time in the most strict prisons, escaping from prison twice, and killing inmates who violated *ponyatiya*. Vasya Diamond died in prison in 1985 under unknown circumstances, which has afforded plenty of room for legends and conspiracy theories to abound. The most popular is that Vasya Diamond was killed by authorities because they were not able to break him. Many songs and works of art are dedicated to preserving his memory.

Postmortem Customs

A *vor*'s importance follows him to the grave. *Vory* are never cremated. Instead, if they die outside of prison, they are buried with great pomp and ceremony. Their coffins are very expensive, made of the best woods and decorated with gold. When it is time for people to pay their respects, middle-level criminals approach first to say goodbye. After them come any natural family members, and lastly, other *vory*. Graves are marked with huge monuments and are often later visited by members of the criminal family. (The most popular gravesite among *vory* in Russia is that of Vasya Diamond.)

Tea Drinking

According to the memories of a prisoner of Gulag, "*Urkas* usually didn't break bread with outsiders. Meals were an important *urka* ritual, and I had heard that allowing someone to eat from the same bowl or sharing a piece of *paika* [food ration], was a rite of initiation into the group."[14] That was the case because back then, food in prison camps was so scarce that people often died of starvation. That is not the case anymore, so this tradition has changed.

Now, one of the central A.U.E traditions, which symbolizes the idea of unity, is drinking an extra strong, energizing tea called *chifir'*. *Chifir'* is typically prepared with five to eight tablespoons (50–100 ml) of tea per person poured into a cup of boiled water. It is brewed without stirring until the leaves drop to the bottom of the cup. During the brewing process, the caffeine breaks down, and the leaves release adenine and guanine into the water, which does not happen during traditional tea-making.

To make it the strongest, baking soda is added. It must be sipped slowly, otherwise it may cause vomiting. It may be left to brew overnight and served either hot or cold. The nature of the brew results in a bitter flavor.[15] It can be addictive, and some inmates continue drinking it even after being released.

An even stronger version of *chifir'—konyachi* (horse's) *chifir'*—is made by boiling tealeaves in already-brewed *chifir'*. This liquid manure is so bitter, it is impossible to drink without adding a lot of condensed milk, and it is very dangerous for people with heart problems as it elevates their blood pressure.

Drinking *chifir'*, participants usually sit in a circle and drink the tea from one cup, with each one taking two sips.[16] Such drinking from one cup shows that everyone trusts everyone else and that they are from upper castes (absolutely unacceptable to drink from the same cup as a member of the lower caste). Also, it is considered very impolite to interrupt a tea ceremony, cross the circle of those drinking, or refuse to drink it without a good excuse (such as having high blood pressure). On a side note, unprepared tea cannot be borrowed and replaced later. It can only be given as a present from one inmate to another.

According to inmates, drinking *chifir'* is not only reserved for special tea ceremonies. It also serves as a daily necessity in many prisons where there are often shortages of food and *chifir'* is an inmate's main source of energy. Because of the tea's bitter and unpleasant nature, living on *chifir'* (and smoking cigarettes) signals a strong person who does not depend on food to survive and so cannot be easily broken by authorities.[17]

Ceremonies

As in any ideological movement, ceremonies serve two goals. On one side they need to highlight their oppositional aspect. After the October Revolution, religious celebrations were prohibited by the Bolshevik government and later, in 1927 so was New Year celebration. As a result, in prison those holidays became actively celebrated. Special food was prepared even in the hungriest Gulag years, and even Christmas trees were often decorated.

On the other side, special ceremonies are institutionalized to enforce a particular ideology. So for the *vory* criminal organization, the most important occasion for *chifir'* drinking in prison is a traditional once a month (on the fifteenth) gathering of all the upper-caste members. The occasion is the celebration of the birthdays of *vory* from the local region and the commemoration of local *vory* deaths. Either the *polojenets* or the *smotryasçiy* in charge of ideology organizes the meeting, and attendance is mandatory. Serving sweets or chocolate or salty dry fish signifies a high-level of respect to participants.

The main goal of this gathering is propaganda, glorifying *vory* leadership and A.U.E ideology. While inmates eat and drink, a *smotryasçiy* of ideology often tells heroic stories about famous *vory* and their contributions to the criminal organization. Usually the day before the event, the *smotryasçiy* for ideology gets an audio message with all the information, including the short stories he will tell to others in the meeting.

Of course all members, and particularly criminal leadership, are serious about those gatherings in public, but in private, talking to someone unrelated to the criminal family like me, they acknowledge how ridiculous it is. One fifty-five-year-old, high-level member of the criminal family told me this story:

> Once I was in the prison hospital in the minimum-security prison camp for first timers [he himself was a recidivist and was housed in another prison camp]. On the fifteenth, a young guy come in and, like an actor, announced, "Can I have your attention please?" Then he started reading from a piece of paper the birthdays and deaths of *vory*. He could not read well in general [was almost illiterate] and reading the names of *vory* correctly seemed absolutely impossible for him. I started correcting him. He also tried to tell some stories about those *vory*. I am old, so I knew those *vory* personally, and again I was correcting him and trying hard not to laugh. When he left, I called the *polojenets* of their prison and asked that, if next month they were going to send someone here again, I would appreciate it if they sent someone literate.

Conclusion

As for any society, communication is one of the most important public goods a government has to offer its citizens. So one of the prison criminal government jobs is to develop a functional system of communication services within the prison and make sure that inmates are connected not only to the outside criminal world, but also to loved ones.

On the other side, effective provision of public services is not enough to garner support for the *vory* rule. So to further enforce their rule and the legitimacy of ideology associated with their government, *vory* leadership promotes a particular culture and rituals. As a result, when an inmate gets involved with the *vory* criminal family, his entire identity changes. He gets a new name, learns a new slang, listens to different music, and sports new tattoos. His values also change to reflect those of the new society he has become part of. And because this criminal culture is so old and rich, for many inmates, it becomes their only reality, a paradigm they will never shake for as long as they live.

8

Conflict with Prison Authorities

Getting Power

In the previous chapters, I talked about how criminal leadership governs prisons that are under their control. But this is not always the case. In some prisons in the former Soviet Union, internal life is fully controlled by prison authorities through their trustees (members of *sherst'* caste). Those prisons are called *krasniye*, or in English, *red*.[1] And to gain power in such prisons, the criminal leadership first needs to take it from the prison administration.

If they are successful, then prison administration relinquishes part of their authority, and *vory* leadership move from the position of opposition to the position of government. Such prisons are called *cherniye*, or *black* prisons.[2] And, as discussed in previous chapters, in black prisons, there is an unspoken agreement between administration and criminal leadership; administration closes their eyes to some things inmates do, and criminal leadership keeps control of the inmate population.

In other words, how the criminal family operates—as government or as governed—coincides with the color of the prison. Inmates who are in leadership positions in black prison (*blatnyje*) are on the bottom in the red prisons, and in the red prisons, it is the *sherst'* from the lower caste (of people working or cooperating with the administration) who have the leadership positions.

Because relations between members of the criminal family and prison guards are in constant negotiation for the balance of power, those systems are not set in stone and sometimes change. It could be that the balance of power is steady through daily life, or sometimes it can change radically, and very abruptly. Like the frontline of a war, it can be in constant flux. If the criminal family inmates want more authority, they will be on the offense and prison administration (and their trustees among inmate population) will be on the defense, or other way around, with the administration aggressively taking the upper hand and the criminal family being subject to it.

So in this chapter, I will discuss what it takes for criminal leadership to take control of a prison (and how strict *vory* criminal ideology aids in this struggle) and how prison administration can try to prevent it from happening.

Criminals, Nazis, and Islamists. Vera Mironova, Oxford University Press. © Oxford University Press 2023.
DOI: 10.1093/oso/9780197645659.003.0009

From Red

Red prisons often operate like a strict dictatorship, and conditions for inmates are usually so unpleasant that those prisons are unofficially called concentration camps. Incoming inmates feel it the minute they arrive.

By law, every new inmate has to spend fifteen days in isolation for medical reasons. In those cells, prison administration try to break new inmates right away by confiscating all of their personal belongings, including their toothbrushes. This is often followed by beatings to near death (and deaths are also not rare). For example, in one such prison, when new inmates arrived, prison guards lined the corridor, and as new inmates passed through, they were severely beaten as they went. If, on the way, an inmate dropped his belongings, he had to start at the beginning and go through the corridor again.

In addition to beating, the prisons guards usually humiliate inmates. It is not rare for prison authorities to make inmates paint the grass green in winter, walk around naked during formation, and formally greet not only prison guards, but also their K9 dogs.

Also, prison authorities usually show power and put psychological pressure on inmates by over-enforcing visible signals of *their* ideology, which is based on the Department of Corrections manual. One red prison does this by having guards meticulously follow all the official rules cited in facility manuals and internal prison memos. This could involve enforcing everyday formations, cadences on the way to work, and mandatory attendance in the cafeteria.[3] Movement is also allowed only in formation, and inmates must always be dressed in the prison's official uniform. And the dress code is taken very seriously. No one can have the top button of their shirt undone, even in summer.

The daily schedule is also followed meticulously, to the minute. According to inmates, "Although everything in those prisons is done according to the law, it is intentionally done so meticulously that, psychologically, it is very hard to handle. It makes you constantly worried, and you cannot relax. They use it as a form of psychological torture."

For any violation of rules, inmates are punished severely. They may be punished according to the rules—solitary confinement, canceled visits, canceled mail, and even extension of a prison sentence—or by other methods, such as beatings and torture.[4] And, according to an inmate who shared a cell with ex-Guantanamo inmate Ruslan Odizhev, "When we asked him how it was in the notoriously bad Guantanamo prison, he would always say that the torture there was nothing compared to what is done in prisons here [at Nalchik in Russia]."

There are several reasons why such methods are employed. First, red prison administrations adhere to the logic that, if inmates are terrified of their prison experience, it will deter them from violating the law in the future. And the conditions in such prisons are also used to terrify those who are free so they will think twice before breaking the law (or standing up against the government as is often the case in former Soviet Union countries).

Second, these methods make it easier for the prison administration to control inmates. That is also beneficial for the prison administration career-wise, because red prisons pass all prison inspections without any problems.

Third, closely aligned with administrative ambitions is the hope for promotion. To get promoted, prison authorities are expected to help solve cold cases and so use inmates to admit to crimes they never committed. Authorities extract these forced confessions by beatings and torture.

Fourth, it makes guards feel powerful. Almost always, people become prison guards by default. They take the job because they could not find work elsewhere. Therefore, they tend to come from the lowest class of society. According to an interviewed political prisoner in Russia, "I was really surprised when I realized that prison guards and the majority of inmates are from the same social group. It is only because of random events in their lives that they ended up on different sides of the prison barbed wire. Basically, if you changed the guards out for the inmates, or the other way around, no one would even notice." And in Gulag times, many prison guards were former inmates themselves who had stayed in the town where their prison camp was located after their release.

Being a guard makes those of the society who choose that route feel important among their peers, and they are only too happy to exercise that power on powerless inmates. It also does not help that members of other law enforcement agencies (such as internal security and police) also look down on those high in the criminal family, and they are often openly jealous of their success and money.

A final reason is money. Prison administration benefits monetarily in red prisons. First, they use inmates as free labor. In prisons were factories still function, inmates work more than fourteen hours a day in terrible working conditions with no pay.[5] Any manufacturing profits go directly to the prison director. In some cases, particularly in Central Asia inmates are also brought to work in the house of the prison director outside of prison.

Prison Administration and Guards

There is a popular joke among inmates that directors of correctional facilities in Russia do not retire. Instead, they are imprisoned for corruption. And it is true. Many prison-camp directors and members of Department of Corrections leadership do eventually spend time in prison on those charges.

Prison authorities also blackmail family members of inmates. In these situations, they are told to pay so that their loved ones are not beaten to death.[6]

And in some red prisons, prison guards also take not only all the food sent to inmates by their families in packages, but also the food left after a family visit.

Another reason life for inmates is very difficult in red prisons is the lack of self-help mechanisms and unity among the inmates. According to an interviewed inmate in a red prison, since it is not controlled by criminal leadership, there is no safety net, *obshyak*, to help with goods that make prison life bearable—things like food, cigarettes, and other basics. "There is also little to no communication between the cells," he said, "So there, everyone is trying to survive on his own."

But in fact, the opposite is true, and prison guards exploit the natural desire of inmates to help each other. If someone tries to protest against prison conditions by helping another inmate, he is beaten for several days. If he still does not give up, they beat others in his cell. They make him feel bad for his innocent cellmates suffering, and it forces him to give up his efforts.

Because the administration of red prisons does not want a regime change, their main enemy is any organized opposition, which means members of the *vory* criminal family following A.U.E ideology. So the administration has two strategies. First is to keep them out of red prisons altogether. When that is not possible, then the plan is to break such inmates before they join the general population. An inmate in one such prison explained the situation this way:

> It is especially hard for *blatnyje* to be here. *Ponyatiya* is not followed almost at all. *Smotryashchiye* are appointed by prison administration and behave very aggressively, especially towards those who stand up against them. Snitching and spying on each other is rewarded. If someone does a minor violation of the official prison rules, the prison authorities know about it immediately and punish the inmate accordingly. The only way left for us [who adhere to *ponyatiya*] is to suffer.

And prison authorities use prison criminal rules and A.U.E ideology to make them suffer. All incoming inmates are first asked to sign a certain document. It looks like other intake papers, but for *blatnyje* inmates, signing it is a crucial issue. Because of the *ponyatiya* rule about no cooperation with prison guards, signing it is very symbolic and means that an inmate not only cuts ties with the criminal family, but becomes *suka* as well as a member of the *sherst'* caste. As a result, members of the upper castes, and particularly those who plan to make a career in the criminal family, like *blatnyje*, will not sign it under any circumstance.

In some cases, prison authorities made all entering inmates sign a document directly rejecting *ponyatiya*, and during late Soviet times, such documents were even published by government newspapers. In 2009, one *vor* imprisoned in a notoriously bad prison camp, #9 in Omsk, wrote, "I, an inmate Khlinov [last name] have been *vor* since 2001, and in the criminal world am known as 'White' or 'Figure' [nicknames]. However, I now reject all the criminal world ideas and traditions because I consider them alien to me."[7]

If getting inmates to sign the paper does not work, inmates are threatened with rape (and some are raped), which in addition to being a type of torture also means a person will be degraded to *petukhi* caste. In one known case, a member of the *blatnyje* caste was asked to sign such a paper, but he refused. Then prison guards brought in a member of the *petukhi* caste to rape him. *Petukh* was taking his pants down when the *blatnyje* took the pen he was given to sign the paper with and gouged out the *petukh* eye.

Those who refuse to relinquish their dedication to A.U.E. ideology and are not beaten to death are moved to the inner prison. There, at least in several prisons, police SWAT teams come regularly to beat inmates. This twofold practice keeps inmates in a constant state of terror and provides SWAT teams with crowd-control practice. One inmate in such a prison said, "SWAT teams (even from other regions) come to beat us two times a week, so we are already kind of used to it."[8]

However, not all abuse of inmates is done by members of law enforcement. If there is something neither SWAT nor prison guards want to do because it is time-consuming or dirty, they will ask so-called *activisty* (activists), fellow inmates, to step in, and they will do the deed without any reservations. According to interviewed inmates, in some prisons, where authorities want to reduce their workload to a minimum, it is *activisty*, not prison guards, who run mandatory inmate formations.

Activisty

In explanation, *activisty* are militarized members of the *sherst'* caste who are used for applying force on behalf of prison authorities. Their history dates back to the *suki* wars of the late 1940s, but their official legitimacy, to later times. According to communist ideology, only someone's peers are able to reeducate him, so in 1957, volunteer prison organizations were officially organized for this purpose. And although, since 2010, these organizations have been outlawed, they are still widely used.

Inmates who become *activisty* have several common traits.

They Want Power

In red prisons, *activisty* inmates are allowed to exercise almost unlimited power. In some prisons, they even participate in searches along with prison guards. According to one ex-inmate, people who join the *activisty* often have personal problems and were hated by others even outside of prison. In his prison, one inmate mentioned, some of the *activisty* were even sent funeral wreaths from their enemies outside who wished them dead.

They Want an Easy Life

Although officially there are no benefits for being an *activist*, the reality is very different. Not only are they able to dress in more comfortable clothes, go unshaven, and own cell phones, they also enjoy benefits that range from extra packages from the outside, extra visitation rights, restaurant deliveries, and access to gyms, saunas, and swimming pools.

They Depend on Administration

Because they have to be in prison for long sentences, they are very dependent on good relations with the administration. It is one thing to suffer for one to three years defending *ponyatiya*, but it is quite another to live like that for twenty-five years.

They Had Problems with Criminal Leadership

Often these are inmates who had a problem with the criminal world and had to ask prison authorities for protection. Once that is done, not only do they they have to depend on prison administration for survival, but they often want revenge against the criminal family.

According to interviewed inmates, the most effective, and most dangerous, *activisty* are ex-criminal leaders—*suki*—who transferred their allegiance from the criminal family to prison authorities. Because these inmates know how the criminal world works from the inside, they are very effective in manipulating it. They usually chose this path if they are accused of violation of criminal rules (especially ideological rules, since for their violation punishment is more severe), but do not want to lose their power and move to the lower social castes. They are also very loyal to the prison authorities. They do not have any other option but to fully comply with their orders because, again, prison authorities become their only protection against the criminal world they betrayed.

Dictatorship in red prisons is supreme, and it is incredibly difficult for an inmate to be moved to another prison. One option would be paying a significant amount of money in bribes to administration. But because most inmates do not have the kind of money required, many hope to get sick so they are sent to a hospital and then, maybe another prison. A third option would be confessing to another crime (they may or may not have committed). It this case, they would first be moved back to the general prison for a new trial and then to another prison, albeit with a longer sentence.

Most inmates then are left to cope with the situation any way they can. According to an interviewed inmate who spent time in those prisons, "The only thing you could do to avoid being killed is cut yourself when you are being beaten. You have to do a deep cut on your wrists with a razor blade and get blood all over yourself. The goal is to make prison guards too squeamish to touch you."[9]

An internal manual distributed by another ideological group, many of whose members are currently behind bars, named self-harm (known as *vskryvatsya*[10]) as the only option to save an inmate's life:

> You should cut yourself individually if you are being tortured (including if you think you could be raped) if you are pressed to start working for the administration (snitch on cellmates or be a witness for prosecution), or prison authorities want you to confess to crimes you did not commit.
>
> You should always have a blade from a shaving razor for that purpose. You should carry it under you lip when you have to go talk to the prison administration because one can never anticipate what could happen there, and an inmate has to have an option of protesting, and in those conditions, cutting his own veins is the only option. Your goal is to make seven- to nine-inch-deep cuts in your wrists. It is most effective when HIV-positive inmates cut their veins. If you do not have a blade, you can also bite your veins, but this will take more time than you will have.

To Black

There are two types of prisons guards. There are those who are strict—who have to be mean to do their job—and those who are sadistic and enjoy unlimited powers over inmates. Of course, there are prison guards who are rational people who want to help, but they are very rare and are constrained by their uniform. So the important rule is to stay away from even the best prison guards. And prison guards respect only very strong inmates (those they cannot break), so you have to be strong to survive.

It is impossible to even pretend that you are not following prison rules, so do not try. On the other side, those who accept all the rules the prison guards make will forever be in the position that anyone can do anything to them. You should not give prison guards any of your freedoms without a fight. And you should always be in the assault position and targeting their weak points. In conversation, you should always have self-respect and self-control. Only with those will you dominate the enemy.

Remember that in prison, you cannot survive without suffering losses. And the only way to stand your ground is in your constant readiness to face danger and your willingness to make sacrifices. Your main defense is readiness to fight back. Neither your position, your physical stance, nor your friends can substitute for that.[11]

As can be imagined, the constant abuse inmates suffer in a red prison eventually drives them to do something about it. This entails acting against prison authorities in a methodical way, and in prison slang, is called "defrosting the prison." According to an interviewed prison guard, "Red prisons have one dangerous side effect. At some point, inmates have enough of that treatment, and then real problems for the prison leadership start."

Dealing with Guards and *Activisty*

But suffering alone is not enough for inmates to start actively protesting, especially in such a dangerous environment as prison. It takes the right combination of personnel to make it happen. First, inmates need a strong person—or better, a group of people—who are willing to take risks and even sacrifice themselves for the goal. According to one interviewed inmate, it needs to be someone with "experience, knowledge, a strong voice and posture, and his eyes should be very serious."

The same inmate mentioned this leader must be trustworthy so that other inmates will follow him: "For any normal individual to follow someone into such a dangerous enterprise, he needs to feel that, when it becomes really dangerous, he will not be left alone." When such an inmate does arrive in a red prison, two to three other strong-minded inmates among the mass will get close to him, and they will be the core for future action.

Potential leaders in a "defrosting" are inmates who want to rise in the criminal world hierarchy, such as aspiring *blatnyje*, who are willing to go against prison leadership and rules. So their goal is to start an opposition movement inside the prison, and even, if needed, be punished for such actions by the prison authorities. Although the punishment will be severe, it will help promote them in the criminal family.[12] It is very hard for prison guards to fight against a person who is looking forward to such punishments as solitary confinement, beatings, and torture.

According to interviewed inmates, sometimes it is enough to have just one such strong and charismatic individual among them to turn a prison from red to black. Even someone who is locked in solitary confinement is able to start protests from there.

In addition to a strong leader, successful resistance also requires communication between cells, or "roads," so that inmates can coordinate their efforts.

A successful defrost also requires support from the outside. Without that support, it would be very hard (if not impossible) for inmates to make radical changes. As a result, the geographic location of the prison plays a big role in the prison's color. Usually black prisons, then, are located in or near big cities, where the criminal world is strong and outside support can work as a carrot-and-stick for prison authorities.

One reason geographic location is so important to a black prison movement is proximity to family. The closer an inmate is to criminal and regular family members, the easier it is to put pressure on local prison guards and *activisty* (after their release). One interviewed inmate was an eyewitness to the following event in one of the main prison camps in Chechnya, an extreme example of family relations because this region's deep tribal structure, cohesion, and traditions.

Despite it being prohibited, everyone has personal phones in prison. Once a prison guard came to an inmate and asked, "Can you please give me your phone so that I could call home? I have some problems there" (prison guards do not have access to their cell phones during work hours). The inmate agreed and gave it to him to make a brief phone call. The guard left with the phone. Four hours later, the guard returned, but without the phone, and the following exchange happened:

Inmate: Where is my phone?
Prison guard: I am a prison guard and I work here so I am allowed to just confiscate it.
Inmate: But you deceived me.
Prison guard: Well, I am a prison guard, so I am allowed to do so. And if you keep talking to me like that, I will lock you in the solitary confinement.
Inmate: Okay. But I swear, you will return my phone to me.

Then the inmate took a phone from another inmate, called his family members, and explained to them what happened. His relatives went to the village where the prison guard was from, met with the village elders, and told them the story, saying, "We bought our relative in prison a phone so that he could call his wife, kids, and old mother, and your relative deceived him and took the phone." After that, the relatives of the prison guard called him and asked him to come to them, where the following exchange happened:

Elders: Is it true? Did you deceive an inmate and take his cell phone?
Prison Guard: Yes.
Elders: You have to return it to him.
Prison Guard: But I am a prison guard! I am allowed to take it.
Elders: Did you hear us? You have to return the phone.

The next day, the prison guard came to the inmate and complained about what his relatives told him.

Prison Guard: Why did you tell your relatives to talk to my relatives?
Inmate: Listen, I told you in the beginning to return my phone.
Prison Guard: But I can't. It's gone.
Inmate: That's your problem, not mine.

The same day, the prison guard was running all over the prison trying to buy a phone from the *baryga* (under control of prison criminal leadership), but he failed. So he came back to the inmate and gave him 3500 rubles (the price of a similar phone), saying, "Here is the money for your phone. Please buy it yourself. I tried to talk to *blatnyje*, but no one wants to sell one to me."

Also, in such regions as Chechnya, because of its complicated social connections and traditions, a simple threat of shaming is sometimes enough. Another time in the same prison, an inmate used the following tactic: when prison guards were doing a search and a guard took something belonging to an inmate, the inmate yelled at him, "Listen, I know the village you live in, and when I get out, I will go to your village and tell everyone there how you behaved in prison and that you basically took the last stuff we had." The guard apologized and returned to the inmate what he had confiscated.

Vory and other high-level members of the criminal family could also blackmail prison authorities. For example, they could record them taking bribes or being part of some other kind of illegal activity, and then use it to their advantage.

Finally, inmates could also easily threaten prison authorities when they and their families live in the town near the prison. According to an interviewed inmate, there was a person in their prison—an ex-military, special-ops soldier who was part of a gang robbing trucks—and prison guards threatened him that if he did not admit to more crimes, they would plant drugs in his wife's car, and she would be arrested. He came to the *vor* for advice, and the *vor* promised to solve the problem by asking members of the criminal world to threaten prison guards outside the prison.

Another interviewed inmate remembered that, after being assaulted by a prison guard, one of the inmates told the guard, "I will not touch you right now. I will not even argue with you. Just keep in mind that my sentence will be over soon, so in a year something could happen to you, something like a nasty car accident."

It is also not uncommon, when something happens inside the prison, that members of the criminal family come to the prison walls armed with weapons. This sends a signal to prison authorities what could happen to them if they keep mistreating their colleagues behind bars.

And often prison guards are also threatened when they are off duty. They could get death threat phone calls, and since in Russia prison guards have to wear their own distinctive uniform (not a regular police one), it happens that they are occasionally approached on the street and told "to watch out."

And those are not empty threats, especially in the Caucasus. In recent years, someone shot up the car of the director of a prison (wounding him and killing his son) in Kabardino-Balkaria, Russia. In Dagestan, a similar attack left the director of a prison and his driver dead, and a prison director in a prison near Moscow was severely beaten.

On the other side, this is the fate of only a small number of directors of red prisons. The main reason for that that majority of prisons are in small remote villages in the north of Russia. And prison directors and their family members have bodyguards, and even helicopters to move around. Also those towns and villages are so isolated that when someone who is not from that community comes there, it is immediately known to everyone. So putting pressure on them is often physically impossible to do for members of the criminal family.

This type of retaliation makes prison authorities afraid of high-level prison leaders. According to a high-level member of the criminal family, "I am used to prison guards watching my every move. I recently went to the prison hospital in another prison, and while I was smoking outside, an inmate was filming me with his cell from the second floor of the opposite building. He was ordered to by prison authorities."

The number of attacks on low-level guards is impossible to count because they do not report such incidents to police. Any investigation of incident might lead to an investigation of their actions in prison. According to an interviewed experienced prison guard, "I am always telling new recruits to be careful and not beat and humiliate inmates for no reason. It is very dangerous."

And such actions against *activisty* are not even paid attention to among the guards. However, it is very often openly shared among inmates on social media and in prison *vory progons*, which say something like, "Inmate so and so from prison so and so answered for what he did."

Often *activisty* are brutally beaten and degraded (sometimes killed) during their transfer to other prisons or when they are released.[13] On the day of their release, members of the criminal family may already be waiting for them outside the prison gates. In these cases, inmates might be released in the early morning (opposed to the regular time in the afternoon) and driven by police to the train or bus station.

And although these small protections allow *activisty* to leave the prison and get home, it does not protect them in the long run. According to an interviewed inmate, "It is not hard to find them because after release, they go back to their old [illegal] business where they will get in contact with people who recognize them from prison times. Also, many of them are drug addicts, so they interact with drug dealers who will also recognize them and notify people who need to be notified."

Another reason proximity to civilization is important in the defrosting process is because it makes bribing the prison administration easier. Such bribing could even look absolutely legal from the outside. For example, a businessman belonging to a criminal family could donate something like food or construction materials to the prison, calling it humanitarian aid. This will help the inmates, but it will also make the prison administration look good in front of their superiors. And the worse the financial situation of a prison is (due to corruption), the more important support from the outside becomes. Working out such deals with the criminal world makes things convenient for prison administration in more ways than one. Not only do they get wealthier, but it looks like they are taking care of their prison, which, again, makes them look good in front of their superiors.

Although it is more difficult for red prisons in rural areas to make the change to black, criminal-family inmates in these prisons still have their own unique set of tools to influence the system. But to be fair, a move from a really red prison to a black prison is extremely difficult because inmates and the criminal family are weak opposition against the strong, dictatorship-like prison administrations. In many cases, it becomes a zero-sum game—either prison leadership will be changed (and could face trial) or the situation for inmates may become even worse. So how is it possible for a red prison to become less red and more black?

Defrosting a Prison

Administration Change

First, there could be a peaceful change of the prison director. For example, an old prison director retires, and a new director from a black prison moves in. In this case, the new director would be used to how black prisons operate and would likely agree on similar arrangement with inmates. According to an interviewed inmate, "When the director changes, he comes to address inmates during the formation. So basically from his first words, if not his appearance, it is obvious if inmates will be able to use him, or if he will be using them."

Vor Negotiation

Second, a respected *vor* should be moved in because he is able to talk to prison authorities not only on their level, but sometimes even from a higher position.

Vory spend most of their time in prison, so basically when a *vor* was promoted to *vor*, a prison guard in the *vor*'s first prison was most likely also promoted to prison director. It is easy for them to talk to each other. They have known each other for decades.

Also when a *vor* moves into a prison, he immediately brings everything needed, not only for the prison, but also for the prison director. He can even help prison authorities get promotions, find jobs for prison guards, family members, and so on. And if the *vor* needs something but cannot get it himself, his criminal family will help him. So coming in with that kind of power, he will be able to talk to the prison authorities and peacefully solve all the problems, making it comfortable and beneficial for both sides.

But when there is no powerful *vor* to negotiate, inmates must try to solve their problems themselves. While inmates have no influence on who will be moved to their prison, they could try to affect the change of leadership. Because beating and torture in prisons are against the law, even if correction authorities are closing their eyes to it, making it known to the general public will force authorities to change their stance. And often when the situation in such prisons is publicized, it costs the presiding prison director his own freedom. As a result, there is a leadership change.

Complaints

To reach that first, inmates could try to follow the rules and write complaints to the highest authority (which in prison slang is called *shaking the regime*). Although *ponyatiya*, *vory*, and *blatnyje* cannot write such complaints, *muzhiki* can. According to one interviewed inmate, in the middle of an active war between prison administration and inmates in his prison, each of the inmates were writing ten to fifteen complaints a day. Usually, each inmate chooses a particular topic, writes a complaint, and then gives it to the other inmates to copy. Another interviewed inmate mentioned that, at one point, all the inmates in the prison coordinated and sent 500 complaints to prison authorities at the same time (it is harder to simply ignore 500 as they might ignore one). Another interviewed inmate used those complaints to his advantage. On the cover of his file, it was a noted that he liked to write complaints, and when he was moved from a prison in Moscow to one in Chechnya, prison authorities approached him and asked him to not write complaints about their prison. The inmate said as long as guards were respectful to him and the other inmates, he would not. The authorities told him they would be. "And you know, it worked," the inmate said. "We had great relations with them. They were very good with me, and during my eight years there, I did not write even one complaint."[14]

However, a manual of sorts, written by experienced ex-inmates to other inmates, took a different stance on complaints. According to it, one could write complaints to the highest-level prison authorities. And, on one hand, prison authorities are afraid of complaints because they could prevent them from rising in their ranks. But on the other hand, there is very little chance that complaints will reach the high-ranked official because prison authorities tend to protect each other. And while an inmate thinks he is doing something to improve his situation by writing those complaints, he will just be wasting his time and energy.

And in absolutely red prisons, this is often true. In an infamous prison in Bryansk (IK6), inmates had asked prison authorities many times for the forms to write complaints to the European Court for Human Rights. And although this form is listed among the items that inmates could ask prison authorities for—a list that is displayed on the wall of every prison building—prison authorities refused to give them out. In addition, if an inmate asked for the form repeatedly, he was threatened with solitary confinement.

Only after inmates were released could they file complaints. For example, by 2013, several ex-inmates sued the correction authorities for violations of their human rights and demanded compensation for physical and psychological damage. Of course, the correction authorities did not acknowledge any moral or physical wrongdoing. They did not even comment on them, and in a closed session, the local court rejected all the claims.

So since it is not clear whether complaints will be effective, inmates need to reach the general public. All interviewed inmates acknowledge that it is almost impossible to make any change inside the prison unless they go public. "Because basically everything that happens inside prison stays there, and prison guards could do whatever to us," one inmate said. "The only thing that could stop them is pressure from the outside."

Experienced inmates recommend engaging media and human rights activists as much as possible because prison leaders fear that if their problems become public, high-ranking authorities will respond using them as a scapegoat and either fire or imprison them. The best example of this happened in a prison in Karelia (Russia), where Mikhail Khodorkovsky—once the richest men in Russia and a prominent opposition figure—served part of his sentence. Historically the prison had been red, but when Mikhail Khodorkovsky moved in, journalists and activists started monitoring everything very carefully. This show of soft power made the situation within the prison much better. As Khodorkovsky remembered in the interview, "Before I arrived, the prison authorities made inmates repeat, 'We do not have *activisty* in this prison' many times during formation. That is how afraid they were that I would report about the existence of *activisty* there."

If the unlawful actions of prison guards are not enough to draw enough publicity to a prison, inmates may take action to draw the public's eye. These actions are limited to the tools they have at their disposal:

Self-harm

The most accessible option is hurting themselves en masse. These tactics might include a group of inmates holding hunger strikes, slitting their wrists, and stabbing themselves in the stomach with construction nails or sharpened toothbrushes.[15] When inmates do physical harm to themselves, in many cases, it cannot be ignored by prison leadership. It will lead to inspections from prison authorities and negative media attention.

Since the main idea of mass self-harm is to draw attention to the prison and support from outside, it helps to make the event coincide with a prison inspection or family visiting day, so that when it happens, there are many concerned family members near the prison gates.

As can be expected, the first counteraction from prison authorities is doing their best to prevent the information about the event from spreading. Most often, however, they are not very successful.

Mass self-harm is only used when most other forms of protest have not worked. It is also usually triggered by something dramatic, like an inmate being beaten to death by prison guards. At that point, the risk calculations among inmates change. They realize that, even if they did not protest, they could be killed, and, as whole, become less risk averse.

On the other side, self-harm only works as a tactic in democratic countries, where society holds prison authorities accountable for human rights violations. For example, as mentioned in the Alexander Solzhenitsyn book, *Gulag Archipelago*,[16] hunger strikes were of no help to inmates of the notorious Gulag under Stalin's dictatorial regime:

> Approximately in the middle of 1937, a new directive came: From now on, prison administration will not in any respect be responsible for those dying on hunger strikes! The last vestige of personal responsibility on the part of the jailers had disappeared! . . . Furthermore, so that the interrogator shouldn't get disturbed, it was also announced that days spent on hunger strike by prisoners under interrogation should be crossed off the official interrogation period. In other words, it should not only be considered that the hunger strike had not taken place, but the prisoner should be regarded as not having been in prison at all during the period of the strike. Thus the interrogator would not be to blame for being behind schedule. Let the only perceptible result of the hunger strike be the prisoner's exhaustion!
>
> Decades passed and the rime produced its own results. The hunger strike—the first and most natural weapon of the prisoner—at the end became alien and incomprehensible to the prisoners themselves. Fewer and fewer desired to undertake them. And to prison administration, the whole thing began to seem either plain stupidity or else a malicious violation.

Rioting

A final tool of protest is a prison riot. Prison administration might be able to hide self-harm from headquarters, but not prison riots. Not only can riots not be hidden from the media and government, when inmates take control of a prison, they have the tools to make the riot even more public. For example, almost always, the first thing inmates do after taking control of a prison building is to climb to the roof with banners (made of bed sheets) with words like "SOS" and "Help" written on them.

Rioting is a last, desperate resort, and inmates will usually try all other options first because riots almost always lead to causalities and increased prison sentences for those involved. According to an interviewed inmate, "In prisons with experienced criminal leaders, riots are not allowed. They will do anything possible to prevent it from happening."

So to go for it, conditions in a prison have to be so bad that inmates prefer the consequences of a riot to the continued suffering of their condition. The advantage to inmates is that prison administration cannot hide losing control of their prison from either their superiors or the press. The main disadvantage of a riot is prison administration has a right to get military and special-operations forces involved in using weapons to quell the riot. It would be naïve to think that prison authorities would not use this right to respond with force to any such actions of disobedience, so inmates go into a riot prepared.

Also, in all manuals and interviews, criminal inmates highlight the importance of secrecy in planning all those protest actions. According to the written advice of experienced ex-inmates to newcomers, there must be a plan in place for any violent action against prison authorities:

> Remember, when dealing with prison guards, you first do something and then demand. With such actions as a hunger strike, cutting veins, publication, and riots, you should not be talking about them, only doing them. Otherwise they will not be taken seriously . . .

There are many examples when spies for the prison authorities among the prison population are successful, and information about a planned riot is leaked and authorities take all the necessary actions to prevent it from happening. One famous prison riot in Kopeysk (Russia) in 2012 was in fact planned for 2010, but *activisty* learned about it and alerted prison authorities. As a result, dozens of key people were locked in solitary confinement.[17]

Terrorist Attacks

Finally, at least in one known case, desperate inmates went as far as threatening prison authorities and the Russian government with a terrorist attack. In 1993, several former inmates of the most notorious prison in Solikamsk gave an ultimatum to the Russian government, saying that "If the extortion, beatings, rape, and starvation [in that prison] does not stop, we will show our protest by different means, including exploding two shells in a public place in Moscow." They considered it the only option they had after their multiple complaints to correction authorities had been ignored. This threat worked, and a special investigative committee was sent from Moscow to that prison.

Although it is very rare, successful inmate resistance could turn a prison from red to black. According to one interviewed inmate who was transferred through a prison in Chelyabinsk in 2011 when it was red, and again in 2014, when it was black (after a riot): "In 2011, there were absolutely no *blatnyje*, and in the transportation cell, prison guards kept us under terrible conditions in very cold rooms without any light. In 2014, I did not even recognize the same prison. The situation there was totally different. Prison guards were trained and behaved well."

Conclusion

Relations between prison authorities and criminal leadership in red prisons are like those of a dictator and his opposition. When prison administration enjoys unlimited power, they can exercise it in different ways: extracting money from inmates, extracting false confessions to get rewarded for successful investigations, or using inmates for forced labor and SWAT trainings. And in case the authorities do not want to get their own hands dirty by beating and torturing inmates, they use groups of inmates to do it for them, a practice very similar to using progovernment militias for human right violations in nondemocratic regimes. Such delegation of inhumane actions also gives administration scapegoats later if needed.

Of course, such a situation makes life for inmates unbearable, and they will try to get the prison director replaced. The success of such a revolution depends on several factors. Internally there should be a strong leader willing to lead it. Preferably, he should be *vor*, but in absence of *vor*, any person or group *blatnyje* with leadership abilities is good enough. Also, not only should inmates be engaged in complaining to the highest prison authorities and human rights organizations through official channels but, in case it does not work, they should be willing to go until the end to reach their goal, which might include doing self-harm (like cutting veins) and starting prison riots.

It also makes it much easier if such a revolution is supported on the top level, such as a *vor* or other high-level members of the criminal family who could reach out to the local prison leadership and negotiate conditions inside the prison.

Since outside support of such a prison revolution is crucial, the geographical position of the prison is also very important. In big towns where the criminal family is strong, prisons are more likely to be black—and in remote, hard-to-access areas, red. Proximity to a populated area makes it easier for the criminal family outside to support those inside and bribe prison guards—but prison authorities are also more afraid because, if needed, it is very easy for criminals to assassin a prison guard on his way home.

In general, conducting a revolution inside the prison to change its regime is possible but, as in a country, very difficult. And to bring it about, extreme measures are often required. And if they fail, it leads to terrible consequences for participating inmates, so inmates riot only as the last possible resort.

9

Conflict with Prison Authorities

Losing Power

Since, as discussed in the previous chapter, it is possible to change a prison regime fròm dictatorial red to more liberal and democratic black, it is also possible to move in the opposite direction. Prison administration could tighten the screws and bring a black prison under their total control.

So in this chapter, I will talk about this process and, in particular, how prison authorities could decrease the power of criminal leadership and what tools criminal leadership has at their disposal to resist such a negative development. While strict *vory* criminal ideology was a group's strength when they were taking power from prison authorities, in this chapter, I show how it becomes a weakness when an ideological organization must defend itself from an outside force.

From Black

Usually, black prisons are more comfortable for inmates, and everyone wants to serve their sentences in those prisons. There is almost no torture, much more order, and relations among the inmate population are much better. There is also a safety net for prisoners (the *obshyak*) to fall back on. One interviewed inmate remembered, "When I got locked in solitary confinement, I immediately got two big bags from the *polojenets*. There was food, basic necessities, and even a phone so I could talk to my family and to him."

Basically, as criminal leadership themselves describe it, the atmosphere in such prisons is homey. Prohibited items (such as drugs, cell phones, and alcohol) are freely available, the prison schedule is not followed, and movement restrictions inside the prison are not enforced. The food is much better because it is bought by inmates from outside. Some prisons even have organic options available. One respondent even grew his own vegetables in the prison yard, using members of *petukhi* caste not only to plow, but to also collect bird droppings from the roof of the prison camp to fertilize the soil.

Relations with prison guards are also relaxed. According to one interviewed inmate, "I have been to a black prison where days would pass without me seeing a prison guard. We could do whatever we wanted to. It was like a summer camp."

Criminals, Nazis, and Islamists. Vera Mironova, Oxford University Press. © Oxford University Press 2023.
DOI: 10.1093/oso/9780197645659.003.0010

Another interviewed inmate added, "In really black prisons, inmates can even beat guards or lock them in cells. For example, once we had a problem with a food package. Some relatives had sent it to the inmate, but he did not receive it. So we, along with the *polojenets*, went to the prison guard in charge. The guard started arguing with us, so the *polojenets* told him, 'If you do not solve the problem with the package right now, you will seriously regret it [referring to being beaten].' The *polojenets* and the prison guard stepped outside, and the issue was solved right away."

On the other side, when inspection from the correction headquarters arrives, inmates do everything they can to help prison authorities pass it. If in the red prisons the conflict is between the Department of Corrections and prison leadership versus inmates, in black prisons it is inmates and prison leadership vs. the Department of Corrections.

According to interviewed members of the prison criminal leadership, "Prison guards keep us updated about the inspection by minutes. When they land at the airport, when they enter prison camp, how many people, where they are, and where they will go next. It is our job to make sure everything in prison is how they want it to be. And we take this job very seriously. No alcohol or drugs at least a week before the inspection, and everyone who is not reliable and could say something to an inspector is, just in case, locked in inner prison. During the inspection, all inmates look sad and miserable, all prohibited items are hidden[1] and prison looks as boring as an illustration in the correction authority's manual."

Since those prisons are under absolute control of the prison criminal leadership *ponyatiya*, its ideological rules, are strictly enforced and castes are segregated. But what is particularly important is that in many cases, prison criminal leadership in those prisons was even able to enforce the criminal caste system on the prison guards, which absolutely ensured them power over their enemy.

First, in many black prisons, prison guards do not want to touch members of the lowest class considering it unacceptable to them, like it would have been for inmates in the criminal hierarchy. Yet it is their job to body search those inmates. As can be expected, inmates use the guards' aversion to their benefit and often ask members of the lowest caste to hide prohibited items. And it is important to mention that since those rules were originally made to help the criminal organization against the enemy, by *ponyatiya*, it is not prohibited to touch things touched by *petukh* if those items are prohibited in prison. Also according to an interviewed inmate, "Whenever prison guards came to do a search, we had a petukh who would run over and threaten to hug or kiss them. It scared young inexperienced prison guards and slowed down the more experienced ones. Either way, it bought us enough time to hide whatever contraband we had."

Second, in some prisons, there are some prison guards who are the only ones to conduct body searches on *petukhi*. And those prison guards are considered the lowest, most degraded class by their colleagues, who often refuse to shake their hands or drink tea with them.

Finally, in the most black prisons, it is not rare that prison criminal rules are so deep in the Department of Correction's system that prison guards inside their own community declare someone degraded because they learn that he, for example, had oral sex with his wife, an action unacceptable by *vory* ideological rules. And they are not even hiding such deep infiltration of criminal ideology rules in their own social order. When I asked prison guards about acceptable ways of having sex with a female, many of them were very clear that oral sex was absolutely unacceptable.

Informants

Such enforcement of ideological rules on the enemy basically gives prison criminal leadership ultimate control over prison guards. In those prisons, the only influence prison authorities could have on prison criminal leadership is through spies among the general population. Although they do not have the freedom to do anything other than collect information and pass it on to prison authorities, these spies come from the same inmate population as do *activisty* in red prisons. These inmates all do the bidding of prison leaders for the same reasons.

Material Benefits

Usually people with long prison sentences and no relatives to support them are chosen by the prison authorities for these jobs. When they go to brief prison guards on inmate happenings, they lie and tell other inmates they have a visitor. As payment for the information, once a month they are sent a package with standard items such as cigarettes, cheap tea, some meat, and sweets. Not to raise suspicion, an inmate usually explains that an old prison friend who is now free comes to visit and sends him the packages. In truth, those packages are filled with items confiscated by the prison guards from the mail of other inmates.

Protection

Another popular source of spies are people who have a problem with inmates and asks prison guards for protection not to be degraded. To protect them, prison authorities transfer them to prison far away from their original prison. By doing so, they put these inmates into the general population and until they are discovered (news about their past reaches new prison), they work for the administration as spies.

Blackmail

Prison guards can degrade a person, film it, and then blackmail the inmate into spying for them. Many inmates would prefer to do that job rather than spend their sentence in *petukhi* caste.

People in this second category are also used to recruit other spies by dubious methods. For example, a person who is secretly working for the prison authorities is asked to play a card game with an inmate the authorities are interested in recruiting. When that inmate loses money (not a big sum, but he still needs help from outside to repay), according to criminal rules, he has a certain amount of time to ask for it from friends and family. However, prison authorities will prevent the money from reaching the inmate with reasons like not being able to schedule a visit. Either that or the money is confiscated after the visit, during an inmate's body search. Once the inmate's allotted time to pay back expires, according to criminal rules, that inmate must be punished. So to avoid punishment, the inmate starts cooperating with prison authorities.

In the past, informants were dealt with in several ways within black prisons. First, no inmates were allowed to meet with prison guards without a *blatnoj* present.[2] Also, if there was a search in the cell and inmates had to leave, the first and last people in the formation were from the *blatnoj* caste. This ensured no messages from inmates were passed to prisons guards. Then, if someone was accused of being an informant, he was seriously beaten, if not killed. One inmate currently in prison for killing another inmate told of how he would always get caught by prison guards while making alcohol in prison until he found out why:

> A friend comes to me and takes me to a hallway in the basement. There, through a thin wall, I could hear another friend of mine—we were so close that we sleep next to each other—talking to prison guards about me. I got back to my bed, and he also came back. He always asked me to teach him martial arts, so I told him to follow me outside so I could show him a move. I hit him so hard that I instantly killed him. Then I went to the prison guard my friend reported me to and asked him to collect the body of his colleague. It should be clear to everyone what will happen to such people.

Now that cell phones are so widespread, it is much harder to monitor informants,[3] so they are usually allowed to exist. But the *blatnyje* usually know who they are, and inmates do not talk about anything important in their presence.

To Red

The relatively peaceful coexistence of inmates and prison authorities is based on unwritten rules, agreements, and compromises. But all that can be destroyed with a change in prison director.

That could happen if one director retires and a new, zealous one arrives. But a change of leadership could also happen because a prison director is arrested for corruption. And if it becomes publicly known that a prison is black and criminal leaders are running it, authorities have no other choice but to replace the prison director.

One interviewed inmate told the story of a totally criminal-controlled prison in Tver region in 1998; it had a factory that manufactured pistols. When someone in Moscow was assassinated, the police traced the pistol back to that manufacturer and found the pistol was illegally made and smuggled out for criminal purposes. Not only were prison authorities immediately fired (and probably arrested), but new leadership took control of the prison.

Prison authorities might try to gain control of the prison by replacing internal criminal leadership with an inmate they have more control of a *suka*. Sometimes prison authorities make a deal with a new high-level *blatnoj* who is moved into a prison to push the old one out from this position. Basically, when he comes in, he solves problems for the inmate population that a previous *polojenets* could not. One example might be making an illegal channel to bring prohibited items inside the prison. Of course, the new leader does this with the help of the administration, but inmates do not understand this and support the new *blatnoj*.

Currently, according to interviewed inmates, this is often done in Georgia where all members of criminal leadership cooperate with prison authorities openly and *smotryashchiye* are divided not by prison barracks, like in other post-Soviet prisons, but by regions that match official law enforcement precincts. For example, in that prison, there is a *smotryasçiy* for inmates from the Ajaria region of Georgia, even if they are housed in different barracks.

Although slowly replacing criminal leadership is the quietest way to solve the problem, it is complicated and time-consuming. So prison authorities often apply quicker and more violent techniques. The majority of black-red changes of regime in prison follow the same scenario.

Step One: Neutralize Leaders

First, prison administration has to neutralize the existing criminal leadership. In the past, they used extermination, done through such methods as contaminating the leaders with tuberculosis. They would have special, humid cells where they put inmates with an open form of tuberculosis. Then they put the leader they wanted to target in a maximum-security ward where his immune system would become weakened due to the bad conditions there before moving him into the tuberculosis cell. In the 1950s, some prisons had a special unit for people sick with syphilis. So if someone did not want to cooperate with prison authorities, he was left in this unit to be raped, thus also contracting syphilis.

Threats such as fake executions were also popular. Criminal leaders were put in formation and blindfolded while several guards stood behind them with rifles. But instead of shooting the inmates, guards would shoot over their heads.

Another way to threaten a criminal leader was medically. A prison doctor did some medical tests on a *vor* and lied to him, telling the *vor* he had a serious illness. The diagnosis was something like cancer that must be treated immediately if the *vor* was to live. Then the administration offers to start treatments, but only if the *vor* repeals his criminal allegiance.

Then, prison authorities discredit the criminal leadership among the inmates. This could be done with any small action, like a guard making a slight expression of appreciation to a criminal leader in front of the other inmates. By doing so, the administration planted a seed of suspicion that a criminal leader was somehow working with administration. This method was most often used during the *Suki* wars (1950s and 1960s). In the worst-case scenario, prison guards threaten to spread rumors about a *vor* that he had become a *suka*. This *vor* would then be moved to another prison where not only would his crown be taken away, but also he might also be moved to the lowest caste or killed. Finally, prison administration instigated infighting. The strategy of increasing conflict among criminal leadership was getting them to kill each other in a race for power.

Of course, that did not always work. For example, in 1950, when there was widespread starvation in the Soviet Gulag, and the war among criminal leadership was the most active, at some point one *vor* (1) stole a food ration from another *vor*, (2) but prison guards planted all the evidence with a third *vor*. As a result, *Vor* 1 accused *Vor* 3 of being a rat and killed him according to the criminal rules. The next day, a prison guard told *Vor* 1 that he had killed the wrong person, and that, in fact, *Vor* 2 was the guilty one. During a criminal meeting, *Vor* 2 asked for permission to commit suicide instead of being killed, but instead, it was decided he should not kill himself, but instead lose his title, so the infighting did not further benefit the prison authorities. In general, however, administrative provocation is very successful, especially when several *vory* were in the same prison and were all vying for supreme control.

Since the fall of the communist regime, those especially ambitious methods are not in use anymore, and the most popular tactic is simple isolation. Prison authorities might transfer those trouble-causing leaders to other prisons to be broken. And for this particular purpose, in the 1950s, special prisons were built, such as the notorious White Swan in Solikamsk. More often, prison authorities simply locked the criminal leadership—*vory*, *polojenets*, *smotryashchiye*, and other *blatnyje*, in the inner prison.

And officially finding a reason for confinement is very easy for authorities to do because in all prisons and all cells, there is an official cleaning schedule for the toilets each week. Of course this schedule is not followed, and the job is done only by *petukhi*, but since the schedule officially exists, anyone would does not do it is violating prison rules and should be sent to the inner prison.

Locking them up, however, is often not enough to disarm criminal leaders. One interviewed *blatnoj* told of his experience in Chita prison in 2010.

> They locked all the criminal leadership in the inner prison, so they were setting the atmosphere from there. Communication was bad, so the decent inmates were only communicating through *balundery* [distributing food between solitary-confinement cells]. Soon these inmates started cutting themselves, but we did not want our actions to affect the general prison population. We did not want prison guards to punish them for what we were doing. But they supported us. Their parents came to prison to protest, and they brought human rights NGOs with them. Yes, and also friends with weapons. The prison authorities did not like it, so they started breaking inmates in solitary confinement. Well . . . then inmates set fire on the prison.

To avoid that kind of response, prison administration could try either a carrot or stick.

Carrot

In some prisons, the situation for criminal leadership locked in the inner prison is much better than it is for the other inmates. According to interviewed inmates, "There could be some kind of an agreement that guys there will live well, like in the black prison (with outside food packages, cell phones, and drugs), but they cannot intervene with what happens in the rest of the prison."

Stick

Prison administration could try to break criminal leaders by force. For example, walls of the inner prison may have been washed in chlorine, making it nearly impossible for inmates to breathe. From time to time, prison guards also might pepper spray a cell or constantly play the same song over the loudspeakers.[4] In the shower, only ice-cold or boiling-hot water is available, making it impossible to shower. Or the cell itself could be flooded with cold water, making it not only cold and humid, but also impossible to stand up in.

In some cases, leadership inmates could even be raped. Prison guards do not often do the rape themselves, but instead have a dedicated inmate from *petukhi* caste who does it for them when needed.

Step Two: Intimidate General Population

While leadership is confined, the prison authorities need to show their power over the general population inmates to deter them from any action. Often, this starts with police SWAT teams doing searches (in the past, prisons have used army personnel). These searches are usually highly theatrical and often involve shooting, screaming, beating, and confiscation of inmates' personal property. According to inmates, "It all looks very scary, and a large group of unorganized inmates without a leader soon surrenders."

Then prison guards chip away at communication both inside prisons ("roads" are cut) and with the outside world. According to an interviewed inmate, "Prison authorities installed anti-cell phone equipment that blocks cell phone, and although we had cell phones, there was only one place where they barely worked. To send a text message you had to type, then throw [the phone] up in the air. That's the same way you received the reply." Free movement inside prisons is also stopped, usually by metal fences between prison camp buildings.

Also everyone who violates even the tiniest regulation (such as smoking in a non-smoking area) is placed in the inner prison. And to make this job easier, all inmates are required to wear badges with their name, unit, and photo. Before the crackdown, an inmate caught doing something illegal could just say any random name and not be punished, but the badges make his identity clear.

Since by that time, prison authorities have decapitated the criminal administration, they use the window of opportunity to replace leadership with someone under their control. So prison authorities prepare *sherst'* to take control of the prison.

The process is simple. Prison guards meet with *sherst'* inmates and tell them that, if they want to make parole, they need to provide prison authorities with the names of two or three inmates a day who are violating prison rules. Usually *sherst'* inmates are afraid to do so, but prison administration assures them they will be protected. And since many of members of *sherst'* already do not like upper-caste inmates, they are happy to get revenge (when protected by prison authorities). But if *sherst'* inmates still refuse to go against criminal leadership and members of upper caste (because they had good relations in the past), prison authorities would transfer *sherst'* caste members from another prison to do the job.

Step Three: The Final Freeze

When general population inmates are left without strong leadership and *sherst'* agree to work in a more violent capacity (as *activisty*), inmates can do little to stand up against prison authorities. So authorities start the final move in *freezing* the prison—changing the ideology. And it is done by visibly changing all A.U.E ideology attributes in prison and replacing them with official prison symbols.

They install their own show-of-force rules. Inmates are made to wear official prison uniforms, make their beds military-style,[5] and participate in mandatory morning sport exercise at 6:00 am. In addition, they dismantle the crux of the criminal ideology—the caste system.

They start by prohibiting inmates from even using the names of the criminal castes. For example, *petukhi* are not allowed to be called that way anymore since it is a considered criminal way of calling them and are supposed to be called *neformal* (which could be roughly translated as a derogative term for someone different from others). They then work on making all inmates of the same caste, of the lowest one. To do so, prison authorities make everyone use the same tableware, meaning tableware that is also used by those in a lower caste.

Inmates consider being made to do actions like these the worst thing prison guards can do, and with good reason. According to *ponyatiya*, eating from the same tableware with *petukh* immediately degrades one into that caste, so is often much more dangerous than any torture or beating inmates might receive. A beating hurts you for a short period of time, but violating *ponyatiya* will hurt every day of an inmate's sentence and any subsequent ones. And according to the norms among old criminal leaders, it is better to commit suicide than to live in *petukhi* caste.

According to an interviewed inmate—a middle-level member of the criminal family, "It is the last step in making a prison red—having the same tableware. If they do it before, there will be a riot. So they do it only when they are sure there will be little resistance, and they will be able to control it."

When such a measure was taken in a prison in Ryazan (Russia), it was not met with cooperation from the prison population. Several prison guards were even beaten. Then, with help from outside *vory*, plans were even made for a prison riot. In particular, the following *vory progon* was supposed to encourage inmates to riot:

> In the prison, we have a disorder made by prison guards and *goats*. So first with this statement, I want to encourage you inmates to unity, because only in unity and cohesion can we stand up against the prison administration. And in prison when there is the same tableware for both *muzhiki* and *petukhi*, I want you to understand one thing—reds are trying to make us all equal to *petukhi*.[6]

A *freeze* is a very hard time for inmates trying to hold on to *ponyatiya*, and not everyone survives. According to an interviewed inmate, "Those are very serious prisons, and other inmates warn us about them. Usually you take your own plastic tableware with you, but guards confiscate it. As a result, you have to refuse not only food in the canteen but also drink. Basically you take only bread and drink tap water.[7] And if you are lucky, you are able to boil this water in your cell with a self-made heater made from razors attached to the electric outlet by wires. So you survive on water, bread, and sugar."

According to another interviewed inmate, one who is aspiring to become a *vor*, "When I learned that I would serve my sentence in Karelia, I already knew that it was going to be bad. The system usually sends inmates there to be broken. And there were leadership changes, which meant new rules. Brothers told me that guards insist on the army way of making a bed, which is, of course, not acceptable to us decent people [upper-caste inmates]. The first day there I refused to do so and was immediately sent to solitary confinement where I was tortured with *restyazka* [held for a long time in a stretched position] and freezing [put in an extremely cold cell]. I also had to do a hunger strike because they used the same tableware for all inmates. I did not eat for two weeks before my cellmates found a way to smuggle food to me."

So if there is no outside food coming that inmates could eat without touching official prison-provided tableware, prison guards might try to refuse them prison food (e.g., in solitary confinement) and not accept packages from outside. In one prison, during a freezing prison guards told inmates that they have to be on formation every day at 6:00 am. When inmates refused, prison authorities stopped all goods from entering the prison. If someone's relatives arrived at the prison with a package, the authorities would turn them away, saying, "Today we are not accepting food packages. Come back tomorrow." That lasted for months. The situation was terrible, and the inmates were basically eating grass in the yard.

In one known case, prisons authorities went even further in fighting the prison criminal ideology. According to an interviewed inmate, in a prison in Irkutsk, a facility infamous for prison authorities' abuse of inmates, they brought a firetruck to a prison formation one morning, made *petukh* pee in the reservoir, then sprayed this water all over the general inmate population, thus rendering them all degraded simultaneously.

Such a basically ridiculous situation became possible because *vory* ideology became so strict that it became the group's weakness. And in private conversations, prison guards often joked that *vory* criminal ideology made it that the most effective weapon against the most powerful *vor* is not weapons or a prison sentence, but a children's water gun filled with urine.

Also, while prison authorities are trying to make all their existing inmates caste-equal, they also need to make sure incoming inmates are degraded the minute they enter. Otherwise criminal prison leadership would be replaced and prison guards might again lose control of the prison.

First, they might put new inmates in conditions that, according to *ponyatiya*, would qualify them for the *sherst'* caste (those who cooperate with prison guards). In the infamous Omsk prisons, all new inmates, while being beaten in quarantine, have to sign a document saying that they will not follow criminal ideology.

Or, in some prisons, all newcomers have to put on red armbands (which those working for prison administration wear), and then prison guards take a picture. Once the photo is taken, prison guards can easily blackmail inmates. In some places, new inmates are given a winter coat with a red armband already sewn to it. So inmate wears it or gets cold. And since A.U.E ideology prohibits putting on this armband, the coats or photos automatically downgrade these inmates to the wool caste. When in the interview I asked why an armband has to be red and not any other color, a prison guard explained, "In the Soviet Union, those bands were red, and by *ponyatiya* it became prohibited to put them on. Of course, we do not care about those armbands or what color they are, but by making them red, we are making a bigger statement. It kind of makes it even more unacceptable by *ponyatiya*."

Other popular options for degrading is making an inmate touch a toilet seat, pick up a doormat, or even water a plant. For example, in an Omsk prison, prison guards say, "C'mon, pick it up and clean after yourself. It is a normal thing to do. Just do it, and we will not touch you." But, according to an interviewed mid-level criminal leader—a former inmate in the same prison, "When they told me that, I said, 'I am ready to die here, but I will not touch it.' Of course I was badly beaten [and lost several teeth], but it is not about cleaning or touching anything; it is about giving up what you believe is right."

Such actions and the fact that criminal ideology became a group weakness is a big problem for prison criminal leadership and the criminal world in general, one they are still not sure how to approach. Should the criminal world still enforce the ideological parts of *ponyatiya* when they are used against inmates, or should rules be relaxed to protect its own members? And while in general *ponytiya* is still enforced, in some circumstances, individual criminal leaders are already reconsidering them. In some instances, there were *vory progons* that said the situation in some prisons (such as ones in Omsk and Saratov, in Russia) were so bad that nothing should be held against inmates coming from there, and they should all be considered members of the upper caste. It also said that inmates who are unfortunate enough to end up in those prisons should do everything possible to stay alive, even if it violates *ponyatiya*. However, not all prison criminal leaders are eager to honor these generalized *progons*. And according to one inmate, some cases can be complicated. One inmate was transferred to a black prison from a notoriously red prison in Omsk, where he had a problem. He got into a conflict with *activisty*, and, in addition to beating and torturing him, they threw urine on him to degrade him. Then he also got urine from the prison *petukh*, and at formation, he threw it on the main *activist* inmate. It was a total suicide operation, but he neutralized him [*activist*] and helped inmates a lot by doing so. Prison guards tried to claim that it was not urine but tea, but it did not help and *activist* became *petukh*. His case is very complicated, so he needs *vory* to solve it. But it is hard because, in some prisons, he is without a cell phone, and most of the time, the prison criminal leadership in Omsk could not be reached either. So until there is a *vory* decision about the caste he should be in, he does not touch anyone and lives in the corner of the *muzhiki* barrack (but not with *petukhi*). And according to a middle-level criminal leader in his new, black prison "to be honest, I am not sure if there is a chance he could avoid becoming *petukh* if this question reaches *vory*, so it is better that he will serve the rest of his prison sentence that way."

And in some prisons, criminal leadership was known to break *ponyatiya* to ensure the survival of fellow inmates. One interviewed member of the criminal leadership told of how, in his prison camp, a normal person would be sent to the inner prison for thirty days, but when he came back, he would be absolutely insane. "He could not talk about what had happened. It even took some time before he could talk at all." In order to figure out what they were dealing with, the criminal leadership chose one inmate among themselves to become *sherst'* so they could get a job in the inner prison. The new *sherst'* could then get information would help leadership decide on a plan of action.

To survive in Omsk prison, prison criminal leadership had to make an even harder decision. When it became clear that the prison was turning red, criminal leadership volunteered to become not just *sherst'*, but *activisty* to protect the rest of the inmates.[8]

Despite ideological tactics, prison authorities are not always successful in their attempts to turn a prison from black to red. The best example of how risky and dangerous a freeze attempt can be is from a prison in Kyrgyzstan, where, at that time, the only Kyrgyzstan *vor* (of Chechen origin) was imprisoned.

In 2004, Aziz Batukaev, known in the criminal world simply as Aziz, was incarcerated in prison camp #31 in Moldavanka. Although the prison was guarded by prison authorities on the outside, inside they had no authority. They were basically afraid to say anything against Aziz. He had full control of the prison and decided all internal matters. He had several bodyguards armed with automatic rifles and hand grenades, and people openly visited him (including those detained in other prisons in the country). In one known case, *polojenets* from other prisons visited him for a meeting, and at least one of them flew on the aircraft to get there, meaning he passed major airport security without any problems.

His accommodations were unprecedentedly homey, even by black prison standards. He lived in a two-story, private building that had around sixteen rooms and also housed his wife and daughter-in-law. And because Aziz had a gastric ulcer, he also had three female horses and fifteen goats he used for milk. He also had a personal garden inside the prison where he got his vegetables and a continual supply of marijuana. Other amenities included fighting dogs (for entertainment), an enormous knife collection, and a stash of weapons. Aziz also did nothing to hide his lifestyle, and there are many photos of him online, enjoying his life.

In 2005, after the revolution, Kyrgyzstan's government decided to show they were fighting corruption, especially in the penal system. They could not ignore the case of Aziz, so on 20 October 2005, the Kyrgyzstan government issued an inspection of his prison. Parliament member Tinichbek Akmatbayev was in charge of it. He was also the brother of Aziz's long-time enemy, Ruspek Akmatbayev, another member of the criminal world. During the inspection of the prison, Mr. Akmatbayev was shot five times in the head and killed, along with his advisor, an invited expert and director from the correction authorities. Two other men, the director of the prosecutor's office for the Alamudinsky region and Mr. Akmatbayev's bodyguard, were wounded and hospitalized.

After this event, the president of Kyrgyzstan personally gave an order to transfer Aziz and several dozen of his closest associates to another prison. But when law enforcement came to his prison to execute the order, they met resistance. For several days, members of law enforcement were not able to enter the prison because inmates, led by Aziz, had barricaded themselves in by parking a firefighter's truck against the prison gates. They also took several inmates' family members, who had come to visit their relatives, hostage.

When negotiation efforts were met with automatic rifle fire, and several members of law enforcement were wounded, police decided to storm the prison. An armored personal carrier smashed through the prison gates, and a Special Operations Force followed on foot, and in a short exchange of fire, several inmates were killed.

Before the assault, Aziz gave an order by phone for other prisons to also start rioting. The first to respond were prisons in the north: #3 in Novo-Pokrovskoye, and #8 in Petrovka. Both were armed resistances that led to several killed and wounded. Prisons in the south of the country also followed the order, although with less enthusiasm. For example, in one prison in Jalalabad, several inmates cut their stomachs open, but later recovered.

Eventually Aziz was moved to another, redder, prison. Following the events, the courts charged several inmates with murder, and they were given life sentences. And although Aziz was charged with organization of the riot (in addition to drugs and weapons possession) and he was given sixteen extra years behind bars, he was released in 2013 based on a bogus cancer diagnosis.

Gray Prisons

The long-term existence of either an absolutely red or absolutely black prison is relatively rare and highly unsustainable. A red regime rarely lasts long without a strong effort from the outside because neither inmates nor prison authorities are interested in keeping them that way. Long-standing red prisons lead to major problems, such as accusations of torture and abuse. But the same things happen when a prison is absolutely black because criminal leadership can also become dictatorial if in power for too long. Also, if either criminal leadership (black) or *activisty* (red) is too powerful, they start getting prison authorities involved in their internal power struggles, and prison authorities want to avoid those situations at any cost.

In general, most inmates just want to serve their sentences quietly without any problems. They would much rather eat, sleep, watch TV, and have occasional access to drugs and alcohol, than to start conflicts with prison authorities.

The same is true of most prison guards. Usually they are people from villages around the prison who simply want to minimize their work, increase monetary profits, and feel safe going home at the end of their shift. For them, working in red prison is especially difficult because their main goal is to reduce the workload (and dangers) and increase the payoff. They are not particularly interested in meticulously enforcing all of the rules and are content to allow inmates to organize themselves. For example, one prison in Yegoryevsk was red until 2009, but prison guards still had problems with several inmates. When one *blatnoj* inmate moved in, and prison authorities saw he was able to control those inmates, the authorities were happy to give him the power to do so.

And then there is the additional equalizer of corruption. For a price, guards are often more than willing to smuggle prohibited items—from food and cigarettes to cell phones, drugs, and even weapons—inside the prison. They will also take bribes to organize unauthorized visitations (not only of family members and prostitutes, but, in many cases, from other criminal family inmates) and relocate an inmate from the general population to the comfortable conditions of the prison hospital. There, instead of staying in an overcrowded cell, a high-level inmate can enjoy his own clean bed, better food, and exemption from the prison schedule. An exceptionally rich inmate, often from the criminal leadership, can have his own renovated room, have restaurant food delivered every day, and even go outside the prison in town (alone) or to different towns (with a company of prison guards) and even travel abroad.

As a result, the majority of former Soviet Union prisons, especially the most stable ones, have found a balance between black and red, and are of different shades of *gray*.

In such prisons, there are a different set of unwritten rules, agreements, and compromises. And all the negotiations and decisions are made on the level of the *polojenets* and prison director behind closed doors, and no information gets out. Prison administrators are interested in promotions and yearly bonuses, and they do not want to be fired (and potentially arrested), not to mention seeing their name in newspapers.

So while prison authorities close their eyes to the comfort inmates build for themselves in prison, inmates keep their part of the contract by not writing complaints to the higher correction authorities and making sure all luxuries are hidden during inspections. There is even a general prohibition by *vory* on posting pictures and publicly discussing life in prisons on social media.

So how do the two sides negotiate and reach the middle ground? Usually, it begins with prison authorities, who have their list of demands. According to interviewed member of *blatnyje*, "In different prisons, there are different things crucial to prison authorities. In some prisons, they do not want to see any drugs; in some, no illegal activities, in some, no gambling or even in one prison, guards were obsessed with having no roads on the windows."

For criminal leadership, the main issue is always *ponyatiya*. In particular, all prison authorities must respect the criminal caste system and other ideologically inspired rules. Once that is established, then there may be demands for free movement inside the prison, civilian and colored clothes, cell phones, packages from outside, visitations, and so on.

When any of these agreements are broken from either side, it is followed by renegotiations. An agreement might be broken from the side of prison authorities. In one prison, there was an agreement that HIV-positive inmates got unlimited packages from outside (there is no appropriate food and medicine in the prison). But while the prison director was on vacation, the guards stopped respecting this agreement.

But most often, agreement breeches are related to visitations and happen on the prison administration side. One inmate's wife might be inappropriately searched, or an inmate's mother would come from far away but be unable to see her son because prison guards had locked him in the inner prison, and so on.

But it is not always prison guards who are guilty. And when inmates do not follow their part of the agreement, it is usually related to drugs. Several years ago in a prison in Klin, prison authorities and criminal leadership had an agreement that inmates could have, among other things, certain drugs. Authorities closed their eyes to hashish but refused to tolerate heroin. However, one inmate smuggled heroin inside the prison and took it on a day he was going to court. The inmate was so high, he could not function. Prison authorities were extremely angry because it created problems with their superiors. Another similar problem in many prisons that agree to allow drugs is inmates overdosing.

Any breach of agreement on the part of an individual inmate brings an undesirable spotlight on the prison that, in turn, causes prison guards to retaliate against the whole prison population. Not only that, violating inmates are also punished by criminal leadership for, according to *ponyatiya*, endangering the other inmates.

When an agreement is violated by prison authorities, inmates also have tools to punish them with. They might protest peacefully, harm themselves, or write a complaint to the highest prison authority. In one prison, when inmates were protesting against something prison authorities did, 400 people went to the canteen at the same time. It was a major problem for the prison administration because usually not more than forty people go there, and that is how much they usually cook. (The majority of inmates cook food themselves from the packages they receive from outside.) So technically, it means that the prison director was not able to feed inmates, which by rules is a major problem and would lead at least to an inspection.

Because prison administration does not want those problems, they go back to negotiations with prison criminal leadership that represents the inmates. And then, according to interviewed inmates, "Criminal leadership will basically give prison administration a list of their demands, and they [administration] would say what from that list could and could not happen."

As a result, the majority of prisons are a very careful balance between black and red powers. That is why they are often called gray because it is a neutral color between the radicals of red and black.

Conclusion

Prison authorities have an option and the tools needed to tighten the screws on the prison regime. For that, they first need to neutralize criminal leadership and those who are respected by prison administration. Then they can lead the mass of inmates. If in the past, eliminating criminal leaders would have been done by killing them, now they are more likely to be isolated or moved to another prison. Second, communication and freedom of movement inside the prison would be limited so inmates could not organize against the prison administration. The general population of the prison would then be threatened by public beatings and torture. They would also be forced to follow rules that are not necessarily important but signal the ability of the regime to enforce them, such as a particular way of making the bed.

Finally, to cement their power, prison authorities will dismantle criminal ideology. They do this by going after its cornerstone—the caste system. They might make everyone eat from the same tableware, which, on one side, signals their unlimited power, and on the other, make everyone equal to the lowest prison caste—*petukhi*. As a result, inmates will no longer be interested in supporting a prison criminal leadership that will regulate them to the lowest possible caste.

Although gaining control of the prison is possible for the prison administration, it is not sustainable. It is very time consuming with no clear benefits, so not many prison directors are interested in doing so. As a result, the majority of former Soviet prisons are considered gray, where governance is done in negotiations between prison administration and prison criminal leadership.

10

Problems within the *Vory* Criminal Organization

It would be a mistake to assume that criminal leadership faithfully follows all of the rules described in previous chapters, and that their leaders are only selfless people out for the good of all inmates. And though selfless and effective leadership was once the norm among the organization, that is not the reality of the organization today.

Although the *vory* movement has been a strong force in the Soviet Union for nearly a century, it has been undergoing major changes since the Union's fall in the 1990s. In particular, they lost their main enemy—the Soviet government—and have no one to fear anymore, which led to the group getting caught in internal problems. And it was not on the prison level, but on the level of the whole criminal family, putting the survival of the entire organization under question.

In particular, many strict out-group relations rules were dismissed and the quality of leadership significantly decreased. These changes have made the organization more internally problematic and, as a consequence, much weaker. And some members of the criminal organization, even those who used to actively support the A.U.E. ideology, are disappointed in what it has become.

Fall of the Soviet Union

The weakening of the Soviet Union in 1960s is associated with major changes in Russia, and in its economy in particular. The communist government began losing their monopoly on economic activities, and, although it was still against the law, many individuals engaged in producing and trading goods and offering services. These new businesses also meant new business opportunities for members of criminal organizations. To fight criminal involvement in those businesses, the government declared war on organized crime, making prisons very dangerous for the *vory*.

As a consequence, the criminal family had to quickly adapt to this new environment. This move was led by a *vor* named Anatoly Pavlovic Cherkasov, also known as Cherkes. Crowned in the infamous Vladimirsky Central Prison in the early 1960s, Cherkes proposed several changes to the existing criminal rules in a

Criminals, Nazis, and Islamists. Vera Mironova, Oxford University Press. © Oxford University Press 2023.
DOI: 10.1093/oso/9780197645659.003.0011

major criminal family meeting in Kiev (Ukraine) in the early 1970s. The changes were ratified soon after.

First, since there was a lot of illegal business going on in the Soviet Union, everything from illegal trade to prostitution, and *vor* Cherkes proposed to tax it. His logic was that, since those businesses were illegal anyway, those involved in them would not turn to the police for protection. That would give the criminal family unlimited taxing jurisdiction.

This wide-open tax racket led money-hungry *vory* to tax illegal businessman mercilessly, and for those businessmen, it became cheaper to hire bodyguards or even organize their own militias than to pay the *vory*. To keep the violent skirmishes from becoming a full-scale war that neither side wanted, an emergency meeting was held in Kislovodsk, and, at this meeting, it was agreed that the criminal tax could not exceed 10 percent.

Then, *vor* Cherkes proposed that, instead of spending most of their time behind bars, *vory* should be free and a specially appointed person—a *polojenets*—should be inside the prison running it. At that time, this was relatively easy to accomplish. There was no special criminal charge for organized crime, and since *vory* themselves did not do anything illegal, there was no crime they could be charged with.

And finally, a direct change to the *ponyatiya* was proposed. Beginning in the 1950s, prison authorities would force *vory* to sign an agreement not to follow *ponyatiya*. By original *ponyatiya*, their signature on that agreement meant that they not only lost their title of *vor*, but they also became *suki*. As a result, in the1960s, a split in the organization between *vory* who had signed and those who had not began. And because this split could have potentially led to a new, so-called *suki* war, that no one in the criminal world wanted, *vor* Cherkes proposed that signing such a paper should not be punishable by *ponyatiya*. His reasoning was that there is nothing shameful in not honoring a word given to police.

Although these changes seemed minor, in fact they turned the whole logic of the criminal family upside down and became a turning point for the organization's development. Originally, the main purpose of criminal leadership was to suffer for its members and taking a leadership position was associated more with dangers and responsibility than with benefits. But these modifications significantly decreased *vory* risks and hardship while simultaneously increasing profit.

And with *perestroika* in the 1990s, the gap between benefits and hardship became even more amplified. At that time, not only was there no law and order in the Soviet Union to fight organized crime, but *vory* also seized the opportunity for even more profit by becoming part of legal businesses and the privatization of state enterprises, and even getting involved in the government.

More Benefits

At this point, very significant sums of money and power became associated with organized crime and its leadership in particular. Membership in the criminal family became one of the fastest ways to get rich with little risk involved,[1] and *vory* started enjoying several benefits not even imaginable before:

Family

Originally, *vory* were not allowed to have a family because its members could be used by the government to apply pressure to the *vory*. But as things relaxed, *vory* started getting permanent girlfriends and having children. Children, however, were not registered in a *vor*'s name, but in the name of his relatives, such as brothers. Soon *vory* stopped hiding being married at all, and now Muslim *vory* even go so far as to openly acknowledge several wives, citing religious permission to do so.

Wealth

It was also believed that a *vor* should not own anything, not even a house, and their true home was always prison. One interviewed seventy-year-old inmate remembers the attitude of *vory* many years ago. "There was a *vor* in my town. When he was offered a car, he replied, 'Why would I need a car if there is public transportation?' "

But now the situation is much different, and *vory* live in luxury. According to another interviewed inmate, "We went to the house of one *vor*, and it was like a castle with guards on the perimeter. Inside there was antique furniture and paintings bought at auctions. And more than nineteen expensive sport cars were parked outside." Many *vory* now also own expensive real estate abroad, and often, they even live there permanently.

Position

When *vory* started increasing their ranks to take control over bigger territory, the profile of potential candidates became less stringent. For example, according to *ponyatiya*, a candidate cannot have served in the military. But now they have hired veterans of the Afghanistan and Abkhazia Wars to perform jobs like racketeering.

Government Affiliation

Because the biggest money is often affiliated with the government, many *vory* became increasingly cooperative despite their own rules. Several interviewed high-level members of the criminal family openly discussed solving even day-to-day problems with the cooperation of top FSB leadership. At the same time, town *smotryashchiye* mediate conflicts between different branches of law enforcement. In some regions, the *vory* have had their own candidates in elections, and some *vory* even took official positions in the government. *Vor* Dzhaba Ioseliani was even a member of the Georgian Provisional Council in 1992.

Less Risk

While the benefits associated with being in a leadership position in the criminal family increased, costs and risks associated with the position decreased, especially within the prison system.

Less Time Incarcerated

In the past, a person promoted to *vor* was someone who had not only spent a significant amount of time in prison but did so on particularly serious charges, like grand larceny. But by the 1990s, *vory* candidates who needed to spend time in prison were doing so for minor crimes, such as illegal weapons possession, and getting a maximum of three years.

Also, some *vory* candidates were even imprisoned on rape charges. In the past, it was considered unacceptable for a rapist to even be in the upper caste. Now someone on such charges can actually be promoted to *vor* if he claims he did not rape anyone, and that it was a police set-up. There are even *vory* who have never been to prison but were still crowned.

Self- versus Inmate-Interest

In the past, the main role of criminal leadership in prison was to protect inmate interests even at the expense of their own interests. But this is often not the case anymore. In the past, to be promoted to the prison criminal leadership, an inmate had to refuse to follow prison guard orders and, as a result, be punished by prison administration. Now if a *vor* is imprisoned, by bribing the administration, he lives a very comfortable life incarcerated while nothing significantly changes for other inmates.

Such a rapid change in the cost-benefit calculation of a potential *vor* eventually corrupted the *vory* criminal organization, and decreasing requirements for the *vory* led to the downward spiral of the whole organization.

As a consequence of the commercialization of the criminal world, it is now possible for a person to basically buy his *vor* title, which is a disappointment to many *vory* who still adhere to strict *ponyatiya*. As one inmate sarcastically noted, “We now have more *vory* than people in prison.” Not only that, being a *vor* is now often a family business with several generations of people crowned in succession, making many *vory* families powerful criminal dynasties.

Also, to make things even worse, in the 1990s, the low-quality leader selection and the increasing desire for entertainment led many leaders of the criminal world to start using drugs. According to an interviewed high-level criminal member, "When everyone around me was poor and just trying to survive, I could afford anything I wanted. I was one of the first people in my republic [part of Russia] to own a Mercedes. So of course, I and everyone around me always wanted more and more. So we turned to drugs."

In fact, the drug usage among *vory* was epidemic and even concerned those who were caught up in it. The same high-level member of the criminal organization explained:

> At one point, Ded Hasan [The most powerful *vor* at that time] himself came to visit our republic. In the morning, all the young *vory* who came with him were hanging out near his hotel room waiting for Ded Hasan's doctor to distribute heroin. Ded Hasan himself did not use. But he was giving them drugs, and they went to my friend's house to cook and use it. It was summer, so they all took off their t-shirts, and all those men, covered in tattoos, were standing around the cooking place, carefully looking to make sure the drugs were distributed equally. Then they started fighting about who would get the first injection and arguing if they got into a vein or not. At that time, even though I myself was also using heroin, I was disgusted and terrified by what I saw. It became very clear to me that it was the lowest point of the organization.

Infighting

Historically, the main purpose of the *vory* criminal organization had been to form a unified front against the enemy and support each other in times of hardship. And it was indeed true when the group had to stand up against the powerful Soviet Union. But as the organization changed, several factors ate away at this original intent and caused major conflicts among *vory*.

Conflicts between Generations

Even in the beginning, not all *vory* accepted *vor* Cherkes changes to the organization, and that resulted in conflicts between the newer generation, who were looking for self-benefits, and the older generation of *vory*, who were against the commercialization of the organization and the corruption of the *ponyatiya*.

In 1990s, the most stalwart example of the old A.U.E. ideology was *Vor* Georgy Chickovani. Although considered the most respectful *vor* of his generation, at the end of his life, he lived alone in a very modest house in his home country of Georgia, a strange concept for the new generation of *vory* who live in luxury. According to him, the newer *vory* were not true *vory*, and "they should be hungry and not be running businesses."

Those feelings were also shared by middle- and low-level members of the criminal organization who had joined before the fall of the USSR. One interviewed middle-level organization member explained how, before the 1980s, people running the organization were trying to help each other survive. They were "generous, brave, daring, and relatively unselfish." By the time the USSR started falling apart, leadership was already using those below them for their own power and enrichment. "When the streets started being big business," he said, "*vory* also became business. And now everyone joins to get money and power. I hate it!"

These disagreements between adherers to both the old and new ideologies were rarely peaceful. Once, in Kislovodsk, there was a high-level member of the *vory* named Altin Shidakov. He spent the majority of his life behind bars in many different prisons all over the country and was known for following the strict old traditions of *ponyatiya*. When he got out of prison and returned to his hometown, a competition had turned into a dangerous conflict—between an Armenian gang (who had working relations with government police and courts) and a Karachaevci (small ethnicity in Caucasus) gang—over the control of the city.

At some point, top members of the Karachaevci left the city, and members of the Armenian gang complained to Altin Shidakov that members of the Karachaevci gang were not following criminal *ponyatiya*. In particular, they did not respect the *vory* organizational structure and often used unnecessary violence. When the Karachaevci returned and went to Shidakov to introduce themselves, he confronted them. Shidakov said, "Who are you? What are you doing here, and how do you dare to break criminal rules?" A member of the Karachaevci gang said, "Why are you talking to us like we are dogs?" and hit Shidakov in the ear (a sign of total disrespect, by *ponyatiya*). In response, Shidakov took out a knife and stabbed him in the hand. The people who were there jumped in and managed to stop the fight. To figure out what to do next, members of the Karachaevci gang turned to another *vor*. That *vor* said Altin Shidakov was actually not a *vor* himself and was not allowed to introduce himself as such and behave that way. He was assassinated soon after.

Conflicts between *Vory*

As the amount of resources accumulated and controlled by the *vory* criminal organization increased, many self-interested *vory* started fighting among themselves to increase their share of those resources. And during the 1990s, those disagreements were open physical conflicts with very real casualties.

According to a member of the criminal organization active during that time, "What was going on was a war, and the goal was to kill your competitors [other *vory*] before they killed you. Ded Hasan just wanted money and did not care much about *ponyatiya*. He killed absolutely everyone who did not totally support him. It's not surprising that he was also killed later."

This approach to gaining power was not only harmful for the organization, it also significantly decreased the quality of criminal organization leadership simply because the most qualified were being killed. This decrease in recruit quality can be illustrated by the following story told by another high-level member of the criminal family.

> In our republic [part of Russia] . . . there was a group of guys from a sport club who were doing some racketeering and had become quite good at it. Ded Hasan approached their leader to become a *smotryasçiy* and invited him to his office in the center of Moscow.
>
> This guy had no idea about the *vory* criminal organization. He also knew he would have to learn about *ponyatiya* and have someone with prison experience, so he asked me to come with him. In Ded Hasan's office, we met with his right-hand man nicknamed Vitamin. In the discussion, the future *smotryasçiy* was so unqualified (had no idea of *ponyatiya*) that I was ashamed I had even come with him.[2] I am sure they [Ded Hasan's people] also understood how bad he was, but despite that, he was appointed and even got an armored Humvee as a present.

These major issues going on at the top of the criminal hierarchy also resonated down through the chain of command. According to an interviewed middle-level member, "When *vory* had conflicts with each other and talked about each other very badly, people under their command were also getting involved. But if *vory* reconciled between themselves, those under them were stuck in this conflict, destroying organization cohesion."

In prison, the situation was not any better. There were many cases when a *vor* was moved to a particular prison, and while his friends send a *progon* that this *vor* was indeed a *vor* and should be treated as such, his enemies (also among *vory*) would send a *progon* telling the *polojenets* not to consider him a *vor*.

It is an extremely dangerous situation for a *polojenets* to decide whether to consider someone a *vor*. Some *polojenets* put into similar circumstances resigned from their positions so as not to have to make this call. Others sided with whichever *vor* was the most powerful. Still others turned off all cell phones in the prison camp so as not to be reachable. Others intentionally violated prison rules so they would be locked up in the inner prison and could avoid making this decision.

Ethnic Conflicts

To survive the dangerous struggles of the 1990s, *vory* started building coalitions. And although in theory, only the criminal hierarchy exists and all other distinctions are inconsequential, many *vory* turned to their co-ethnic *vory* for support and, as a consequence, segregated by ethnicity.[3]

Soon that resulted in open conflicts between different ethnic groups of *vory*. The most famous conflict was the war between Slavic *vory* and those from the Caucasus, and it resulted in a significant number of causalities.

Also, to increase their relative power, other groups of *vory* increased their numbers by giving *vory* titles to those who were loyal to them.[4] Not only did this increase the conflict between groups, but it decreased the quality of *vory* even further. So to stop this practice, Ded Hasan prohibited any new crowning of *vory* for a time.

This ethnic division among the *vory* also resonated through the whole criminal organization, even to the lowest members. Low-level members of the organization began looking at *vory* through the lens of ethnicity, and, as a consequence, middle- and lower-ranking members of the criminal organization started segregating themselves beneath *vory* of their own ethnicity. This was feasible for many reasons, one of which was because *vory* acted as judges for disputes. According to one ethnically Russian *blatnoj* inmate,

> You could not openly say you wanted your problem solved by a *vor* of a particular nationality, but you could make it happen. When some Slavs come to me, they say, "If it is possible, can this problem be solved by a Slavic *vor*?" I always reply, "Of course it is possible, and I will do my best." There is no problem with fairness, but there is an opinion that Georgian *vory* are bloodthirsty, Azeri ones are more pragmatic, and Chechens are unpredictable. But with Slavic *vory*, you kind of know what to expect. It is also well-known that it is really hard for a Slav to get a *vor* title, so Slavic *vory* are always more experienced.

Finally, there is at least one known recent case of ethnic discrimination among *vory*. In Kirgizstan, for a long time the most influential *vor* was Chechen Aziz Baturkayav. Everyone acknowledged his fairness in distributing positions in the criminal organization between the Kyrgyz and Uzbeks. But later, in 2013, when Baturkayav had to leave the country, and a Kyrgyz *vor* took his place, many

Uzbeks were removed from their positions and believe they were discriminated against.

Prison Regulation Changes

It is not only the *vory* criminal organization that has changed throughout the years, but government and its laws and regulations have as well. Since the fall of the Soviet Union, laws and treatment of prisoners have also been modified, impacting life inside the prison. In the time of Gulag, for example, it was clear to inmates that the only way to survive in prison was by supporting each other. The prison administration worked hard to divide them, and there was no one else to help.

But that is not the case anymore, and the absence of a dangerous enemy led to the criminal organization inside the prison falling even deeper into internal problems. Or as one interviewed high-level member of the criminal organization noted, "The better prison authorities behave towards inmates, the harder it is for us to maintain our power."

Better Treatment of Inmates

In the 1960s, the Russian government declared war on organized crime. As a result, conditions in prisons became terrible for people who claimed to follow A.U.E. ideology. Notoriously brutal prisons, such as White Swan in Solikamsk, were opened to house criminal leadership, and for those lower in the criminal chain of command, prison authorities put a special mark (a stripe) on the prison criminal leader's case file, and they were tortured and segregated in every prison they were sent to. According to one interviewed inmate who was in prison at that time, "I was known as someone who had started a riot, and I had also killed another inmate [a snitch]. I have not seen what was written on my file, but no prison wanted to take me in. So I was moved from prison to prison and basically spent a year in the prison train." At that point, everyone thought this mistreatment would be the end of the *vory* criminal organization. But the opposite was true, and the criminal organization grew stronger.

One of the biggest problems the criminal organization had to solve was ensuring that only the best people were promoted to leadership positions. And promotion in the criminal family was closely related to an individuals' behavior in prison. According to one high-level member of the criminal organization, "If you want to know something about a person, you ask about his behavior in prison. If you, for example, do business with him outside [prison] or meet for coffee, you cannot learn much about him. But being in the same cell for twenty-four hours every day and going through its dangers and pressures, you will know everything about him."

So to be promoted years ago, inmates not only had to survive the hardships of prison, they also had to be so-called *objectors*, meaning they had to refuse to follow any directive from prison guards or other authorities. This led to more torture, extended sentences, and even death. And if members of the criminal organization cooperated with prison authorities in even the smallest way, like cleaning a floor, they were immediately kicked out of the organization, if not killed. Even in the case of a *vor*, the minute he showed weakness and would not stand up to prison authorities, his title would be taken away and he became a *suki* (and likely killed), or, in the case of a *blatnyje*, he would be moved to the *sherst'* caste.

Such prison brutality became a good screening mechanism and helped identify the strongest candidates for promotion to criminal leadership. One interviewed inmate explained that during a beating, a strong, sportsy newcomer might "cry like a baby and . . . tell police everything they want to hear." Meanwhile an old, skinny, illiterate inmate newcomer will not say a word, even when he is tortured. "You never know who is who when they come in," the inmate said. "But after they'd go through police brutality, you know who is worth what."

The harsh behavior of prison authorities helped ensure that, at any given time, only the strongest people were in charge. In addition, the *vory* ability to withstand such abuse earned both the leaders and members a lot of respect. Knowing what they went through, other inmates trusted not only their judgment, but also their loyalty to the group. They were the people everyone could rely on.

As a result, when prisons conditions improved in 1990s, it was a negative development for the criminal organization because their crucial screening mechanism was eliminated. According to a member of the criminal family, "Even when one by one prisons started turning from red to black, we never complained about prison authorities beating inmates on arrival (to make them sign cooperation papers). It helped us to understand who was who before they even joined the prison's general population." But then, under pressure from human rights organizations, when this practice was eliminated in some prisons, it made it more difficult to distinguish between the weak and the strong inmates. As one interviewed *blatnoj* inmate explained:

> Because now in our prison no one is beaten on arrival, we try to compensate for that. We have to basically do the pressing ourselves. By putting psychological pressure on a new inmate (by making him believe he will be degraded to the lowest caste), we get to see how he reacts. He has to, at the same time, stand his ground and avoid escalating conflict. Although it works, it is, of course, a very poor substitution for the prison authorities' beatings and torture.

Parole

In the USSR, and particularly during time of Stalin, it was unimaginable that an inmate would be released before the end of his sentence. (Sometimes, a person was not even released when his official sentence was over.) Now, the situation has changed. At least theoretically, an inmate could be released early on parole. However, since it is the prison administration who writes the recommendation, any possibility of parole requires an inmate to be in good standing, which is impossible for an objector. Since most inmates want to be released as soon as possible, following the original radical *ponyatiya* has fallen out of favor, and *ponyatiya* itself has become more liberal.

This is a fairly recent happening. Until early 2000, it was not acceptable for a decent inmate to leave prison early by going on parole because it required application and signatures on official court documents. This was considered cooperation with authorities. Later, applying was permitted for members of the *muzhiki* caste, but, to be on the safe side, an inmate would have still needed to inform the *polojenets* and get his consent. Getting that consent assured the inmate that if he was released and then returned to prison, there would be no question about whether he had cooperated with authorities, which might cost him his prison caste and status.

Now, even criminal leadership openly desire early release. As a result, instead of provoking them as they had in the past, *vory* now minimize their conflicts with prison authorities. This does not mean that they have started following all the official prison rules, only that they try harder not to get caught violating them. According to an interviewed inmate, "Eight out of ten *blatnyje* allow their *snir* to use their cell phone. It sounds like a nice gesture, but really, if there is a search, it is the *snir* who is in charge of hiding the phone. Which means that if he gets caught, he will be the one punished and not its actual owner—the *blatnoj*."

So if in the past, *blatnyje* were defending the rights of other inmates and suffering for the *muzhiki* caste, now it had become other way around. *Muzhiki* are often suffering for *blatnyje*. That further decreases the leadership's reputation and, as a consequence, criminal leadership's authority in prisons. According to another interviewed inmate who had spent forty of his seventy years behind bars, "It was much better before the parole in terms of relations between inmates. Now everyone is stepping on each other to get home earlier."

Separation of First-Timers

In 2010, a law was passed in Russia that separated those who were in prison camp for the first time from repeat offenders. This became a major problem for the *vory* criminal organization. Experienced criminal inmates could no longer educate the next generation or choose the most qualified among new inmates for promotion. Now the only place where those two groups can interact became the prison hospital (because there is usually only one for several prison camps), which is not enough.

Consequently, the quality of *ponyatiya* among first-time offenders has decreased, which has also decreased inmate respect for the *vory* and criminal organization in general. One inmate who, before being moved to the prison camp for first timers, had spent a significant amount of jail time with recidivists and had even lived in the same cell with a *vor* was able to give a glimpse at the situation:

> Understanding of *ponyatiya* among first timers is terrible. They punish inmates for something that a person should not be punished for and even degrade him, destroying his life. And the so-called *blatnyje* there have no idea how to control inmates and ensure law and order. There were two boxes for *obshyak*—one for a group of guys from Central Asia and one for the rest of the prison population. Such division is simply not acceptable. Also, the barrack was very dirty. The *smotryasçiy* openly told me he has no idea what to do.
>
> I had to enforce *ponyatiya*, which almost led to a fight. I aggressively approached one Central Asian inmate who was officially in charge of cleaning and told him that he had one day to perform his duties and that everything had to sparkle. His fellow countryman came at me with a knife to defend him. Then I also had to explain that, according to *ponyatiya*, one could not just come to a meeting with a weapon because threatening is not allowed, and if he would not use it against me, I would have to use it against him. It all was just a mess.

There is a loophole in this prison rule, though, which can be beneficial for the criminal organization. According to Russian law, if a person serves a prison sentence abroad—including in ex-Soviet Union countries—and is then arrested in Russia, he is still considered a first-timer. That way, experienced inmates sometimes end up in first timers' prison and are able to teach and indoctrinate the new generation of inmates. This, however, is not a desirable position for recidivists. According to one such inmate, "It is like a kindergarten there [in first-timer's prison]. Of course, I am in charge, and I do all I can to govern it, but I feel like a teacher in middle school."

However, not all such inmates are as interested in promoting the *vory* ideology as they are in using the situation to their own benefit. This further exacerbates the problem and decreases the reputation of the *vory* criminal organization. Sometimes, these inmates use their experience to show off in front of inexperienced inmates.

A middle-level member of the criminal family told the story of a time in a first-timer's prison, when an older, more experienced inmate said he was a respected *blatnoj*. The first-time inmates believed him, but the middle-level member went to the hospital (he was a recidivist, but the hospital was on the territory of the first timers) and confronted the so-called *blatnoj*, asking him what prisons he had been in and who could vouch for him. He gave a name, and the middle-level member asked him to call that person. He pretended to call but said he was not able to reach him. The middle-level member also knew that person, and called from his own phone. The person on the phone said the other inmate was lying. Not only was he *not* a *blatnoj*, but he was a *snir*.

Longer Sentences

In the past, an inmate who killed another inmate would have his sentence extended by approximately three years. Now, that sentence is ten years. And because it is a significant difference, fewer people are willing to sacrifice their freedom by executing a *vory* order to kill someone. This has further decreased criminal leadership control over the prison's general population.

Relative Trust of Judicial System

During Soviet times, the judicial system was not independent of the government, and its judgments were not considered fair. But after the fall of Soviet Union, the situation started to change, and people, including members of the criminal family, increased in their trust of the system (or in their ability to bribe it to get decisions in their favor). According to a *blatnoj* inmate, "When the USSR fell apart, we decided we could work with the government and fight the system *through* the system itself because it was not biased against us anymore."

The original *ponyatiya* does not allow *vory* to use the judicial system for anything, but now the situation is different. Not only *blatnyje*, but even *vory*, use the system openly. *Vory* claim that because they are not physically going to court themselves—their lawyers are—then they have not violated *ponyatiya*. And this reasoning has opened up the world of law for the *vory*.

Oversight of Prisons

In the past, particularly during Gulag times, prison guards and administration were free to do whatever they wanted with inmates with little oversight from their leadership and no media or human rights interference. Now, if information about any kind of abuse or torture becomes public knowledge, directors of prison camps can be fired for mistreating inmates.

As a result, the *ponyatiya* rule that prohibited writing complaints about prison guards has also changed. Right now, the *vory* allow *muzhiki* to make such complaints, but *vory* and *blatnyje* are still not able to do so. At least officially. According to one interviewed inmate in charge of helping inmates write official paperwork, "Everyone writes all kinds of complaints and appeals, even *vory* themselves." One interviewed lawyer had even written a complaint for a *blatnoj* to the European Court of Human Rights.

Corruption of Courts

According to the original *ponyatiya*, bribing court officials to get out of prison time was considered interaction with authorities and, as a result, prohibited. Instead, *vory* were expected to spend significant time in prison. But since it is now considered acceptable for *vory* to bribe officials and avoid prison sentences, it is now rare that they become guests behind bars. Following their example, middle-level members of the criminal organization have also started bribing courts to avoid prison sentences. As a result, the majority of members of the criminal organization currently behind bars are mostly poor drug addicts who are not able to buy their way out. Not only do these inmates not care about the A.U.E. ideology, but they are willing to do anything for drugs, even if that means cooperating with prison authorities. This has brought the quality of the prison criminal leadership to a new historic low.

Changes within the *Vory* Prison System

Such major changes in both the criminal world and governmental policies have also had major effects on the prison criminal government. It sent the organization into a downward spiral of ideologization and made their ideology and caste system counterproductive liabilities.

Commercialization

Commercialization of relations in prisons shaped the new prison criminal organization on many dimensions.

During Soviet times, the traditional criminal hierarchy did not allow for commercial relations, which limited corruption. In fact, those imprisoned for white-collar crimes (who were usually wealthier than the average prison population) often were in the lower caste. But in the 1990s, when business relations between inmates began, people who had money were also getting power in prison.

Mixing Castes

According to *ponyatiya*, it is not acceptable for a member of the lower caste to play cards with a member of the upper caste because it makes them equal. But now in many prisons, looking for ways to increase income for the *vory* fund (which is technically collected only from the tax on gambling), prison leadership not only allow inmates belonging to different castes to play between themselves, but they have also started collecting taxes from gambling inside lower castes.

Punishment

Strict rules that were the base of inmates standing up against prison authorities are also partially corrupted. Currently, there is widespread financial punishment for inmates. If an inmate violates criminal rules, he has to pay additional money into the criminal mutual fund, which itself has become less mutual and more for the prison criminal leadership.

And in the past, not paying card-game debt on time was a major violation of *ponyatiya* for which a person was beaten and moved to a lower caste. But now it often happens that a *blatnyje* will pay the card debt on time for an inmate who will repay him later. According to an interviewed inmate, "The rule was changed to get more money. When one is degraded, he does not need to return the money (basically his debt is gone), but this way, he borrows the money and has to pay back."

Other times, such corruption is even more open. For example, in one prison in Osh, Kyrgyzstan, an inmate was a librarian. Then he was moved to another prison in Jalalabad, where he was beaten and downgraded to the *sherst'* caste because the librarian job was considered working for the prison authorities. His family paid a significant amount of money to prison criminal leadership and had the inmate moved back into the *muzhiki* caste. Such upward movement is considered absolutely unacceptable by the original *ponyatiya*, not to mention that it was done for money.

In another prison in Russia, an inmate testified against his co-conspirator during a trial, which is also a major violation of *ponyatiya*. But after paying the *polojenets* a significant sum of money, not only was the inmate spared a beating and being downgraded to *sherst'*, but the *polojenets* protected him, particularly against the person he testified against who was also in the same prison camp.

Cooperation with Prison Authorities

In many prisons, on the issue of commerce, criminal leadership started working in conjunction with the prison administration. For example, many inmates have computers and smartphones, which allow them to run their criminal enterprises. Prison guards allow these enterprises to continue, as long as they get a cut of the business. In one prison, an inmate was actually conducting criminal activities using the prison director's computer.

Outdated Criminal Traditions

Some attributes of *vory* traditions are considered problematic by many and have led to further disappointment. The biggest issue is the ideological explanation for the caste system. For example, in the past, when inmates were serving sentences for several decades in remote Siberian forests where there was no access to females, the caste of *petukhi* was justified. However, the need for that caste has largely disappeared. Now inmates can easily get prostitutes within the prisons to satisfy their sexual needs. And according to one of the biggest madams in one Central Asian country, inmates are her most frequent clients.

Many inmates consider active homosexuals (members of the prison criminal leadership who use sex services of *petukhi*) as gays (something forbidden by prison criminal leadership) and think it is hypocrisy for passive homosexuals to be in the lowest caste while active homosexuals may remain in the upper castes.

A similar complication has arisen with drug dealers, or those who are in prison for selling drugs. In the past, drug dealers would have been in the lowest caste. Now they are in the *muzhiki* caste but are still considered slightly lower because their drug crimes broke two criminal rules. First, it is considered dishonorable to destroy someone's health, and second, drug dealers often cooperate with police (e.g., helping them catch other drug dealers), which, as mentioned, is also considered a major violation of the criminal code of conduct.[5]

In general, a drug dealer's status and quality of life depend on both the particular prison and the person himself. Usually drug addicts and low-level drug dealers (especially those who are first-time prisoners) will have to pay some mandatory amount of money to prison criminal leadership[6] or make an extra effort to help the inmate population by volunteering for low-level criminal prison jobs. High-level drug dealers will be used by the criminal family leadership because they are generally rich and usually know important people in the drug-trafficking industry. So they would be made to pay or bring drugs to prison. And many do not agree with such low classification and mandatory payment for several reasons.

First, *vory* and the criminal world in general get a huge share of its income from drug trafficking and dealing, so many people consider putting drug dealers lower than others in the *muzhiki*'s caste as hypocrisy.

And second, because in the present day, former Soviet states' law enforcement often plants drugs on people to incriminate them, it is not clear who is really a drug dealer. As a result, now in prisons, it is up to the *polojenets* to determine whether a particular person was dealing drugs, using them, or was framed by police. And since this decision is in hands of one person, it leads to another problem—this decision being considered unfair and biased. According to interviewed inmates in this caste, "Criminal leadership is just using this old archaic criminal rule to intentionally put us into a lower status, and then make us repay it to them."

And though, in the past, drug dealers once made up a relatively small number of inmates, now, most inmates currently in Russian prisons are on drug charges. This leads to them becoming a serious opposition to the criminal prison leadership. According to an inmate on drug charges, criminal leadership pressed for money as soon as he got to the prison camp. He quelled the situation by becoming a *smotryasçiy*, which increased his status with the leadership.

Now this *smotryasçiy* uses his position to help new inmates with drug charges: "I can explain how to behave so as not to be pressed by criminal leadership for money. My goal is to sabotage the criminal leadership because what they do to us [drug dealers] is unfair."

To complicate the issue, the majority of those sentenced for drug dealing are Muslims from Central Asia,[7] and this also makes this particular issue of harassing drug dealers feel like ethnic discrimination.

Quality of Prison Criminal Leadership

The quality of people being promoted into the top criminal ranks within the prisons has also significantly decreased. In the past, the majority of *blatnyje* were the most dedicated objectors. But now, following the lead of *vory* outside of prison, many live better than the rest of the prison population. One interviewed inmate gives his account:

> Those *blatnyje* live like kings in our prison camp, and it is disgusting. They have many *sniri* who cook and clean for them. And they will even yell and beat their *snir* for not making coffee the way they like it. Also, instead of spending time in the inner prison (being punished defending inmates), they make a deal with prison authorities and live in the building for visitation (which is basically a hotel on the prison territory). And often, they live there not alone but with wife or a girlfriend. We barely see them. Also, sometime to show their power in front of inmates and increase their ego, they even meet members of the Department of Corrections inspection holding a cell phone (a prohibited item) in their hand. Of course that leads to problems for the whole prison, but it looks like they don't really care.

In some black prisons, the leadership has even become dictatorial. One interviewed inmate explained that most *muzhiki* inmates are afraid to say anything at shodka. Even though those meetings are supposedly democratic, *muzhiki* fear sharing their opinion and are sure it will not make a difference anyway.

In rare cases, the dictatorial behavior of criminal leadership was even worse than prison authorities in red prisons. For example, in one prison, leaders demanded that 90 percent of what inmates got from the outside (food packages) were given directly to them. Inmates did not even have a chance to see what their relatives had sent before it was taken. At the same time, members of the prison criminal leadership never shared their food with others, even those who did not have anything.

In another prison, the *blatnyje* insisted that inmates with money pay them on a monthly basis, and they would confiscate everything of value. For example, if an inmate got a phone inside the prison, they would take it. And they would behave that way only with inmates from the upper caste since, by *ponyatiya*, those inmates were not allowed to complain to prison guards.

This dictator mentality was so bad in some prisons that, in central jails where cells were so overcrowded inmates took turns sleeping in three shifts, *blatnyje* would not allow anyone else to sleep in their bed near the window. This behavior was particularly despised in the summer when it was so hot, and older inmates were suffering from lack of fresh air and even dying from heart attacks.

To make things worse, if in the past it was absolutely prohibited for any drug user to be anywhere close to the mutual fund, now many inmates with drug addictions aspire to rise in the ranks and gain access to the mutual fund as a way to support their drug habit. And as drug users do gain access into the higher ranks, it decreases the quality of the prison criminal organization even further by affecting the following.

Security

Such widespread drug addiction among the leadership is a weak point that has already been exploited by law enforcement. In one prison, guards intentionally flooded the prison with heroin for a time and then abruptly stopped the supply. Prison criminal leaders were so weak due to withdrawal that correctional authorities were able to turn that black prison into a red one basically overnight.

Ponyatiya

Several interviewed ex-inmates mentioned how drug addict *blatnyje*—responsible for judging conflicts between inmates—would play favorites with those who were supplying them with drugs. According to one interviewed inmate, a gift of drugs to the *blatnyje* before the trial will ensure they rule in your favor. He also recounted the story of an inmate who had been a major drug dealer and who had multiple counts of rape in his charge. "Despite that, he is a *blatnoj* because he brings drugs into prison," the inmate said. Then he mentioned that, "in the same prison, two drug dealers were degraded when their family stopped sending them money."

Non-Universal Application of Standards

Many interviewed mid-level *blatnyje* do not consider their drug consumption a problem. According to one interviewed *blatnoj*, "It is not a problem if criminal leadership uses because they are smart enough to behave appropriately. The problem is when stupid people take it, lose control of themselves, and cause problems between us and prison authorities. So although it could be prohibited for *muzhiki* and other castes, it is okay if *blatnyje* use it quietly." Such a double standard not only causes the lower castes to feel the inequality, but also turns the prison's general population against its leadership.

As a result of these issues, often the criminal governance within the prisons has become very ineffective. One former inmate who, in sum, spent ten years behind bars, shared his reflections on the changes he had seen in his time:

> It was very hard for me to go back to prison [from 2014 to 2019] after I was there from 2000 to 2006 and to see that everything related to *vory* had basically became *suki* in just ten years. The old people are gone, and young people think the A.U.E. is some kind of pop culture. Now everyone is joining organized crime to be successful. They do not even know how it was before. They have never even seen how a *vor* helped the sick and poor, and how proudly he could walk through the prison. Everyone honestly called him Father, a man who would help when needed and punish but not hurt. Even prison authorities respected

the old *vory*, and looking at what is going on now, say, "In the old days, the *vory* would not have allowed it."

Fixing the Problem

The current leadership of the *vory* criminal organization is aware of many of these problems and, in an effort to maintain power, has initiated some changes in the last few years. For example, to solve the problem of low-quality *vory* getting titles (and sometimes buying them), in 2015, the moratorium on new *vory* was reinstated.

Also, there is currently an ongoing war on drugs in the criminal world, and people in leadership positions, either inside or outside of prison, are absolutely prohibited from using drugs. According to an interviewed high-level member of the *vory* criminal organization, "Everyone who would not stop using drugs was forced out of important positions. And if someone came to a meeting under the influence, he was told to 'go rest and then come back.' So we all had to choose [between drugs and membership]. Many people never came back."

In fact, during the late 1990s and early 2000s, there were even special drug rehabilitation centers for members of the criminal leadership, such as one in Bishkek (Kyrgyzstan). According to one high-level member of the criminal organization who had been treated there several times, "In this rehab, there were rooms especially for *vory*, who were treated for free. On their doors, there were pictures of *vory* stars [the tattoos that a *vor* gets when he gets his title]."[8]

And currently while other inmates are allowed by the criminal leadership to drink alcohol and take drugs in prison, a *blatnoj* is never allowed to do so. He must always remain sober and sharp, so he can perform his duties whenever necessary.

Other organizational issues are more deep-rooted and, as a result, are more difficult to solve. One such problem is the massive number of members in the lower castes (*sherst'* and *petukhi*) who were degraded in the 1990s when many *blatnyje* were showing their dedication to the *vory* criminal ideology. According to one inmate who has spent forty years behind bars, "We have a whole barrack of *sherst'* and a whole barrack of *petukhi*. We simply cannot have more. They will just overthrow us." So now, *vory* leadership is only allowed to degrade a person in very special circumstances.

However, this prohibition on degrading has caused another problem: the loss of a major punitive measure that was central to the *vory* power structure—a measure that had always been extremely effective. All interviewed inmates indicated that the worst thing that could happen to an inmate was being degraded.

If in the past, criminal leadership could move an inmate to a lower caste for any small infraction, now they are told to avoid downgrading an inmate at all costs (basically only unless he is caught being a passive homosexual). And because inmates know that they can now get away with more, the *vory* authority has been weakened.

This rule has also led to the decrease in the quality of inmates in the upper caste and has affected the number of people working as *sniri*. Although historically, *sniri* is a subcaste of the upper caste, they have now become the new lower caste (inside the upper caste). The logic behind this change is that erring inmates cannot be equal to people in the upper class, but since they cannot be put in the lowest caste, a new caste identity has been forged between the two. According to an interviewed inmate, "In the past, a rat [who had stolen from another inmate] would immediately be kicked out of upper and into the lowest caste. But now, he is beaten and left in the *muzhiki* caste as a *snir*." Although this time, this new subcaste is not serving all members of the upper caste as a public good (as *sherst'* and *petukhi* do), but mostly the prison criminal leadership.

Despite these changes to the criminal organization, many interviewed inmates feel that the changes are too little and too late, and that the system is already in a downturn.

Machnovshina

With the decrease in the quality of the *vory* criminal organization governance, inmates openly voice their dissatisfaction and even challenge its power. As a result, in addition to the red-black changes of the prison regime, a third type of governance began to appear in 1990s—independent gangs. This movement is often called *Machnovshina*, or the "Machno movement." This word was originally used to describe an independent anarchist army led by Nester Machno, who had fought against both the White and Red Armies in the early 1900s.

In such prisons, the inmate in charge is not a member of the *vory* criminal organization, but an independent gang leader. This can be the leader of a group of *sherst'* that prison authorities lost control of, a group of rouge drug dealers, a group of friends from one neighborhood, people of a particular ethnic background, or just a group of strong men.

In some cases, a gang could also be former members of the *vory* criminal organization who had problems with its leadership. For example, *vory* members who had worked for the organization for a long time, but because of internal clan politics, a group was kicked out. Like the original *Machnovshina*, these rouges are against two powerful forces; they are still against the government prison administration but have also turned against the *vory* organization and have organized their own gang. And when a group like this takes power, they are not constrained by anything, including *ponyatiya*, and are free to establish their own rules.

According to an interviewed inmate, "The difference between the *vory* criminal organization and those gangs is that *vory* get their power because of their authority, but gangs get it by force." By *ponyatiya*, for example, it is prohibited to come to meetings outside of prison with weapons. Gang members, however, have no problems doing so. It is a similar situation in prisons. By *ponyatiya*, it is unacceptable to hit someone during a meeting. "For the gangs," this inmate said, "it is acceptable to hit someone during a conversation to shut him up."

These takeovers occur if there are problems with prison criminal leadership and prison authorities either cannot or do not want to take full control of the prison. This was the situation in one prison in the Tver region. There, the *blatnyje* were all drug addicts who stole all the money from *obshyak* and then started collecting money from *muzhiki*. The situation became so terrible for ordinary inmates that a group of strong inmates under the leadership of a local criminal beat the *blatnyje* and had them moved to a separate building.

After taking power, a gang could install their own rules. But in the case mentioned above, the new leadership did not alter the existing prison criminal governmental structure. For example, each building still elected their own *smotryashchiye*, and if there were problems with particular inmates, it was discussed on a meeting. They also kept the names of castes and activities the same.[9]

One notable change the new gang did institute was a more commercialized system, and for luxuries like a phone or good alcohol, inmates had to pay. Previously, those items had been paid for by the criminal mutual fund.

As ambitious as a gang-related regime might be, they lacked one key element that has kept the *vory* system active for so many years: outside support and a wide network. According to an interviewed inmate who had observed gang governance in Smolensk, "It was okay under them, but it was not sustainable. They have power today but who knows about tomorrow? They have no one to back them up."

There are usually two strategies *vory* used to regain control of such prisons. First, they may try force. As a result, the majority of prisons run by non-*vory* gangs are in very remote areas where criminal leaders are rarely sent to serve their sentences. But if they are not able to overpower the dissenters, they tried to integrate them into their structure. This is illustrated by the story of Evgeny Vasin (nicknamed Jam). He was born in 1951 in a small town in the Chita region. When Jam was a teenager, he organized a soccer team and was its captain. His goal was to win the regional championship, but that did not happen. So instead, he used his cohesive team of young men to engage in criminal activities like racketeering. Eventually, he and his teammates were arrested and imprisoned.

While in prison, he and his team actively fought the prison administration and *activisty*, and in the 1980s, they tried to build their own criminal organization called the Union of True Inmates (Soyuz Istinnykh Arestantov).[10] The *vory* were not comfortable with such an independent organization and because it was already powerful, they decided to incorporate them into the *vory* criminal organization by giving Jam the status of *vor*.

Conclusion

When the government of the USSR was strong, so was the *vory* organization that stood in opposition to it. But with the fall of Soviet Union, the government and criminal organizations established working relationships, and, in the long run, these connections tremendously decreased the quality and reputation of the *vory* criminal organization.

In addition to the dissolution of the communist regime—the *vory*'s main enemy—other changes helped its decline. The new government no longer targeted adherers to A.U.E. ideology. This resulted in better conditions in prisons, less arbitrary sentencing, and conditional releases, all of which made inmates less antagonistic against government authorities. This governmental softening also made it possible for criminal leaders to not only come out of hiding but to even become legitimate civilians and take part in the normal life, business, and even government.

But the downside of it was the whole organization increasing internal problems. In the absence of existential threat, money and power started playing a bigger role in the criminal organization, eventually corrupting it. The new generation of *vory* were only interested in self-enrichment, which also led to the drug epidemic among group leadership. Now the *vory* criminal organization is trying to at least partially stop the downfall of the organization, but have not, until this point, been very successful. Meanwhile, independent gangs have begun challenging *vory* power in prisons.

11
Prison Islamist *Jamaats*

At the same time the *vory* criminal organization was experiencing difficulties and losing some prisons to independent criminal gangs, a new and different group of inmates began to appear. These were radical Islamists arrested after the Second Chechen War in 2009. They were mostly from the Caucasus, but because the government feared them breaking out of prisons there, many were sent all over Russia to serve their sentences. And there, these Islamists became the seed for a new power structure inside the prisons.

After that wave, the imprisonment of Islamists only continued to grow. In 2003, the Supreme Court of Russia criminalized membership in seventeen organizations because of their alleged extremism, which further increased the population of radical Muslims in prison. Later, these inmates were joined by people accused of violating article 282 of the Russian criminal code: inciting ethnic hatred. Then the war in Syria began in 2012, and even a larger group of radical Muslims were arrested, as were those accused of providing material support to terrorist causes.[1]

The situation is similar in other formerly Soviet countries. According to interviewed inmates in a prison in Muslim-majority Kyrgyzstan, there were not more than 100 people praying on a daily basis before the Syrian conflict. But beginning in 2016, when many people coming back from Syria were arrested, "All of a sudden, in like a month, 600 to 700 people started going to the mosque," remembered one of the interviewed inmates.

These Muslim inmates formed their own groups called *jamaats*. But unlike everyone else in a *black* prison, these jamaats refused to follow *ponyatiya* or operate under the *vory* criminal organization leadership. Rather they established a parallel structure with the long-term goal of taking total control of black prisons and turning them *green*, because it is considered a color of Islam.

Original Leadership

Originally, the founders of the prison *jamaats* had been veterans of the Chechen Wars in Russia and the Afghanistan War (on the side of *mujaheeds*) in Central Asia. These fighters were not only very respected among the criminal inmates,

Criminals, Nazis, and Islamists. Vera Mironova, Oxford University Press. © Oxford University Press 2023.
DOI: 10.1093/oso/9780197645659.003.0012

they also had many qualities and goals that easily overshadowed those of prison criminal leaders.

First, the *jamaat's* goals were similar to that of the original *vory* organization. In the beginning, the goal of the *vory* criminal organization was to present strong opposition to the government. However, many inmates see *vory* leadership now as coconspirators with, rather than opposition to, the government. These are criminal leaders who can easily be bought with money. According to a former inmate, "The original *vory* were against the government, but not anymore. They simply discredited themselves with corruption and cooperated with the government for money."

However, the Islamist veterans of different wars are seen as true leaders of opposition who will not make concessions for any reason. Their defiance is clear and absolute. The leader of one prison jamaat was Abdul Malik. At some point, he was driving his car at night and was stopped by the traffic police. They were rude to him, and it probably got to the point of them trying to hit him (not a rare event in Russia). As a result, he killed both of them, put them into the trunk of his car, and drove to the police station. There, he opened the trunk and, pointing to the dead bodies, told the police officers there, "This is your meat."

A second notable quality is their bravery. While criminal leaders are now more often seen as weak people looking for quick and easy self-enrichment, Islamist veteran inmates are seen as people who will achieve their goal at any cost, which includes sacrificing their own lives. This quality is particularly visible because many Islamist inmates with combat experience were severely wounded and are visibly disabled. One ex-ISIS foreign fighter inmate in Kyrgyzstan explained their outlook in this way:

> We tried to overthrow terrible corrupt regimes that everyone hates but no one dares to do anything about. Also everyone portrays us as so-called terrorists who are extremely dangerous, yet so many people here think we are their only hope against the (governmental) injustice.

According to a mid-level, non-Muslim criminal leader—a *smotryasçiy* of a barrack in one prison in Caucasus—"Because they are not afraid of death, when they see unfairness, they stand up against it without thinking about the consequences for themselves. It [their bravery] attracts strong people to them."

In addition to bravery, many Islamists veterans are qualified to resist the government, meaning they have the combat skills required to achieve their goals. Some criminals may use weapons in their day-to-day work, but their experience is nowhere near the level of those who fought in Chechnya, Afghanistan, and Syria. Other inmates—including criminal family members—are usually extremely impressed with Islamist inmate fighting skills.[2]

For example, one interviewed inmate admired an Islamist veteran in his cell who, in addition to fighting in Syria, had combat experience from the Islamic Movement Uzbekistan in Afghanistan. According to the inmate, the Islamist veteran "knew so many tricks that everyone in prison was in shock." Not only could he untie (in seconds) any knots the other inmates tried to bind him with, "On his way from the prison [to court], he managed to open his handcuffs, hit a guard, and run away." This obviously impressed even more inmates.

Another impressive quality was their behavior among other inmates. While criminal prison leadership is now often seen as troublesome drug addicts, Islamists who started *jamaats* movement in prisons not only do not use drugs but also do not drink alcohol or even smoke. According to interviewed inmates on criminal charges, those accused of fighting for Islamist insurgencies or terrorist groups often behave differently than the general prison population. They are usually very polite, and even their appearance is different. They are considered to be very well groomed and to take very good care of themselves. In the prison in Kyrgyzstan, according to interviewed inmates, while other inmates only wash their clothes one time a week, Islamist veterans inmates wash them twice.

The Islamist inmates' behavior with prison authorities is also an admired quality. While prison criminal leadership now have closer cooperation with prison authorities—so they can serve their sentence in comfort and even luxury—this is not the case with Islamist veterans. Because they have grievance against the government, they refuse to cooperate with prison guards. In one known case, an Islamist veteran inmate in Chechnya went so far in objecting to prison guards he would not respond to anyone speaking the Russian language. According to an inmate in the same prison camp, "He hated Russia and its government so much that he even hated the Russian language and wanted to forget it."

This is especially poignant in standing up to the tyranny of prison guards. And where criminal leadership had traded their opposition for cooperation—and thus early parole—Islamist veterans make no such concessions. Based on the Russian law, inmates on terrorism and extremism charges are never eligible for early release,[3] so they have no incentive for good behavior and nothing to lose by standing up against prison authorities' injustice.

And even if Islamists wanted to increase cooperation with prison authorities to improve their own life in prison, it is not possible because prison guards are often biased against them. Many prison guards had served their mandatory military service on the frontline in Chechnya, so in prison, they are either looking for revenge or are afraid of people on terrorism charges. For example, according to former inmates in Kyrgyzstan, after Islamist inmates have visits from family members, guards check them an extra time to make absolutely sure that they did not bring anything prohibited, often joking, "So did you already bring the bomb inside?"

And in many cases, those fears are not baseless. "Because of their connections to Islamists still outside the prison," one inmate remembered, "they could just say that a particular prison guard bothered them to their colleagues outside, and they would beat or even kill him [the guard]. While in prison in Nalchik, fifty-eight members of the insurgency were imprisoned there, several prison guards who were not nice to them were killed."

Since altruism, bravery, and military prowess are respected by both criminal leadership and Muslim inmates, ex-Islamist fighter inmates are very respected by the prison population in general. According to a criminal inmate who has spent more than fifteen years behind bars, "Those people started prisons jamaats as a copy of jamaats they saw fighting in the insurgency. Those founders were honest, ideologically strong, brave, and experienced. They were real people who naturally attracted other people."

When I asked inmates to describe an ideal candidate for the leader of a prison *jamaat*, the following qualifications were mentioned: (1) at least basic religious knowledge; (2) well spoken and able to persuade others to follow him (be a true leader); (3) diplomatic and, according to one inmate, "able to negotiate with other prisoners and prison administration"; (4) experience fighting in Chechnya, Afghanistan, or Syria (especially in major battles); and (5) will defend not only himself but also those in his *jamaat* and *Ummah* (general Muslim community).

It is important to notice that, with the exceptions of religious knowledge and fighting experience, theoretical requirements of a good *jamaat* leader are similar to those of a good *vor*.

This similarity in qualifying characteristics mean that if Islamist veterans had wanted to rise within the ranks of the *vory* criminal organization, they could have done so with relative ease. However, they chose not to. And instead of becoming part of the criminal family, Islamist veteran inmates not only stayed apart, they developed a parallel power structure with the ultimate goal to squeeze out and then replace *vor* criminal authority in prisons.

As a result of Islamist separation in many prisons, the *vory* criminal organization already deals with *jamaats* on equal footing. They no longer have, as in the past, jurisdiction over every inmate. Now, if the criminal family has problems with members of the *jamaat*, they cannot just take action. Instead, they have to address it to the *amir* of the *jamaat*, who then decides what to do with his subordinates according to their own rules. And the decisions that an *amir* might or might not be in line with criminal *ponyatiya*. In some prisons, *jamaats* are already successful at becoming more powerful than the *vory*.

As a downside, with such significant expansion, *jamaats* were not able to maintain the quality of their membership, and quickly it significantly decreased as it had with the *vory* criminal organization in the past.

Internal Organization

If in the previous chapters, I talked about how the *vory* criminal organization works inside the prison, a similar question arises now: How does this new *jamaat* organization function? And the answer is, much the same way. If not identical to the *vory* organization, the *jamaat*'s internal government structure and non-ideological rules are very similar. This is the case for two reasons.

First, the rules for opposition groups are the same, no matter who the opposing parties are. The in-group cooperation and out-group relations rules, laws, and regulations developed by the *vory* criminal organization work exceptionally well against the strongest enemies in a complicated environment. So for another organization to survive in that same environment, their rules, laws, and regulations would have to be very similar. According to a Muslim inmate who had been a member of both groups—first, at a high level in the *vory* criminal system and currently the member of a *jamaat*—"The most sustainable and successful *jamaats* are basically a copy of the criminal organization."

Second, the *vory* system is the only system known to inmates, so they copy it without even realizing it. As a result, the two parallel organizations are almost identical in structure. So how do the *jamaats* justify their existence? By having not just a different ideology, but an opposite one: Islamists are religious and pure in purpose, whereas the *vory* criminal organization, according to Islamists, is anti-God and based on vice.

As a result, the two organizations look very different in the outside—one's identity is portrayed as purely criminal and the other's, as religious—but in structure, essential rules, internal organization, and goals, they are very similar. While they are opposite in their form, the *vory* organization and *jamaats* are equal in substance.

And some members of *jamaat* even openly talk about this similarity during an interview. One member explained, "The leader of the *jamaat* should be someone who knows the prison environment well and has experience managing inmates. His knowledge of religion is less important. A religious guy could be something like his advisor for example."

Designations

Although *jamaats* claim to follow Sharia law instead of manmade *ponyatiya*, the Sharia-flavored rules Islamists offer the prison population are not much different from those of the criminal world. Islamists simply rebrand *ponyatiya* rules and norms and call them by Islamized names. For example, members of the *jamaat* call themselves (the in-group) *Muslims* and refer to each other as brothers and members of the out-group as *kafirs* (non-Muslims) just as members of the criminal world call themselves *people* and out-groups *non-people*. Similarly, the criminal family divides something permitted from something forbidden by calling them either *zaskvarinoye* or *zaskvarinor*, respectively, while *jamaats* divide those categories into *halal* and *haram*.

The similarities continue. According to criminals, the official enemy government is called *police state*, and for Islamists, it is called *tagut* (dictatorship). Muslims working for the prison administration are called *murtads* (those who left the religion) and are punished for their departure. In the criminal family, those people are also punished but are called *suki*. Conflicts inside the prison inmate population are called *fitna* by Islamists and *intrigue* by criminals and are prohibited in both circles.

The upper classes in both groups also have servants, but they have different reasons for their existence. Criminal leadership says that a *snir* is an inmate repaying criminal society for his mistakes. *Jamaat* leadership points to religious history for their justification because slaves existed in the time of the Prophet Mohamed. The only difference is that in the *jamaat*, slaves are called *kafirs* (nonbelievers) or *mushreeks* (polytheists).

The government of each system is also similar. The Islamist counterpart of the *vor* and *polojenets* is called an *amir*, and while a *vor* relies on the *blatcommittee* (a group of respected *blatnyje*) to discuss important issues, an *amir* relies on a *shura* (a group of respected Muslims, members of *jamaat*). They even meet in similar rooms, one being an office of the blat committee called the Kremlin and the other, either in a mosque or a praying room for Muslims.[4]

The mutual fund of those two coexisting groups also works similarly because to survive, both groups must have an internal mutual fund. In the criminal world, this fund is called *obshyak*, and in the *jamaat* world, *Bait al-Mal*.

While the criminals tax businessmen on the outside to increase the criminal budget, under Islamic rule, those same businessmen would pay *zakat* (if he is Muslim) or *djizya* (if he is not Muslim) to help the brothers.

Jamaat rules

As with the *vory* criminal organization, the Sharia-inspired rules *jamaats* claim to live by consist of three main parts: those specifying interaction with the enemy, those specifying interaction within the group, and the ideological rules. The rules for interaction with the enemy (prison authorities) and inside the inmate society are similar for any sustainable organization in opposition and, as a result, are basically the same for the criminal organization and *jamaats*. They both have

	Criminal Organization	***Jamaat***
Leader	*Vor/Polojenets*	*Amir/Imam*
Decision-making groups	*Blat* committee	*Shura*
Leadership Meeting	*Shodka*	*Majlis*
Office of the leader	Kremlin	Mosque
In-group/Out-group	People/Not People	Muslims/Non-Muslims
Servant	*Snir*	*Kafir/Mushrik*
Person turned to an enemy	*Suka*	*Murtad*
Law	*Ponyatiya*	Sharia
Order from the leadership	*Progon*	*Fetwa*
Allowed/Not Allowed	*Zaskvarinoye*	Halal/Haram
Internal Conflict	Intrigue	*Fitna*
Fundraising	Contribution to the mutual fund	*Zakat* payment
Mutual Fund	*Obshyak*	*Bait al-Mal*
Government and Prison Guards	Police State	*Tagut* (Dictator) State

Figure 11.1 Names used by criminal inmates and members of *jamaats*

to stand up against prison authorities and get along with each other, so those rules are similar. But it is a different situation with ideologically inspired rules.

Although ideological rules serve the same purpose in both organizations—to show that the organization could enforce even the most bizarre rules—their audience is slightly different. The criminal organization has to show their power only to inmates and prison authorities, whereas *jamaats* need to show their ability to enforce rules first to the criminal leadership. As a result, to make their demonstration of power highly visible, their ideological rules need to be opposite those of the criminal organization.

Interactions with the Enemy

Rules and norms that regulate inmate interaction with government employees, prison authorities, and courts are very similar in both *ponyatiya* and Sharia-inspired rules. In theory, both groups reject any cooperation with government institutions, but in practice both vary from moderate to radical. And both tend to move from radical to moderate when they see that the government system is not targeting them.

The *vory* criminal organization originally rejected any cooperation with government institutions. But in the 1990s, when courts stopped being biased against *vory* (and could be bribed), *vory* made the *ponyatiya* more liberal in its dealings with the government institutions that were once sworn enemies.

Islamist *jamaats* are now also going through this same warming-up process, but since they appeared later, and the Russian government is still largely biased against them—which is evident in the absence of due process, excessive prison sentences, and bad treatment in prisons—their journey to moderation is moving slowly.

And similar to the conflict between old and new *vory* traditions, there is an active discussion (and disagreement) among both Islamist religious scholars and their followers about whether interacting with government courts is allowed and to what extent. Islamist opinions range significantly from the view that being a court judge is no problem to the view that entering a court for any reason immediately makes one a *kafir*, or non-Muslim.

First, there are Islamist moderates who believe interaction with government courts should be permitted. They are no different from people of other religious or social groups in that they turn to civilian courts for any legal problem they encounter and follow its judgment.

Second, there are those who use religion to justify strategic interaction with the court. This group tries to avoid court, but when it is not possible, they feel at liberty to do anything necessary to defend themselves or friends. For example, it is acceptable to go to court as a defense witness for a fellow Muslim, but not to testify against a Muslim.[5] This position is in sync with *ponyatiya*, which allows a *vor* to testify for a brother's defense, but not against him. People in this category would also use lawyers as an intermediary between them and the court. This way, if asked, they could say they did not interact with the court; it was their lawyer who did.

Next are the more radical groups. According to their understanding of Islam, interaction with a *tagut* court is absolutely prohibited,[6] and even hiring a lawyer is questionable. Someone could hire a lawyer for consultation, but not to represent a defendant in court. Basically, he could not be doing *kufr* because in court, he would have to defend his client based on *tagut* laws, which would basically legitimize those laws.

Similar to more radical members of the *vory* criminal organization, people who follow this interpretation of Islam also prohibit interactions with police, prison guards, or any other law enforcement. So currently, all complaints to correction authorities are prohibited as is listed on a popular Islamist website Q&A page:

> ***Question 1***: A Muslim is in prison and his prison does not have adequate food. Can he complain to the correction authorities?
> ***Question 2***: Let's assume a Muslim is in prison and guards ask him to do something against prison rules. Is it *kufr* to tell the prison guard that his actions are against the law of the country, and that he is obliged to follow them?

Answer: No, you could not say either. It is prohibited. You could not complain to prison authorities and answer in a way that tells the guard to follow *tagut* laws. For example, you could not tell him, "You do not have a right to do something because you are breaking a government law," because, in that case, you want them to live according to *tagut* law and do *kufr*. And you need to remember that helping someone do *kufr* is also *kufr*, so reminding someone about the government law makes you a *kafir*. I am honestly not sure how to advise you because you obviously could not tell him, "You should not do something because it is against Sharia law." That will lead to much bigger problems. We have to pray to Allah, and if he wishes, he will give us a solution.

Members of *jamaats* who consider interaction with courts and prison authorities prohibited are also divided between more and less radical.

The fourth group are those who, despite the prohibition on interaction with courts, will allow a Muslim to defend himself if there is an *Ichrach*—an extreme necessity, such as a life danger.

The fifth group are ultra-radicals. They consider even attending a trial in the court *kufr* because everyone has to stand up to give respect to the *tagut* judge and "a goddess of fairness and justice, Femida [a personification of the moral force of the judicial system]." Doing so is considered *shirk* (polytheism).

Consequently, people in this group absolutely prohibit *any* interaction with the government court or law enforcement. According to Ahmad ibn Umar Al Hazimi, "If you are losing your life, you still cannot turn to the tagut court to save you. If you have to choose between turning to the court or losing your life, you will have to lose it because you are not allowed to turn to the court."

And although people in this radical last category are rare, they still exist. According to an inmate in a main Russian prison in Rostov for people on terrorism and extremism charges, "We had guys [Islamist inmates] who were total objectors. They refused to stand up, talk, or sign any papers not only in court but also when interacting with prison authorities."

Ideological Rules

Because the goal of the *jamaat* is to squeeze out, and ultimately replace, the *vory* criminal authority, their leadership needs to do two things. First, they delegitimize *vory* power inside the prison—*jamaats* need to discredit the existing criminal prison ideology. For example, here is a message that is widely distributed among members of *jamaats* in different prisons:

> Too often in prison you meet people who consider themselves Muslims and, at the same time, follow the A.U.E. ideology. For those who does not know, A.U.E. and *ponyatiya* are rules basically everyone who "comes to the *vory* home" [prison] has to live by. . . . But I could not even imagine a more disgusting culture than *ponyatiya*. Here are several things that it rewards: 1) stealing, 2) drugs, 3) alcohol, 4) adultery, 5) homosexuality, 6) arrogance, 7) impudence, and 8) card games.
>
> Also, it is impossible to describe the immorality of *ponyatiya* without mentioning that, by the A.U.E. religion, the *vor* is the most respected person on the planet. But who is the *vor*? In 90% of cases, he is a drug addict and alcoholic. And in honor of those people, every month, inmates raise a glass of *chifir'* to wish them long life. And everyone has to reply "Forever [when there is a toast of "Life to *vory*"]!" Can you even imagine this? What have *vory* done for Islam that you are meeting every month to honor them? Why are you not thinking about what you are doing and ask yourself, "Will I be rewarded for this, or will I be punished for it [on the judgment day]?"
>
> Why am I saying this? Because a big number of ethnic Muslims live in prison following *ponyatiya* and dream of rising in the ranks of the so-called "people." They are intentionally learning prison slang, 60% of which is swear words, and the rest are deformed regular words. Are they already fluent in Arabic or English to care about this language? I only wrote just a small part of what I wanted to write, but I am already so disgusted . . . .

Second, they have to replace A.U.E. ideology with anything of their own Islamist ideology that will reinforce *jamaat* leadership power. So where to start? At the crux of the *vory* prison criminal organization's power—the caste system (which is how they divide and conquer, by terrifying inmates); card games (which provides the main income for the criminal leadership); and vices like cigarettes, alcohol, and drugs (which are used to basically bribe regular inmates to support the criminal regime).

To simultaneously deprive criminal leadership of support and show their own power, the *jamaats* prohibit all these things. And these prohibitions, like everything else in *jamaat* rules, are rationalized by the Islamist ideology. And in lieu of these rejected criminal rituals, *jamaats* make other traditions—consequently traditions that undergird their own authority—mandatory. For example, prayer and religion classes are mandatory for all.

One of the popular messages circulated by *jamaat* members gives a clear illustration of this ideological battle.

Religion of *Vory*

I want to dedicate this work to a topic that is not covered well, but is crucial to many Muslims. First it is relevant to those Muslims who are in prison and second, all other Muslims because you never know what will happen to you later [when you get in prison]. Many Muslims do not understand the main idea of Islam and think that it is only a mandatory prayer and *haj* and, because of that, do things that are in fact destroying religion.

If a person thinks that something prohibited by God is allowed, he is doing *shirk* [polytheism]. And if a person, in addition to that, himself prohibits something allowed by Allah or allows something prohibited, he is *tagut* who dares to make laws himself. In addition, he is also a *kafir* even if he says *shahada* [statement of God's oneness], prays, fasts during Ramadan, and does other good things.

And this is often the case in prisons among people who claim to be Muslims. They get positions in the *vory* religion (yes, it is indeed religion, along with democracy and communism), and, as a result, become preachers in this religion instead of becoming preachers of Islam. They are participating in meetings of the sin [criminal gatherings], promoting *vory*, prohibiting things that are allowed by God and allowing things that are prohibited. Would you tell me that it is not true? If a *vor* says that you have to tell everyone his words (for example, give permission to use drugs), would you not do that?

Shouldn't you be using your position in the criminal world to prohibit something that is prohibited by God, like alcohol? If you would say, *That it is not possible*, then why did you join them in the first place?

Everyone should know that it is *shirk*, and being a *smotryasçiy* or *polojenets* in this criminal system equals leaving Islam [becoming non-Muslim]. I expect that people say they are doing it to make life in prison better for Muslims. But that is not true. They are simply afraid of the hardship affiliated with distancing themselves from *shirk*.

Now, lets talk about the words:

A.U.E.: It is obvious that it is prohibited for Muslims to pronounce those words because they mean *shirk*, *kufr*, drugs, alcohol, and adultery with both females and males. And if someone thinks it is allowed for him to say those words, although he could be judged only by God, he should not consider himself Muslim.

Life to vory: Or in other words, *Life to tagut*. I think that a person who considers himself a Muslim will not say those words, ever.

Also, the *vory* ideology is a hierarchy:

Vor is the main *tagut* in the system, and the one who calls himself *vor* could not be considered Muslim.

Blatnyje are those who aspire to become *vory* and promote the ideas of *vory*. So those people could call themselves Christians, Jews, or Buddhists, but they have nothing in common with Islam.

If *muzhiki* (Men) refers to the criminal meaning of this word [the name of the caste], then it is *kufr*. Because according to criminal rules, a function of the *muzhiki* is to support a "common goal [of inmates in prison]." If one is using this word as a regular word, then it is not *kufr*, but it is still better not to use it at all. It could be understood in relation to the criminal system.

Also, in prisons, inmates contribute to the criminal *obshyak*. If a person who gives money there knows that there is *kufr* (because its purpose is not to spread the religion), then giving money there is also *kufr*.

The saddest thing to see is that these things are also being done by people who did great things for religion and even jihad while outside of prison. So why did they do them back then if now they are acting against Islam?

As shown by the message above, *jamaats* are against the higher castes—such as criminal leadership and those who support them—because the people in those castes are their main competition. But what about people in the lowest castes? The situation with them is very different. Even though, theoretically, *jamaats* are against the criminal caste system, they have found a way to use it for their own benefit.

On one side, *jamaat* leadership says there should be no castes because for a person who has accepted Islam, it does not matter what he did before, and all Muslims are equal. On the other side, while *jamaats* absolutely prohibit its members from having sex with a member of *petukhi* caste, they still use them to clean toilets and do other dirty jobs they do not want to do themselves.

Also, with time, *jamaats* holding power has resulted in ideologization and corruption of their leadership. They also started using *sniri* to cook and clean in their barracks. When asked how this inconsistency is possible, interviewed members of the *jamaat* rationalize it by saying the Prophet Mohamed also had slaves. Furthermore, sometimes members of the *jamaat* pay *sniri* for their services in cigarettes—because this is the type of payment they demand—even though the *jamaat* interpretation of Islam prohibits its members from touching cigarettes.

Economy

Like everything else *jamaats* do, their economic rules serve two purposes. They not only want to increase their own funding, but they also want to decrease funding for their main competition, the *vory* criminal organization. And of course, like everything else they do, all their economic regulations are justified with religious doctrine, and if one does not follow these regulations, he becomes a non-Muslim (and has to leave the *jamaat*).

First, since the main income for the mutual fund and criminal leadership fund come from the gambling tax, *jamaat* leadership prohibit card playing for their members. Because gambling is not allowed in Islam, this is easily accomplished.

Second, according to their interpretation of Islam, not only are drugs and alcohol prohibited, but so is smoking. So when members of *jamaat* are not buying anything illegal, including cigarettes, through the criminal system, this also reduces the *vory* criminal income.

Third, all inmates from the upper caste contribute to the *obshyak*. It is where inmates can get support in a time of hardship. But since it is the main budget of the *vory* system, *jamaats* want to decrease it by not allowing their members to contribute to it. And as shown by the message above, the explanation for this lack of contribution is based, again, on religion. According to *jamaat* leaders, since money from that fund is used for things prohibited by Islam, contributing to it would make an inmate a non-Muslim.

Fourth, to maintain inmate cohesion, criminal leadership prohibits free trade inside prison. On the other side, they ensure that necessary goods are delivered inside prison and are in the *obshyak* for those in need to take for free or buy through their *baryga* (dealer). *Jamaats* however, claim trade is allowed in Islam and openly sell and resell goods inside prison. This also has serious negative implications for the criminal family economy and mutual fund.

And since *jamaat* prices are not controlled by prison criminal leadership, *jamaat* leaders are free to increase prices as much as they want. Not only does this variable pricing practice increase *jamaat* income, it seriously hurts prison criminal leadership and other inmates in the long run by making many goods not accessible to inmates.

The main side effect of these *jamaat* rules that target criminal leadership is that the criminal mutual fund also funds inner prison public goods provision (like bribing prison authorities). *Jamaats* then are not only freeloading on this system (by using public goods but not contributing), they are actively sabotaging it. And by doing so, they decrease the well-being of all prison inmates.

Culture

For something as radical as moving from traditional A.U.E. ideology to Sharia-rationalized rules, it is not enough to just change the group's leadership from *vor* to *amir*. A successful long-term sustainable change also requires a shift in the norms and customs surrounding and reinforcing each system. This means change within several key areas.

Islamist Family

The *vory* criminal organization not only labels those in the same prison as family, but it derives pride and power from being a strong force all over the world. Similarly, members of a *jamaat* consider the prison *jamaat* a family—calling each other brothers and claiming that it is mandatory to help each other—as well as the bigger *Umma* (community) that spans different countries. So even while in prison, members of a *jamaat* are very involved in Islamist affairs all over the world, from regions of the former USSR to Afghanistan, Iraq, and Syria. Many Islamists stay involved within the *Umma* by spreading propaganda, and many leave to active battlefields after they are released from prison.

For example, even before the rise of ISIS in the Middle East, young radical Dagestani inmates (charged with theft) made it known that part of the money they stole was sent home for *jihad*, according to their cellmates. Many inmates around that time were even giving allegiance to armed groups over the phone. The most famous case was an ethnic *Chuvash* (Christian) who converted to Islam after befriending a person from Dagestan. He was imprisoned for forming an eighty-person *jamaat* in his hometown and sentenced to thirteen years in prison in the Ulyanovsk region. In 2007, when the Caucasus Emirate (an Islamist insurgency in Russia) increased in strength, so did the Ulyanovsk *jamaat*. Its leader pledged the *jamaat*'s allegiance to the insurgency's group leader, Doku Umarov, by phone. After the *jamaat* leader and some of its members served their sentences and were released, they joined the armed group in its insurgency activities in the Caucasus Mountains.

As ISIS emerged, the affiliation of members of *jamaat* with armed groups became even more common. With their cell phones, Islamist inmates showed other inmate videos of ISIS making explosives and fighting against Russian forces. And when ISIS declared caliphate in Syria, all the prison *jamaats* were extremely excited, hoping that ISIS would also take over the former Soviet Union. Many vowed to go to Syria after their release, and many did go and fight. Interviewed inmates remembered that many of them died there.

Language

In prison, slang has always held an important place in the criminal family subculture, and being fluent in it sent a signal of belonging to conversing parties and made it easier for two members of the criminal world to identify each other. So uprooting this criminal language required Islamists to not only avoid the language, but to replace certain phrases with new Islamized terms. This includes the overuse of Arabic words like *Inshaalah* (if Allah wills it), *Bismillah* (in the name of Allah), and so on. Those Islamized words are particularly used in well wishes and greetings, which immediately signals membership in a *jamaat* instead of the criminal family. The Islamic greeting *salam* is widely used because, in addition to being Islamic, it also fits nicely with criminal customs because a *muzhiki* cannot greet people from the lowest caste, but it is acceptable to wish them *peace* (the English translation of *salam*).

The main mottos of criminal family inmates are "Life to *vory*," or "A.U.E." They are used not only to express happiness, but to identify who might be in a nearby, unseen cell. In those conditions, *jamaat* members would substitute these phrases with their own *Allahu Akbar*, which, when translated from the Arabic, means *God is great.*

However, because the Islamist movement in Russian prisons is relatively new, it has not yet developed the sophisticated slang that covers all spheres of prison life, and so still has to often use criminal slang instead.

Names

In the criminal world, inmates use nicknames alone or with actual names, and so do *jamaats*. All *jamaat* members have an Arabic-style, Islamized nickname or even a *kunya*. The new name could be a regular Arabic name like Muhamad or Imran, or it could be a *kunya*, a more complicated name like *Abu Mohamed* or *Abu Fatima*, which means *a father of Mohamed* or *Fatima*.

Appearance

Since *jamaat* leadership wants its members to visibly signal their association with the group, they have also developed a particular dress code. For example, they are required to have a beard and no mustache, and to never wear shorts, only shortened pants. Sometimes they also wear Afghani-type dress and checkered headscarves. Particularly, radical members of the *jamaat* will not wear clothes with pictures or brand logos on them (they either remove the logo or sew something over them) because, according to their understanding of religion, those images are *shirk*.[7] Also, a special strong perfume, *musk*, is often used by members of the *jamaat*.[8]

Heroes

Like in the criminal family culture, Islamist culture has its own heroes. When a particular *vor* is considered a hero, inmates pass stories about him onto the new members of the criminal family; it is the same in Islamist culture. But Islamist heroes are often radical Islamist preachers (particularly ones currently in prison), slain fighters from the Chechen wars, or Russian-speaking ISIS leaders. And the main hero for non-ethnic Muslims who converted to Islam (to join the *jamaat*) is usually Said Buryatsky, the son of a Buddhist father and a Christian mother who converted to Islam and became a prominent ideologist of the Islamist insurgency in the Caucasus. According to interviewed inmates, "His writings and video addresses are all over prisons in Russia."

Music

Since specific criminal music (*blatnya pesnya*) is basically a symbol of the criminal world—celebrating its rules and highlighting the suffering of inmates—Islamists have to replace it with something that serves their goals. And since the criminal family music is very deep in the prison culture, such change is occurring gradually.

With the first wave of Islamist inmates (after a Second Chechen war), Timur Matsurayev, a Chechen who sings in the same style as criminal songs, became popular in prison. However, instead of the suffering of the members of the criminal world, he sings about the suffering of Muslims fighting Russian forces in Chechnya. His most popular song among inmates, "Islamic Umma," has the following lyrics:

> *We are not looking for the benefits in this life;*
> *we are getting wounds on the battlefield*
> *because it clearly says in Quran*
> *that jihad is mandatory.*

Later, when the Syrian conflict started, it became a commonly accepted opinion among Islamists that any instrumental music was prohibited in Islam, and only *nasheeds* (male acapella songs) were allowed. At the same time, ISIS and other armed groups in Syria started to mass-produce high-quality *nasheeds*, and suddenly, Timur Matsurayev songs were considered *haram* (not allowed). Consequently, his music was replaced by *nasheeds* within the prison systems. Now *nasheeds* are so common, they are sung by the inmates.

Activities

While the criminal family inmates spend their time playing cards and reading entertaining literature, Islamist rules dictate that time should be spent reading and studying religious literature. In their public speeches, radical sheiks often propose that "God gave you time in prison to study Quran, so you need to use it wisely, and not just read it, but memorize it. You have enough time to spend it with benefit—you could actually memorize the Quran" (according to a popular sheik's address widely distributed by inmates on social media).

And many Islamists following this advice. *Jamaats* in some prisons hold mandatory religious classes.[9] According to a letter from one of the ex-inmates of a St. Petersburg prison, "Cells where Caucasian and Russian Muslims are spending time studying the Quran have become a norm. You cannot harm a Muslim by killing him or breaking him in prison because where the body of a dirty criminal is rotting, the spirit of a Muslim is just getting stronger."

Celebrations

Since celebrations and commemorations are ideological events, the leadership of *jamaat* prohibits members to participate in criminal family events, such as the celebration of *vory* birthdays on the fifteenth of every month. *Jamaat* members are allowed to celebrate only religious holidays.

And since *jamaats* have little to do with religion, and the only real reason for those celebrations is to show power, the real problem arises when prison criminal leadership organizes celebrations for Islamic holidays for everyone in the prison camp. It puts *jamaat* leadership in a very ideologically complicated situation. On one side, they need to claim exclusive ownership of the ideology and use it to oppose *vory* ideology. But on the other side, they cannot refuse to attend the celebration since it is a religious holiday and refusing to celebrate it would go against their own ideology. According to an interviewed member of the prison criminal leadership, it poses a difficult situation for the Islamists:

> Once we organized such a celebration—we brought halal food, set up tables, and invited everyone. The *jamaat* guys did not know what to do. They did not want to attend, but they could not find a legitimate excuse not to. So they came but felt very uncomfortable, and we could hear their leadership discussing how they should not be there because they were setting a bad example for their members, by celebrating together with criminal leadership. The next year they made a totally fake excuse related to the meat we were buying, claiming that

they could not be sure it was halal, and then celebrated those holidays inside their *jamaat*.

Competition

The *vory* criminal family has an almost absolute monopoly on their criminal ideology and does not have any other gang try to claim it for its own. But that is not the case with *jamaat* Islamist ideology. They base the legitimacy of their rules on their variation of a known ideology, namely Islam, and, as a consequence, face several competitors.

Official Islam

According to one ex-inmate, "Once [in the prison], they were showing a meeting between the Russian prime minister and the official Muslim leadership on TV. The hate towards those Muslim leaders among Muslim inmates was so great that Muslim [inmates] started yelling offensive terms, and the TV had to be turned off."

One Islamist Sheik, Abu Ali Al-Anbari, whose statements are widely distributed in prisons, makes this distrust of mainstream Islam leaders very clear with warnings against Islamic scholars on TV. He reasons that, because the scholars are televised (even on their own channel), they must have, at some point been approved by the government. He reasoned that, "If they [scholars] would actually say true things about tagut government, they would be in prison and not on TV." He went so far as to say, "Allah is not pleased with them. And those people [scholars] are either saying something tagut is pleased with, or are silent about the truth. About those people, the Prophet said, 'I only fear for my *Ummah* [community] from the misguiding A'immah' [Tirmidhi 2229]."

Official Imams

These are religious leaders assigned to a prison. However, they are simply not recognized by the prison population. When a prayer room opened in one of the prisons, and an official imam came for the first prayer, almost no inmates showed up to join him. In another prison, where one imam entered the prison he was appointed to, he was immediately told, "You are not a true imam because you are not an inmate, and you are outside the prison [have freedom]." According to Islamist inmates, if you are an imam, you also have to be an inmate (be suffering with others, particularly for your religion) and be in opposition to the prison rules. Because of that, official imams are usually afraid of prison imams, especially those who have been imprisoned for terrorism or extremism.

In more radical cases, if a prison mosque is under the control of an official prison imam, praying there makes one *kafir* (non-Muslim) according to members of *jamaat*.

Traditional Islam

Jamaats have to defend their interpretation of Islam against other, less radical interpretations of Islam (basically ethnic Muslims who consider themselves Muslims but do not want to join *jamaats*). This is one of the most common problems between Islamist members of a *jamaat* and those who were born and raised Muslim and follow their own Islamic traditions. In one prison, White Swan in Pyatigorsk in the Caucasus, they historically have many conflicts between Islamists (on extremism and terrorism charges) *jamaats* from North Caucasus and other Muslims (such as Uzbeks, Tatars, and Azeri), and the latter often complain about discrimination. In particular, those in the worst situation are people who have had religious education because they are seen as a dangerous competition to *jamaat* leadership.

For example, Muslims from the Caucasus would not pray with other Muslims, essentially showing that they do not consider them Muslims. In other cases, where Islamist *jamaats* were more powerful, the radical Islamists beat up those who followed traditional Islam. In one prison, where Islamist *jamaats* were particularly strong, even an imam was beaten when he mentioned celebrating the Prophet Mohamed's birthday (not allowed according to Islamists' interpretation of Islam).

Other Islamist Groups

Jamaats also have to defend their interpretation of Islam against other Islamist groups that are also using Islam to rationalize their existence and aspirations for power. For example, in the black prison in Kyrgyzstan, Islamist veteran inmates who fought in Syria and Waziristan have a major problem with those affiliated with Hisb-al-Tahrir (another recognized terrorist organization, but one that did not participate in fighting). These conflicts are often big and very loud. When that happens in black prisons where *jamaats* are weak, criminals—who do not distinguish between different types of Muslims but have to keep the peace—usually quietly watch from a distance since, by criminal rules, intervening in someone's conflict unasked is prohibited by *ponyatiya*.

In Tashkent prison in Uzbekistan, there were conflicts between Salafi inmates and Akramits (followers of the religious teachings of Akram Uladshev). According to a Salafi inmate with fighting experience in Syria, "In my cell there was an Akramit, and he believes he is allowed to miss a prayer and simply redo it later. So when I wake up for the morning prayer and see that my cellmate is sleeping, I wake him up. It makes him angry! He runs to the doors to get prison guards inside and accuses me of forcing him [to pray]."

If either party in one of these conflicts were to complain to a *vor* or *polojenets* (in prisons where Islamists are weak and do not have parallel power structure yet), he could intervene, listen to both sides, decide which side was wrong, and carry out the judgment—usually five hits in the chest. But such things happen very rarely because, for a radical Salafi, turning to a non-Sharia judge is prohibited.

What rarely happens are conflicts between people who fought in Syria for different groups. This is because those group differences are not applicable outside of Syria, and these inmates clearly understand that the use of Islamism is only to get power. Also, many of the inmates did not know each other in Syria and, as a result, have no Syria-based grievances against each other. According to an interviewed ex-ISIS foreign fighter, "In prison, I met many ex-foreign fighters from different armed groups who were all from my hometown but whom I did not meet in Syria."

The conflicts that do happen, however, are a serious factor that prevents Islamists from increasing their power in prisons. Because of this, many famous and influential Islamist sheikhs try to stop the infighting by issuing different statements. Here is one example:

> Brothers, I wish Allah frees you!
>
> It is one of the worst punishments for a Muslim to be in *kafir* prisons. May Allah put those so-called judges in hell forever! Brothers in prison, please unite! You are under *kafirs*. If you are Muslims (even *bidaatchik* [referring to traditional Muslims]), you need to support each other so that *kafirs* will not defeat you. You have to unite so that criminals do not control you. I am getting many letters from prisons that some brothers are not praying with each other [do not consider each other Muslims], call each other different offensive names, and do not eat each other's food sent from outside [do not consider each other Muslims]. Brothers, you are in such a position that you cannot afford to segregate.
>
> Let Allah free you and punish those who did judgment upon you to put you in prison.

Conclusion

When members of Islamist armed groups from the former Soviet states were imprisoned en masse, they changed the power structure behind bars. If, in the past, the *vory* criminal organization enjoyed a monopoly on power behind bars, it is not the case anymore.

While many Islamists had qualities that would have made it easy for them to rise in ranks of the *vory* criminal organization, they chose a different path. They started developing parallel power structures known as *jamaats*. Using their ideology and claiming that their religion did not allow them to follow *ponyatiya*, they rationalized the existence of a parallel ideological organization. And since the *vory* criminal organization proved to be not only sustainable, but also an effective opposition organization inside prison, *jamaats* had no option other than basically copying its structure and rules.

The only thing they did not copy were the ideologically inspired rules and traditions of the *vory*, all of which legitimized the criminal leadership. And to delegitimize and squeeze criminal organization even further, *jamaats* replaced it with Islamist-inspired rules and traditions. They took this visible change of ideology very seriously and even the words from criminal slang were replaced with Islamized words.

But although the two organizations look very different from the outside—one's identity being purely criminal and the other's religious—in structure, rules, internal organization, and goals, the two groups are very similar.

12

Islamist *Jamaat* Rise to Power

In the previous chapters, I talked about what Islamist *jamaats* look like and why they sprung up in prisons in the former Soviet Union. What is still not clear is *how* these *jamaats* managed a quiet takeover—how each began and grew, what problems they faced, and how leadership was able to overcome them. So in this chapter, I will talk about how, step by step, some prisons went from a handful of religious inmates to a serious force that *vory* criminal leadership have to reckon with.

Phase One: A Silent Insurgency

Islamist Perspective

In the very beginning of the *jamaat* movement in prisons, it was the work of experienced and battle-hardened ex-fighters from various insurgencies who were responsible for Islamist proliferation. These were men who hated prison guards (and the government in general) and were not afraid to stand up against them. They also had a very acute sense of fairness and were very disciplined and polite. According to one inmate in a prison in Chechnya, "There are some idealists in the criminal world, but there are many more in *jamaats*. Members of a *jamaat* would never do something against their *jamaat* to get an early release from prison (like spying), but [members of the] criminal family will." These Islamist veterans were often mentally and emotionally stronger than prison criminal leadership and were very respected, which placed them in a position to strongly influence their fellow inmates. How were they able to get first followers?

In Soviet times, one of the main ideologies of the criminal world was their strong anti-government stance. But now, because the criminal world is linked very closely to business and politics, there is little real interest in opposing the government, with criminal members often involved in one or both. So inmates with anti-government grievances are easily led to seek out Islamist ex-fighters. According to an interviewed inmate in a prison in Chechnya, "People who join *jamaats* here are the ones who are really pissed at law enforcement and the government. They see there is no real justice on earth, and that only God can establish justice in the afterlife."

Criminals, Nazis, and Islamists. Vera Mironova, Oxford University Press. © Oxford University Press 2023.
DOI: 10.1093/oso/9780197645659.003.0013

In other cases, the desire for justice that pushes an inmate toward the *jamaat* is his immediate surroundings, namely the prison. In 2003, a thirty-five-year-old, middle-level member of a criminal family was imprisoned for smuggling and selling drugs. In his cell there also was a Tajik imprisoned on the same, drug charges. His father was an imam in a small mosque in Tajikistan, and he and his Tajik friends were very religious and prayed regularly.

Prison was in Siberia, where the days were long, and at night, this Tajik was not sleeping but sitting on his bed waiting for darkness to arrive so he could do night prayers. He was short, so he fit standing between the second level of the bunk bed and the ceiling. His friends were praying sitting on their beds.[1]

At night, prison guards were usually walking around, looking for someone to punish. When they saw him praying, they beat him. This happened several times, but it never stopped the Tajiks from praying. Then as a criminal inmate explained:

> At some point, I [a strong guy holding a respected position in the criminal world] stood up and told the guards, "WTF is wrong with you? He is not doing anything bad. Let him pray." The guards stopped. After that, when they were again coming to beat him, they saw me staring at them from the first-level bunk bed, so they did nothing and moved on. In fact, I also had to defend those poor Tajiks from the criminal leadership because they were drug dealers [and, as a result, low in the criminal hierarchy].
>
> Then, at some point, the Tajik came down to my bed and very politely and respectfully asked me, "Do not you think it is time for you to also start praying?"
>
> It was not the first time someone had told me that. For a long time, my family tried to make me follow religion, but I refused. In fact, I thought that something was seriously wrong with religious people—they were simply nuts!
>
> He came with a notebook in which a prayer was written in a very nice handwriting. Then he got me a book called *Russian translation of the Meanings of the Quran with Commentary.* I had nothing better to do, so I started reading it and asking myself different questions. In fact, I was shocked. There I found many answers to my questions.

It is a common knowledge that inmates locked within the four walls of a prison cell have a deep need for hope and are very keen to get involved in something superstitious as one way of getting it. According to one interviewed inmate, "Inmates are all sick and are looking for something like a magic cure." The need to get involved with something that might help their family also drive inmates to seek something that could allegedly help their families.

Some individuals who practiced no religion before being imprisoned learned to pray behind bars simply because they felt better referring to God in the time of their worst despair. Basically, all interviewed inmates confirmed that praying made them feel better. One interviewed inmate told the story of when he first came to the prison, the *polojenets* asked him if he was baptized and wore a cross; "When I said no, he gave me a cross. When at night I was standing on the road [communication between cells], he gave me books on Christianity. It was very interesting to see someone as important as a *polojenets* praying every day, on his knees, in front of icons."

Inmates not only turn to mainstream religions in prison, but also to obscure theories and sects. According to one inmate, "We had a guy working in the library who found a book by some crazy magician, Mr. Lazarev. The inmate was obsessed with this [magician's] theory and forced everyone to read it. Many in fact did and also started following him, until they saw a program on TV that [proved] he was a charlatan."

In the case of Islam, inmates who want to turn to it (such as ethnic Muslims) are hijacked by Islamist veterans and their interpretation of the religion. And while the majority of inmates lack any real religious knowledge, those imprisoned on terrorism and extremism charges usually have at least some. And they successfully use it in their recruitment efforts, making other inmates approach them with spiritual questions.

According to one inmate with fighting experience in Syria, proselytization—or doing *dawah*—in Uzbekistan's main prison in Tashkent was a natural result of his own religious activity:

> In the beginning, I was praying by myself. But then someone gave me a book in Arabic, which I learned while fighting in Syria. So I started reading it out loud. It was just a normal religious book, not radical and not prohibited by prison rules, but I was reading it as one is supposed to read religious books—very nicely, melodically, and poetically. Then I noticed that two people in my cell started looking at me as if they saw something magical. I immediately understood that their hearts were open to religion, although both were in prison for killing people. So I asked, "Do you want me to teach you how to pray?" They agreed, and I first taught them how to pray and then told them more about religion.

Also, taking into account that *inmate* is a very specialized category of people, Islamist veterans carefully persuade inmates that their interpretation of religion is particularly catered to what they are looking for. According to an interviewed former drug addict inmate who claimed to convert to Islam in prison, "I stopped doing heroin, but in the afterlife, I can do as much heroin as I want to. I will do it from the boobs of *houris* [virgins who accompany the faithful in heaven] because it will be allowed there."

This first step in attracting inmates to Islam is easy because *ponyatiya* ensures freedom and respect of religion among inmates. For example, if there is a religious Muslim who does not smoke in a cell, others in the cell, out of respect, will only smoke next to the window or in the toilet area.

What is harder to do is to convert this interest into power for future *jamaat* leadership. To do this, Islamist veterans have to get inmates to start following Islam-inspired rules. One Islamist ex-foreign fighter (in Syria) who is now an inmate in Kyrgyzstan said criminals who self-identify as Muslims in Muslim-majority Kyrgyzstan would approach him with questions about religion and the afterlife. "That," he said, "is a great opportunity to explain why they need to start praying and then following Sharia law."[2]

However, getting inmates to move in that direction is not an easy task in black prisons under total control of criminal leadership. So to succeed, Islamists are very careful in their early attempts to exert influence. According to interviewed Islamists, there are several rules they have to follow to do dawah in black prisons.

One important element is showing inmates that their interpretation of Sharia law is, for the most part, in line with criminal rules. This keeps criminal family leadership from feeling threatened by an internal fifth column. And to illustrate their point, Islamists use examples of similar rules related to behavior with the enemy and inside the group. "We figured out that Sharia and criminal rules are very close," commented the Islamist inmate. "One could not kill and should not use swear words. According to Sharia, if a person steals something, his hand should be cut off, and by criminal rules, the thief's hand should be broken; in the criminal world if someone is lying, his jaw should be broken, and by Sharia, it is also punishable."

This approach of highlighting the parallels between the two sets of rules can be illustrated in the story of an Islamist inmate, an ex-foreign fighter in Syria, imprisoned in Kyrgyzstan. When he first got to prison, a criminal leader asked why he was in prison. I told him it was for fighting in Syria. The leader explained the criminal prison rules to the ex-fighter and said that he could pray and other "religious stuff" as long as he obeyed their rules. When the ex-fighter explained that he lived according to Sharia law, the criminal leadership initially saw him as a direct threat. But once the ex-fighter explained the substance of Sharia law, the laws appeared to be close to criminal laws, so they allowed them.

Criminal norms in such prisons also restrict what Islamists can say about their religion at this first phase. According to Islamist inmates, they can talk about praying five times a day and the importance of building a caliphate, but subjects like card playing, drinking, and smoking—all things prohibited by Sharia but allowed by prison criminal leadership—are taboo. Nothing they teach can go against criminal rules.

A second important element in the way Islamists veterans do dawah is also in line with *ponyatiya*'s basic rule of respect. For example, if someone does not want to talk to an Islamist veteran about religion, or criminal leadership has asked the veteran to stop doing so, he would apologize and leave. But Islamist veteran inmates quickly figure out how to get around that problem.

In one case, an Islamist veteran inmate was put in a cell with nine inmates. Since it was his first time in prison, he openly began doing *dawah*, and trying to enforce sharia law within his cell. He was immediately told to stop and not to express his opinion about how things were done unless he was asked. He complied immediately and switched tactics.

Without saying a word, this inmate began by quietly doing ablution in the cell. One of his cellmates who did not know what ablution was (but was an ethnic Muslim) asked the Islamist inmate to teach him how to do it. He did. The next day, two other cellmates asked him to teach them how to pray. Within a month, all nine of his cellmates were regularly praying.

So often the effectiveness of such insurgency-style *dawah* in such a complicated setting depends largely on the skill and creativity of the inmate doing it. Because, according to criminal rules, everyone has a right to their own opinion, one Islamist inmate in a black prison in Kyrgyzstan used that rule for *dawah*. Any time there was a party in his cell, he would tell his criminal cellmates, "Sharia law says that is prohibited, but this is your choice, and only you will have to answer for that [behavior] in front of God." He would then not participate by lying down on his bed and covering himself with a blanket.[3]

The next day during his prayers, he would pray loudly enough for all his cellmates to hear: "God, forgive the sins of people around me" (referring to the previous night's party). This showed the other inmates that the Islamist inmate cared enough about them to pray, and that was something they appreciated. As a result, the praying inmate's standing increased in the eyes of his cellmates, something that served to further that *jamaat*'s ultimate goal.

A third element in leading people closer to Sharia-inspired rules require introducing the ideology gradually. This makes its growth less visible to the criminal prison leadership. It is also more effective since any turn from one belief system to another is difficult for people to adapt to quickly.

This makes for interesting transitional stages where criminal and religious rules are mixed. For example, a person may be praying and conducting all the other mandatory rituals while at the same time hold a position in the criminal system that requires him to do things prohibited by *jamaat* rules. He may be a *smotryasçiy* in the prison criminal system and happily yelling "*Allahu Akbar*" when something important happens, but not praying or fasting during Ramadan; or he could be praying regularly but also smoking regularly; or he could get Islam-inspired tattoos instead of criminal ones. It is also not unusual to see inmates drinking *chifir'* and making toasts, the first-time toast with the cheer, "Life to *vory*," and the second time with, "Allahu Akbar."

All of these things—holding a position in the criminal government, not observing Ramadan, smoking, tattoos, and drinking—are all forbidden according to the Islamist interpretation of Islam, yet in the beginning, the compromises are allowed to persist because, according to Islamist inmates, if a person starts moving toward Islamic rules, customs, and habits, he will not turn back and will eventually completely abandon the criminal code.[4]

Basically, at this early stage of going from black to green, Islamist veteran inmates carefully follow criminal rules, pay attention to what is allowed and what is not, and try to fit *dawah* into the small space they are given. They are also trying to portray themselves as better human beings than those in the criminal leadership so that other inmates have a good opinion of them and the Islamism they represent.

Criminal World Perspective

At this point in an Islamist takeover, members of the criminal family have little understanding of a *jamaat*'s ultimate goal. As a result, they have no real means or desire of deterring them. According to *ponyatiya*, everyone is allowed to practice his religion and express his opinion. Islamist veterans take full advantage of these rules and are allowed to operate because they are not considered dangerous. It is only if they violate *ponyatiya* that they are punished by criminal leadership, just as any other inmate would be.

For example, once in Kyrgyzstan, an inmate with Syrian fighting experience was going to be moved to another prison. His relatives wanted him to stay close to home, so they made a deal with the prison manager for the inmate to stay. But in return, he had to work raising chickens for the prison kitchen. According to *ponyatiya*, this made him *sherst'*. Despite this arrangement, the inmate was eventually moved into another black prison where, because of his *sherst'* status, three criminal family inmates beat him by lifting him high in the air and throwing him down on the concrete three times.[5]

And under no circumstances are Islamists allowed to go against the decision of criminal family leadership, even if that decision is against their understanding of Islam. This was exemplified in one black prison in Central Asia when an inmate lost a lot of money playing cards and was not able to pay it back. According to *ponyatiya*, the offending inmate was to be beaten, but his Islamist cellmate tried to stop this beating, an act that is considered merciful according to Islamist beliefs but not allowed by criminal prison rules. So the Islamist was also beaten. In addition, when the gambler eventually died from the beating and someone had to take legal responsibility for the killing, it was a person with a life in prison sentence,[6] but the criminal prison leader decided the Islamist inmate should help the lifer until the end of the Islamist's sentence by doing things like sharing any food relatives might send him.

At the same time, while still strictly enforcing *ponyatiya* rules, criminal leadership also tries to accommodate Islamists in their growing demands, which still seem purely religious to the criminal leadership. This is illustrated in the story of two ethnic Muslims who, after being incarcerated, decided to become religious. When they realized that following Islam required them to be circumcised (and they were not), they looked online how to do it themselves, found and made all the required tools for the procedure, and conducted it in prison, assisting each other.

Had they done the circumcisions only to themselves and not to each other, everything would have been fine. But according to *ponyatiya*, touching someone else's penis is a gross violation of one of the most complicated ideological rules there is. As a consequence, the two men were immediately moved to the *sherst'* caste while this straightforward rule turned into a political debate that went outside of the prison, to high-level *vory*, to be decided. After more than six months of deliberations, the two inmates were declared innocent. The criminal leadership basically told them, "Okay, we should not draw our attention to this case, but please do not do it again," and offered them to move back to the *muzhiki* caste.[7]

This once incident shows how *ponyatiya* was bent to fit Islamist behavior. To further confirm it, I asked one of the criminal leaders involved in this decision what would have been the verdict if those inmates were not Muslims performing mutual circumcisions but regular criminal family inmates doing a very popular in-prison procedure called "balls," which is basically placing small polished plastic balls (made from, for example, a toothbrush handle) under the penis skin.[8] This is a very complicated procedure that is extremely difficult for a person to perform himself without assistance.[9] He replied that, in that case, there would have been no discussion. Both inmates would be degraded to *petukhi* right away because "Guys who did circumcision did it to be closer to God, while those who did balls did so for pleasure, like animals." This indicates that criminal leadership themselves made an exception for members of *jamaat* to violate *ponyatiya*, and by doing so, discounted their own ideology. In other cases, for example in prisons in Kazakhstan, prison criminal leadership did not downgrade inmates who violated criminal prison rules because they had been on *haj*, a Muslim religious pilgrimage, before being incarcerated. Because people who go on *haj* are very respected in the society, criminal leadership decided they could be excluded from some criminal rules.

Not having had previous experience with Islamists, criminal leadership makes a fatal mistake in assuming the main goal of Islamists is more religious freedom when it is, in fact, power. Their assumption is that by giving Islamists more concessions to their ideological demands, they will remain under criminal leadership, and prison criminal leadership is willing to do everything possible to keep them there. *Vory* leadership also try to incorporate them into prison decision making, so they will be more engaged with prison criminal values.

For example, while Islamists will not participate in elections for any key criminal positions in prison (considering elections against Islam), the criminal leader of the prison still demands their presence at those meetings because usually prison rules are being discussed there, and he wants Islamists to also know and follow them. And although Islamists do not vote, their opinion about appointments is both solicited and considered by the leadership.

Outside Perspectives

At this point, this silent Islamist insurgency is still considered minor, if visible at all, to prison authorities, and they have no intentions of getting involved. In truth, prison authorities have less understanding than the criminal leadership does at this stage. According to interviewed prison guards, they think it is just a religious question of several inmates and not a potential seed of a major problem. And because the rest of the related world outside of prisons—the media and NGOs—are not aware of those issues, these quiet movements attract no outside attention.

Phase Two: A Parallel Structure

Islamist Perspective

Once Islamists veterans have recruited a sizable following, phase two commences. At this point, a *jamaat* leader officially announces it existence, leadership, and rules. In some prisons, they physically segregate, for example, onto one floor or in one barrack. And all incoming inmates, while still on mandatory quarantine, have to decide with whom they want to live and, as a consequence, whose command they will be under. At that stage, *jamaat* leadership also often collects money and builds a mosque or praying room in prison to have a physical headquarters for their group.[10] And although it is officially a room for all Muslims in prison, it is often the case that it is used only by members of the *jamaat*, and other Muslims are prohibited from entering.

In addition to physical separation between Islamists and criminal leadership, separate jurisdictions also result. While *jamaat* leadership solves conflicts related to *jamaat* members (according to their interpretation of Sharia law), criminal leadership solves problems arising among the rest of the inmates. And according to one interviewed Islamist inmate, "We do not get into criminal rules and try to stay as far from them as possible." Similarly, only an *amir* can punish a member of a *jamaat*, and only a criminal leader can punish members of the rest of the prison population.

In one black prison, this separation of jurisdictions began the following way: two Muslim inmates got in conflict with each other. Like any inmate is supposed to do to solve it, they went through the whole chain of *smotryashchiye* and ended up asking the *polojenets*. He made a decision. Then thrity Muslim inmates with the imam of the prion mosque came to the *polojenets* and told him that the dispute was somehow connected to religion, so he had no authority making a judgment. He backed down from his ruling, although it is not clear why (whether he was bribed or threatened). From then on in that prison, Muslims solved their problems themselves without even the knowledge of criminal leadership.

Although at this point a *jamaat* has independent governance, in terms of economy, they are still freeloaders on the criminal family system. They withdraw from contributing to the mutual fund (claiming that it is against their religion), but still use the public goods provided by prison criminal leadership. This loophole allows *jamaats* to rapidly increase their own savings while depleting criminal organization finances.

Also, because the majority of inmates do not realize that provision and main governance is still the responsibility of criminal leadership, they begin to think the *jamaat* is a better option. After all, inmates do not experience the constant conflicts they associate with criminal leadership fundraising efforts with *jamaat* leadership, and they attribute that to *jamaats* being a superior system.

At this point, a new phase of more aggressive mass recruitment begins. For those who are being recruited, the draw is several benefits not available to them within the criminal family.

Personal Benefits

Because *jamaats* freeload on the public goods provided by prison criminal leadership, they are in a position to offer more benefits to *jamaat* members. In addition, Islamist inmates are, very often, wealthier than their low-level criminal counterparts. Usually, criminal family inmates are from poor families and have been in and out of prison their whole lives. Often, their families and friends turn away from them and do not support them financially.

However, many inmates doing time on extremism or terrorism charges are first-time offenders, and their families care about them deeply and show it in their financial support. And because the majority of inmates on those charges are from Caucasus, where being in prison is considered a regular occurrence, the inmate's whole family—and sometimes his whole home village—cares for him and sends financial support. One inmate explained that if an indigent inmate wants to eat something other than prison food, he can either turn to criminal leadership or turn to Islamists. The inmate explained: "If he turns to criminal leadership, they will most likely make him work for food [as a *snir*]. But if he turns to Islamists, the only thing he will be asked to do is prove he is an Islamist, which is basically praying. This is obviously much easier than working every day."

New Norms and Customs

Again, because *jamaats* are freeloading on what the criminal organization provides, they do not need to raise money among inmates—an activity that the general inmate population does not like. Of course, the criminal family makes inmates pay as long as they are part of their system, so for many of them, switching to the *jamaat* is, at least in part, a financial decision.

Another example of an undesirable, money-making criminal custom is gambling. Because it is a major source of income for prison criminal leadership, inmates are strongly encouraged to participate. But if an inmate identifies himself as a religious Muslim, he can avoid attending traditional night card games, claiming that gambling is against Islam. According to an interviewed Islamist inmate in prison in Kyrgyzstan, "There are low-level criminals who become religious simply to sleep at night and not have to play cards."

It is also a similar situation with other criminal-family mandated prison responsibilities. According to an interviewed *smotryasçiy*, self-centered inmates are especially likely to join: "They think, 'Why should I sleep during the day and not at night? Why should I take a shift standing next to the door to alert people when a prison guard is coming? Why should I take care of the road?' So those people, by joining the *jamaat* and claiming that those public good activities are against their religion, can avoid taking part in them and free ride."

Reputation

Because *jamaats* are very respected, many incoming inmates want to join simply to increase their status in front of peers (inside and outside of prison). One interviewed inmate observed that at one prison in Dagestan, the majority of new inmates were joining the *jamaat* instead of the criminal world: "These were young guys with petty charges like stealing, but they found it cool to be in an Islamist *jamaat*. They did not even follow all the rules [they were secretly smoking in the restroom], but were proudly telling their friends that they were religious Muslims suffering in prison for their religion and that their *amir* is a veteran of jihad."

Protection

Because of their separate standing and a respected position, *jamaats* start offering protection to inmates from the upper caste who are not satisfied with their treatment in the criminal family. Who are upper caste inmates who feel discriminated against by criminal leadership and are looking for protection?

Drug Dealers. By prison criminal rules, people on drug charges are considered the lowest in the upper (*muzhiki*) caste, and usually have to pay a special tax to the criminal mutual fund. They are obviously not satisfied with that situation, but they cannot do much about it inside the criminal organization. In addition, those people are often long-time drug addicts, which makes them especially psychologically weak and unable to dispute their position. So becoming a *jamaat* member not only means a step up on the prison's social ladder (since members of the *jamaat* are considered regular members of the *muzhiki* caste), but it also protects them from the criminal leadership's imposed tax. One interviewed Christian inmate in on drug charges explained it this way:

> Drug dealers who come to the prison camp are immediately pressed for money. And many, right away, understand that those drug dealers who become religious Muslims have a much better life than the others. [When they convert,] the prison criminal leadership immediately stops harassing them. Maybe there are people who really start believing in Allah after they get here, but when a drug dealer tells me (another drug dealer) that, for a long time, he was choosing between Christianity and Islam, and then in his sleep he saw the crescent and decided that the right choice is Islam—sorry, but I just do not buy it.

And since the war on drugs began in the early 2000s, drug dealers have become a large chunk of the prison inmate population, the majority of which are ethnic Muslims from Central Asia.[11] Their membership in *jamaats* significantly increases its numbers.

Sniri. These inmates are in a similar position to drug dealers. Although they are still considered members of the upper (*muzhiki*) caste, they are not highly respected in the criminal hierarchy and have to work basically as servants. So membership in the *jamaat* is also the only way for them to improve their situation. In a prison in Chechnya, there was a normal but very weak inmate. He did not talk much, and if you asked him something, his answer would be hard to understand. The criminal leadership made him a *snir*, but then the *jamaat* guys took him in. When criminal leadership noticed it and asked the guy, "Why didn't you cook us dinner or clean?" the *jamaat* guys said, "He was praying with us." The *blatnyje* had nothing to say about that, and let the guy go.

And *jamaats* do not just depend on their reputation to bring people in. Members make it a habit to approach newcomers. A new inmate comes in and is, understandably, very frightened by the environment. So members of the *jamaat* first invite him to their table, offer tea and food if he does not have any, and then offer to help with something like getting a cell phone to call his family. Next, they give him religious literature to read, motivating him by saying that in prison, he has tons of time to read. And finally, he joins the *jamaat*.

If an inmate in the *jamaat* gets in trouble with the criminal system, the *jamaat* will protect him whether he is right or wrong. Islamists also often tell inmates that when they finish their prison sentences, their Muslim brothers will not leave them but will continue to help them. And this also becomes a very important selling point for an inmate who has no family and nowhere to live once he is freed.

Separate Jurisdiction

Jamaats also target other inmates who do not agree with their position in the criminal caste system. But because this system is a cornerstone of criminal prison ideology, *jamaat* leadership still proceed with great caution. In the example above, Islamists were recruiting inmates low in the *muzhiki* caste, but *muzhiki* is still considered an upper caste.

The situation is different with the lower castes. Because *jamaat* members are still very careful about how far they stretch *ponyatiya* and criminal leadership patience, they do not reach out to lowest caste, per se. To do so would violate one of the most ingrained criminal rules, and they are not strong enough to challenge the criminal system on that level. And it is not even a case in a particular prison but in the ex-Soviet Union prison system in general. For example, according to an interviewed member of the *jamaat*, "We are not against taking people, even from *petukhi*, but what will happen if we do so? They will be hanging out with us. And then what if one of us is moved to another, very black, prison? It will be very bad for him there."

Jamaats will, however, offer an opportunity to convert to Islam and join the *jamaat* to inmates about to be degraded to the lower caste but are not there yet. At that time, this inmate is still in the upper caste, but it is obvious he made a big mistake, and being degraded is just a matter of the time it takes the *polojenets* to get to his case. So there is a window of opportunity while the *polojenets* is still busy and has not made a decision.

In one of the black prisons in Russia, a Christian inmate stole someone's cigarettes.[12] Based on the criminal rules, he becomes a rat and should be kicked out of the *muzhiki* caste and into the *sherst'*. But before the whole investigation was over, *jamaat* leaders came to him and offered him protection if he would convert to Islam. He did convert, and *jamaat* leaders gave their word for him and saved him from being downgraded. Soon that inmate was actively propagating Islamism.

At the same time, *jamaats* still do not cross caste boundaries, so if an actual member of *sherst'* says he is a religious Muslim now, often members of the *jamaat* congratulate him, but they still keep him at a distance and do not take him inside the *jamaat*. And when *petukhi* become religious, they pray separately.[13] Also, members of the *jamaat* will greet these converts with the Islamic greeting, "*Salam* [Peace]," but not with "Hi" and "How are you doing?"

According to an Islamist veteran member of one of the most powerful *jamaats* in Russian prisons, "*Petukhi*, even if they become religious Muslims, should be praying separately. If one person's actions will cause problems for his brothers [Muslims], he has to avoid those actions. So he has to understand that in the current situation [in former Soviet Union corrections system], he cannot be praying with us."

In this second phase, while *jamaats* already have more to offer than in the first phase, they still do not require much of converts (although more than in the first phase), especially anything that would be counterproductive to long-term plan of power. Since converting to Islam and joining a *jamaat* actually has little to do with Islam as a religion—it is more about being part of an organization with Islam-inspired rules—the only thing required is an inmate's outward demonstration of dedication. He has to pray five times a day; fast during Ramadan; refrain from drinking alcohol, smoking, and gambling; start using Arabic words instead of criminal slang, especially in greetings; and perhaps change his name. All this signals an inmate's membership in the group.

And such lack of conviction in *jamaats* is common knowledge among inmates. One ethnic Muslim member of the prison criminal leadership openly mocked new members of the *jamaat* and told the story of a group of Buryats (half of them Buddhists and half pagans) who converted to Islam and joined the *jamaat*. Yet they had no idea about Islam and were barely able to memorize *shahada*. All they really wanted was to live separately (*jamaat* had its own barrack), have more freedom (not strict *ponyatiya*), and enjoy better food. They were also very surprised (and upset) when they found out smoking was not prohibited in the *jamaat*. Despite publicly calling them brothers (fellow Muslims) out of respect, no one in or outside of the *jamaat* took them seriously.

Because *jamaats* are an easy alternative to the criminal system, the quality of recruits decreases significantly in phase two of a *jamaat*'s development, and the dedication level becomes either equal or lower to that of the parallel criminal hierarchy. As a result, inmate behavior becomes worse and harder for *jamaat* leadership to control.

Criminal World Perspective

By this point in phase two, the criminal family leadership clearly understands that they are rapidly losing power, and that the shift is getting dangerous for them.

First, they realize they are being used by the *jamaats*. *Jamaat* inmates do not contribute to *obshyak* like the other inmates do, yet they are still benefiting from the public-goods provision. They also do not work criminal jobs, like on the roads, yet they still use them. Criminal world inmates also complain that *jamaat* members do not support criminal members who are in inner prison, but when their *jamaat* members are there, they receive support from criminal leadership. And it is not only about the money for the goods to support *jamaat* inmates. A criminal family inmate also takes the risk of being caught and punished for delivering goods there.

According to an interviewed inmate, "Our internal prison criminal system is like a labor union. Some people leave it, and it is immediately beneficial for them. But in the long run, it is bad for them and for everyone else."

Second, because of the different jurisdictions, the *polojenets* finds he is losing control of what is going on with all the inmates, yet he is still responsible for all of them before the prison authorities. This is a problem not only for the prison criminal leadership, but for all inmates.

Third, the inmates who have remained under the authority of the criminal leadership become extremely dissatisfied with the situation. One Christian drug dealer wrote a lengthy message about the issue that was widely distributed among inmates:

> While we are always told that, in prison, we are all equal under the *vor*, where is it [the equality]? Why do drug dealers who turn Muslim live a normal life and drug dealers who do not turn Muslim are discriminated against? We had a new guy on 228 [drug charge according to Russian criminal code]. He absolutely denied that he was selling drugs and claimed he was just a drug user who was set up by the police. After several days, we get a call from the jail where he was before that said this guy was lying and needed to be punished. His parents are rich, so he gave someone [in prison criminal leadership] money and was left in the *muzhiki* caste. But now he had two problems in his bio: 1) he is drug dealer and 2) he lied. So he turned to Islam.

> Soon two respected Muslims—one from Dagestan and one Russian convert—came to the *smotryasçiy* of our barrack and told him, "Because this new drug dealer guy is our brother [Muslim], we want him to be put on the first level of the bunk bed near the Dagestani guy." And the *smotryasçiy* agreed! But how is that fair?
>
> I have been in prison for four years, actively involved in its life [helping criminal leadership run it], and I was offered a low-level bunk bed only half a year ago. And even older people not on drug charges who have been here for more than five years could not get that place.
>
> So we even had a meeting for people on drug charges who did not turn to Islam [and stayed with criminal leadership], to discuss such discrimination. I proposed a strike. If we are bound according to *ponyatiya*, we also need to use it to our advantage. For example, when we are told to do something like make *chifir'*, we should answer, "Of course, no problem." But why am I doing it for like the fifteenth time while Mohamed or Ali (hypothetical Muslims) are never asked to do it?
>
> If *ponyatiya* says that everyone is equal, it should be the case. But of course, drug dealers are afraid that they would be threatened or even beaten, so everyone [criminal family inmates] is still just sitting here quietly increasing grievance inside and not doing anything in protest.

At this point, however, there is little criminal leadership can do to peacefully reverse the process, because not only it is hard to change *ponyatiya*, but some aspects of it—like making drug dealers pay extra to the *obshyak* (a big selling point for the *jamaat*)—are essential for funding prison-wide goods.

To make things worse, since criminal leadership and many inmates already understand where the *jamaat* movement is going, they are afraid of what is to come. Although they are still not showing any hostility toward the criminal world or other inmates, everyone is already cautious about them. According to a regular inmate, "Those people in *jamaats* behave very respectively, are groomed, and dress nicely. But looking in their eyes, I am sure they could kill me anytime they wanted without any hesitation."

Outside Perspectives

Phase two is also when conflict between prison administration and the *jamaat* begins. When the criminal world had the monopoly on prison life, the majority of inmate-prison authority disagreements—in addition to crucial issues such as beating, torture, and money extortion—were over symbolic problems crucial to A.U.E. ideology; things like the way an inmate made his bed, using different tableware for different castes, and skipping mandatory morning physical exercises. Now *jamaats* start asking for their own ideological demands. Regular demands include cooking their own halal food (though cooking in the cell is prohibited by prison rules) and having scheduled time for pray five times a day (which also goes against official prison schedule).

While both groups of inmates will usually protest together for general demands and to defend their human rights, how those groups treat the ideological demands of the other is more nuanced. Criminal world inmates will stand up for the Islamists' religious demands, but the other way around is not always assured. For example, in one prison, authorities did a search in the *jamaat* room and disrespected a religious book the Muslim inmates had. When members of the *jamaat* started complaining and were beaten by guards, criminal inmates immediately came to their defense and started a riot. And interviewed *jamaat* members said that it is exactly what criminal leadership was supposed to do because it is their job to defend all the inmates. But members of *jamaats* do not always help criminal leadership do so.

In some prison *jamaats*, *jamaat* leadership understand that if they do not help criminals defend their ideological demands, prison authorities would later refuse Islamists their own demands. In prison was in Karelia (IK7), there was a problem with tableware. Prison authorities wanted upper-caste inmates to eat from the same tableware as *petukhi*, which was absolutely unacceptable. And the *jamaat* members totally agreed with criminal leadership on this issue. They thought that if prison authorities were making this move now, later they would not allow them to fast during Ramadan. So an aspiring young member of a criminal family and a Dagestani member of the *jamaat* (sentenced for supporting terrorism) were the first people to start a hunger strike in protest, and prison guards even ended up force-feeding them.

But in other cases, despite being helped by prison criminal administration, *jamaat* members will try to hurt criminals by not helping them demand more from prison administration and not even respecting already hard-won criminal demands. According to a Chechen (ethnic Muslim) inmate who was a *smotryasçiy* in a cell, the main problem with Islamists was they freely give prisons guards what has cost the criminal world blood for years. For example, it is a norm not to report to a prison guard when he enters a cell. Prison guards tried to force criminal inmates to do it, but they eventually gave up. In a cell where half the members were the *jamaat* and the other half members of the criminal world, the *jamaat* simply do not care. They had signed an agreement (with prison guards) about obeying internal prison rules, so they do report to guards when they enter a cell.

But for criminals, this is unimaginable, which creates conflict within the cell. Prison authorities see this division and start using the divide-and-conquer tactic and say that if everyone does not sign the agreement, they will take something from the cell like a TV or a refrigerator.

Because a basic tenant of the criminal world is that an individual is ready to suffer for all inmates, they will not sign. But, according to Chechen inmate, *jamaat* members will not stand with them because they care only about themselves or maybe other members of the *jamaat*.

Conclusion

Starting with strong, respected Islamist leadership—who from the very beginning exploited the liberties of *ponyatiya*—the *jamaat* structure was able to separate from the criminal one. At first, criminal leadership did not understand what was going on and believed Islamists just wanted more religious freedom. And even if criminal leadership was not happy with this arrangement, according to *ponyatiya*, the religious freedoms of inmates had to be respected. As a result, this rule provided a window of opportunity for a religious (on the surface) organization that would later develop into a parallel power.

Then, as a relatively small, separate organization belonging to the general inmate population, they were able to freeload on the public goods still provided by criminal leadership, using religion as an excuse for doing so. This gave *jamaats* time and opportunity to become even stronger and more respected because they required no money or responsibility from the prison population. Also, since they already separated from prison criminal leadership, they started recruiting individuals who felt discriminated in the prison criminal hierarchy and by that, significantly increased their ranks and became a serious challenger to the *vory* monopoly of prisons in the former Soviet Union.

13
Jamaat Conflict with the Criminal Organization

Starting with the description of the *jamaat* lifespan, in the previous chapter I talked about how *jamaats* rose to power and secured their existence outside of the prison criminal leadership control. In this chapter, I will continue this discussion and talk about how as *jamaats* underwent ideologization, it made them weaker. Step by step, I will look at how, after securing their independence from the *vory* criminal family, they increased in their internal problems and the conflicts it led to in prisons.

Phase Three: A Shift of Power

Islamist Perspective

By this point, the *jamaat* already has a strong position in relation to both the prison criminal leadership and prison authorities and can now enforce their own rules in prisons and even on the prison's criminal world. And this has been their goal from the beginning: to increase their own well-being, to decrease the well-being of the competitors—the criminal family community, and to become the only real force in the prison. This is done two different ways, either peacefully or by force.

Muslim-Majority Regions

In Muslim-majority regions, *jamaats* very quietly enforce their Islamized rules on the rest of the inmate society, and basically push the criminal world to be ideologically closer to *jamaats*. Their end goal is to slowly raise the level of Islamization in the criminal world and to squeeze out *vory* ideology and ideological rules altogether. The other option is to keep an Islamized version of criminal ideology but distance their prison from the rest of the criminal world.

As a first step in prisons with a Muslim-majority population, *jamaats* usually lobby to get rid of some of the *vory* criminal world traditions prison-wide. For example, in Chechnya, the Muslim majority successfully prohibited any form of homosexuality, one of the oldest traditions in the criminal world. That meant

Criminals, Nazis, and Islamists. Vera Mironova, Oxford University Press. © Oxford University Press 2023.
DOI: 10.1093/oso/9780197645659.003.0014

that even though the caste system and *petukhi* remained, no one was allowed to have sex with them.

Jamaats also put increasing physical pressure on those who still follow unacceptable criminal prison traditions. For example, when a self-identified Muslim from Tatarstan who was not religious (drank alcohol and did not pray) was imprisoned, he started earning his living by doing tattoos. But soon he was pressured by members of the *jamaat*. They told him that by Sharia, tattoos were prohibited. He refused to stop, however, so they started beating him regularly.

And in some cases, like one prison in Chechnya, the Islamist leadership basically separated the prison criminal leadership from the bigger criminal family. In those prisons, there often are no *progons* from *vory*, which in other prisons are mandatory. Islamist leadership explained that having such a *vory* statement is *shirk* (polytheism) and, as a result, not acceptable.

So even if in such prisons some attributes of the criminal word remain (such as a simplified caste system), with time, the criminal hierarchy gradually follows the same ideological rules of the *jamaats*. And in doing that, *jamaats* inherit all the public goods provision infrastructure from criminals and continue supporting it without decreasing the quality of life for the inmate population.

On the leadership level, they also reach an agreement, and, according to members of the criminal world, ethnic Muslim *vory* from the Muslim-majority regions help mediate conflicts between *jamaats* and the criminal world. In return, outside of prisons, *jamaats* often help criminals by serving as militia.

Non-Muslim Regions

Prisons in non-Muslim-majority regions, however, have a very different situation. In those regions, Islamists take power by force. They understand that they will not be able to turn everyone to their interpretation of Islam simply because some inmates are devout Christians or Buddhists. Their plan then is to subdue the prison criminal leadership by fear. So in these regions, their strategy is to simply make the criminal leadership as weak as possible and dependent on the *jamaats* for all rules and decisions. There are several strategies a *jamaat* uses, individually and in tandem, to turn the tables on the criminal family. They do so by targeting three main areas: the money, the ideological rules, and the traditions.

First, in previous phases, *jamaats* were only peacefully withdrawing from prison criminal mutual fund contributions and growing a fund of their own. Now they feel strong enough to openly stand up against the whole prison criminal economy system. They begin with free trade, which is prohibited by prison criminal rules. This move both substantially increases *jamaat* income and drastically alters the criminal economy.

Jamaats also sabotage the criminal communication system (the road) by "freezing" cells, meaning they do not participate in passing messages and packages. This is a big problem because, in many cases, some cells can only be reached through other cells, and when cells are frozen, other cells suffer, which is a problem for the whole communication network. Here again, *jamaat* members use religion as an excuse. After all, there may be drugs and cigarettes in those packages, and it is against Islam to take part in delivering them.

Members of the *jamaat* may even try to sabotage everyday prison activates with the sole purpose of demonstrating their power. For example, according to an interviewed inmate, "In my prison, a *jamaat* leader gave an order that if Muslims [members of *jamaat*] are in the cell with members of the criminal hierarchy, they should not clean the cell, even if all inmates take turns doing so."

Another way *jamaats* sabotage the criminal family is by ending the ideological transition phase during which inmates are allowed to combine both Islamist and criminal ways of life. Now they want the boundary of the *jamaat* clearly demarcated, meaning that its members have to fully turn to the *jamaat* way of life and reject the criminal world's ways. We see this in a teaching from one of the Islamist sheiks, widely distributed online:

> *Dim* [Arabic word for religion] does not only mean official religion like Christianity and Buddhism, but it is any system of rules and laws that guide a person in his life. So for the religion of criminals, people who make rules and say what is allowed and what is not are criminal leadership. As a result, it is clear that those who live in prison according to criminal rules set by *kafir* leadership are mushriks, even if they pray, fast in Ramadan and say that that they are Muslims. . . . Those [criminal] people have two faces and, as a result, are *munafics*. Those people do not consider it prohibited to defend the honor of a criminal leader in a fight, and some of them go even further and attack Muslims who try to stand up against criminal rules. And then there are cases when a Muslim refuses to defend the honor of a criminal leader. Then those fake Muslims [members of criminal world who self-identify as Muslims] could beat the true Muslim for that, simply because he went against those devil traditions.
>
> Those fake Muslims are almost not distinguishable from *kafirs* because they are emulating them in everything: clothes, manners, words, shaving their beards, wearing long pants, and everything else.

A final strategy is to maximize the size of the *jamaat* by both lowering their recruitment standards and breaking the cornerstone of the criminal caste system at the same time. Because everyone who was willing to join the *jamaat* from upper castes has already done so, the *jamaat* begins to accept inmates from the lower caste. Even though *jamaat* leadership understands that many of those people were moved to a lower caste for a reason, they are willing to take a chance and admit them. According to an interviewed member of *jamaat*, "We know that those people made some mistakes in the past, but they are not a problem for a well-run *jamaat*. They could still be useful or, at least, increase our numbers."

Using the equality of Muslims in Islam as an explanation, *jamaats* accept members of the *sherst'*—and even in some cases *petukhi*—caste within their ranks and start treating them as equals. This swell in ranks leads to increasing ideologization and a laundry list of problems for *jamaat*'s internal operations.

First, the quality of *jamaat* members becomes lower than that of the criminal organization because, by definition, it accepts those who were on the lowest rung of the criminal ladder.[1] Also because those new members of *jamaat* do not care about Islam—and only use privileges that *jamaat* leadership originally won for them—they start misbehaving, doing things like watching porn or doing drugs in the prison mosque (prison guards are less likely to search for contraband there).

As a result, to monitor commitment and control group membership, *jamaat* leadership has to tighten the screws. So *jamaats* starts enforcing strict and mandatory requirements inspired by the ideology, including religious classes with exams and a strict prohibition on drinking and smoking, rapidly ideologizing the group. With time, those rules also become counterproductive.

Second, because *jamaats* recruited inmates who were kicked out from the upper level of the criminal hierarchy (such as drug dealers, *sniri*, *sherst'*, and even occasionally *petukhi*), those inmates have an increasing grievance against the criminal leadership. If originally, *jamaat* leadership mostly wanted to take the power inside the prison, now *jamaats* members also want revenge on criminal leadership. And because *jamaats* have separate jurisdiction and protect its members, some members of the *jamaat* feel empowered to attack members of criminal hierarchy, which increases tension between the two groups.

Third, the overall situation for all inmates in the prison rapidly deteriorates. The quality of the goods provision decreases for the whole prison. Although *jamaats* themselves are not capable of governing the prison and providing public goods, they will not help criminal leadership do it. Not only that, they actively sabotage the system.

Also, *jamaat* inexperience in prison governance and building relations with prison guards leads to the increase of prison authority power, which hurts all inmates. In one prison, to decrease the prison guards' motivation to do searches, the *polojenets* prohibited inmates from buying back phones that had been confiscated. Members of the *jamaat*, however, completely ignored the order and were still buying them. This behavior obviously led to more searches and confiscations.

Interestingly, real Islamists, those with insurgency fighting experience, become increasingly disappointed in *jamaats* at this point and leave by turning back to the criminal hierarchy. One Islamist veteran of the Second Chechen War, who is seventeen years into his sentence, lives with members of the criminal family. According to him, "We have those so-called *jamaats* who live according to imaginary Islam mixed with prison culture. They are like kids in a kindergarten, so normal people should simply ignore them."

This exodus from the criminal word to the *jamaats* has two major consequences. First, it further decreases the *jamaats* average quality of the membership. According to an ethnic Muslim inmate who has spent more than ten of the last twenty years behind bars, "At first, prison *jamaats* were real *jamaats*. They had substance. But later, all of it was wasted. Now it is like a parody of its past self."

Second, as departing senior members vacate *jamaat* leadership positions, those looking for power inside the *jamaat* are promoted. They are not qualified to run the *jamaat* but are being selected because they managed to portray extreme religiosity. As a result, not only are all previously mentioned problems compounded, but the corruption within the *jamaat* also increases. If the original *jamaat* founders were very modest and more interested in the well-being of their members, now *jamaat* leaders are only interested in luxury for themselves. For example, they surround themselves with *sniri* who cook and do other work for them. Basically, they begin to repeat the same mistakes the *vory* criminal organization did before them, and it leads to the same consequences.

Criminal World Perspective

In Muslim-majority regions, the criminal hierarchy slowly becomes more Islamized and, as a result, separates from the rest of the criminal world outside. They do not have conflicts with the *jamaat*, and the boundaries between *jamaat* and criminal family are blurred. But this is not the case in non-Muslim regions. Those prisons experience real tension between decreasing criminal leadership and increasing *jamaat* power.

In those prisons, the discontent among inmates in the criminal hierarchy is extremely high. As a result, criminal leadership tries to keep the peace by stabilizing relationships with their remaining inmates and not reacting to provocations from the side of Islamists. For example, once a conflict started in a prison in Sverdlovsk region. A senior criminal leader in Krasnoyarsk wrote in a *progon* that "There is only one set of rules in prison, and there should be no differences by nationality and religion. And we have to keep it that way."

This reply was in response to criminal leader attempts to change prison rules because Muslim inmates objected to them. Examples mentioned in the *progon* were conflicts about pork being cut in the kitchen, making knives dirty for Muslims; and going to the communal shower naked—Muslims were taking showers in their underwear and made others do the same. At the end of the address, it highlighted that top ethnic Muslim *vory* would be working on solving this problem.

On the other side, some prisons' criminal leaders tried other ways to reduce the power of *jamaats* and their ideology by copying an official prison strategy used against A.U.E. ideology. In one case, an inmate member of the *jamaat* from Dagestan was moved to a different black prison, and the *blatnyje* there tried to force him to sign a prison statement (*molyava*) that he "recognizes criminal ideology as his only ideology." The *jamaat* member refused, saying, "I do not live according to the imaginary rules of people, but only by the rules of God. And this is not your territory, but the whole world, including this prison, is God's territory." A conflict started, but he was lucky there was another Muslim who knew criminal rules and norms very well and managed to settle the conflict for him.

However, when the situation has reached this phase, it is a common opinion among prison criminal leadership that only very radical actions will bring the prison back into the hands of the criminal world. For one interviewed *blatnoj* inmate, the biggest problem with Muslims was them allowing *sherst'* and *petukhi* to become equal to *muzhiki*. According to him, doing so empowers *sherst'* to take revenge and collapses the whole criminal social order. Because of this *jamaats*, according to the *blatnoj*, can only be dealt with by careful force, so the situation does not turn into a full-scale war in and outside of the prison.

So the only thing criminal leadership can really do at this point is damage control and try to negotiate with *jamaats* to foster a peaceful coexistence. However, now criminal leadership tries to do so from a weaker position. A sure sign of this is criminal leadership often trying to work in line with Sharia-inspired rules, a reversion of what the *jamaat* did when it was operating within the framework of *ponyatiya*.

One *smotryasçiy* explained how, in his thirty-person cell, there was one very young Islamist. He refused to participate in the life of the cell or do anything for the benefit of other inmates. The majority others in the cell were regular elderly blue-collar workers who have been in prison criminal life for a long time. They understand why criminal world norms were in place, and they respected them. They contributed to the cell mutual fund and worked on the "road." But the young Islamist did nothing but sleep, or talk on his phone the whole day, because, according to his understanding of Islam, everything is *haram*. "So how, as a *smotryasçiy*, should I solve this conflict and explain what is going on to the others in the cell?" complained the *smotryasçiy*. "It is my job to deal with it, so I have to find a way to compromise between what is needed for the cell and his religious ideas. We did make a deal that he would contribute to the mutual fund, but only to things that are not *haram*."

Outside Perspectives

At this point, prison *jamaats* become very visible and draw attention from several sources. Prison authorities, both local and regional, become aware, and as information about them spreads, often the Federal Security Services, NGOs, and media also get involved. Then the issue goes to the national agenda.

Despite their competition for internal power, both the criminal world and *jamaats* do have the same main enemy—prison authorities—and they still cooperate when it comes to resisting them. So in conflicts with the authorities (on issues not related to ideology), *jamaat* and criminal-world members usually stand side by side. One interviewed inmate described the situation as "a turtle swimming across a dangerous river with a poisonous snake on its back. If either the turtle tries to throw off the snake, or the snake tries to bite the turtle, they will both drown. So they just keep moving together."

For example, one of the reasons a *jamaat* does not want to officially take control of the prison and unseat the *polojenets* (even a puppet one) is because then prison authorities will take a strong action against them, and the *jamaat* will suffer. According to an interviewed inmate, "The *jamaat* needs the *polojenets* because without him, there would be problems with prison authorities, and the prison would be made red, and there would be no *jamaat*."

So why do *jamaats* still need the criminal family as a buffer between them and prison authorities? There are several reasons. First, prison *jamaats* are still a relatively new entity, and they have less experience in building dialogue with administration, which makes them less effective than criminal leadership in major protests.

Second, prison authorities are often afraid of conducting negotiations directly with *jamaats* because of their Islamist and terrorist affiliations. They are also afraid of how it will be seen by the Department of Corrections. At one point, a prison in Nalchik was under total control of Islamists on terrorism charges. When an inspector from Moscow came and asked the warden how the situation was, he replied, "Everything is fine. We are in agreement with them [inmates]." Although this would have been an acceptable reply if the criminal family inmates were in control, the inspector was furious and fired the whole prison leadership. Authorities in Moscow simply could not understand how prison authorities could dare to make the same agreements and give the same concessions to so-called terrorists as they do to the criminal family.

Because members of a *jamaat* understand this negative view of them, they usually do not attempt mass resistance. For example, even in the prison in Chechnya where the *jamaat* was undoubtedly the strongest entity when a riot happened,[2] it was led by the *polojenets* and members of the *jamaat* faded into the general mass of the prison population.

Third, according to Islam, self-harm and suicide are forbidden. As a result, it puts restrictions on one of the most successful resistance tactics among inmates: cutting their veins ad stomachs. However, as long as the *polojenets* is in charge, general inmates can continue to use this tactic.

Finally, since prison guards are often afraid of *jamaat* members and do not understand how to negotiate with them, they are more likely to apply excessive force if they lead a riot. This played out in 2016 in red prison IK-25 in Hakasia, where 50 percent of the inmates identify as Muslims. An Islamist *jamaat* started a riot, and, according to local law enforcement, the leadership of the *jamaat* were citizens of Kyrgyzstan, Armenia, and Tajikistan, who were there for low-level criminal activity like stealing cars, robbery, and theft. They were also joined by inmates from the criminal hierarchy and totaled around 250 people. They threatened to cut their veins, and their demands were the following: permission to pray any time of the day, no wearing patches with prison identification numbers, no closing the top shirt button, no working in prison because it was against religion, and permission to smoke inside the buildings.

For one night, more than 100 inmates held control of the sleeping quarters in one of the prison buildings. Through the local media, the government announced that inmates were trying to get cell phones inside the prison so they could connect with other prisons in the region and start a mass uprising.

Members of the SWAT team who came to retake control tried to negotiate with prisoners, but those negotiation did not bear any fruit because, according to one prison official, "The religious group did not follow traditional criminal-administration-relation norms, so the usual negotiations techniques and compromises were not successful. Storming the building was required." A SWAT team then climbed to the third floor and used gas explosives to disorient rebels inside. From the ground, they were supported by cold water from water cannons.

Later, one of the members of prison administration openly explained, "Islamists are the least controllable group of inmates. Because they do not drink or smoke or take drugs, it is very hard to reach an agreement with them. In addition, because they are not following criminal rules [which prevent inmates from complaining to authorities], they constantly complain to correction authorities and to human rights activists."

Phase Four: War

Many prisons in Muslim-majority regions quietly and peacefully turn green as the border between the criminal family and *jamaat* is blurred, and there are no conflicts between the two groups. But prisons in non-Muslim regions—where the only way for *jamaats* to take control is by force—the situation becomes more complicated, and tension between the inmate groups runs very high.[3]

Jamaat Inmate Perspective

Many inmates join the *jamaat* because of the discrimination they experienced under criminal leadership. As a result, members of the *jamaat* (from the lowest member to leadership) feel extreme animosity toward the criminal family. For example, in many prisons, Islamists intentionally irritate inmates left in the criminal hierarchy. For example, before each of the five prayers, there is an *azan* (call for prayer), and after each prayer, there is a call between prison cells of "Allahu Akbar." By initiating these calls daily, *jamaats* signal their size and cohesion.

Some members of a *jamaat* outside of the prison go even further and record threatening video messages and circulate them within prisons. For example, on one of those videos, a person wearing a mask and a combat uniform and holding an automatic rifle is filmed in a forest, declaring a death sentence to *vory* and prison criminal leadership.

Jamaat members are also willing to act on their grievances. But that is only half of their motivation. The other half is fear. These inmates fear being kicked out of the *jamaat*—which would leave them defenseless against the criminal hierarchy and their retribution—so they are very loyal to *jamaat* leadership and will follow any orders just to remain a part.

This loyalty plays out in many ways. Although according to Islam, all Muslims are equal, an unofficial caste system also exists in *jamaats*. And with increasing ideologization of the *jamaat*, the caste becomes more and more visible. For example, even though a *jamaat* contains inmates from all ethnicities, inmates from the Caucasus are still most often in leadership positions, as are people with previous fighting experience.[4]

As a result, those lower on the ladder are willing to do anything to increase their status. This is particularly the case for those who have no fighting experience and have converted to Islam in order to join the *jamaat*. These inmates often feel an additional pressure to prove they are no less Muslim than their ethnic Muslim brothers.

Leadership then often uses this loyalty to further their power. For example, they rely on these inmates to provoke conflict with criminal family members. According to interviewed ex-inmates, this consists of leadership usually telling these inmates something like, "That person [criminal family inmate] does not like Allah." This is enough to provoke those inmates to action. And although they will be most likely punished, it does not bother them. They get defender-of-the-religion status, which increases their reputation, not only inside the prison *jamaat*, but often in the outside Islamist community.

One interviewed inmate explained how leadership capitalizes on this loyalty. They often target physically strong, non-ethnic Muslims to convert to Islam, so they can join the *jamaat*. Then they use them for the dirty and dangerous jobs. The inmate explained, "I saw how the *jamaat* in my prison used a young, stupid Russian convert to start a conflict with criminal leadership. As expected, he was very seriously beaten, but *jamaats* did not care since it was basically what they wanted." Afterward the *jamaat* hailed him as a hero for defending the religion, but it was clear to the interviewed inmate the convert was only being used.

Criminal Inmate Perspective

Regular inmates on the criminal side are extremely disappointed with the parallel structure's double standard and their leadership's waning authority. In particular, they are irate about those once in the lowest caste now demanding to be treated equally and often using their *jamaat* status to settle old scores. This causes individual conflicts almost every day. In one prison in Nalchik, there was a despised member of the *sherst'* caste who turned to Islamism and became a leader in the *jamaat*. Once the *polojenets* bribed a prison guard to be let through the fence to another part of prison, and there he stabbed this *amir* in his leg with a knife. In fact, he had tried to kill him, but prison guards stopped him.

On their other side, the criminal world's hands are tied. Not only can they not put *jamaat* inmates in their place, they cannot even afford an equal action against these provocations because they are afraid of escalation. Any escalation, they understand, will lead to causalities, increased prison sentences, prison guards tightening the screws, and the prison becoming red. Not only that, but because they are still officially in charge of the prison population, they would be blamed for any conflict.

The Clash

By this point, both groups understand the volatility of the situation and have no illusions about how long the thinning veneer of peaceful coexistence will last. Both groups prepare for the possibility of a big confrontation. This preparation includes making homemade knives and other weapons that might be needed for mass fighting. In addition, the *jamaats* up their emphasis on physical performance. For the members of the *jamaat*, playing sports is an important aspect of their life in prison, and they practice their sport very hard.[5]

And as predicted, in 2017, one prison conflict exploded with such force that it went from being first a prison-, then a country-, and finally to a region-wide problem. It has been, so far, the biggest violent conflict between criminals and Islamists, and it began in a prison camp in Kizil (Tuva region of Russia).

In March of 2016, a twenty-nine-year-old ethnically Georgian *vor*, Ruslan Gegechkori "Hat Junior" (a son of a powerful *vor* Roland Gegechkori "Hat"), was arrested in Moscow on drug charges. Since he was a *vor*, he immediately took the highest place in the criminal hierarchy when he arrived in the prison. There he encountered a group of Dagestani inmates who did not agree with his new leadership position. According to inmates familiar with the situation, Ruslan Gegechkori asked them, "Do you accept criminal authority in prison, and will you follow the criminal rules?" They replied, "We are Muslims, and we have our own rules." This answer did not satisfy Ruslan Gegechkori, and the Dagestanis were beaten. This conflict was short and without any consequences for Ruslan Gegechkori because, in that particular prison, the *jamaat* was very small and weak.

Later, Ruslan Gegechkori was transferred to prison #4 in Kizil.[6] Right away, he made one of the inmates (an Armenian) his close associate, but this inmate had a preexisting conflict with people from the prison *jamaat*, which was strong and powerful there. In his new status as a person close to Ruslan Gegechkori, the Armenian inmate tried to give orders to Muslim inmates from Chechnya, Dagestan, and Ingushetia, which resulted in the Armenian being punched in the face. Ruslan Gegechkori took his associate's side and invited the inmates from the Caucasus to discuss the issue.

The meeting took place in the prison hospital, and the whole prison criminal leadership was present. At first, the members of the Islamist *jamaat* behaved peacefully. They said they recognized the leadership of Ruslan Gegechkori but could not change their attitude toward his right-hand man. They explained that the Armenian inmate had always been disrespectful to Muslims, particularly when they were praying, and would say inappropriate things to members of the *jamaat*.

However, the only question that Ruslan Gegechkori kept asking the members of *jamaat* was whether they hit the Armenian inmate, and that it was an action that was unacceptable by the prison criminal rules. Then, allegedly following the discussion, Ruslan Gegechkori mentioned he had interacted with a lot with Chechens outside of the prison and only had bad to say about the nation in general. The conversation was not even finished before Gegechkori himself was punched in the face. After that, members of the Islamic *jamaat* retreated to the mosque for prayer.

Gegechkori then collected twenty close associates from the criminal hierarchy (some sources say many more) and went to the prison mosque where Muslim inmates were meeting after prayer. A fight ensued. As a result, eight members of the *jamaat* were seriously beaten, and the mosque was destroyed. Two more members of the *jamaat* were ambushed outside the mosque, stabbed with sharp objects, and beaten with metal bars. They were all admitted to the hospital, one of them in a critical condition. Some of others medically treated were Muslim Timarov from Chechnya, who was in prison for terrorism, participating in a non-state armed group, assault on a police officer, and illegal weapons possession. Another injured Muslim inmate was Arsen Isaev in prison for racketeering, assault on a police officer, and illegal weapons possession.

Ruslan Gegechkori also made a statement in prison, officially denouncing the five people of the *jamaat*, who were now all in the hospital, as *gad* (someone who went against inmates), and said criminal inmates should deal with them accordingly in the future.

According to *ponyatiya*, hitting a *vor* is punishable by death, so by those rules, Ruslan Gegechkori did the right thing. The problem was that Islamists, both in and outside of the prison, do not recognize those criminal rules, and the conflict escalated further.

Once Ruslan Gegechkori realized the potential consequences of this conflict, he tried to calm the situation down by immediately decreeing that no one should touch members of the *jamaat* anymore, and that their religious beliefs should be respected. He also ordered all cell phones in the prison to be confiscated so the information would not spread to other prisons and destabilize the situation further. But this only made the situation worse. News did spread, and it immediately became a major event, affecting not only relations between criminals and Islamists in prisons, but also people in the country outside of the prisons.

Many prisons all over Russia were officially put on high alert, expecting the conflict to spread. A *blatnoj* inmate in another prison explained that things got very tense after the Gegechkori event. "Everyone was ready to jump on each other with knives. Everyone had them prepared and ready to use. However, it was clear that doing that would also have major consequences, so we decided to do nothing and wait to see how the event would play out."

According to a *vor* candidate who, at that time, was imprisoned in another prison with similar tense relations, "Under no circumstance should Gegechkori have done what he did. It was very dangerous for our prison camp. If he is really qualified to be a *vor*, he should have solved it peacefully."

Top criminal leadership was extremely concerned. Not only did a *vor* being punched cause a problem between the *jamaats* and the criminal hierarchy, a rift formed between non-Muslim and Muslim *vory* because Ruslan Gegechkori had destroyed the mosque. In the days following, meetings between members of the Islamist community, Caucasus elders, and the criminal world were taking place not only in Russia where the incident happened, but also in several foreign countries.

To solve the problem before it was too late, national and international criminal leadership related to the Gegechkori family were actively seeking a person to negotiate the conflict that both sides would respect—a *vor* respected by the criminal world who was also a Muslim from the Caucasus. Among the proposed names was *vor* Ahmed Dombaev (Ahmed Shalinsky), who was currently in prison in North Ossetia.

He absolutely refused to take this role however because, as criminal rules stated, one could not advocate for another side (the Islamists) no matter what his nationality and religion were, and such advocacy might destroy his own reputation.

They also talked to the respected Chechen *vor* Aziz Batukayev, the highest criminal leader in Kyrgyzstan, who was wanted there and so lived in Chechnya. According to someone in the criminal world, "Aziz could solve this problem. No one needs war now. But it is obvious that without a public apology from Ruslan Gegechkori in front of the beaten inmates and Muslims and Chechens [communities], it will not be solved. Only that will help to calm the situation down."

And this problem had to be solved quickly. Religious leaders and members of different ethnic groups from the Caucasus had a meeting in which they laid out Ruslan Gegechkori's offenses: (1) offending the whole Chechen nation because of a personal conflict, 2) punishing those who hit him should have not happened in the mosque, and 3) destroying the mosque was absolutely unacceptable. The final outcome of that meeting was issuing a death sentence for Ruslan Gegechkori.

Members of the criminal world from Chechnya not only agreed with the decision, but also made it clear that, in line with criminal rules, not only did Ruslan Gegechkori need to be dealt with, so too did his father Roland Gegechkori and others close to them who would try to stop the retribution. And according to members of *jamaat* in prison in Caucasus, even the president of Chechnya, Ramzan Kadirov, expressed that Ruslan Gegechkori should be punished.

So law enforcement immediately increased the numbers of police officers in the Moscow neighborhood where they expected confrontations between the criminal world factions.

Because Ruslan Gegechkori was constantly getting death threats, and his assassination was being planned in several different prisons, prison authorities got involved to keep him from being killed. At the same time, however, authorities took advantage of the opportunity to further damage the unity of the criminal world and moved Ruslan Gegechkori to a red prison. They also wanted to break Ruslan Gegechkori, so there he was intentionally placed in a cell with a significant number of people from the Caucasus. He was continuously beaten by cellmates and prison guards, and according to his lawyers who were able to visit him, he was also tortured.

Finally, Gegechkori was moved to the prison hospital in Krasnoyarsk. However, that was not the end of his suffering. There he met two other *vory*, Konstantin Borisov ("Crutch") and Sulhan Mzhavia (Sulhan Kutaisski),[7] who belonged to different criminal clans. Because of past clan conflict, Gegechkori had once signed a death sentence for one of those men so, according to the criminal laws, when they encountered each other, neither of them had an option. They each had to try and kill the other. The attempt, however, was thwarted by prison guards. Both parties were moved, but they were moved together to another prison hospital in hopes of exacerbating the conflict not only between Islamists and the criminal world, but also within the criminal world.

After this, those two *vory* wrote a statement, circulated among members of the criminal world, saying they no longer recognized Ruslan Gegechkori as a *vor*. Here is an original *vory progon* written according to criminal rules (see Chapter 4):

> Vory Statement
>
> Welcome inmates. We wish peace and well-being to our common house with wishes of good and health. Freedom and all wordly goods to you.
>
> We Thieves are letting you know that you should not treat Ruslan "Hat" as a vor.
>
> We wish you unity and mutual understanding.
>
> With respect, Vor "Crutch" and Sulhan Kutaisski

Although this statement was only a recommendation to other *vory*, Ruslan Gegechkori losing his status would mean totally losing his immunity in the criminal world. He would be treated like a regular inmate, which meant another death sentence. However, many *vory* did not sign this statement. Instead, they accused *vor* "Crutch" and others who had signed this statement of helping the government divide the criminal world. At least, these *vory* said, Gegechkori was not doing that.

Meanwhile, everyone waited for the word of the most respected *vor* alive, an Azerbaijani named Lotu Guli (living at that time in Turkey). But he said he would not intervene in the conflict.

At the same time, trying to prevent such problems in the future, *vory* from all over Russia increased their efforts to unite inmates under their leadership. For example, many of them signed the following *progon* widely distributed in prisons:

> We *vory*, who are proliferating our word [rules and norms], work towards one goal—everyone's well-being. Having no other option, I am reaching out to you with this writing, trying to unite you! But in order to restore the situation to how it is supposed to be, wishing is not enough. We need support to turn people to the right way! As a result, [those of you] in jails and prisons, show more interest and connect with *vory* and those who live by criminal rules. Explain to young people and new inmates the rules of the criminal prison world. . . . Show brotherly care and attention to each other's needs . . .

Miraculously, Ruslan Gegechkori lived to finish his prison sentence, and in 2018, he was deported from Russia to his home country of Georgia. He later moved to Cyprus.

The members of the *jamaat* who had participated in the initial incident enjoyed a boost in their reputation among the Islamist world. When in 2019 one of them was released from prison, he was met as a hero by his fellow Islamists who arrived in a ten-black-car convoy. Someone even made a tribute video of him going home—complete with ISIS music in the background—which was widely distributed on Islamist social media.[8]

Conclusion

When one *jamaat* felt empowered enough to take full control of a prison with an ethnic Muslim majority, it started enforcing Islamized rules on the criminal hierarchy, replacing criminal traditions and moving them closer to the *jamaat*. With time, this prison turned green as the border between criminal hierarchy and *jamaat* became more and more blurred. And while de jure leadership of the prison was still the *polojenets*, the main decision maker was the *amir* of the *jamaat*.

The situation in non-Muslim-majority prisons was different. *Jamaats* clearly understood that they would not be able to enforce their rules on the majority of the population, so their goal was to leave the criminal hierarchy in place but to control them by fear and force.

They started by maximizing the number of *jamaat* members, going as far as recruiting members of the lower caste. And to control those new group members who, by definition, already had a history of violating prison rules, *jamaats* had to increase the enforcement of ideologically inspired rules, which led to a rapid ideologization of the group.

Because the attention on the groups' ideology increases, new group leadership started being promoted based on their dedication to the group's ideology instead of on management qualifications. As a result, unqualified but power-hungry people reached leadership positions. And since these inmates came from the lower caste of the criminal hierarchy and are now in a position of power, they wanted revenge on prison criminal leadership, which led to a conflict between those two forces.

14
Vory Criminal Organization Resurgence

By now it is clear that *jamaats* are not just a headache for prison criminal leadership. In some cases, issues arising from the parallel structure lead to fatal consequences, and that makes the problem of controlling them existential for the *vory* criminal organization. Not only do *jamaats* compete with *vory* for power inside prisons, but having such a division inside the prison population could lead to inmates as a whole becoming weaker and unable to stand up against prison authorities. As a consequence, a prison in this dilemma could easily turn red. And that in turn makes it an existential problem not only for the criminal organization, but also for the criminal leadership personally. In red prisons, nothing prevents guards from using beatings and torture to break them.

So can *vory* save their prisons and decrease the role of *jamaats* late in the game, especially if a prison is already green? The answer is yes; theoretically, it is possible. But practically, recovering lost power is both difficult and dangerous.

So in this chapter, I will talk about what problems criminal leadership faces trying to decrease *jamaat* power by using the example of one particular prison, not only because such cases of success are very rare, but also because of its geographic location. The prison is located in Kalmykia, on the border between majority Muslim and majority non-Muslim regions of Russia, and, as a result, the inmate population is mixed. This makes it a clear example of the life-and-death dynamics of a *jamaat* in a religiously mixed prison.

Rise to Power

Before 2010, this prison was, as inmates say, "as red as a fire truck." Mostly locals were housed there, and prison guards, who were often drunk, regularly beat and tortured inmates to extract money from them. It was one of those Russian prisons all convicts were terrified of being relocated to. In addition, the geographic location meant there were constant problems not only with food, but also with water.

The prison was so corrupt that a female who worked in the accounting office was killed under suspicious circumstances on her way home from work.[1] After that, the situation in the prison became unstable as a parade of prison directors—all involved in different scandals—were moved in and out of the position.

Criminals, Nazis, and Islamists. Vera Mironova, Oxford University Press. © Oxford University Press 2023.
DOI: 10.1093/oso/9780197645659.003.0015

Then, in 2010, a new group of inmates moved in, sixty ethnic Muslim inmates from Dagestan. They had no intention of serving their sentence in such terrible conditions, and during the first prison-wide search, they started a riot.

The situation rapidly evolved. Inmates started cutting their wrists. One HIV-positive inmate tried to bleed on the prison guards but was neutralized before he had the chance. Because prison guards were mostly drunk and unable to resist the inmates, a SWAT team was brought in. They locked all inmates into the prison club building, threw gas grenades inside, and were only letting them out one by one, to beat them. In response, however, a group of young people still inside the club building used chairs to smash through the wall of the building, then ran onto the soccer field and started fighting with the SWAT team. The situation got so bad that armored vehicles were called in. SWAT team members were beating the inmates so badly that some prison guards even turned sides and protected inmates, afraid that they might be killed.[2] Still, there were several casualties.

When prison guards called for backup, so did inmates, and soon vehicles full of friends were on their way from Dagestan to help. Although police were able to stop the vehicles before they reached the prison, it sent a strong message to local law enforcement and the corrections department: do not mess with inmates from Dagestan.

When the inspector from Moscow arrived, he fired the old prison director and appointed a new one. The new director clearly understood that even if police were successful in stopping that particular riot, they did not have control over the new inmates, and it was just a matter of time before the next riot happened. He also did not want to attract anymore unnecessary attention to the prison, considering its history of corruption and the suspicious death.

To save his job, and perhaps his life, the director decided to make an unofficial agreement with inmates. It was the usual agreement for turning a prison black—inmates could run the prison, but it would be their responsibility to make sure that nothing attracted Moscow's attention. No complaints would be sent to correction authorities and neither the agreement nor the situation inside the prison would be made public. Inmate leaders agreed, and the notoriously red prison was finally *defrosted*.

But it soon became clear that, among those who took power of the prison, the Islamist influence was stronger than the criminal family influence. Before the Dagestanis had come, there had only been a small group of Muslims who occasionally prayed in the corner of the prison club building. Now an official Islamist *jamaat* organized, *azan* was done five times a day, and religious classes once a day.

The person in charge of the *jamaat* was an inmate from Dagestan named Hasan who was imprisoned on terrorism charges (member of an Islamist insurgency in the Caucasus). His tenure as *amir* was not long, and just a year later, he was released. His place was taken by a fellow Dagestani, a twenty-five-year-old inmate named Shahban who had been charged with illegal weapons possession.

Under his leadership, the *jamaat* became strong and was basically the only real force in prison. Although the majority of inmates (around 70%) were still members of the criminal hierarchy living by *ponyatiya*, they were much weaker than the *jamaat*, so *jamaat* leadership largely determined how the prison functioned.

According to one interviewed inmate, "Shahban knew how jihad should be done and how a successful fighting *jamaat* should function. I think he saw it somewhere before . . . like in the forests [Insurgency in Caucasus]." He knew how to organize and control a group of even misbehaving criminal inmates. For example, although some members of his *jamaat* were in on rape charges—which is the lowest possible level in the criminal hierarchy—they did not cause any problems for Shaban. According to one ex-inmate who was in prison at that time, "Under Shaban, members of criminal world and the prison guards knew their place. But he was also into fairness, so if someone from the *jamaat* did something wrong, he would punish him and kick him out."

In fact, members of the prison criminal world were terrified of the *jamaat* but could do little about it. The *polojenets* liked to drink alcohol, and members of the *jamaat* would openly beat him for it. One time they found weapons (handmade knives and sharpened metal bars) in the criminal leadership barrack. They asked the *polojenets* "Why do you have these? If it is to fight prison guards as you claim, then why would you not tell us that something was wrong, so we could also prepare?" Then they contacted the *vor*, and the *polojenets* was changed.

In addition, Shahban was a good negotiator and was able to successfully talk to prison administration to solve everyday problems. And as a main force in the prison, they also took the job of providing such prison public goods as maintaining communication on the roads upon themselves.

And because he was not constrained by *ponyatiya*, Shaban also made a deal with prison guards to smuggle cell phones into the prison and was selling them to inmates. Other members of the *jamaat* also started selling other, less expensive things (such as food) to fellow inmates—members of the criminal family. This business ensured members of the *jamaat* good and stable income.

Under Shahban's leadership, the *jamaat* were on top of their power, and its members were a very respected.

Jamaat Membership

In 2013, Shahban was released.[3] But before that happened, he appointed a replacement, a Dagestani inmate named Ali (name changed), his right-hand advisor. The majority of inmates who knew him did not like him. He was a very business-oriented person, and his main goal was power; religion and the *jamaat* were nothing more then just ways for him to get that power. As a result, the situation with the *jamaat* deteriorated very quickly. This was mostly a result of the change of *jamaat* membership.

If in the beginning, the core of the *jamaat* consisted of professional, qualified, honest, religious, and brave people—which is how the *jamaat* was able to defrost the prison and gain such a good reputation—after the Islamist veteran leadership left, the average member profile changed almost overnight.

In particular, members of *sherst'*, who had nothing to do with religion, started joining in big numbers. So did others who had problems with criminal leadership. They were attracted by the benefits *jamaat* life offered including better food and being part of a so-called privileged group.

To make things worse, the *jamaat* made no attempt to screen newcomers, and they also ignored screening previously done by *blatnyje* (such as distribution to different castes). In addition to members of *sherst'*, prison administration informants were also joining in big numbers. According to an interviewed member of the *jamaat*, "As we later learned, there were so many snitches that they even had their own codes. For example, if one of them came in the *jamaat* barrack saying to another one, 'I need your information to receive a package [an inmate has a limit of 20kg per month, but could transfer unused weight to another inmate],' it meant that the prison director wanted to talk to that person."

To feel powerful even outside the prison gates, members of the *jamaat* were also considering themselves part of ISIS, and all visible attributes of the subculture were very prevalent in the *jamaat*. Its members were wearing Afghani-style clothing, listening to *nasheeds*, watching videos from the Middle East, and celebrating ISIS victories. And although *jamaat* leadership publicly encouraging such an affiliation, they clearly understood it was a joke. Their group of former drug addicts in prison for rape, drug smuggling, and killing while under the influence had very little relation to those fighting in the Middle East. When a friend of the *amir* privately mentioned that ISIS was not a good organization, the *amir* said, "Of course you are right, but please do not talk like that here. Others will not like it."

At that point, it became obvious to intelligent inmates that religion, along with ISIS affiliation, became only a cover for the existence of the *jamaat* in the first place and a tool used to enforce order and obedience within the group. Previous religious lessons that inmates were free to attend had now become mandatory for *jamaat* members. And according to religious inmates, "What they were studying in those classes had very little relation to religious education. Instead it was random information without any logic or context that everyone had to memorize." At the same time, the *jamaat* was very strict about attendance, and after the classes, members of the *jamaat* had to pass an exam.

Also, according to interviewed inmates, the person in charge of those classes was the least knowledgeable about religion in the whole *jamaat*, but the most power-hungry. One *jamaat* member said, "The person conducting the exam had no idea or interest in religion, and his only goal was to rise in ranks in the *jamaat* leadership." And he realized that to show his dedication to the *jamaat*, he had to show excellence in following ideology and that position was the best for his purpose. This position did show that he cared about *jamaat* ideology and that he could enforce it on other members of the *jamaat*.

And because many *jamaat* members joined the group for the sole reason of power, everyone was very sensitive about the issue of the leading positions in the *jamaat*, which, considering its religious cover, meant those who lead prayer during mandatory Friday prayer.

While it was the leader of the *jamaat* who led the prayer in the prison mosque, it was not determined who led the prayer in any other circumstance. For example, when there was something going on in prison such as an inspection, and doors between different parts of the prison were closed, many members of *jamaat* did not go to the mosque to pray but prayed inside the living quarters instead.

And for every mass prayer, there should be someone standing in front and leading the prayer, an imam. Who led prayers was a constant source of conflict, and it was the worst members of the *jamaat*—who had no idea about religion and only wanted power—who always wanted to do it.

According to one religious inmate, "While technically, you can pray behind anyone if you do not know him, in prison, because you know everyone, there are some people you do not want to pray behind." So members had a say about whom they wanted to pray behind. This had little to do with religion, but instead became a kind of popularity contest. The aspiring *amir* who had the most people who wanted to pray behind him won.

Seeing all this, Islamists with previous fighting experience who care about religion want nothing to do with the *jamaat*. One older inmate—who was not only a regular fighter in Caucus insurgencies but was also in a unit in charge of assassinating policeman as a member of its intelligence wing—had been in prison for eighteen years.[4] He refused to be involved in the *jamaat* in any capacity.

Even support for ISIS did not unite *jamaat* members and strong Islamists. Those of them who also openly supported ISIS chose to support it separately from *jamaat* members. The smartest among the ex-fighters were also concerned that "We are teaching all those bad people and *sherst'* all our codes [how to behave to be identified as Muslims], and it is dangerous. They will get out of prison and then go to the mosque where they will easily be able to blend in."

Those inmates who had not been involved with an insurgency but were religious and cared about Islam did not want to live with them either. "As a person who cares about Islam, I was pissed that something that important to me [his religion] is being misused by those idiots," commented one of the religious inmates about the *jamaat*.

And because such a situation with *jamaats* was common in many other prisons across Russia, religious inmates transferred from other prisons also refused to be part of the *jamaat* without even getting to know about it. One interviewed inmate explained, "I wanted to live with people who did not abuse my religion. They [the criminal family inmates] maybe do not know it, but at least they respect it. I do not care if they are smoking or drinking in a room. I can tolerate that."

Many religious people also agreed and wanted to do the same.

At that point, even prison authorities understood what was happening, and in their counter extremism work, they started paying more attention to Muslims who are religious but are not in *jamaat*.[5]

Relations with the Criminal Hierarchy

As mentioned before, because of the parallel relationship between *jamaats* and the rest of the prison population, criminal leadership does not have authority over members of the *jamaat* and cannot punish them, or vice versa. Only the leadership of an inmate's own group is allowed to punish based on that group's rules. However, originally, the *jamaat* in this prison was stronger, there was not equal power distribution. For example, if a conflict arose between criminal and *jamaat* inmates, the whole *jamaat* would stand up to defend their comrade.

So many new *jamaat* members abused this power structure. They did so under the cover of religion and declared *takfir* (calling non-Muslim) on Muslim inmates not in the *jamaat*. According to their logic and interpretation of religion, they looked at non-members of the *jamaat* as second-class people.

And since many people who joined the *jamaat* had long-term grievances against criminal leadership (for being moved to the lowest castes), they used their newfound protection as an avenue to be aggressive and offensive towards inmates in the criminal hierarchy.[6]

Such behavior also moved them even closer to the *jamaat* leadership, because now they had no illusions that if they were kicked out of the *jamaat* and went back into the criminal hierarchy, they would be seriously punished. So to avoid that, inmates were willing to do anything from memorizing religious lectures to doing the job of *snir* to conducting illegal activities on behalf of the *jamaat* leadership.

At the same time, since members of the *jamaat* did not really believe in Islam and had little interest in following the *jamaat's* strict religious rules, they were secretly (but regularly) asking inmates from the criminal hierarchy for everything that *jamaats* prohibited. While *jamaat* members were strictly prohibited from smoking, the majority of them smoked anyway. And because they were hiding it, they did not have their own cigarettes and were always asking members of the criminal hierarchy for them. This situation became extremely irritating because cigarettes are considered a public good, and the criminal leadership invests a lot in bringing them to the prison so everyone has enough. According to interviewed inmates, "This is totally freeloading on the side of the *jamaat*, and since they also smoke, they and their leadership have to make sure that they are also moving cigarettes inside the prison and not taking them from the criminal *obshyak* that they do not contribute to."

There is a similar situation with drugs. One time a thirty-year-old member of the *jamaat* came to the *polojenets* asking for heroin. When the *polojenets* confronted him about being a Muslim (who is not supposed to do drugs), he told the *polojenets* it would not be a problem. In this case, the *polojenets* mentioned it to the *jamaat*'s *amir*. When the *amir* confronted the inmate about doing drugs, he denied it and said the *polojenets* was lying.

At that point, it became way too much. Because this inmate was doing drugs that violated *jamaat* rules *and* wrongly accused the *polojenets* of lying, he was immediately kicked out of the *jamaat*, beaten, and moved to *sherst'*.

By this time in the *jamaat's* cycle, all members of the criminal hierarchy have not only lost respect for members of the *jamaat*, they openly hate them. But there is not much criminal inmates can do. Not only were they afraid of the *jamaat*, non-Muslims were afraid to be seen as people discriminating against Muslims. In other words, they still did not understand that the main goal of the *jamaat* was power, not religion.[7]

However, religious Muslim members of the criminal hierarchy saw the true face of the *jamaat*, but they were still cautious, hoping that as the *jamaat* members studied Islam, they would understand it, and the situation would improve. According to an ex-fighter in an insurgency in the Caucasus who did not join the *jamaat*, "I tried to educate those kids [members of *jamaat*] on how true religion and a *jamaat* should look. It did not help. But at least we have azan and religious people in prison."

As a result, nothing was done to put the *jamaat* in place. In some instances, members of the *jamaat* beat criminal inmates and criminal leadership did not respond in any way.

Corruption in the *Jamaat*

Since those left in the *jamaat* were there only for personal benefits and power, corruption was a big issue. According to an interviewed inmate, "At first, *jamaat amirs* lived like Mahatma Gandhi [in modesty]. Now they live like the king of Saudi Arabia [in luxury]." Like their criminal counterparts, *jamaat* leadership secured private rooms for sleeping, had individual offices, and were surrounded by *sniri* willing to do any job for them.

Also, members of the *jamaat* were willing to do anything for financial gain and had no ethical limits on their profit-generating activities. In addition to reselling goods to other inmates (at an increased price), they were reported to be involved in extortion. For example, when they knew someone owed money to someone else, *jamaat* members waited for the borrower to win in a card game and then pressed him to pay the lender back what he owed. Then the owner would give the *jamaat* members a cut.

Within their group, *jamaat* leadership also institutionalized all kinds of monetary punishments for members who violated internal rules. For example, they might sell someone a cell phone for money down and say the whole price needed to be paid by the end of the month. And if at the end of the month the *jamaat* member was a little short, the leaders not only took the phone back, they also did not return the money the inmate already gave them.

Jamaat leadership also charged fines for violations of ideological rules. In one case, a *jamaat* member had a girlfriend visit him. He had agreed she would bring drugs in for the *blatnyje* at his request, and that he would deliver them after the visit.

But the girlfriend came to visit for several days. At some point, the criminal hierarchy got tired of waiting and sent a *sherst'* who was cleaning floors in the visitation building to check on them and to get the drugs. Instead, the *sherst'* told the story to the *jamaat* leadership.

When the *jamaat* member's visit was over, *jamaat* leadership was waiting. After confiscating the drugs, they took him to a half-constructed restroom on the prison territory and beat him. Then they not only kicked him out, they also said, "We know that you have an expensive car at home, so you have to give it to us." When asked on what grounds they were demanding the car, one leader replied, "We thought he was our brother, but he ended up being an untrustworthy guy."

Religious people in the prison were furious about those "half *sherst'*, half radical fanatics [the *jamaat* leaders]" because, according to them, the banished inmate's so-called brothers should have prayed for him and tried to help him quit drugs, not beat him and try to extort his car.

And the fear of being kicked out of the *jamaat* was so frightening for some, that they regularly paid the *amir*. They knew that in that case they would be first immediately downgraded to *sherst'* caste (and have to work) and then, most likely, seriously beaten. While they were in the *jamaat*, they were showing off and being offensive to those in the *muzhiki* caste. They knew that if they got back under the criminal leadership authority, revenge would follow.

Other inmates were suspicious about one inmate who behaved really badly toward others, yet the *amir* would not allow anyone to touch him. "So either that inmate was paying him [the *amir*] or prison authorities asked the *amir* to protect him," commented one of the inmates.

Finally, since inmates who joined the *jamaat* were not only dishonest but also greedy, prison business was not enough for them. So they got involved in illegal business on a much larger, countrywide scale. What was their business model?

An *amir* distributed phones to members of the *jamaat*, and they organized several phone scams.

In one scam, *jamaat* members would look for advertisements on the internet from people who had lost documents, and then call the people and say they had found their documents. Scammers would then ask the elated document owners to meet them at a designated place near where documents were lost so they could return them. Once the owner arrived, the scammer would tell the owner (via text or call) that he was not sure whether the documents were stolen, so he did not feel comfortable returning them himself. But he was going to send a child who would come bring them in a few minutes. Then, the scammer would ask the owner if the owner would mind, while he was waiting, if he would send the reward money to the scammer's phone number (in Russia, the phone number could work like a bank account/cash app).

In another scam, *jamaat* members would call random numbers and say, "We are calling from the police station. Your son is with us and has been accused of drug possession. It is in his best interest for you to send us money as soon as possible." And being familiar with corruption in Russian law enforcement, such a scam is not as ridiculous to those who receive these calls as it seems to a Western reader.[8]

Scammers might also send a text message to a random cell number that they had accidently put money on that person's pre-paid phone account (all phone accounts in Russia are prepaid) instead on their own, and then ask if they would mind putting the same amount of money on the inmate's account (like a refund).

These scammers are also known to meet a married female online, flirt with her, persuade her to send a nude picture on the phone, and then use the picture to blackmail her.

According to interviewed inmates, between 2017 and 2019, the monthly income from phone scams in that particular prison was about $20,000. Who participated in this enterprise? Mostly ex- *sherst'* who had become part of the *jamaat*. Instead of the physical work they had done as part of *ponyatiya* and the caste system, that job allowed them to lie on the bed all day with a cell phone and make money.

This large-scale, profitable business was under the control of an *amir*, who protected those involved from other inmates and negotiated (by paying a cut) with prison administration. In return, prison guards ignored the places in prison where those scammers were working and did not confiscate their cell phones (prohibited to own in prison).[9] Even the local branch of Russian security service (the FSB) were getting a cut and closing their eyes, ignoring multiple complaints from victims.

For a long time, this enterprise was successfully kept secret from everyone who was not involved. It was kept secret from those who cared about *ponyatiya* because it is against *ponyatiya* to scam innocent people. In fact, there is a special *progon* that says inmates are not allowed to scam people outside of prison. It was also kept secret from some members of the prison authority. It was even kept secret from some members of the *jamaat* because "if a real Muslim would have known about it, he would have killed everyone involved," said one interviewed inmate.

Running a *Jamaat* from a Distance

Although the illegal business was still not known to the broader prison population, relations between the *jamaat* and criminal hierarchy worsened every day. One particular event was the final straw for criminal leadership. A *balander* (person from *sherst'* caste who distributes food) was in the kitchen causing problems, and a member of the *jamaat* hit him. The *amir*, Ali, immediately came to the *balander*'s defense and hit that *jamaat* member very hard.

This was strange for several reasons. First, it is very unusual for a *jamaat* leader to personally defend a low member of the criminal hierarchy, especially against a *jamaat* member. Second, such actions were not according to *ponyatiya*, which would have solved that conflict peacefully. Also, by crossing the division between criminal and *jamaat* jurisdictions, it was obvious that Ali followed his own interests and is breaking prison relations and rules. This was a major problem for both criminal leadership and the *jamaat*.

To keep from being beaten (or killed) by prison criminal leadership, Ali took the only other option he had. He asked prison guards for protection. In particular, he asked to be locked in the inner prison. According to all prison norms, doing this is most dishonorable action an inmate can do.[10] And despite being in a more confined area of the prison, Ali was still trying to run the *jamaat* from there.

However, with so many power-thirsty members of the *jamaat*, this was difficult, so Ali appointed a puppet *amir* who would be taking orders from him. And because all inmates who were at the prison understood the situation, Ali decided to choose a new inmate who did not understand what was going on, and who would look to Ali for guidance.

At that time, a group of new inmates from Kabardino-Balkaria had come to the prison, and among them were several potential candidates for such a puppet *amir* position. According to one of the interviewed inmates, they were considered candidates in part because they prayed whole-length prayers while being transferred from prison to prison (which was viewed as strong signal of their dedication).[11] Those candidates included:

(1) A drug addict who was a religious Muslim. While in prison he remained clean from drugs but would relapse immediately on release, which had already happened several times.
(2) An inmate in his early to mid-thirties in on drug charges. He smoked, but also had two wives and had been in the *jamaat* in the previous prison.
(3) A thirty-five-year-old inmate also in on drug charges. In his previous prison, he had lived in the criminal hierarchy but was also close to *jamaat* members.
(4) A religious inmate in his fifties. He was also an ex-drug addict on drugs charges but was close to the *vory* criminal family.

In quarantine, when the new inmates met each other, it become clear who was who, and the new inmates decided between living with the *jamaat* or the criminal family. Then during one of the Friday prayers, when both newcomers and *jamaat* members went to the mosque to pray, the position of *amir* was offered to the thiry-five-year-old inmate who had previously lived with the criminal family whose name was Mohamed. He agreed and started following Ali's orders.

The other inmates watched as Mohamed and those close to him began to wear expensive clothes and carry expensive cell phones. In retrospect, inmates understood that he had also became part of the illegal business controlled by the *jamaat*, but at that time, it was still not known.

Once Mohamed got comfortable, he took steps to secure his position by eliminating any potential competition. Those who questioned his decisions were accused of being against Islam and were kicked out (to the criminal hierarchy). He was especially wary of respected inmates who were knowledgeable about both religion and the criminal world. He could control *jamaat* members who were offensive to members of criminal hierarchy because they would do everything told just to stay inside the *jamaat*, but that was not the case with those not afraid to go back to the criminal hierarchy. Without that fear, those inmates were free to challenge *jamaat* leadership.

Each barrack had a *smotryasçiy*, each barrack had a Muslim leader. One such Muslim leader also had a particularly nasty friend—an Azeri ex-drug addict, who was born Shia but converted to Sunni Islam in prison. To show that he was not less than ethnic Sunni Muslims, he was constantly calling his family members and accusing them of being *kafirs* (non-Muslims).

Once a new guy in the *jamaat* who pointed out that something was against Sharia. He was right, and one inmate, Amin, supported him. Because Amin was not young and easily manipulated, the Muslim leaders did not want to get into an open conflict with him, so they told him to leave the *jamaat* because he was breaking the order. Amin agreed and said he would leave as soon as there was a free bed in the criminal hierarchy section.

Then the Azeri member of *jamaat* kept saying out loud, without referring to anyone, "Why do we have people in the *jamaat* who do not belong here?" Amin could not tolerate it, so he said, "Are you talking to me? You are a disgrace and have absolutely no relation to religion."

"Of course, everyone supported the Azeri inmate," Amin commented in an interview, "because they are terrified of being kicked out of the *jamaat*. Inmates from the criminal hierarchy would eat them alive for everything they had done."

Then Amin was asked to follow *jamaat* leadership to their room used for meetings. There was an *amir* and others from the leadership. It was a shura, similar to a criminal blat committee. They questioned Amin about what he had initially said.

Amin said, "Because this is how it is according to Islam, and this is how it is according to *ponyatiya*, and also it is the same based on common sense. You are the only ones who see it differently. Also, why are you torturing people with all your crazy rules and absolutely useless pseudo-religious classes? Just to make everyone busy and show your power?"

"You are always saying things against the *jamaat* politics, and it is bad for discipline," replied one leader of the *jamaat*, "And your opinion about ISIS is not popular [he did not support it]. So if you are not with us, could you please move away from the *jamaat* to the criminal section of the barrack?"

Then Azeri inmate told Amin to keep in mind that from then on, Amin would have to be subordinate to him. "After those words, I basically had two options," remembers Amin, "Either I could beat him [the Azeri inmate] or peacefully leave. He was not worth it, so I left."

Amin moved to the criminal hierarchy where he was immediately given a privileged space on the first level of the bunk bed close to the *blatnyje* because, even though he was in the *jamaat*, he was very respected among the prison criminal leaders. Before long, many members of the *jamaat* started coming to him for advice. The *jamaat* leadership hated it because they saw this inmate as competition, but there was little they could do because he was no longer under their jurisdiction.

Eventually, the situation between criminals and members of the *jamaat* approached the level of armed conflict. Everyone prepared self-made knives in case of mass fighting, but the leadership was still able to avoid it. First, the situation with *vor* Gegechkori happened in another prison (as described in the previous chapter), and no one wanted a repeat of that violence. Second, the *polojenets*, who was also from Dagestan, clearly understood that if there would have been mass fighting, Islamists would portray it as religious discrimination and not only would their friends from outside come armed to prison gates, there would also be problems for him back home. But after another experience, the criminal leadership decided it was enough.

At some point, the prison administration refused to allow huge *obshyak* packages—several hundred packs of cigarettes, hundreds of kilograms of tea, and the like—into the prison. The *polojenets* already had an agreement with the director of the prison, but he was not at work that day, and his deputy had refused it. So the *polojenets* ordered everyone to go to the prison cafeteria for lunch. On the average day, only 10 percent of inmates eat in the cafeteria, meaning that is the amount of food usually prepared. So when a mass of other inmates showed up to eat, the cafeteria did not have enough food to feed them. For the prison authorities, this was a serious violation, and the central corrections authority would mete out substantial punishment to those in charge of the prison.

It was a good plan, but despite the order from the *polojenets* for everyone to take part, not everyone showed up. In fact, the *amir* refused to give a similar order to the *jamaat*, so they did not participate. To make things worse, while the strike was going on, *jamaat* members were defiantly playing soccer in the prison yard.

Since this strike was to increase the well-being of all inmates, the criminal leadership took the *jamaat*'s refusal to participate very seriously. They interpreted it as the *jamaat* cooperating with prison guards against other inmates. Everyone in the criminal leadership agreed that, in order not to lose the prison to the authorities, serious action had to be taken against the *jamaat*. And the sooner, the better.

New Leadership

Everyone was working hard, trying to figure out what to do. The prison desperately needed strong people to take leadership of both the black and green sides of the inmate population to stabilize the situation. Luckily, soon new inmates were moved in, and among them were a thirty-five-year-old Dagestani inmate, Hasan, who was accused of killing someone in a fight. In his previous prison in Dagestan, Hasan had been in the *jamaat*, but then separated himself for all the same reasons religious Muslims in this prison had. When he left, half of the *jamaat* had also joined him. According to inmates, he was a very strong person, very religious, and fair.[12]

Another new inmate was an ethnic Armenian. He was related to a very respectful clan of *vory*, his father was a *vor*, and he was one step away from getting a *vor* title himself. Immediately, he took criminal leadership of the prison (although officially he did not become *polojenets*) and took this job extremely seriously—partially because his actions were very important for his future *vor* title. According to one inmate, "He was very experienced, modest, smart, and rational. And although he was a practicing Christian, he was interested in other religions, including Islam."

The key to success was both of these inmates openly drawing a line between religion and the *jamaat*. While basically everyone else was afraid to touch such a sensitive issue, Hasan especially left political correctness aside and took action. According to inmates, when he saw what was going on in the prison with the *jamaat*, he told other religious Muslim inmates that *jamaat* members needed to be beaten. When they said it could not be done because those *jamaat* members were Muslim brothers, Hasan replied, "They are neither Muslims, nor brothers. And we have to clean this mess up."

Several meetings ensued with other respected inmates and even Islamist veterans who had left the *jamaat* when it had become corrupted. They all agreed Islam was a religion that had nothing to do with the rules within prison, and that the caste system should be reinstated.

At the same time, the FSB had also taken a particular interest in the prison. First, they started charging members of the *jamaat* with additional crimes for positing ISIS propaganda online.[13] Second, the scamming operation was revealed. The FSB was faced with so many complaints from victims that they simply were no longer able to close their eyes, and they had to act.[14]

Meanwhile, the puppet *amir*, Mohamed, could not handle the pressure. Realizing he needed immediate protection, he did as his predecessor had and turned to prison authorities. He cut his wrists and was moved to the safety of solitary confinement, where he stayed until his release.

Because of the illegal business scandal, many members of the *jamaat* were quietly transferred to other prisons, and an inmate, Alim, took the position of *amir* in the slowly dying *jamaat*.

De-*jamaat*ization

At the same time, members of the criminal leadership, with the help of religious Muslims, were conducting their own investigation into *jamaat* activities for the sole purpose of completely destroying it.

Using his high-level contacts, the aspiring *vor* collected information (including from law enforcement and prison guards) about who exactly had been involved in the scamming business and in what capacity. Those inmates were then interrogated by him and Hasan. When they confessed, they were punished according to *ponyatiya*. In this way, the *jamaat* was losing between one and three members daily.

Many of these inmates were seriously beaten, and some were sent to *sherst'* caste where they started working cleaning prison floors, doing landscaping and such. Other inmates became *sniri*.

However, as information continued to be uncovered, not everyone was lucky enough to stay in the upper caste as *sniri* or even to become *sherst'*. Many of them were downgraded even further. For example, three passive homosexuals were discovered in the *jamaat* (two Russian converts[15] and one ethnic Muslim), and there had been several other *jamaat* members (active homosexuals) using their services. Because these inmates, who should have been in the *petukhi* caste had looked down on inmates in the *muzhiki* caste while they had been in the *jamaat*, there was no mercy for them.

Allegations of passive homosexuality are very serious according to *ponyatiya* and need to be proven. A secret operation was organized when an inmate named Rulka[16] said that one *jamaat* member had come to him and asked to change roles in sex. Such acts in that prison usually happen in the room for drying clothes, so the group had a small inmate hide in one of the huge bags of dried clothes while the others remained close by. When Rulka and his client started the act with reversed roles, the small inmate jumped out of the bag and called the others to the crime scene.

After that, in line with *ponyatiya*, the passive homosexuals were moved to the *petukhi* caste, and those who had known about the passive homosexuality but had not informed criminal leadership (active homosexuals) were sent to *sherst'*.

Other minor problems uncovered, in addition to smoking, were *jamaat* leadership and other members not only drinking alcohol but using heavy drugs, even in the prison mosque.[17] They were also sent to *sherst'*.

However, it was an unexpected event that put the final nail in the *jamaat*'s coffin: the death of a criminal inmate within the inner prison. This inmate—who had been a member of the criminal hierarchy and was a relative of a powerful *vor* from Dagestan—had his head smashed open by two members of the *jamaat*.[18] Strangely enough, *Amir* Alim was also in the inner prison, but in another cell.

It was never clear exactly what happened. According to interviewed members of the *jamaat*, "Although *Amir* Alim says he had no idea what was going on, he was on the phone with someone at the time of the killing. The guy was killed on Alim's order because, by Sharia law, members of a *jamaat* can't kill anyone without the permission of the *amir*."

According to the criminal leadership version of events, "One of the *jamaat* members was asleep and the criminal inmate was inappropriately touching him, so he was beaten. Then he died from the beating. It was an accident."

At the same time, the victim's Dagestani *vor* relative vowed the killers would pay for what they did. To save their lives, the two killers remained under prison guard protection within the inner prison until the end of their sentences.

At this point, the criminal leadership considered two options. They could either close the *jamaat* altogether or leave it but make it a puppet *jamaat*. They chose the second option. The criminal leadership explained their decision this way: "Who would dare to totally get rid of them? We would immediately be [verbally] attacked not only by Islamists outside of prison, but also human rights NGOs for discrimination against Muslims. Also, it would be kind of strange not to have a *jamaat*. Everyone is already used to its existence. So we decided not to kill it totally but to leave a small puppet one, but one cleaned up."

The question then became who would be the next *amir*, and what should be done with the previous *amir*, Ali, who was still in the inner prison? Changing the *jamaat* leadership, they knew, could be a sensitive and explosive issue. They had to find the right person.

While Muhamed, the puppet *amir*, had still been in power, he had accepted one of the *balanders* (a *sherst'* working in the kitchen) who had originally started the trouble in the *jamaat*. This *sherst'* was an ethnic Russian convert to Islam. He memorized key religious words and movements but, according to other inmates, "had neither knowledge nor interest for religion." He knew just enough to be able to conduct a *hudba* (Friday prayer).

But he was very business-oriented and smart. For example, he learned about bitcoins and, using his phone, rented a server somewhere and was earning money that way. It came to light later that he had also been part of the defunct illegal phone scam business, was still under the control of Ali, and was suspiciously close to prison authorities and FSB. However, it was he who took the position of *amir* of the *jamaat*.

At first, he was just leading a prayer, and there were no problems. But with time, he tried to increase his power. In fact, he was getting more and more dictatorial. And because he was afraid of repercussions from the criminal leadership, he began cultivating an anti-criminal attitude within the *jamaat*. For example, he was against members of the *jamaat* hanging out with members of the criminal hierarchy. Basically, he was trying to cut the puppet *jamaat* free from its strings.

But his plans were not to happen. People within the *jamaat* informed criminal leadership about what was going on. It was also leaked that, after Friday prayer that next week, the new *amir* wanted to have a shura (special meeting) to get rid of those in the *jamaat* who did not 100 percent support him. He was preemptively approached by criminal leadership, who reminded him he was put in place to quietly read *hudba* once a week, nothing else.

This deterred the *amir*, but only for a while. He did not give up on the idea of distancing his members from the criminal hierarchy and told his supporters that "[*jamaat*] members are in bed with members of the criminal hierarchy, and we need to do something about it." He even had former *jamaat* members who had been released call those still inside and threaten to hurt them if they got too close to members of the criminal hierarchy.

Again, the criminal leadership had enough, and the *amir* was given the option to "either very quietly leave the *amir* position and go to *sherst'* yourself, or we [criminal leadership] will help you." He did not resist. At first, from time to time he still went to the mosque to pray, but soon, he even stopped doing that and completely forgot about the religion he had been so zealous about in the past.

Although it might not seem as such from outside, this was an extremely dangerous maneuver on the side of criminal leadership, and it was done with a surgical precision. There were several things that made it dangerous. First it was crucial to avoid any open conflict with the *jamaat* because it might have led to a major countrywide war between the criminal world and Islamists. And as a consequence, such war would also lead to infighting in the Russian-speaking criminal world (as in the case described in the previous chapter).

Second, the Russian internal security (FSB) who had been involved in the *jamaat*'s illegal business were particularly unhappy with the criminal family's interference because they lost a lot of money with the closing of the business and most likely also lost intelligence.[19] The last thing criminal leadership wanted to do was to garner more unnecessary attention from Moscow for the prison. Doing so could lead not only to additional prison sentences, but even to them being killed.

Third, it was dangerous because any escalation of the conflict or increase in attention from Moscow would lead to the prison turning red, which likely meant it becoming a place of beating and torture. And since many of those involved still had long sentences to serve, the change in the prison color would have been a disaster.

Fourth, it was highly possible that some members of the *vory* criminal family were aware and even involved in the *jamaat*'s large-scale illegal activities. When the majority of inmates in the prison were from Dagestan, the *vor* (on the outside) and his *polojenets* were also from Dagestan, and it was likely that even if they were not part of that illegal business, they were aware of it, and had closed their eyes. In retrospect, one indicator to criminal leadership was that when they wanted to deal with ex-*Amir* Ali, who was safely locked away in the inner prison, the Dagestani *vor* would stop them.

So when the new respected criminal leader had come, his first challenge was to carefully navigate the top-level politics to change the *vory* criminal family. They knew that while the Dagestani *vor* was in charge of the prison, they could not do much in relation to the *jamaat*. And because the aspiring *vor* was close to a particular clan of *vory*, to get rid of the *jamaat*, he had to move the prison criminal leadership to the side of that *vory* clan. He was very good and experienced in negotiations, and was able to persuade the Dagestani *vor* that "we on the ground here see things more clearly," and by that, reduce the Dagestani *vor*'s involvement.

Once this was accomplished, they were even able to declare Ali *gad*, which, by *ponyatiya*, meant he should be very seriously beaten and, if he did not die, be moved to the *sherst'* caste. Since Ali has been released, it is not likely this punishment will happen outside of prison,[20] but the next time he is imprisoned, it will be waiting for him.

This cleaning operation was major and resonated even outside of prison. For example, information about its success was even known to civilians in the nearest town. According to one former inmate, when he was released and was taking a taxi from the prison to the train station, the first question the taxi driver asked him was, "How did you guys manage to shut up those idiots from the *jamaat*?"

And because this event was a big deal for both the Islamist community and the criminal world outside, its fallout accompanied inmates outside of prison walls. Criminal inmates who participated were told, "We will deal with you when you get out of the prison."

For *jamaat* members, it was the revenge of internal criminal leadership that caught up with them. There was a case of one released inmate who had been disrespectful to criminal family inmates the entire time he was active in the *jamaat*. And, despite portraying himself as a devoted Muslim, his first order of business outside of prison was not going to the mosque, but to a drug dealer. Because his drug addiction was known, one criminal leader asked dealers in that town to call him when the former *jamaat* inmate came again. One dealer did, and while the *jamaat* member was standing there, the drug dealer handed him the phone. After the criminal leader and *jamaat* member talked, the drug dealer beat him on the orders of criminal leader. The former *jamaat* member later even moved to another city because he was afraid for his life.

The criminal leader who beautifully executed this complicated operation was praised by the *vory* community, but, because of internal politics inside the criminal family, he was never given the title of *vor*.

Coexistence

After all the changes in the *jamaat* personnel, the next step was its internal reform. First of all, the *jamaat* no longer had strict requirements for its members.

There were neither mandatory religion classes nor different rules inside the group. From then on, the only law in prison was *ponyatiya*, which even included permission to smoke, drink, and do drugs because, according to *ponyatiya*, no one could judge another person's lifestyle.

These changes were accepted without any problems, and because *jamaat* membership no longer came with any immunity or other benefits, not many people were eager to join, so making membership artificially costly with such requirements (i.e., not drinking or smoking) was not necessary anymore.

Although *jamaat* members were still allowed to sell items, the prices were now controlled by prison criminal leadership. Sellers of cell phones were no longer able to put an arbitrary price tag on their product. Prices were fixed at costs just slightly higher than outside prices (plus what it cost to have prison guards to smuggle them in).

Even religious issues were negotiated between members of the *jamaat* and criminal leadership. For example, while there was still azan in prison, because early morning calls were bothering non-religious inmates, calls were made quieter.

The caste system was also reinstated and very strictly reinforced. For example, there was an inmate degraded by prison guards for killing the director of another prison. But he was also a practicing Muslim and a member of *jamaat*. New inmates who did not know his status often tried to shake his hand, but he refused, then telling them his caste, as he was supposed to do by *ponyatiya*.

That was an easy solution to complying with caste status within a *jamaat*, but not every issue was so clearly defined. This same inmate practiced *sadaka* (Islamic charity) by buying bottles of water and giving them to other members of the *jamaat*, and some members were taking the bottles directly from his hands. If the *jamaat* had been stronger, they would have most likely lobbied to make an exception to the rules about interacting with the degraded, but that was not a case anymore. This inmate was told to only give water to fellow Muslims in the degraded caste because those in the *muzhiki* caste could not take anything from him.

Also, after the last *amir* quietly left his position, once again, the criminal leadership was faced with the tough decision of who would lead Muslim prayer. With no better candidate in sight, they chose a Dagestani inmate, Abdullah, to do it. Although Abdullah was basically an alcoholic, he was still a better option than the rest.

Once he was in place, the situation in prison stabilized for a short time. Unfortunately, the criminal leadership had won the war but was unable to sustain the peace for several reasons.

First of all, the criminal leader who had successfully reduced the power of the *jamaat* was released so, once again, the prison criminal leadership was starving for top management talent. For example, although the aspiring *vor* had a relative in prison (accused of murder) who was also very experienced in the criminal world and could be a *polojenets*, rumors that he had been *sherst'* while in a juvenile prison kept him from being appointed. And although by *ponyatiya*, one who is *sherst'* while in juvenile prison could be in the upper caste later on, it is still a stretch for someone with such an issue on his criminal resume to get the highest criminal position in the prison.

A second disturbance was that, even though the *jamaat* had been neutralized, there was still a great distrust of the *jamaat* among the other inmates, which manifested in daily interactions.

And finally, members of the criminal hierarchy still held grievances against *jamaat* members for past offenses, which kept relationships from moving forward.

So history repeated itself, but this time with members of the *jamaat* as victims while members of criminal hierarchy became the perpetrators. Criminal members were still afraid of the *jamaat* and also wanted revenge, a dangerous and unpredictable combination that could cause a massacre at any moment. And to make it worse, there was no peacekeeping force to stand between them. The following sequence of events basically happened within a week.

Once night a *jamaat* member and a criminal inmate began fighting, and everyone in the building rushed in, including the leadership from both groups. The conflict was over something trivial, so it basically died down immediately after everyone arrived. But as everyone was leaving, Abdullah hugged the highest-ranked criminal leader, Umar (names changed) from Ingushetiya, who was the *polojenets*'s right-hand man and gambling *smotryasçiy*. When *Amir* Abdullah hugged Umar, he felt a knife under Umar's t-shirt. *Amir* Abdullah was angry and told Umar he should not come to meet with his brothers armed with a weapon.

On one side, the *amir* was right. *Ponyatiya* explicitly prohibits bringing weapons to meetings. However, Umar had a weapon on him because he was coming to an incident that could potentially have become fighting between the two groups. Either way, the incident sparked more distrust between the two groups.

Two days later, Umar was involved in another incident. While drunk, he hit a Chechen who was with a small group of *jamaat* members. The victim was an illiterate and despised thirty-three-year-old inmate. He was hated because he was disrespectful and resold cigarettes (something prohibited by *ponyatiya*). Despite that, Umar still had no right to hit him. According to *ponyatiya*, he had not right to beat anyone without a criminal trial. He also had no right to beat a member of the *jamaat*. And finally, it was prohibited for criminal leadership like Umar to drink alcohol.

After that event, the criminal leadership was fearful of revenge from the *jamaat*. Umar and his people did not spend that night in their barracks, but rather in the prison factory where they made sharp metal objects that could be used as weapons. When they returned in the morning, they distributed hundreds of weapons to members of the criminal hierarchy.

Fortunately, prison guards were on high alert, and, as it turned out, the *jamaat* did not plan to attack them, so a war was avoided. However, the *jamaat* did expect Umar to be punished by the criminal leadership. And since it was, potentially, a very dangerous situation, it was immediately taken up by the top *vory* in Moscow. The plan was to do a conference call between the *vory* in Moscow, prison criminal leadership, and *jamaat* leadership to decide how to punish Umar and reinstall peace.

But one of the criminal leaders who was supposed to take part was not reachable. Allegedly he was in an inner prison somewhere else in Russia. Everyone decided to wait, but during the interim, the prison authorities intervened and many members of the *jamaat*, including its leadership, were transferred to another prison.

But members of the *jamaat* did not believe the story about the unreachable *vor* and felt the *vory* were just covering for Umar. It seemed suspicious they would wait for this particular *vor* if any *vor* could have solved the problem. Weren't there hundreds of *vory* in the criminal world that could answer the phone? And it was hardly believable that there was no phone in inner prison in a black prison camp. "What they were doing was buying time for Umar to be released," one *jamaat* member said. And it was true that Umar was released before he was punished.

At the same time, for the inmates who remained in prison, the *vory* played the incident down, portraying it as a simple ethnic problem. According to them, instead of a conflict between the *jamaat* and the criminal world, it was a personal conflict between an Ingush and a Chechen, two ethnic groups from the Caucasus. This strategy was relatively successful, and the conflict did not spread behind the prison walls. At least not until the next incident took place.

On November 15, 2019, a video of a man beating another man near the entrance of the prison camp went viral on social media. Unsurprisingly, the perpetrator was Umar, and the victim was a *jamaat* member from Dagestan. This victim was one of the few members of the *jamaat* present during the incident between Umar and the Chechen who had not been transferred to another prison.

To make things worse, Umar was only kicking him, which, according to *ponyatiya*, is very dishonorable to the victim and signals that he is *gad*. Within minutes, this video was reposted by almost every Russian-language Islamist channel with the following message:

> Today we got a message from a prison where there was an incident between a *blatnoj* from Igushetiya and our brother from Chechnya. . . . One *shaitan* [devil] *blatnoj*, may Allah humiliate him, under the influence of alcohol, started

> bothering a Muslim who was just passing by. *Blatnoj* provoked our brother and then hit him. Of course, our brother hit him back....
>
> Today, this *blatnoj* was released, and . . . on this same day, our Muslim brother was released. So this *blatnoj* and his friends caught him at the gate and beat him up, saying it was revenge for the previous incident. They also recorded it on video and sent it to their friends inside the prison camp who were laughing at it.... I am asking all brothers, no matter their ethnicity or skin color, please revenge your brother and also record it on video. And Inshallah, you *blatnyje shaitans* will get a video on which your *blatnoj* brother will be begging for mercy. Wait, and we will also wait.

The response inside the prison was polarizing. Some inmates came to Umar's defense. According to members of the criminal leadership, "Ethnically-Muslim Umar is not against Muslims although he does not pray. He believes in God and knows that, what he is doing now, he will have to answer for to God later. We have a disabled fifty-five-year-old ex-Islamist fighter in the inner prison who was badly tortured by law enforcement[21] and Umar helped him."

Others were more pragmatic. "I do not care if he beat the guy and why, but he should not have done it right in front of the prison, and he shouldn't have recorded it. He was showing off and not thinking about the consequences, especially for those left inside." "The prison guards are very concerned about this incident," commented another inmate.

Amir Abdullah carefully choose his words when he commented on what happened. "The Ingush and Chechen had personal problems. But we understand that from the outside, it looks different. So in the future, the Ingush might suffer from actions of some brothers." Another member of the *jamaat* had a more radical outlook. According to him, "Umar was always against Islam, and for the last year we ignored him and never even said hi to him. I am sure that the ones who will kill Umar will climb the ranks in the *jamaat*."

Indeed, the immediate reactions on major Islamist social media platforms were asking for exactly this:

> A tagut soldier (Umar from Ingushetiya)—along with his friends who came to pick him up from prison—beat a Muslim. Thanks be to God that there are lions in our Umma who want to help our brother.... The video that you (Umar), a dog, recorded, you will be watching multiple times from the phones of those Muslim brothers who will catch you. You will watch as they beat you....

How the situation played out in a long run, however, was interrupted by a major counter terrorism operation less than a month later. The majority of prison *jamaat* members were taken by FSB and charged with a new crime in connection with ISIS. According to an official statement of the Investigative Committee of Russia shown on all major Russian television channels:

> The Investigative Committee of Russia opened a criminal case against twenty-two people, according to a 205 criminal code article [organization of a terrorist group and taking part in it]. In 2013, a native of Dagestan, serving his sentence for illegal weapons possession in [that prison], organized a terrorist group with a goal of supporting terrorist activities. Since 2013, more than 100 inmates of this prison camp who supported his goals joined him. The Investigative Committee of Russia—together with the FSB, local police, and corrections authorities—conducted an anti-terrorism operation in Dagestan, Kabardino-Balkaria, the Krasnodar and Volgograd regions. They searched the houses of those under investigation and their family members, and in the office of the deputy director of Department of Corrections [of the region]. As result, five people were arrested outside of the prison camp, and seventeen inside were charged.

Those arrested inside the prison camp were moved away for interrogation and a trial. Included were all the main characters of the story including active members of the *jamaat.* Both previously released *amirs* (Ali and Mohamed), and even the director of the prison who hid the *jamaat* phone scamming business were also arrested. According to a prosecution office, part of the money the *jamaat* collected from their business operations had been sent to support ISIS terrorist activities.

15

Neo-Nazis behind Bars

In 2009, a new twist on an old ideology sprung up on Russian soil, an opposition movement known as neo-Nazism. In particular, three regional groups rose to prominence: the Orel Partisans (in the town of Orel), the Primorsky Partisans (a village in Far East Russia), and the NS/WP (National Socialism/White Power) in Saint Petersburg.

The main motivation of members of neo-Nazi groups is like that of radical Islamist forces—opposing the Russian government by any means necessary. Like Islamists, neo-Nazis see violence as the only way to fight government corruption and, since their inception, have assassinated immigrants, attacked law enforcement officials, committed acts of terrorism, and even attempted a short-lived guerilla war in 2010. The main difference between Islamists and neo-Nazis is what happens once they achieve the ultimate goal of defeating the government. For Islamists, it would be Muslims who take over the governments, and for neo-Nazis, it would be the Russian Slavs.

As expected, it was not long after inception that many of those group members were arrested and entered the prison system, further diversifying the inmate population and adding a new color to the prison spectrum. In addition to the existing red, black, and green, the neo-Nazis became the *whites*.

It would seem that the situation with whites in prison would be similar to that of the greens—they would construct their own organization within the existing prison system and increase their membership from among the inmate population. But the reality of their prison experience is very different. Not only are they not able to do what Islamists did, but they actually lost members to the *vory* criminal organization, the *jamaats*, and even prison administration if they become collaborators (as members of the *sherst'* caste, or even their violent counterparts, *activisty*). So in this chapter, I will talk about why neo-Nazis, when compared to Islamists, are not able to increase their ranks in prison and actually end up losing members during incarceration.

Islamists and neo-Nazis are unified in their hatred of the current government, their goal to overthrow it, and their violent discrimination against those in their out-groups. For Islamists that out-group is *kafirs* (non-Muslims), and they openly fight against them, while neo-Nazis target non-whites as their out-group.

Criminals, Nazis, and Islamists. Vera Mironova, Oxford University Press. © Oxford University Press 2023.
DOI: 10.1093/oso/9780197645659.003.0016

However, such similarities between the two groups are often not noticed by the public eye. Islamists operating in the former Soviet Union are able to tout their desire to deliver people from a hostile government while downplaying their holy war against unbelievers, while neo-Nazis are not. As a result, Islamists are often considered freedom fighters who do not attack innocent civilians while neo-Nazis are considered terrorists. When most people think about neo-Nazis, they think about the deaths of innocent non-white people, not that the main goal of their activities is an attack on the government.

According to an interviewed neo-Nazi imprisoned on terrorism charges, "Maybe we started with just hitting random non-white people, but we quickly realized how dumb that was. We realized that it was not the fault of those folks, but a bigger problem with the government and started organizing to conduct actual operations against the government."

Culture

Like any other social movement, neo-Nazis have developed their own culture complete with language, music, and religion.

Language

Although neo-Nazis have not developed their own slang yet, their everyday language is filled with German words. Nicknames that members of the group take are often stylized to resemble German names. For example, if the original name of a female is Olga, she might change it to Helga. Most telling of their allegiance is in their greetings to one another, which are usually either the usual "Heil Hitler" or the more creative "14/88."[1]

Music

A rich musical culture has developed around neo-Nazism, and the most popular band is *Kolovrat*. The name of the band is the word for the Slavic pagan symbol of the sun, which resembles the swastika. Their most famous album is called *Blood of the Patriots*, where a song with the same name has the following lyrics:

Krov' patriotov chistaya	The blood of the patriots is pure.
Clovno rosa alaya krov' vnov' vytekayet iz rany	Like dew, scarlet blood flows out of the wound again.
Mortvyye stonut, i my slyshim ikh golosa	The dead moan and we hear their voices.
Tonut v ariyskoy krovi yevropeyskiye strany	European countries drown in Aryan blood.

Dress Code

To visibly distinguish themselves from out-groups, neo-Nazis have adopted a particular dress code. Both males and females usually wear black. Often, the men's heads are shaven, and they only wear particular brands of clothing and heavy military boots with white shoelaces. Their image is also often completed with tattoos, usually of German words, Scandinavian script, or pictures of fighting dog breeds.

Emphasis on the Non-Material

According to neo-Nazis, National Socialism is not just a form of government, but a spiritual ideology that denies the importance of material value. To support that claim they often use the following quote from Adolf Hitler: "Anyone who sees National Socialism only as a political movement, does not understand anything about it. National Socialism is the will to create a superman."

Religion

Many neo-Nazis claim to be modern pagans (*rodnovery*) following the pre-Christian religions of the Germanic, Scandinavian, and Anglo-Saxon peoples. Neo-Nazis are skeptical about Christianity, as Adolf Hitler was, in part because they believe Jesus was a Jew whose Christian religion was part of government propaganda. In fact, many of their terrorist operations even target Christian churches.[2]

Gender

Neo-Nazi gender roles are similar to those of many other radical movements, including Islamists. In-group females are expected to be modest and submissive to their husbands and, most importantly, to uphold their ideals of honor and dignity. Her role in the society in general is limited to helping her husband (and other males of the community) in the struggle for the white race and raising children according to neo-Nazi ideology.

Broader Community

Neo-Nazis in Russia see themselves as part of the much bigger community, one involved in a worldwide, racial battle of whites against non-whites. This community identity is even highlighted in a one of their songs, dedicated to Serbs in Kosovo:

Nashim serbskim brat'yam pomoshch' tak nuzhna	Our Serbian brothers need so much help.
Im odnim seychas ne ustoyat'.	They alone cannot resist.
Belaya pobeda- kak ona vazhna,	White victory, how important it is,
Kosovo albantsam ne otnyat'.	Albanians would not take Kosovo away.

Whites in Prison

Despite their similarities to Islamists—in goal and method—neo-Nazi positioning within black prisons is far from the privileged status of *jamaats*. The main reason for this difference is outside perception. Most inmates do not see neo-Nazis as a group who fights against the government (how Islamists are seen). To them (and most other people), neo-Nazis fight against innocent civilians because of their differing religions and ethnicities.

The criminal *ponyatiya* are very clear about hate crimes based on individual nationalities or religions. Discrimination is not allowed because the *vory* criminal organization does not recognize nationality or religion. And while Islamists are able to downplay the out-group (non-Muslim) part of their activities, neo-Nazis are not. This automatically puts neo-Nazi inmates at odds with the criminal leadership and their criminal rules.

So when a neo-Nazi is arrested and imprisoned, where does he end up? In a black or gray prison, guards place such an inmate in the *muzhiki* caste cell where his fate will be determined by the prison criminal leadership. A neo-Nazi's original crime and attitude are usually the best determiners of their fate.

Upper Caste

If an inmate was not personally involved in killing an innocent civilian on racial grounds and does not openly voice his ideology, he has the opportunity to remain in the *muzhiki* caste, although it would be on the lower end. In particular, he might remain in the *muzhiki* caste as a *snir*. He would have to clean floors and cook, but he would still be included in their society.

Lower Caste

If a neo-Nazi inmate is very open about his racist opinions or had been personally involved in killing an innocent civilian, he would be beaten and degraded to the *petukhi* caste.

If a person is a neo-Nazi and openly voices his racist opinions but is *not* incarcerated for a racist crime, he will only be beaten and kicked out of the upper caste cell and told to "Go live with your people." He will then go to prison guards and explain that he was kicked out and needs to be placed in a different cell. Then prison guards would have to place him with either the *sherst'* or the *petukhi*. There have been cases where prison guards place such an inmate in a *sherst'* cell, but members of that caste also won't take him in, and prison guards have to relocate the neo-Nazi inmate again, this time to a *petukhi* cell.

From time to time, neo-Nazi inmates cannot handle being degraded and take their own lives. In 2010, a twenty-one-year-old neo-Nazi named Dmitry Antipov was sentenced to nine years for several assaults on African immigrants. Soon after his incarceration, he was found hanged in his cell. His friend explained the situation:

> There were only people from Caucasus in his barrack, and the *smotryasçiy* was also from there. The day before his death, he called me to say goodbye. I asked him what happened, and he said that non-whites wanted to degrade them [him and another neo-Nazi]. Prison camp authorities did not do anything. He said that they would prefer to honorably die in fighting then to go through the shame of being degraded. At 6:30 am, non-white inmates attacked them, and my friend tried to fight back a sharpened object. Eventually then, prison authorities interfered and transferred them to another prison, where he was found dead later.[3]

Personal Indicators

What is a neo-Nazi inmate's strategy when entering prison? He cannot remain in a neo-Nazi group since it does not exist, so he will join another group. But the choice of the group will largely depend on the reasons he joined the neo-Nazi movement in the first place, as follow.

Racism

For some, their main interest in neo-Nazism is racially motivated, and it is something they adhere to deeply. These inmates make no attempt to hide their neo-Nazi status. In one prison, a neo-Nazi inmate in the office of prison guards took office scissors from the table and stabbed himself in the neck saying, "I am for Russia, and refuse to be in prison with non-whites!"

In these cases, neo-Nazis inmates are safer in a red prison. In a black prison, any actions based on discrimination would violate *ponyatiya* and would be punishable, whereas they would not be in a red prison.

These inmates are not only safer in red prisons, but they even thrive there. By joining activist inmates—violent collaborators with prison administration—they can enjoy leadership positions among the inmate population, take revenge

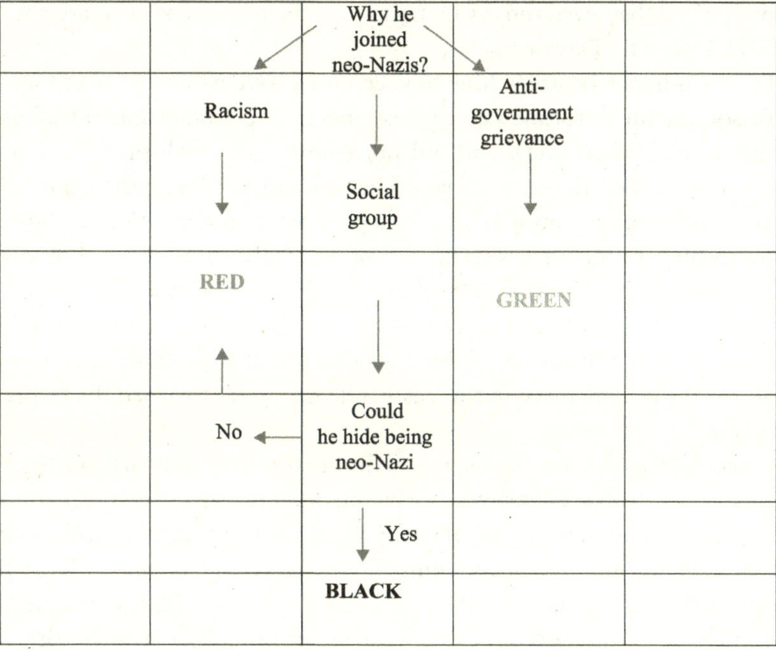

Figure 15.1 Options neo-Nazis have in prison

on criminal leadership, and discriminate against (by beating and torturing) non-white inmates, many of whom have leadership positions in the *vory* criminal family.

But if a blatant neo-Nazi is not lucky enough to get into a red prison, he could still join the *sherst'* caste and work for the administration in a black prison. In that case, although he would be low in the prison caste system, he would be, at least partially, protected from the prison criminal leadership by the prison administration.

Social Group

If an inmate joined the neo-Nazi movement simply as a social group without any ideological reasons and is able to hide his previous involvement, he has a chance of remaining in the prison criminal hierarchy, and maybe even advancing there.

Interviewed inmates explained that it was not hard to identify neo-Nazis because they do not hide it, or they are not good at doing so. They dress differently. They wear particular shoe brands, short jeans, and short jackets. They also have visible neo-Nazi tattoos on their hands—pictures of pit bulls and words written in German. Some of them also openly talk about their racist opinions.

There have also been neo-Nazi inmates who, on entering prison, openly declared their unwillingness to listen to non-white people, even after considering that very often members of prison criminal leadership are non-white. One inmate added that "even those who try to hide their neo-Nazi ideas are not very good at it when they are drunk."

But for others who are willing to keep quiet, have no neo-Nazi tattoos, are in prison for the first time (so it takes longer for prison criminal leadership to check his background), and did not commit any high-profile crimes, it is possible to hide their neo-Nazi affiliation and become part of the upper caste of the criminal family. That is also possible for an inmate who had committed a high-profile neo-Nazi crime but was still a minor when it occurred because, according to *ponyatiya*, underaged offenders are not responsible for their deeds. In either case, a neo-Nazi, by default, will be in the *muzhiki*'s caste on arrival to the prison. Even if his true identity comes up later, he has a good chance of remaining in this caste if he has already earned the respect of his peers.

A neo-Nazi inmate could even rise in the ranks of the criminal hierarchy. One former inmate who spent ten years in prison on terrorism charges (against non-whites) is now part of the criminal family. He did so by being very careful to keep his racial views and opinions to himself. He also considers himself lucky that, "from the beginning [of his sentence], I was in the cell with the *vor*. He liked me, and [when I was moved] he would call before my arrival in other prisons, so I would not only be safe there, but respected." This inmate eventually moved to a prison camp where they never had a *vor*, but because he had at least been in the same cell with one, and had learned from him, he was considered a respectable authority.

Anti-Government Grievance

Many neo-Nazis joined their movement because their grievance centered on the current government and their main goal was to overthrow it. So for them, the closest group with government grievances in prison is Islamist *jamaats*.

This can be well illustrated by a story of a famous Russian neo-Nazi, Kirill "Vegan." In 2009, he was accused of taking part in the terrorist attack in the metro in Russia. In particular, according to the prosecution, his role was drawing swastikas and writing "Hasis" (the last name of the person from the Caucasus accused of associations with a Russian journalist and lawyer) on the bomb. He was also accused of recording a speech on video when a group of other neo-Nazis killed an African immigrant. He was sentenced and imprisoned.

In propaganda, Vegan was basically made a hero by his fellow neo-Nazis. For example, they published the following messages about him online: "Kirill is a true revolutionary. He and his comrades fought against the Putin regime as true revolutionary should—fanatically and without compromise—until victory or until death." And in an interview, he also confirmed that his main grievance was always against the Putin regime.

In 2011, he again stood before a judge for an extension of his sentence (for violating prison rules). After being sentenced to two more months in prison, the court guards were escorting him to the car when he decided to make a statement. Everyone expected him to say, "Heil Hitler" or something along those lines, but that is not what he said. Instead he yelled, "*Shahada*—There is no God but Allah, and Muhammad is the messenger of Allah" (in both Russian and Arabic). Two of his friends (also neo-Nazis turned Islamists) were there, and, according to the Islamic rules, they said, "Witness that you are our brother."

In fact, often relations between neo-Nazi and Islamist insurgencies are usually positive, even outside prison walls. First, neo-Nazis respect Islamists for their actions against the government. When asked who the main heroes in the fight against the Russian regime were, several interviewed neo-Nazis named Islamists Said Buryatsky[4] and Anzor Estimirov.[5] According to an interviewed neo-Nazi ex-inmate, "Before I was arrested, I was putting stickers on walls in my town that said, 'Slavs, kill police; Chechens, kill police; Dagestanis, kill police,' and it had a swastika on it."

Second, neo-Nazis see Islamists as a more experienced and successful force they could learn from. As a result, they look to them for guidance on insurgency operations and ideological inspiration. They even read their literature and news websites. One former neo-Nazi inmate explained, "When preparing for our operations, we always looked at Islamists fighting in the North Caucasus because they were successfully doing exactly what we wanted to do—fight the central government. We even wrote messages to their [Islamist insurgency] website with support, and they published them."

Often Islamist literature is also found on neo-Nazis during law enforcement searches. According to another interviewed neo-Nazi, "I was always reading the Caucasus Emirate [major Islamist group] website. They have the best and most objective information, better than ours or the government propaganda. They even had the best reporting on crimes we did."

Neo-Nazis also see Islamists as their colleagues in the fight against the Russian government and are sure that this opinion is mutual. According to an interviewed neo-Nazi who was imprisoned for putting an explosive in a police station, "On video, Said Buryatsky said that they would support whites fighting against the government. This video was widely distributed on the internet, but the FSB did not like it and altered it. So now it looks like he said we will only help whites if they convert to Islam, which is not true." Although it is not clear if his statement itself is true or not, it shows how he thinks about members of Islamist groups.

Another interviewed neo-Nazi inmate remembers meeting a famous Islamist, who had previous insurgency experience and was in prison for killing a judge and attempting to kill a government official. According to an interviewed neo-Nazi, he was very impressed that when an Islamist was asked whether his group would help neo-Nazis in organizing potential operations against the Russian government, the Islamist said they would be happy to.

Also, in the famous video address from members of the Primorsky Partisans, who started an insurgency war in Russia shortly before they were arrested or killed in 2010, they said their goal was to get rid of a government that was oppressing people. They also addressed insurgents in the North Caucasus, greeting them and calling them honest and brave people.

Despite the sympathy the two groups have for each other, they almost never interact in person outside of prison. Incarceration, however, gives them this opportunity. One widely distributed and fascinating neo-Nazi letter gives an idea of the nature of these relationships:

> Statistically, my cellmates are most often Muslims. For at least half of my prison sentence, I listened to Muslim prayers five times a day. Recently, I spent a month with a Wahhabi [radical Islamist] guy, and because I am interested in everything that the system [government] is afraid of, I started carefully studying the worldviews of the followers of Al-Wahhab [with the Wahabbi inmate's help]. We were both learning from each other, since I was the first pagan, Russian neo-Nazi Russian he'd met.

Often in the evenings, we played chess. By a mutual agreement, I always played the white side and he, the black. We both saw it as natural. We studied each other, sharing opinions, asking pointed questions and not hiding answers, like two space aliens might have studied each other on their first encounter—that is how different our worldviews were. But we also found a lot of similarities.

For example, we perfectly understood how hostile the system was to us, and that we are both dangerous to it. And this system could do nothing to us or the ideas of either Russian nationalism or radical Islam other than the old fashioned and ineffective method of imprisonment. We were even imprisoned in the same place and investigated by the same people who tried to persuade, trick, and scare both of us. The only difference is that prison guards promised to put him in the cell with "crazy skinheads" and me with "wild people from the Caucasus." To both of us, they gave their official word that our life in prison would be painful.

We both survived criminal leadership who promised to make our prison lives terrible because I am an extremist, and he is a terrorist. But we both stayed calm and managed them. I did it by a logical conversation; he did it by a fight. Both of us also have females outside, waiting for us. Me, a wife and him, a girlfriend. Our food was in the same refrigerator, but on different shelves. Pig's fat [popular Russian snack] and halal meat—like a symbol of unity of opposites.

Every morning until lunch, we did different sports. He did martial arts and I practiced fencing with a piece of plastic used to cut food. During the day, we studied foreign languages. English is important for me, and Arabic is necessary for him.

I read his Islamic *hadiths* and he read my newspapers, *Right View* and *Russian Truth*. We both preferred the television to be switched off. He was surprised to see the Bible and Quran on my bookshelf, and for me, his anti-Semitism was unexpected.

Sometimes it happened that we barely exchanged several words during the day, but when we sat down to play chess, our conversations would flow. In our slow conversations, he would highlight that we both refused alcohol and cigarettes, and I would be surprised at how we were both against the system. Sometimes our peaceful conversations could get heated over such topics as terrorist attacks in airports and the metro [done by Islamists], war in North Caucasus [done by Islamists], riots in center of Moscow [done by neo-Nazis] and killings of immigrants [done by neo-Nazis]. At those points, the prison guards would knock on our doors, so we tried to avoid those discussions.

In our conversations, we did not find compromises. Multi-culture is not for us [neo-Nazis]. I on the other side was thinking about his opinion that we could work together against drug trafficking, pedophilia, prostitution, and everything else that is harmful for both of our nations. On those points, I felt that if

> our chessboard had a third side, we would, without hesitation, unite together against the common enemy. Thanks to law enforcement, the Wahhabi guy learned the truth about Russian nationalism and I, about *mujaheeds*. Without them, we both would still have been held hostage by media propaganda.

Many interviewed neo-Nazis also mentioned that Islamists had helped them in prison. One interviewed neo-Nazi inmate remembered, "In my prison, the most important person was an Islamist named Sidik, and his best friend was a *polojenets*. I did not usually talk to him because we disagreed about religion, but when my girlfriend was arrested [also on neo-Nazi charges], Sidik called a Chechen prison guard working in her prison and asked to make sure she was okay."

Often neo-Nazis even convert to Islam and join *jamaats* in prison. For example, according to interviewed neo-Nazis, the majority of imprisoned members of the Primorsky Partisans[6] converted to Islam and joined the *jamaats*. They realized that since Islamists are the most organized and effective in their anti-government activities, they would be better off joining them to act on their grievances. One interviewed inmate even had both Adolf Hitler and the ISIS flag tattooed on his chest. He served his first prison sentence for a neo-Nazi crime but is currently incarcerated for an attempt to join ISIS.

It is actually very easy for a neo-Nazi inmate to join a *jamaat* because he does not have to hide his neo-Nazi history. As discussed in the previous chapters, *jamaats* take everyone who claims to turn to Islam because, according to their teachings, what happened to the person before he turned to Islam is not important. Like any member of the lower caste, a neo-Nazi can advance in the prison society if he converts to Islam and joins a *jamaat*.

How do neo-Nazi peers view a conversion from pagan white nationalism to Islamism under the leadership of non-whites? Some are in agreement. According to one radical neo-Nazi who spent ten years in prison for terrorism, "I believe that Primorsky Partisans could be right to join Islamists, but I myself just do not want to betray the culture [pagan religion] I have followed since I was thirteen years old."

Others are less favorable in their opinion of converts, but they do understand. According to another interviewed neo-Nazi who spent three years in prison on extremism charges, "The guys who converted to Islam totally betrayed our ideas and our friendship. We were sending them birthday and New Year's cards in prison, and they would make fun of them and throw them away.[7] Only weak people from our movement turn to Islamists because they are stronger. But I understand it. They want to overthrow the government more than anything else."

Building a (White) Parallel Structure

The majority of neo-Nazis in prison do not want to be under the command of prison criminal leadership. According to an interviewed neo-Nazi, it was unacceptable for them to listen to "a gay drug addict from Georgia [non-white]." He also pointed to a corrupt and hypocritical leadership that uses heroin but prohibits it for the other inmates. "They [also] could not survive without cooperating with prison administration, but they try to hide it," the interviewee said. "We, on the other hand, are openly working with them [as *sherst'* and *activisty*], so why does it make us worse than them? At least we are honest."

They are also concerned that other ethnic groups within the *vory* criminal family are cohesive and support each other while whites do not have anyone to look after their interests. According to an interviewed inmate, "In my prison, we had a group of Tajiks. One of them lost money in a card game and was not able to pay back on time. So his fellow Tajiks collected money and paid for him so he was not kicked to *sherst'*. They all stood up to protect him."

Another neo-Nazi told a story illustrating how hard it was for them to ensure that some ethnic groups are not favored in their prison. One time, all the inmates in the barrack left, but he and his friend stayed behind. A group of new inmates came in, and among them were several people from Central Asia on rape charges. This is a bad charge, so as inmates are supposed to do by *ponyatiya*, they investigated it. They separated new inmates and started interviewing.

At first, they said that they did not rape anyone, and it was a police set-up. "But we were sneaky," explains the interviewed inmate, "so we kept asking the same questions over and over again, rephrasing them. Then we asked one of them, 'What did she say when you were raping her?' He replied, 'Just do not kill me.' At that point, it was clear that they really did what they were being accused of." And as they were supposed to do by *ponyatiya*, they beat them and sent them to a *petukhi* barrack.

But when everyone came back from work and found out what happened, there was a scandal. "It was clear that if we were not there at that time and did not do what we did," said the inmate, "their fellow countrymen would have saved them from *petukhi* caste."

So the majority of interviewed neo-Nazis, when asked what their goal in prison was, said they wished to have their own group following their own rules (like *jamaats*). According to an interviewed neo-Nazi inmate, "We are afraid of losing our white identity. We want to have our own group and not follow criminal rules because they were made by [non-white] people from the Caucasus. But then together with criminals and *jamaats*, we of course would work against prison leadership."

An example these inmates often mention is that in the history of the Russian prison system, there was a time when that was the case. For example, after WWII, many pro-Nazi nationalists from the Ukraine and Baltic states were imprisoned in the Gulag system where they lived separately as a powerful, strong, and cohesive group that was very respected by other inmates.

So is it possible for neo-Nazis to also build a parallel to the prison *jamaat* structure outside of the criminal leadership jurisdiction? Currently, there are several issues that prevent that from happening.

Obstacles

Bad Publicity

Neo-Nazis are aware of the bad PR their organization has had, especially as compared to the Islamists. This hurts them both in and outside of prison. According to an interviewed neo-Nazi inmate, "Nazis and Islamists do very similar things, but everyone thinks Islamists are defending religion and are fighting a war [so civilian rules do not apply to them], so it is allowed. It is hypocrisy." So in their official statements and unofficial forums, neo-Nazis highlight the urgent need to change their image.

Missed Opportunity

In comparing neo-Nazis to Islamists, it is clear neo-Nazis missed a criminal *ponyatiya* loophole that Islamists have long since exploited. When finding a way to circumvent the *vory* system, Islamists were clever enough to highlight their religiosity as a reason for a *jamaat*'s existence. This worked because, especially in the beginning of their insurgency-style *dawah*, the growing *jamaats* were largely ignored by criminal leadership. Initially, the *vory* criminal organization did not fully understand what was going on and were also cautious about intervening in what was labeled as religious affairs. By the time the criminal family did realize what was happening, it was too late; the concept of separate *jamaats* were already established. Neo-Nazis lost this opportunity to do the same thing and use their own religion—modern paganism—to carve out their own identity within the prisons. Now they will have to find other ways to separate.

Little Outside Support

Because Islamists in general have a strong hierarchy and are geographically segregated into large groups (to North Caucasus region for example), it makes it much easier for them to coordinate with one another. Neo-Nazis, on the other hand, are widespread across Russia and have little interaction with one another outside of prison. As a result, they are much less organized, not only in their activities against the government, but even in their help for their imprisoned brothers-in-arms. So while Islamists are able to increase outside support with claims of discrimination within the prison, neo-Nazis are not. According to an interviewed neo-Nazi inmate, "The White Movement is very divided, but we are not a small number. We are, in fact, many people who just need to get united." Another former neo-Nazi inmate agreed with the need for more outside support: "In 2009, even Doku Umarov [an Islamist leader of insurgency in the North Caucasus] said that we need to help our people in prison [Islamists] so that they have maximum comfort there if we cannot get them out. We should take the same position."

The need for outside support and an improved public image is illustrated in a document published by one of the main neo-Nazi groups, NS/WP Novgorod. Below (numbered as in original document) are three of five key decisions the group made in January of 2011:

3) Because of the constantly increasing pressure on members of NS/WP Novgorod currently on trial, we call for members of other neo-Nazi and revolutionary groups to publicly campaign, both legally and illegally, in solidarity with those arrested and to put pressure on the repressive regime [government] by all possible means.
4) We've collected a dataset of prison criminal leaders, law enforcement, and FSB members who were involved in torturing inmates (name, photo, family members, addresses, their role in tortures). We will distribute it first through our secret channels, and then will make it publicly available. If you are able to contribute to it, please do so.
5) We again call to avoid any actions based on religious and national intolerance against civilians and any actions that will give a bad reputation to our movement (and would only benefit government and law enforcement). By our example, we want to show the new generation of NS/WP activists that it is time for a change.

We have to change the negative stereotypes that our members are underaged maniacs. It is time to dedicate our efforts to fighting an occupational regime by attacking those who work for it and not those who are its product (like illegal immigrants and homeless people).

Addressing NS/WP activists, we want to wish a more fruitful use of resources and more thought-out choice of targets in agreement with other members and the civilian population in general.

Revolution or death! Forward to the victory!

Little Military Experience

When Islamists first entered the prison system, they were already experienced and battle hardened. As a result, they were respected and able to talk to prison criminal leadership at the highest level. This authority helped them separate from the criminal hierarchy and build their own group. Neo-Nazis, on the other hand, are often arrested before they have fighting, or even life, experience. They often enter the prison system very young and unseasoned, so they are not taken seriously nor are they respected.

Internal Division

Neo-Nazi inmates are extremely divided, even within the prisons. Some of them are in the prison criminal hierarchy, some are in *jamaats*, and some are even working for prison authorities. Although this fact further prevents them from organizing into a separate group, some interviewed neo-Nazis do not think so and are trying to benefit from this situation. According to interviewed neo-Nazi inmate, "It doesn't help much if all of our guys join the criminal hierarchy, but it would help our cause if they joined *sherst'* because it would make our relations with prison authorities easier. It is absolutely okay that they [neo-Nazis] are doing so when imprisoned."

Forging an Identity

Despite the many complications, some neo-Nazi inmates are taking steps toward organizing whites in prison into one group. But it has to be done extremely carefully. In fact, even more carefully than the first imprisoned Islamists. One former neo-Nazi inmate commented in an interview that when whites were as powerful as Islamists, "we will also tell the prison criminal leadership that we are against their institution. But we are not in such a position now. We may be an insurgency now, but later we will reject both blacks and reds."

Another neo-Nazi inmate explained that they were trying to organize by having fellow whites from the upper caste [*muzhiki*] and *sherst'* meet together to drink tea. They also shared literature, food, and even a cell phone. He added: "Our minimum-security prison bordered a medium-security prison where there was one of our people, so we also made sure that he was with us."

Another inmate added, "I have good relations with neo-Nazis who became members of activist. In my prison, there were two neo-Nazis—one red and one black. Then several more came in. I was organizing our meeting (with tea and sweets), but to avoid problems, I asked everyone to bring their own teacup [not to mix castes]. We agreed that to survive and potentially grow, we needed to stick together, read, do sports, and so on." When I asked how other inmates viewed such meetings, he replied, "Inmates from the Caucasus [members of *jamaats*] were okay, but Russians from criminal leadership really did not like it."

Changing Perception

With time, however, this situation could indeed improve for neo-Nazis. First, the beginnings of their own identity even began in one prison with a respected neo-Nazi who was capable of changing the perception of the movement. In the past, absolutely all whites were sent to the *sherst'* caste or even degraded, but thanks to one person, it is slowly changing now. There was an inmate named Nikola Korolev, who was in prison for explosions in the Cherkizovo bazaar.[8] In 2006 or 2007, he was in prison in Moscow and prison guards put them in a cell where he was supposed to be beaten by inmates working for administration. But he was a good fighter, so he beat them, which surprised prison criminal leadership. They had tried to take control of that cell in the past but were not able to. They started respecting him so he negotiated that prison criminal leadership would not fight neo-Nazis, which significantly improved the situation for neo-Nazis in that prison.

Advancement in *Vory* Criminal Family

Second, several other neo-Nazis have gained respect and risen through the ranks of the criminal family. Usually these inmates are individuals who had committed crimes while underaged (and so were not punished according to *ponyatiya*) and spent a lot of time behind bars, which allowed them to both gain respect from the *vory* criminal world and learn the craft of running a prison government. In some cases, they are able to help incoming neo-Nazis avoid some of the harsher elements of the prison criminal system.

Other times they are not. One neo-Nazi inmate who had risen among the *vory* criminal world explained how he was able to help one neo-Nazi stay in the *muzhiki* caste, even though he had killed an immigrant. But it was not always that easy, especially for young guys that "sometimes are really dumb":

> There was another Nazi guy in Butirka. For being a Nazi, the criminal leadership made him a *snir*. He agreed, but later wanted to stop doing this job. . . . Although I knew it would be impossible to get him out of the job, I wanted to make sure he was at least treated well. The problem was the idiot was lying to *blatnyje*. . . . There is absolutely nothing I could do to make life for this idiot less of a hell.

Education

A third factor that may help neo-Nazis find their place in prisons is the education they gain there. Incoming neo-Nazis are often placed with or near Islamists accused of terrorist attacks, and spending time together with them, they learn. According to one interviewed neo-Nazi inmate who spent ten years in an inner prison for terrorism, "I was in a cell with another neo-Nazi, and our cell was nicknamed 'Third Reich.' Next to us was a cell with Islamists called 'Caliphate.'" And according to an interviewed member of the criminal leadership, "Often guys on terrorism charges, both neo-Nazi and Islamists, are in the inner prison. There, those Islamists teach those neo-Nazi kids everything from sports to how to run an organization, and when they finally get back out into the general population, they are very dangerous people."

Alliances

Finally, the internal politics inside the highest level of the criminal world may also benefit neo-Nazis. Recently, several Slavic *vory* realized that neo-Nazis have become friendlier with them. Since the 1990s, Slavic *vory* have been losing power to *vory* from the Caucasus. They also see Muslim *vory* cooperating with Islamist *jamaats*, who, if needed, could be used as militias. So the Slavs have started checking to see if they would be able to use neo-Nazis in the same way.[9] One interviewed neo-Nazi started working with *vory* in prison and is now an aspiring *vor* himself. He gave his opinion of the situation:

> Slavic *vory* need to be very careful about cooperating with neo-Nazis. *Vory* accept Nazis now, but they cannot say so. . . . It is now obvious to everyone, including *vory*, that multiculturalism does not work, and the only thing that will work is a return to nationalism. Georgian *vory* want to hang out with Georgians and see them prosper, and the same is true with Slavic *vory*.
>
> At the same time, I managed to communicate to fellow neo-Nazi inmates that we are in prison, and here we cannot fight based on skin color. It does not matter who is next to you in the cell. Your only enemy is the system. And in prison, the system is prison guards. If you do not like to eat from the same plate as non-whites, it is your choice, but we cannot be enemies with them here. And the majority agreed with me.

Leaving *vory* family politics aside, some members of the criminal family are increasing in their anti-government grievances and are becoming interested in neo-Nazi ideology. For example, one of the imprisoned members of Orel Partisans is son of the criminal *smotryasçiy* of the town of Orel.[10] This also potentially helps drive neo-Nazis and the criminal family closer to each other.

Conclusion

While Islamists are able to separate from the criminal hierarchy, neo-Nazis are still not able to do so, but are instead relegated to the lowest class of the inmate population. Because they do not have respected and battle-hardened leaders and strong support from the outside, they have been unable to earn the respect Islamists have. As a result, the *ponyatiya* rules that prohibit violence based on someone's ethnicity or religion cause neo-Nazi inmates to be punished—often beaten and sometimes degraded to *petukhi* caste.

So if an inmate cannot hide being part of the neo-Nazi group, they have few options other than looking for protection from either prison authorities (by becoming *sherst'* or *activist*) or from Islamists, which they do by joining *jamaats*.

This situation, however, could change in the near future. Slavic *vory* have noticed Muslim *vory* benefiting from cooperation with *jamaats* and are exploring the option of using neo-Nazis the same way—as a violent wing to increase their standing in the criminal family. But due to the extremely weak position of white supremacists in prison, until they increase in the respect—which they are urgently trying to do—such cooperation will be handled in a very secretive way.

Conclusion

In this book, I looked at the hundred-year history of Soviet and former Soviet prisons and their inmate community. First, in opposition to the Bolshevik communist government, there appeared the *vory* criminal organization with their own rules.

The Bolshevik Revolution of 1917 was led by those in the lowest class of society, including members of the criminal underworld and former inmates newly released from czarist prisons. As a result of the revolution, the social order of the country was changed, and when the Bolsheviks gained power, those deprived of resources had no option but to move underground. Eventually, they found themselves behind bars where they lived following their own *vory* criminal ideology, a code of prison-specific, ideologically inspired rules that became crucial to the *vory* criminal organization structure.

After taking full control of the country, the communist regime started an extremely ineffective governance, which, in turn, led to more people falling into the lowest class with no rights in that social order. It did not take long for the communist government to realize that its lowest class could soon challenge their rule. And in response, they turned to mitigating its symptoms by incarcerating people en masse. While behind bars, those people joined the *vory* criminal family, which soon declared total control of the prison's internal governance throughout the Soviet Union, and *vory* criminal ideology became the only ideology behind bars.

During its early years, the Soviet Union had a war with crime, and the situation in prisons for the *vory* criminal family was extremely difficult, and it fought for its survival. But that all changed at the end of the Soviet Union. When the country and its law enforcement became weak, the *vory* criminal organization became so strong that not only were they not just an underground secret group anymore, but they became a part of the legal business world, and even the government.

One would expect that legitimization, in many respects, made the *vory* organization stronger. But just the opposite occurred. The absence of an existential threat led the *vory* criminal group into getting stuck in the internal problems. Power-hungry leaders vied for leadership positions in the prison organization and succeeded by claiming to be exceptionally loyal to the groups' ideology. And as a consequence, inequality inside the organization increased, and within the prisons, more and more people became members of the lowest caste for violating strict ideologically inspired rules.

Criminals, Nazis, and Islamists. Vera Mironova, Oxford University Press. © Oxford University Press 2023.
DOI: 10.1093/oso/9780197645659.003.0017

Inmate dissatisfaction with the *vory* prison regime and its social order continued to increase until the early 2000s, when a new ideological group appeared in the prisons. They offered inmates an opportunity to challenge the century-old *vory* prison social order.

Islamist *jamaats*, claiming to be the antithesis of an unfair and corrupt *vory* criminal ideology, wanted to—if not take prisons over—at least share control of them. And they became successful, significantly increasing their ranks and eventually taking power in at least some of the prisons.

However, those Islamist *jamaats* that took power were also not immune from internal problems. When they secured their rule in prisons, they turned to making ideological, Sharia-inspired rules for their members much stricter and, at the same time, started promoting people who excelled in following them instead of those qualified to lead. That led to the group's decline, and in some prisons, the *vory* criminal organization was able to reinstall its power.

Deradicalizing Prisons

Above I talk about the situation inside prisons in the former Soviet Union. But like with a Russian nesting doll, a bigger society encapsulates those prisons, which encapsulate inmates, who are also citizens. That bigger society is the country.

And who are the most delegitimized, lowest-level class members of any country? The prison population. First, their status is so low, they are physically isolated from the rest of the society. Second, by definition, their rights are restricted. And finally, they are under the total control of the prevailing power because of the closed environment and lack of oversight in the penal system. This basically puts inmates at the total mercy of the system. They themselves often can do little to improve their situation, and in many cases, they cannot even make their situation known to others.

Such a position makes inmates very important to look at in terms of potential challengers of a country's system, especially in countries like the former Soviet Union, where many inmates are behind bars for political reasons. As a result, prisons have become an incubator for the rise and spread of radical ideologies with inmates becoming future combatants who could challenge the existing social order. That is the place where those who start radically opposing government due to their position as prisoners (those arrested for regular crimes) meet those who are imprisoned because of radical opposition.

These become very dangerous connections for several reasons. First, because when people who oppose the government but follow different ideologies meet behind bars, they join forces and either make one ideological group stronger or become allies against the common enemy. Usually outside of prison, these people never have the opportunity to meet and discuss their goals and grievances, but prison gives them just such an opportunity.

Second, those imprisoned for radical opposition to the government also inspire non-ideological inmates to join their group. And finally, political prisoners learn new skills from those imprisoned for non-ideological crimes—skills like killing, how to use weapons and explosives, stealing, and scamming. Also, radical opposition members meet people who have ties to illegal businesses such as weapons smuggling. All of these connections could tremendously increase the power of an opposition movement against a government.

Such interaction between groups could be well illustrated by the story of one Uzbek member of ISIS who had been imprisoned several times in his small hometown. First, he was briefly arrested for a minor theft. But while behind bars, he learned a lot from his more experienced cellmates. He was also beaten by law enforcement officials, which increased an already existing grievance against the government which pushed him toward Islamism, and ISIS in particular. When he was freed from prison, he started stealing from supermarkets and reselling the merchandize to collect money to send it to ISIS before eventually going to Syria himself.

He was only there for a short time before he returned to his hometown and established an ISIS cell. His ambitious goal was performing terrorist attacks and potentially taking control of the country on behalf of the group. Using his contacts with the criminal world made while in prison, he bought weapons, something that is very difficult to do in that country.

This man was not successful is his terrorism enterprise, nor was he able to conduct any attacks. Instead, he was arrested. But that did not stop his zeal, and now in prison, he continues to radicalize others, trying to persuade them to support ISIS.

And in such efforts, he is supported from outside. Another Islamist, currently in hiding from law enforcement, who started a project called Zandinistan[1] to support Islamists behind bars in the former Soviet Union, said, "As in any insurgency war, we will have people who get arrested, and they will be very good members of the group. So our goal is, first, to support them while they are there, but also to help them continue working for the benefit of the group by recruiting more people. So our job is to provide them with halal food and our [Islamist] literature, so they can do their job."

Interestingly, the situation in prisons can also be used as a recruiting ground by outside enemies. Even in recent Russian history, it has been exploited by all regimes and groups. On one side, foreign enemies have tried to use Russian inmates against the Russian regime while, on the other side, the Russian government has tried to use foreigners they had in their prisons to spread their ideology abroad.

In 1919, at the eighth meeting of RKP(b), Lenin talked about spreading communism in Europe. He said that by sending ex-military members of Western countries—recruited from Russian POW camps and instructed in communism—back home, Russia could "make a virus of bolshevism to take over those countries."

In 1942, Nazi Germany also developed Operation Zeppelin to recruit Russian prisoners of war in Europe who would conduct espionage and sabotage Soviet operations. Part of this plan, developed by Russian prisoner of war Brigadier commander Bessonov, was to conduct a naval and air invasion of Siberia, targeting the Gulag prison camps and recruiting anti-Soviet forces from among the inmates who had grievances against the government. In this way, they wanted to open a second front in the war between Nazi Germany and the Soviet Union.[2]

Currently, there are radical Islamist groups trying to recruit inmates. For example, between 2000 and 2010, a radical imam named Marat Kudakaev (with the Tatarstan Islamic Council) worked as a liaison between the council and law enforcement. As such, he enjoyed the official religious authority to legally go into prisons and spread radical Islam among ethnic Muslim members of the criminal family. According to him, because the criminal leadership was running the prison society, the easiest way to spread radical Islam was through them, and the best *mujaheeds* would be inmates who already had experience killing people. Kudakaev appointed prison imams from those in upper prison castes who had not worked (and would not work) with prison administration. Finally, in 2012, Kudakaev was arrested for planning to assassinate the official imam of Tatarstan.

More recently, several inmates, after being released, went to Ukraine to fight because they saw it as the fastest way to exact revenge on Russia. What is interesting is that one of those former inmates is a neo-Nazi who converted to Islam in prison and was a member of the *jamaat* while there.

On the other side, interviewed former inmates of one prison in Chechnya said that while watching the news from the frontline in the Ukraine, they recognized one of their former prison mates fighting on the side of Russian separatists as part of a special Chechen battalion. In prison, he had been a member of *sherst'* (working for the administration) who left prison on parole before the end of his sentence. According to them, "For years, the government was observing him in prison, and they probably decided he would be useful on the frontline and loyal to them, so they offered him an earlier release if he would go fight for them." And there is nothing new in such government behavior because the same strategy (but on a much bigger scale) was used by the Soviet government during WWII.

So what could be done to at least slow down radicalization in prisons? Currently there is major policy discussion about how to house people accused of extremism (e.g., members of ISIS) in prisons. One opinion is they should be segregated in separate prisons, so they do not have interaction with the general population of inmates. But in this case, there is a real danger that they would radicalize each other and, when they are finally released, would be much more radical than when they had been imprisoned in the first place.

However, on the other side, mixing them together with people sentenced for other law violations would make it impossible to prevent radical opposition groups from recruiting more members and learning from others.

This is a problem that cannot be solved, and as a result, there has been no universal policy. For example, in Uzbekistan, Islamist inmates are housed separately in special prisons, while in neighboring Kyrgyzstan they are housed together with other inmates. In Russia, the situation is even more complicated. While individuals sentenced for extremism (e.g., membership in ISIS) are in the same prison camp as other inmates, they are usually not mixed with the general population in barracks but are housed in smaller cells in the inner prison. Even there, according to interviewed inmates incarcerated on extremist charges, "We are both mixed and segregated at the same time. Technically, we are mixed, and out of twelve people in a cell, we'll have six inmates on radical Islamist charges. But if we reach a bigger ratio, the prison authorities will mix us again. They do not want too many of us together, and at the same time, they do not want us to be with non-Islamists."

And although this quandary of how to house radical opposition has no resolution, it does not matter much. Neither way is helpful in the long run for either stopping or slowing the spread of radicalization. As long as members of the lower class continue to feel underprivileged and helpless to change their situation by legitimate means, there will always be people willing to join Islamists (and other) radical group(s) that claim they will change the existing social order.

And since many former Soviet Union regimes already have turned to imprisoning the mass of malcontents in an effort to control them, any attempts to treat the symptoms of the problem are as ineffective as a regime's initial attempts to quell the problem. More of the same makes it impossible to reverse the situation.

However, some different attempts could still be made. To start with, a regime could assure the treatment of inmates is according to international standards, and that their human rights are respected. By doing so, even though inmates are still in the lowest class, they would not feel so desperate as to grab at any opportunity to take revenge against the government.

Second, there should be ways for inmates to improve their status as the lowest class of the society through official channels. For example, there should be a way they could peacefully challenge their treatment via official courts, non-government organizations, and unbiased media. This would make inmates less likely join radical groups in prison. As shown by the example of the *vory* prison criminal ideology, their worst time for recruitment was the 1990s, when courts were unbiased against the criminal family, and prison-guard behavior was more tightly controlled.

At the same time, similar improvements should be made outside of the prison gates, in the society in general. As long as the lowest class of citizens feel powerless and look to radical organizations as their only salvation, they idolize those in prison as heroes who suffer on their behalf. By satisfying even the most basic rights of the general population, a government can deprive radical groups of its new members and turn the tide. Instead of feeding the groups new recruits, a government could actually deprive groups of them.

If nothing among the underlying conditions that led to the radicalization of the lowest class changes, another way to affect a society is to change from one opposition ideology to another like from Islamism to democracy, or from monarchism to neo-Nazism. In that case, those behind the new ideology should be seen as more effective in achieving its main goal—changing the existing social order and being better organized internally. If this happened, the core of dedicated members would switch their allegiance, and others would soon follow.

On the other side, to conduct any operation in relation to ideology, people who are in charge in a correction authorities should be well versed in each opposing group's ideology and how it is instrumentalized by the group as well as its internal dynamics. This approach, however, is a major problem in many countries and, in particular, former Soviet countries. Not only is there a lack of this knowledge, their carte blanche permission to law enforcement to use excessive force only continues to empower radical groups.

This can be illustrated by what happened in one of the most secret and brutal prisons in a former Soviet country located in Central Asia. One day all inmates were standing in formation, and the prison director came in and said, "Tomorrow, an official imam from the government department of religion will come to the prison. So if you are interested in Islam and want to meet with him to discuss religious questions, please raise your hand."

Around twenty people did. Those were mostly young guys who did not even care about religion. They were either just curious to talk to a new outside person and learn something new, or they wanted to complain about the mistreatment in prison since this imam represented a higher government authority. By the next morning, all of them were gone. They were moved to another prison where they were really badly beaten and tortured.

"Can you even believe that?" asked my respondent, a twenty-six-year-old ISIS member imprisoned there, laughing. "The KGB honestly thought that people who wanted to talk to an official government imam were radical Islamists who were dangerous enough to single out. When I was going to sleep that night, I was sure they would take us—those who were visibly religious but did not raise our hands [and by that, showed no interest in a government imam], but they did the exact opposite. I am sure those poor guys, if they survive the torture, will want to join us now. That [incident] also showed us everything we wanted to know about the total inability of the KGB to understand who they are dealing with and how easy it is for us to take power."

Notes

Introduction

1. Also, compared to communism, Islamism, and neo-Nazism, the most widespread ideology in prisons is the *vory* criminal set of beliefs, an absolutely artificial ideology not based on any known philosophy or written text. It exists only in the former Soviet Union criminal world. That fact makes this prison research settings even cleaner, reducing the influence of outside events, ideological debates, preexisting opinions, and even prejudices on the sides of participants, researcher, and readers.
2. In addition to the ethics committee in an American institution (IRB) guidelines, I worked closely with local investigative journalists and human rights organizations and activists who, for many years, have constantly worked with former inmates in their countries.
3. To avoid conflicts between regular inmates and former members of law enforcement, if later they are sentenced to prison, they serve it in separate prisons.
4. The hardest part of the fieldwork was getting access to the leadership of those organizations, and it was possible to do only after spending a significant amount of time talking to low-level organization members. They, after feeling comfortable with me, introduced me to those higher in the organization chain of command. After some time, I was able to reach the top of the hierarchy. Sometimes, high-level members of those organizations reached out to me themselves to check what I was doing asking questions. After rather long explanations and them not finding anything suspicious in my questions, they themselves became respondents. The only thing they cared about was me not working for prison authorities, which I did not. That I was a US citizen living in the United States even further persuaded them that I did not work for Russian law enforcement.
5. 18.2% rossiyan imeyut sudimost', Kommersant, 22.09.2008.

Chapter 1

1. If a major criminal leader is behind bars, it is a big benefit for the prison population due to his high-level contacts and resources, but he does not automatically take the place of the prison leader. Although by his rank his has veto power on everything happening inside the prison, he is not involved in the day-to-day operations. Those tasks are considered too menial for his status. Instead, he is usually solving

organizational problems on a regional or countrywide scale and running a business outside of the prison, all by phone.

2. It is also not uncommon, when something happens inside the prison, that members of the criminal family come to the prison's walls armed with weapons. This sends a signal to prison authorities what could happen to them if they keep mistreating their colleagues behind bars. Prison guards are also threatened when they are off duty. They get death threat phone calls and are told "to watch out."

Chapter 2

1. Gurov Aleksandr Ivanovich, Professional'naia prestupnosť, Moskva: Iuridicheskaia literatura, 1990: 108. Cited in Federico Varese, "The society of the *vory-v-zakone*, 1930s–1950s." Cahiers du monde russe (1998): 515–538.
2. Maximilien de Santerre, Sovetskie poslevoennye kontslageri i ikh obitateli (Munich: Institut po izucheniiu SSSR, 1960), 60–61 cited in Federico Varese, "The society of the *vory-v-zakone*, 1930s–1950s." *Cahiers du monde russe* (1998): 515–538.
3. <IBT>Gurov Aleksandr Ivanovich</IBT>, 108; see also ibid., Krasnaia mafia, Moskva: Miko Kommercheskii Vestnik, 1995, 104. cited in Varese, Federico. "The society of the *vory-v-zakone*, 1930s–1950s." *Cahiers du monde russe* (1998): 515–538.
4. Prestupnyy mir Moskvy. Pravo i Zhizn', editor Gernet M. N., Rzhev 1924
5. This slogan was first used by V. Lenin, 24 January 1918
6. Sovetskaya derevnya glazami VCHK–OGPU–NKVD. 1918–1939. Dokumenty i materialy, editor. A. Berelovicha, V. Danilova. M., 2000. Volume 1, pp. 363–364
7. Shabelnikova Natalia, "The fight against anti-state crimes in the Russian Far East during the 1920s." *gumanitarnyye issledovaniya v vostochnoĭ sibiri i na dal'nem vostoke*, no. 3 (2016): 70–77
8. Dal'nevostochniy put' [Far Eastern way], 14 May 1922. (in Russ.)
9. In his research on the difference between *vory* and criminal organizations before it (*artels*), historian Federica Varese highlighted that, compared to the *vory* organization, *artel'* was just a group of people involved in the same business who organized and accepted the leadership of a fellow member. It also exercised a localized monopoly over a certain sector of the underworld. Federico Varese, "The society of the *vory-v-zakone*, 1930s–1950s." *Cahiers du monde russe* (1998): 515–538.
10. Cited in Sidorov Alexander, Velikiye bitvy ugolovnogo mira. Istoriya professional'noy prestupnosti Sovetskoy Rossii. Kniga pervaya (1917–1940 g.g.), Mart 1999
11. Na zashchite otechestva: Iz istorii Upravleniya FSB RF: Vospominaniya sotrudnikov organov gosbezopasnosti Khabarovskogok kraya, editor V.V.Bogaĭchuk. Khabarovsk, 2001. S.14.
12. Alexander Sidorov, Velikiye bitvy ugolovnogo mira. Istoriya professional'noy prestupnosti Sovetskoy Rossii. Kniga pervaya (1917–1940 g.g.), Mart 1999
13. The noble origins of those criminal leaders are even illustrated in the nicknames of the first criminal world leaders who died before the 1960s: Count San'ka Chukotka

(Alexander from Chukotka), General Tolik Kievlyanin (Anatoli from Kiev), Baron Ryazansky (from Ryazan), Count Barnaulsky (from Barnaul), Count Vas'ka Moskvich (Vasily from Moscow), Count Kol'ka Pitersky (Nikolay from St. Petersburg), Count Yurka Vorkutinsky (Yuri from Vorkuta), Count Rostovsky (from Rostov), and Count Yurka Ivanovsky (Yuri from Ivanovo).

14. A great deal of emphasis on honor and courts of honor was places by General Vrangel and its army while in exile. Vrangel issued one order in July 1920 re-establishing courts of honor among the formations of his army, then in November the same year, after arriving in Constantinople from the Crimea, another order doing almost exactly the same thing. In 1923 he issued yet a third set of instructions for courts of honor. Hundreds of such courts sat in judgment of exiled officers in the interwar years. One of Vrangel's successors commented in 1928, "Personally I consider courts of honor especially important and consider them the basis of our existence." Paul Robinson, "Courts of honour in the Late Imperial Russian Army." *The Slavonic and East European Review* 84, no. 4, Modern Humanities Research Association (2006): 708–728,
15. Dmitrii S. Likhachev, "Cherty pervobytnogo primitivizma vorovskoi rechi: Iazyk i myshlenie." In *Elements of primitivism in theves' speech*, Proceedings of the USSR Academy of Science, III–IV (1935), here p. 55. Cited in Federico Varese, "The society of the *vory-v-zakone*, 1930s–1950s." *Cahiers du monde russe* (1998): 515–538.
16. Former Thief in Law Sasha Sever, in his interview to Russian TV in 2016, also expressed an opinion that those rules came from White officer's heritage.
17. It is possible that this rule was a reaction to the CK RKP(B) prohibiting communists from reading newspapers published by White movement.
18. In the second half of 1920s, an instruction came from White officers in emigration in Gensan (China) to the leadership of criminal groups in Far East Russia that prohibited confiscation and even search of the farmers property and promised an execution on the site for such actions. Rossiĭskiĭ gosudarstvennyĭ arkhiv sotsial'no-politicheskoĭ istorii, daleye—RGASPI. F. 372. Op. 1. D. 158. L. 155
19. This increase of potential underground manpower also coincided with former White officers increasing their criminal activities at the end of 1920, when their funding from abroad decreased. From Natalia Shabelnikova, "The fight against anti-state crimes in the Russian Far East during the 1920s." *gumanitarnyye issledovaniya v vostochnoĭ sibiri i na dal'nem vostoke*, no. 3 (2016): 70–77
20. In 1921 there was a special "committee to improve children lives" formed, under the leadership of Felix Dzerzhinsky, who later became chief of secret police.
21. Oleg V. Khlevniuk, *The history of the Gulag: From collectivization to the great terror* (Yale University Press, 2004).
22. Members of the vory criminal organization believe this word means "privileged," and comes from the German word *blatt* or a Dutch word *blat*, which means a piece of paper. In the time of Peter I, there was a list of privileged people (aristocracy) who were excluded from many requirements such as shaving beards and wearing German-style clothing, so the word *blat/blatt* (paper) was associated with privilege.

23. Petr Filippovich Yakubovich, *V mire otverzhennykh. Zapiski byvshego katorzhnika.* "Russkoye bogatstvo,"press house of B. M. Vol'fa, 1896–1899
24. Aleksandr Isaevich Solzhenitsyn, *The Gulag Archipelago, 1918–56: An experiment in literary investigation*. Vol. 3 (Random House, 2003).
25. Taushkanov Yuri, *Thieves-Bitches*, Gorno-Altaysk 2000, International Memorial Archive, Fund 2, Inventory 5, File 138.
26. According to top secret letter #146 from the third department of the GULAG, "On conducting systematic searches of prisoners in the corrective labor camps and corrective labor colonies of the NKVD, 31 July 1939": " A simultaneous search of all prison barracks, initiated by the third department of the Temnikovsky NKVD camp, revealed a huge number of items that was forbidden to store. For example, the search retrieved 111 axes, 11 crowbars, 38 saws, 110 hammers, 828 knives, 52 razors, 34 mock grenades, 7 dumbbells, 2 passports and 12,983 rubles."
27. Many of them, even while in prison, did not lose their trust in the Soviet communist government and even believed they were imprisoned by mistake, but everyone else sentenced on the article 58 were rightfully accused.
28. Stefanskaia, Militsa Cheslavovna, *Chernoe i beloe*, (Moscow, 1994).
29. Olga Adamova-Sliozberg, *My journey: How one woman survived Stalin's Gulag* (Evanston, IL: Northwestern University Press. 2011), 312.
30. As of December 1, 1937, one prison camp (Ukhtpechlag), out of total 54,947 inmates had 24,461 prisoners convicted of counterrevolutionary crimes (6,080 followers of Trotsky; 3,184 spies; 466 subversives; 180 traitors; 1,318 terrorist; 15,233 other counterrevolutionary activities). Khlevniuk, Oleg V. *The history of the Gulag: from collectivization to the great terror*. Yale University Press, 2004.
31. The word *urka* comes from the word *urok* meaning lesson. During Czar times, prison labor was called a lesson, and inmates, because they performed it, were called *urki*.
32. Aleksandr Isaevich Solzhenitsyn, *The Gulag Archipelago, 1918–56: An experiment in literary investigation*. Vol. 3 (Random House, 2003).
33. Fyodor Vasilevich Mochulsky, *Gulag boss: A Soviet memoir* (Oxford University Press, 2012).
34. Aleksandr Isaevich Solzhenitsyn, *The Gulag Archipelago, 1918–56: An experiment in literary investigation*. Vol. 3 (Random House, 2003).
35. Olga Adamova-Sliozberg, *My journey: How one woman survived Stalin's Gulag* (Evanston, IL: Northwestern University Press, 2011), 312.
36. Taushkanov Yuri, *Thieves-bitches* (Gorno-Altaysk, 2000), International Memorial Archive, Fund 2, Inventory 5, File 138
37. Janusz Bardach and Kathleen Gleeson, *Man is wolf to man: Surviving the Gulag* (University of California Press, 1999).
38. Bardach, Janusz, and Kathleen Gleeson. *Man is wolf to man: Surviving the Gulag* (University of California Press, 1999).
39. Fyodor Vasilevich Mochulsky, *Gulag boss: A Soviet memoir* (Oxford University Press, 2012).
40. On 28 April 1941, the order was amended and it also excluded citizens of countries at war with USSR- Latvia, Lithuania, and Estonia.

41. Those sentenced for counter-revolutionary political activities were still ineligible.
42. Their causality rate was three to six times bigger than that of regular battalions. Also, by construction there were no medical personal assigned to punishment battalions, which further contributed to the death rate.
43. The most popular charge for them was not having proper documentation for their military unit property, which in the eyes of government was equal to the stealing state property and meant a long prison sentence.
44. Now, this word is more often used as an offensive word similar in meaning to an English word *bitch*.
45. Varlan Shalanov, *Kolyma tales*. Vol. 913 (Penguin UK, 1994).
46. Demin Mikhail, *Blatnoy*, Interbuk (Novosibirsk, 1994).
47. Demin Mikhail, *Blatnoy*, Interbuk (Novosibirsk, 1994).
48. Vysotskiy, Vladimir i Leonid Monchinskiy. Chernaya svecha. Moskovskaya mezhdunar. shkola perevodchikov, 1992.
49. Taushkanov Yuri, *Thieves-bitches* (Gorno-Altaysk, 2000), International Memorial Archive, Fund 2, Inventory 5, File 138 and Vysotskiy, Vladimir i Leonid Monchinskiy. Chernaya svecha. Moskovskaya mezhdunar. shkola perevodchikov, 1992.
50. Chechens were one of the people groups that, on Stalin's order, were deported to Central Asia.
51. Sidorov Alexander, Velikiye bitvy ugolovnogo mira. Istoriya professional'noy prestupnosti Sovetskoy Rossii. Kniga pervaya (1917–1940 g.g.), Mart 1999
52. Vladimir Konstantinovich Bukovskiĭ, *To build a castle: My life as a dissenter* (Ethics & Public Policy Center, 1988).
53. Janusz Bardach and Kathleen Gleeson, *Man is wolf to man: Surviving the Gulag* (University of California Press, 1999).
54. Federico Varese, *The society of the vory-v-zakone, 1930s-1950s*. Cahiers du monde russe (1998): 515–538.
55. Sidorov Alexander, Velikiye bitvy ugolovnogo mira. Istoriya professional'noy prestupnosti Sovetskoy Rossii. Kniga vtoraya (1941–1991 g.g.), Mart 1999.
56. Other possible translations include *Convict's/Prisoner's Practice (way of life, law), Codex is Unified/Universal/Uniform,* or *Prisoner's/Career con/Thug Unity/Solidarity.*

Chapter 3

1. They had to have this status for more than three years.
2. The most respected (and now very rare) *vory* are those who get their title in prison. Often, a new *vor* was crowned in the prison hospitals and would have to get there by either paying bribes or pretending to be sick.
3. Although origins of that symbol are not clear, some members of criminal family consider it a legacy of the White Movement. It resembles the symbol for the Order of St. Andrew the Apostle of the First-Called, which was the highest order in Czarist Russia

before the revolution in 1917. In the Czar's family, a boy was awarded this order when he was baptized. A *vor* is awarded it when he is baptized into the criminal family.

4. Also, according to interviewed inmates, it is not rare for *vory* to help prison authorities and prison guards with personal problems. Several respondents mentioned that, at times, *vory* found jobs for relatives of prison guards and, in one case, helped a relative of the prison guard solve a problem with custom taxes on import of goods. No need to mention that the problem was fixed illegally.
5. In 2017, there were around 432 *vory* incarcerated within Russia and Ukraine alone (318 others were free, 114 in prison, 31 on trial, and 19 wanted). Skol'ko gruzinskikh vorov v zakone naschitali v Rossii i Ukraine, Sputnik, 9 August 2018.
6. When promoting a *polojenets* to *vor* status, inmates from his prison are called and asked how he performed his job. A good recommendation from the inmates goes a long way to helping his case.
7. Criminal leadership does not even use the word "*smotryasçiy*," but "answering for" in reference to this position. This fact further highlights that there are more responsibilities with the position than there are benefits for it.
8. Also, if something happens to *polojenets* and he cannot fulfill his responsibilities, his position would be temporary taken by *smotryasçiy* of *obshyak* until either the *polojenets* returns or a new one is appointed.
9. In prison camps majority of inmates live in barracks, but there are also prison-inside-prison areas where there are cells used for solitary confinement or to house several inmates. In special cases, including violation of official prison rules, an inmate could be placed there.
10. It is important to mention that although this rule basically exists only on paper and criminals very rarely do anything to support their families and even mothers. Federico Varese, "The society of the *vory-v-zakone*, 1930s–1950s." *Cahiers du monde russe* (1998): 515–538.
11. In the USSR, not having an official job (outside of prison) was a criminal offence, so many members of the criminal organizations had documents claiming they were medically disabled.
12. First in the USSR and now in some former-USSR countries, such registration is mandatory. By not registering, a criminal had a better chance of eluding police or other authorities who might come looking for him. This would allow the criminal to be free longer.
13. Just because criminal inmates do not cooperate with authorities does not mean they are belligerent. Criminal inmates are respectful in court and with authorities. According to one interviewed inmate, "I am allowed to stand up in court, although it is a gesture of respect to the judge, and I should talk to him very politely. What is the point of showing off and cursing him and getting a longer sentence? *Ponyatiya* are about knowing what you are doing and showing by your behavior that you are a respectful human being and that they [court administration] are not."
14. It is interesting to note that this freedom for homosexuals was ensured by *ponyatiya* even when homosexuality was against the law in Russia and many were imprisoned for it.

15. Although it is called cake, it has little resemblance to regular cakes. It is made from everything sweet one has in prison and usually looks like biscuits with condensed milk between and candy of top.
16. When one wants to highlight someone's criminal experience, the most important wording is that he had "lived" with *vory*.
17. It is interesting to note that there are also so-called *torpedoes*—people used for the most dangerous and costly tasks (basically similar to suicide bombers). They have to do the task even if it will cost them their lives or significantly increase their prison sentence. But those people do not come from the same group of *bulls*. One could become a torpedo, for example, after losing in a card game where life is at stake.
18. In many prisons, they also have to follow prison guards who enter cells to make sure they do not plant anything in the inmates' drawers or steal anything from them.
19. One way would be to get an official prison job. In that case, the *snir* would not physically be able to continue working for the *blatnyje*. On the other side, in many prisons that are run by criminal leadership, the *blatnyje* are close to the prison administration and could ask them not to give his *snir* an official job, and the prison authority would most likely agree (unless a *snir* is willing to offer something, like information).

Chapter 4

1. In Russian, the word "goat" has a gender, so they are actually called "female goat."
2. In Gulag times, they also helped prison guards guard other inmates.
3. Another hypothesis is that *sherst'* ("wool") comes from Gulag times, when, if an inmate agreed to work for prison authorities, he was given a woolen sweater.
4. Although beating an inmate is a less extreme approach to the crime than blatantly killing him, the beatings are so severe, they sometimes result in death. Even the Russian verb that an interviewed inmate used to describe the process is not "beating" but "killing" (although in regular Russian language the word *killing* is used only as a perfect action, and a victim is dead).
5. It is important to mention that it is also prohibited to steal from prison guards. He would not be considered a rat for doing so, but it may lead to something like a mass prison search. This then becomes a punishable violation under the criminal code because the thief's actions would be causing hardship for the other inmates. On the other side, it is a common joke to steal a lighter from the pocket of the prison guard and then publicly return it.
6. A regular inmate's release date is written on his bed and tag, but a parole date is known only by him and prison authorities.
7. Because everyone on rape charges was always automatically degraded in the past, law enforcement has indiscriminately misused this charge to further punish non-rapists. So criminal leadership now does their own investigation to determine whether a thus-charged inmate is really a rapist before determining whether to degrade him.

8. Prison authorities disgusted by those types of crimes often support prisons leadership in degrading those inmates. When an inmate sentenced for holding a child hostage for a month for sex was about to enter a prison, the prison's director invited the prison criminal leader to his office and said, "We know you guys are waiting for him, and we have no problems with it." As expected, when the offending inmate arrived, he was very severely beaten and rendered degraded. Prison guards did not intervene.
9. This might happen by an inmate slipping while using the hole-in-the-ground toilet and coming into contact with fecal matter.
10. Once both a teacher and his students from an orphanage were in *petukhi* caste in the same prison. He was there because his crime was considered immoral, and his students were there because they had been raped.
11. Interestingly, this job is considered not acceptable even for members of the *sherst'* caste who work in prison maintenance and help prison administration.
12. While conducting fieldwork, one of the challenges I faced was interviewing high-level criminal inmates after interviewing members of this caste. While opinions were divided (some inmates thought that by doing so, I could pass untouchability to them), we agreed it was acceptable as long as I follow other rules such as not physically touching them or anything they had touched.
13. It is not uncommon to see a long line of inmates at the upper-caste toilet or washstand and no one at the one allocated for the degraded. No man would dare use it, no matter how long the wait.
14. Among them are Grigory Hrapov, who killed seven people, and Vasily Kulik, who killed thirteen people.
15. Janusz Bardach and Kathleen Gleeson, *Man is wolf to man: Surviving the Gulag* (University of California Press, 1999).
16. According to inmates, "[*Petukhi*] are always paid well and on time, and it could often be the case that members of this caste are richer than members of higher castes in the same cell."
17. Application no. 36463/11; X against Russia; lodged on 20 April 2011.
18. Inmates sentenced to life are separated into their own prisons.
19. It also works the other way around. If an inmate is in a maximum-security prison but is behaving well, he could be moved to a medium-security facility.
20. Technically he could not be called a *smotryasçiy* because, being from the lowest caste, he is outside of the criminal leadership structure.

Chapter 5

1. One example of unlawful crowning was *vor* Beso Rustavsky, who then lost his title when it became known that he had hidden parts of his biography: while in Butirka jail in 2006, he had hit a decent inmate and was beaten by *vor* Elgudza Turkadze (Gudza Kutaissky), also an inmate in that jail.

2. Outside of prison, killing a *vor* by snipers or explosives is popular. Inside the prison, it is usually done in the factory of the prison. There, the victim has "an accident" and gets stuck in machinery, is electrocuted, or has something heavy fall on him.
3. For a person to be moved to the degraded caste, he has to be raped with a penis and not an object such as a bottle or a stick, which was often used by police and prison guards in former Soviet countries.
4. Ratting, stealing, and more serious problems do not end here, and one is heavily beaten by plank and stool.

Chapter 6

1. For that reason, if food distribution started with inmates close to the door one day, the next day it would start with inmates located the furthest from the door.
2. If a problematic inmate was not transferred, he might have been beaten or even killed, and prison guards did not want to explain why they were notified by the elder about a problem and did not react.
3. Fyodor Dostoyevsky, *Memoirs from the House of the Dead* (Oxford University Press, 2001).
4. In some regions, such enthusiasm among youngsters is so high that they collect donations for prison funds at school, often giving their lunch money.
5. Although this way of getting drugs and alcohol into prison is less expensive, it is very dangerous. For example, bottles of alcohol are catapulted into the prison at high speeds, and someone has to catch it. And although to do so inmates usually wear heavy winter coats and use their bodies to catch the package, it is not uncommon for inmates to have flying bottles smash into their heads. Another danger is packages landing near the prison fence where someone has to go retrieve it. Because prison guards are allowed to shoot any inmate too close to the prison wall, it is a very dangerous task, and usually members of *petukhi* caste are made to do it. And if those throwing goods over the walls are caught, they could get up to ten years in prison themselves.
6. On the other side, this fact is also being misused by members of the criminal family. One former inmate high in the criminal family offered me the advice that if I would ever wanted to buy drugs, I should say they were for the prison because it is the only way for an inexperienced person to ensure the quality of the product.
7. Yakubovich, Petr Filippovich V mire otverzhennykh. Zapiski byvshego katorzhnika. "Russkoye bogatstvo" (Press house B. M. Vol'fa, 1896–1899).
8. Anton Chekhov, *Sakhalin island* (Alma Books, 2018).
9. When the *vory* criminal organization took control of prisons, card games took on another meaning: their popularity among criminal leadership became associated with the former officers of the White Movement. Historically, before the Bolshevik revolution, card playing was a privilege reserved for nobility and played in the houses

of elites and officers' clubs, but Bolshevik government officially prohibited gambling with a special order on 24 November 1917.

10. D. S. Likhachev, "Vospominaniya [Memoirs]. St. Petersburg" (Logos, 1995).
11. Fyodor Dostoyevsky, *Memoirs from the House of the Dead* (Oxford University Press, 2001).
12. This is the best time to buy cell phones in prison. Cell phones are the only valuable thing an inmate has behind bars, so if he is not able to pay his card debt on time, he sells his cell phone. And since all the card payment deadlines are at the same time, it reduces the average price of cell phones due to the excessive supply.
13. In rare cases, if a person does not have money to pay after he loses a game, he could be also degraded. In Gulag times he also could have been ordered to do a particular job (including a killing).
14. This is not a recent development. According to Chekhov, in 1890 "In Alexandrovka, there are several casinos; in one of them there was a scandal that a prison guard who lost money shot himself."
15. Drugs may also be provided for public safety purposes. At least in one Central Asian prison, criminal leadership permanently provides heroin to long-term heroin addicts inmates to keep their behavior in check.

Chapter 7

1. One respondent also said that in his prison, a cat was used to move messages and drugs from prison to the prison hospital. Messages were hidden in its collar.
2. Because of their nocturnal life, a *polojenets* often negotiates with prison authorities for people working on roads, so they are not bothered during the day. For example, these inmates are not required to attend mandatory formations.
3. By *ponyatiya*, everyone was required to assist a messenger in his mission, and he was protected by his status. No one was allowed to touch him, no matter the content of the message.
4. Information about birthdays usually comes in the beginning of the month and information about deaths at the end of the month.
5. It is allowed for one *vor* to sign for another one if he could not physically sign it himself and gives his permission.
6. This might be because, very often, wives and girlfriends break up with men once they are incarcerated (especially recidivists), while mothers always support them.
7. This word has a complicated history. During Gulag times inmates were used to build White Sea–Baltic Canal that was crucial for national security and when government delegation visiting the construction site, they started calling inmates canal builders. Because Gulag administration followed every word of their Moscow leadership, they starting calling all inmates that.
8. For more information on prison slang, see *Soviet prison camp speech: A survivor's glossary*, compiled by Meyer Galler and Harlan E. Marquess. (Madison: University of

Wisconsin Press, 1972), 216; and Yurii Dubyagin and E. A. Teplitski. "Kratkii anglo-russkii i russko-angliiskii slovar'ugolovnogo zhargona." Concise English-Russian and Russian-English Dictionary of the Underworld.

9. Rules about writing the word "game" (as in the card game) led to a philosophical debate between my respondents. Several members of the prison criminal leadership said that it should be underscored with one line as something essential to the life of criminal family. Other expressed an opinion that the game itself is not a core of the criminal family values, but what is crucial is an agreement between players to honor the result of the game. And as a consequence, "Game" should not be underscored at all.
10. Now it is often used as a joke with inexperienced people who are in prison for the first time.
11. Usually there are many real spiders in a prison cell because they are respected by inmates. They are not allowed to kill a spider, and if a spider's web is inconveniently located, an inmate can only relocate him.
12. There is an opinion that the epaulets are elaborated replicas of high-ranking military shoulder pieces used during Czarist Russia.
13. Those tattoos are obviously hated by the prison guards and, according to interviewed inmates, during conflicts, inmates tattooed with them are usually beaten the most by prison guards.
14. Janusz Bardach and Kathleen Gleeson, *Man is wolf to man: Surviving the Gulag* (University of California Press, 1999).
15. As an experiment, I made this tea at home with an experienced former inmate. The taste was so bitter, I could not imagine anyone drinking it in a normal life.
16. No one interviewed was able to explain why exactly two sips, but if one takes three sips as a joke, he will be called *sherst'*, meaning that he is thinking only of himself and not the broader prison community.
17. In many prisons, and especially when locked in inner prison, you may or may not have food every day. So in prison culture, it is valued when an inmate can remain mentally strong even with a shortage of food.

Chapter 8

1. Red refers to the color associated with the communist regime.
2. There are several hypotheses as to why those prisons are called black. First, some people think that it is a legacy of the White Movement origins of organized criminal organization. They changed their organization's name from "White" to "Black" for General Wrangel, a commanding general of the White Army during the latter stages of the civil war. According to Red Army propaganda, Wrangel was nicknamed the "Black Baron" or "Black Bandit," probably referring to death. Another version of the origins of the name is the color of the prison robe. Often *blatnyje* wear black uniforms while other inmates wear gray or dark blue uniforms.

3. Because food in the cafeteria is often of a very bad quality, inmates who have family supporting them with packages do not usually eat there. They might only go from time to time for bread if it is of good enough quality.
4. In one known case, a chain-link kennel was erected in the prison yard between the manufacturing and living quarters. Punished inmates were locked in there, regardless of age or physical health. Sometimes there would be thirty people locked in this two-square-meter cage. In the winter, prisoners were locked in the cage in their summer uniforms, making it even more unbearable. A humane prison guard might allow an inmate to go to the restroom; otherwise, he could be standing there for eight hours with no place to relieve himself.
5. According to interviewed inmates, despite those prisons being red, access to drugs (such as heroin and methadone) is very easy and openly facilitated by prisons authorities because use of those drugs increases work productivity among inmates.
6. In some prisons, the amount of money asked from each inmate was calculated based on several factors. First, prison authorities had access to official information about inmates, so they could roughly estimate how much each inmate could afford to pay. Also inmates were befriended by pro-authority inmates to find out about their lives before prison—if they have relatives who cared about their well-being, how well-off their relatives were, and so on. Then, the amount of money demanded also depended on the charge (e.g., the highest amount of money was demanded from people convicted of financial crimes and drug charges). In other known cases it was openly announced how much each inmate had to pay monthly. Sometimes there were even official meetings every day dedicated solely to collecting money from inmates.
7. Although he was let out of prison after making this statement, he was soon killed by fellow criminals.
8. Usually these policeman do not have weapons when they enter. Only the ones who remain on the perimeter outside do. They are afraid that inmates will take their weapons and turn them on police.
9. Other interviewees warned that, in some prisons, not only this does not work and prison guards do not stop beating them, but the guards may even provide the inmate with a sharper razor, advising him to kill himself.
10. It comes from the verb *vskryvat*, which means opening something intentionally closed like a box or a can.
11. Internal prison memo written by experienced inmates for new inmates.
12. One of the interviewed ex-inmates, an aspiring *vor*, proudly highlighted in the interview that he spent only three hours of his ten-year prison sentence with the general prison population. The rest of the time he was detained in the inner prison for violations of different prison regulations and conflicts with prison authorities.
13. When those inmates are being transferred, there is a special mark in their file to ensure they are not housed with other inmates (for their own protection). But very often, prison guards forget to notice the mark and place them in the general population.
14. In that particular prison, authorities were so afraid of him writing complaints that even after he was released, prison administration kept asking him (though friends

still in prison) whether he planned to complain to human rights organizations since he was free.

15. In the past, swallowing sharp objects was also widespread.
16. Solzhenitsyn, Aleksandr Isaevich "Gulag Archipelago Three." (1979).
17. It became known only after another, more successful riot in 2012 when during the following trial, inmates and prison authorities were asked about the previous, failed one.

Chapter 9

1. In one black prison, when director of Russian Department of Corrections visited, inmates had so many prohibited items to hide that the prison director together with the *polojenets* came up with the idea to dig a hole in the ground inside prison factory and hide them there.
2. In one prison, the library was located in the same building as prison administration, so inmates were not allowed to go to the library alone and always had to have someone from criminal leadership with them.
3. Now catching an informant with a "smoking gun" happens only by accident. For example, one inmate who was spying for prison guards took money from someone (through online banking) and lost it in online betting. The other inmate was angry and started accusing him. The thief started panicking and wrote a text message to his guard saying that he was uncovered (although he was not). When prison criminal leadership took his phone to check money transfers and online betting history, they found that text message.
4. And to make thing worse, in several prisons, the song of choice is Boris Moiseev's "Blue Moon," which was considered a joke about gays in former Soviet countries. Knowing the widespread hate of inmates to gays, it is a type of psychological operations.
5. This style involves putting a white sheet on top of the blanket and means that you could not sit on the bed during the day.
6. Kots Aleksandr, Bunty v koloniyakh: Provokator v zone - ushlyy "vor v zakone," Komsomolskaya Pravda, 30 January 2006, https://www.kp.ru/daily/23650/49406/.
7. In those places tap water is usually of a dangerously bad quality.
8. According to an interviewed member of the criminal leadership who was there at that time (but refused to become *activist*), "It did not help much because they still had to follow prison guard's orders."

Chapter 10

1. Even famous scientists, such as Moscow State University mathematician Boris Berezovsky, chose to leave the university to work with the criminal family, and many

children, when asked what they wanted to be when they grew up, said they wanted to be *vory*.

2. He asked Ded Hasan to settle a dispute in his region between two groups of businessman about owed money. But the lender had already gone to police with his claim. According to *ponyatiya*, a party can turn to either police or to *vory* to settle a dispute, and if you turned to police even once, you could never ask the *vory* organization for help again.
3. Historically, *vory* in the former Soviet Union represented all ethnic people groups, even the smallest minorities (such as Yazidi-Kurds). Currently there are still *vory* of the following nationalities: Georgians (250), Russians (53), Armenians (31), Azeri (15), Abhazi (11), Chechens (8), Jews-Ukrainians (7), and Greeks (5); and several from the following regions: Tatarstan, Uzbekistan, Ossetia, Kazakhstan, Ingushetia, Bashkiria, Kirgizstan, Moldova, Belorussia; and of Talish, Lezgin, German, Dargin, Balkar and Avar ethnicities.
4. By *ponyatiya*, to give a *vor* a title, several *vory* have to approve it.
5. Theoretically, according to criminal rules, in prison, pimps and those accused of kidnapping have the same status as drug dealers, but their overall numbers are very small.
6. In Kyrgyzstan prisons, new inmates on drug charges are encircled and hit with big bottles of water until they promise to start fundraising from outside sources. However, if even after that very painful and almost torturous experience, an inmate does not agree to pay—most likely because he has no outside resources—he will be let go.
7. This is mostly the case since the majority of drugs come from that region.
8. That rehabilitation center was also a place for networking in the criminal world. For example, according to one interviewed inmate, all his main contacts made with criminal leadership (that allowed him to rise in ranks) were made there.
9. In some cases, a gang does not want to use *vory* criminal organization vocabulary (*fenya*) and introduces its own.
10. According to their manifesto, their goals were: (1) to place their own trusted people in important prison positions, (2) to ensure communication with those outside prison, (3) to support those in the inner prison, (4) to establish a mutual fund, (5) to do ideological work with kids, (6) to make sure the whole criminal world of Khabarovsk region [their region] was under control, and (7) to be careful with every move and have control in all prisons and prison camps.

Chapter 11

1. Currently, there are close to 30,000 Chechens in Russian prisons charged with "participation in an illegal armed formation," the charge usually leveled at militants, for funding militant groups. Chanturiya Kazbek, *Chechens and mobsters in Russian*

prison blood feud, OC Media, 10 March 2017, https://oc-media.org/chechens-and-mobsters-in-russian-prison-blood-feud/.

2. It is interesting that several inmates on criminal charges mentioned that, surprisingly, ex-fighters never talked about their experiences in Syria, though those who were also in Waziristan are happy to talk about their training there. Some of the criminals think "there is some kind of an agreement among those from Syria not to talk about it." Ex-fighters from Syria also refuse all requests from other inmates to teach them what they learned while on the battlefield.
3. In many cases they are not even released when their sentence is finished. The government is afraid of what they will do with their freedom and often adds fake charges to an inmate's file to keep him in prison almost indefinitely. In Uzbekistan many inmates on those charges say that they are often afraid to go to sleep at night because they might be killed by fellow inmates working for prison administration.
4. It is important to mention that, despite it being labeled a room for Muslims, in prisons often only members of a *jamaat* occupy it while other Muslims pray in a different place.
5. It should also be mentioned that because Islamists do not recognize courts, they often also feel no ethical responsibility to follow the justice system's laws. That means when working with courts, they are under no obligation to tell the truth. Instead, they will say anything to turn the judge's decision in their favor.
6. They use the following lines in Quran to explain their position: "Have you not seen those who claim to have believed in what was revealed to you, [O Muhammad], and what was revealed before you? They wish to refer legislation to Taghut, while they were commanded to reject it; and Satan wishes to lead them far astray" (4:60). "But no, by your Lord, they will not [truly] believe until they make you, [O Muhammad], judge concerning that over which they dispute among themselves, and then find within themselves no discomfort from what you have judged and submit in [full, willing] submission" (4:65).
7. In particular, the Nike logo is unacceptable since the brand name comes from the name of the Greek goddess of victory.
8. Many inmates complain because, in addition to applying it on themselves, Islamic inmates also saturate their clothes with it. According to one prisoner, "We had a guy in our room who had strong allergies and he had to be moved to another room because the smell was unbearable for him."
9. Islamist literature, which is prohibited by law (on extremist grounds), is also not hard to get inside prison. Prison authorities not only do not know which literature is prohibited and which is not, but they also definitely do not follow the update of the prohibited literature list.

Chapter 12

1. It is allowed by Islam to do prayers sitting if it is impossible to do them standing. And in some red prisons, inmates only pray with their eyes.

2. For some inmates who have committed particular crimes, the *jamaat* interpretation of Islam also offers an explanation that absolves them of their guilt. Even if a Christian person killed his wife's lover (or his wife whom he saw having sex with another man), he could look at the *jamaat* interpretation of Islam and think, "In fact, I did not even commit a crime. Instead I did the right thing by punishing someone for doing something prohibited by God."
3. In rare cases, at such an event an Islamist inmate could be made to take a piece of bread from the table as a sign of participation, but nothing more.
4. There have even been cases when *smotryashchiye* who lived based on criminal law but, at some point, turn to Islamism, and when they were released, they appoint a member of the jamaat as a *smotryasçiy*. He would happily accept the position and immediately, the cell would become more jamaat-friendly, often leading the whole cell to walk in Sharia-inspired rules.
5. As a result, the inmate became disabled. He now works in the prison factory, lives separately, and does not talk to anyone.
6. It is a usual procedure in such events for a person already sentenced to life in prison to take the responsibility for a killing because they will not be negatively affected by getting another charge.
7. It is interesting to note that they refused to move back, saying they were sick and tired of *ponyatiya* rules and criminal leadership and preferred to stay with *sherst'*.
8. Allegedly it increases satisfaction of the partner during sex.
9. Usually it is done by members of *petukhi* caste because, by definition, they are allowed to touch the penis of an inmate of the higher caste, and the higher caste inmate is allowed to have his penis touched by *petukhi*.
10. Prison authorities usually enthusiastically welcome the addition of a mosque or praying room because, without doing anything themselves, they can show human rights advocates and the Department of Corrections that they support the religious needs of inmates in their prison.
11. The main drug traffic road from Afghanistan to Russia goes through Central Asia.
12. If there is a suspicion that someone is stealing cigarettes, inmates might put sulfur into them, so if someone takes and lights such a cigarette, the sulfur make a small explosion, making it immediately obvious who took it.
13. It is similar to how, during Christian prison services, lower-caste members must stand together behind everyone else, and in at least one known incident, a conflict arose because a member of the Man caste refused to kiss the same cross *petukh* had, and requested another cross.

Chapter 13

1. Criminal-world inmates consider the whole *jamaat* as part of the *sherst'* caste, and, for example, become squeamish at the idea of even entering their barrack.

2. One of the inmates found hidden cameras in the room for long visitations. Inmates demanded an explanation and their removal.
3. Prison authorities add fuel to the fire by trying to use inmate conflicts to their favor. In some prisons, authorities take the side of criminals because, compared to Islamists, criminals are not looking to increase their power, while Islamists are. In other (black) prisons, authorities want conflicts between inmates and, as a result, support radicals Islamists, increasing their power so they can challenge criminals.
4. In one Russian prison, a group of *jamaat* members asked the most respected Islamist sheikh advice about ex-foreign fighter inmates and their relationship to other members of *jamaat*. And he, in very strict language, made a video address explaining that first, participation in *jihad* does not even mean automatic admission into heaven; and second, all Muslims are equal, so *mujaheed* fighters should be good examples to others to increase their proselytization efforts.
5. Also while there was a general ban on sport drinks and food in prison, many *jamaats* were getting protein food supplements in big quantities to help with strength training.
6. There are around 1,000 inmates in Kizil for serious crimes such as murder, robbery, extremism, and terrorism.
7. That was most also likely a prison-authority set-up.
8. When that happened, interviewed members of the criminal world commented that he should not have done so because any middle level member of the criminal family who wanted to be promoted could now easily kill him.

Chapter 14

1. Although several inmates admitted doing it and were sentenced, there was almost no evidence of their guilt. Instead, evidence suggested she was killed by prison guards. This is also what her family believes.
2. Those prison guards later resigned from their positions in disagreement with the treatment of inmates.
3. Soon after that he was killed by the FSB because, according to them, he participated in the insurgency in Caucasus and was killed in an anti-terrorism military operation. His death did not surprise anyone. According to many interviewed inmates, "Everyone who was able to organize a strong *jamaat* inside prison were killed immediately after their release, and those who were members of such *jamaats* were rearrested, often on fake charges."
4. He was sentenced to life in prison, but through connections with high-level law enforcement, his sentence was reduced.
5. As a consequence, several ex-members of the insurgency in this prison did not even attend mass prayers, but prayed on their beds with their eyes (so it is not visible from outside) instead. They did not want to attract unnecessary attention from the prison guards or the FSB.

6. This was truly annoying to members of the criminal hierarchy because in prison, as compared to the outside world, inmates could do more provocations because they know that, in the worst-case scenario, they will be protected because there are cameras everywhere, and prison guards will intervene if things get too violent. That would not be the case outside prison, however, where they would be killed immediately.
7. Many times during interviews with prison criminal leadership, Christian inmates asked me, since I studied this topic, if I could tell them what were those *jamaats* were about and what they wanted.
8. For example, my own mother, who still lives in Russia, got such phone calls several times. According to her, they were so persuasive that she would have believed them if she did not know I was living in the United States and could not have been detained in Russia.
9. They even got their own room where they could work uninterrupted and other inmates in prison would not see them.
10. Many times, criminal leadership asked Ali to come out of the inner prion to talk, but he always refused and was there until his release. He clearly understood that he had nothing to say in his defense, and in the very best-case scenario, ho would be seriously beaten.
11. Prison authorities do not look favorably on those who pray, so while some (even) religious inmates were shortening prayers when they traveled (which is allowed in Islam), they did not. Also, it is allowed in Islam to shorten and in some cases even stop prayers when traveling.
12. Later, he was moved to another prison where he became famous in the region. In that prison, those in charge were dictatorial drug-addicted *blatnyje* who were terrorizing inmates. He organized inmates to beat those *blatnyje*, prohibited drugs, negotiated with prison authorities for the freedom of movement inside the prison, and reinstalled the system of roads, basically defrosting the prison.
13. According to one interviewed inmate, "I was always telling those kids [young members of *jamaa*] to stop pretending they were suffering for religion and posting about ISIS, but they were so dumb, they kept telling me I was old and did not understand technology and that they weren't posting under their real names. Well. . . now they've got two more years to sit here and become smarter."
14. Some inmates got extra time in prison for doing it (three to five years). Several members of the prison's authorities were also arrested.
15. One of them had a twenty-year sentence for murder.
16. In fact, his real name is very traditional Russian name Ivan, and when he joined the *jamaat*, he took the Muslim name Imran. Now that he was degraded, his nickname was *Rulka*, which in Russian sounds very humiliatingly.
17. Based on the *jamaat* member's story, it was criminal leadership who was giving drugs to the jamaat leadership to destroy the *jamaat*. They also made *jamaat* leadership kick out inmates that criminal leaders wanted to punish.
18. The two got an additional eleven and fourteen years in prison for the killing.

19. In fact, according to interviewed members of the criminal leadership, it seemed like prison authorities were actively helping *jamaats* in this conflict because when someone was going against *jamaat* leadership (particularly the *amir* in the inner prison), that inmate was transferred to another prison.
20. When he was released, he was so afraid that he would be beaten or killed, ten cars filled with friends met him at the prison gates to safely escort him away from the region.
21. He was tortured with electricity, so he could not sleep; when he fell asleep, his hands and legs extended upward.

Chapter 15

1. The number fourteen here refers to the fourteen-word slogan, "We must secure the existence of our people and a future for white children," and eight is the number of the letter "H" in the alphabet, making the abbreviation for Heil Hitler eighty-eight.
2. According to a pagan neo-Nazi inmate imprisoned for a church explosion: "In Belyaevo [Moscow Neighborhood] there was a boulder, and I liked the energy there. Then I learned that someone had once moved it, and I thought it was done by the nearby church, and that they did it intentionally against our pagan religion. I was pissed for like three days, and then decided to take revenge on the church." But he also added, "You need to take into account what times those were. We honestly thought that revolution against the government would happen at any moment, and we just needed to be the first spark."
3. https://www.rosbalt.ru/piter/2011/02/19/821194.html.
4. A famous convert to Islam and a member of the insurgency in the Caucasus.
5. A leader of the Islamist group in the Kabardino-Balkarian Republic of Russia.
6. The most famous neo-Nazi group that started a guerilla war against law enforcement.
7. Celebrating non-Muslim holidays such as birthdays and New Year's Day is prohibited in Islamist ideology.
8. The biggest bazaar in Moscow. This bazaar was a symbol not only of the *vory* criminal organization power, but also of ethnic gangs from Caucasus and Central Asia.
9. It should be noted that, in 2009, other Slavic *vory* had written a *progon* saying that neo-Nazis should not be anywhere close to prison criminal leadership. Although the reason for this *progon* is not known, interviewed neo-Nazi ex-inmates speculate that those *vory* wanted to get closer to *vory* from the Caucasus and were signaling their allegiance.
10. Such potential cooperation is also of interest to Russian law enforcement. Another neo-Nazi added, "Russian intelligence and law enforcement are afraid that neo-Nazis, who are not very organized and spread over the huge territory of Russia, will get organized through *vory* criminal families."

Conclusion

1. This word comes from the Persian word *zindan*, which is the name for prisons located underground and were, in the past, used in the Caucasus.
2. The trial operation was conducted on 2 June 1943, when twelve former Soviet POWs, trained by the Germans and dressed in NKVD uniforms, were airdropped in the Komi Republic. But this small operation was not successful, and on 9 June, the group was uncovered by real NKVD troops. Two of the plants were killed, and the rest were taken captive.

Bibliography

Arias, E. D. (2006). *Drugs and democracy in Rio de Janeiro: Trafficking, social networks, and public security*. University of North Carolina Press.

Bakke, K. M. (2014). "Help wanted? The mixed record of foreign fighters in domestic insurgencies." *International Security* 38, no. 4: 150–187.

Bardach, J., and Gleeson, K. (1999). *Man is wolf to man: Surviving the gulag*. University of California Press.

Biondi, K. (2016). *Sharing this walk: An ethnography of prison life and the PCC in Brazil*. Chapel Hill, NC: UNC Press Books.

Blaydes, L., and Rubin, L. (2008). "Ideological reorientation and counterterrorism: Confronting militant Islam in Egypt." *Terrorism and Political Violence* 20, no. 4: 461–479.

Bloom, M. (2019). *Small arms: Children and terrorism*. Cornell University Press.

Böhmelt, T., and Bove, V. (2020). "How migration policies moderate the diffusion of terrorism." *European Journal of Political Research* 59, no. 1: 160–181.

Chanturiya, K. (2017). Chechens and mobsters in Russian prison blood feud, OC-Media. https://oc-media.org/features/chechens-and-mobsters-in-russian-prison-blood-feud/.

Chekhov, A. (2018). *Sakhalin island*. Alma Books.

Cook, J. (2019). Women and terror after 9/11: The case of Islamic State. In *Handbook of terrorism and counter terrorism post 9/11*. Edward Elgar Publishing.

Crewe, B. (2009). *The prisoner society: Power, adaptation, and social life in an English prison*. New York: Oxford University Press.

Darke, S. (2018). *Conviviality and survival: Co-producing Brazilian prison order*. Cham, Switzerland: Springer.

Davenport, C. (2015). *How social movements die*. Cambridge University Press.

Demick, B. (2010). Nothing to envy: Ordinary lives in North Korea. New York: Spiegel & Grau.

Demin, M. (1994). Blatnoj. Novosibirsk: Interbook

Dostoyevsky, F. (2001). *Memoirs from the House of the Dead*. Oxford University Press, USA.

Gambetta, D. (1993). *The Sicilian mafia: The business of private protection*. Cambridge, MA: Harvard University Press.

Gambetta, D. (2009). *Codes of the underworld: How criminals communicate*. Princeton, NJ: Princeton University Press.

Gernet, M. (1921). *Moscow criminal world, jurisprudence and life*. Rzhev.

Hegghammer, T. (2010). "The rise of Muslim foreign fighters: Islam and the globalization of jihad." *International Security* 35, no. 3: 53–94.

Johnson, A. (2017). *If I give my soul: Faith behind bars in Rio de Janeiro*. New York: Oxford University Press.

Kaminski, M. M. (2004). *Games prisoners play: The tragicomic worlds of Polish prison*. Princeton, NJ: Princeton University Press.

Khlevniuk, O. (2004). *The history of the Gulag: From collectivization to the great terror.* Yale University Press.

Kramer, M. (1999). "Ideology and the cold war." *Review of International Studies* 25, no. 4: 539–576.

Kruttschnitt, C., and Gartner, R. (2005). *Marking time in the golden state: Women's imprisonment in California.* New York: Cambridge University Press.

Kotz A. (2006). Riots in prison camps Komsomolskaya Pravda. https://www.kp.ru/daily/23650/49406/.

Kuran, T. (2004). *Islam and Mammon: The economic predicaments of Islamism.* Princeton University Press,

Kuran, T. (2012). *The long divergence: How Islamic law held back the Middle East.* Princeton University Press.

Lessing, B., and Denyer Willis, G. (2019). "Legitimacy in criminal governance: Regulating a drug empire from behind bars." *American Political Science Review.*

Liebling, A. (2004). *Prisons and their moral performance: A study of values, quality, and prison life.* Oxford, UK: Oxford University Press.

Lihachov, D. (1995). *Memories.* Logos.

Maimonides, M. (1956). *The guide for the perplexed.* Vol. 351. Courier Corporation.

Malet, D (2013). *Foreign fighters: Transnational identity in civil conflicts.* Oxford University Press.

Mironova, V. (2019). *From freedom fighters to jihadists: Human resources of non-state armed groups.* Oxford University Press.

Mochulsky, F. (2012). *Gulag boss: A soviet memoir.* Oxford University Press.

Owen, B. A. (1998). *In the mix: Struggle and survival in a women's prison.* Albany, NY: SUNY Press.

Pickenpaugh, R. (2013). *Captives in blue: The Civil War prisons of the Confederacy.* Tuscaloosa: The University of Alabama Press.

Sanín, F., and Wood, E. J. (2014). "Ideology in civil war: Instrumental adoption and beyond." *Journal of Peace Research* 51, no. 2: 213–226.

Shalanov, V. (1994). *Kolyma tales.* Vol. 913. Penguin UK.

Skarbek, D. (2008). "Putting the 'con' into constitutions: The economics of prison gangs." *The Journal of Law, Economics, & Organization* 26, no. 2: 183–211.

Skarbek, D. B. (2010). "Self-governance in San Pedro prison." *The Independent Review* 14, no. 4.

Skarbek, D. (2011). "Governance and prison gangs." *American Political Science Review* 105, no. 4: 702–716.

Skarbek, D. (2012). "Prison gangs, norms, and organizations." *Journal of Economic Behavior & Organization* 82, no. 1: 96–109.

Skarbek, D. (2014). *The social order of the underworld: How prison gangs govern the American penal system.* New York: Oxford University Press.

Skarbek, D. (2016). "Covenants without the sword? Comparing prison self-governance globally." *American Political Science Review* 110, no. 4: 845–862.

Solzhenitsyn, A. (1975). *The Gulag Archipelago.* Vol. 2. Trans. Thomas P. Whitney. New York: Harper.

Stefanskaia, M. (1994). *Chernoe i beloe.* Moscow.

Sykes, G. M. (1958 [2007]). *The society of captives: A study of a maximum security prison.* Princeton, NJ: Princeton University Press.

Trammell, R. (2012). *Enforcing the convict code: Violence and prison culture*. Boulder, CO: Lynne Rienner Publishers.

Vale, Gina. (2019) A minor issue? Trajectories of Islamic States underage members. *Handbook of terrorism and counter terrorism post 9/11*. Edward Elgar Publishing.

Varella, D. (1999). *Lockdown: Inside Brazil's most dangerous prison*. London: Simon & Schuster.

Varese, F. (2011). *Mafias on the move: How organized crime conquers new territories*. Princeton, NJ: Princeton University Press.

Varese, F. (2001). *The Russian mafia: Private protection in a new market economy*. New York: Oxford University Press.

Visotsky, V., and Monchinsky, L. (1992). *Black candle*. Moscow international translators school.

Wang, P. (2017). *The Chinese mafia: Organized crime, corruption, and extra-legal protection*. New York: Oxford University Press.

Yakubovich P. (1896). *In the World of outcasts: Notes of an ex-Katorzanin*. Printing house of Wolfe B.

Index

For the benefit of digital users, indexed terms that span two pages (e.g., 52–53) may, on occasion, appear on only one of those pages.

activisty, 127, 131, 140, 147, 156, 273
A.U.E., 24, 47–48, 49, 75–76, 117–18, 220–21

black prisons, 7, 127, 138, 145–46, 180

card playing, 104, 105, 176, 209
caste system, 5, 13–14, 22, 28, 56, 64, 127, 153, 177, 182, 196, 252
Central Asia, xi, 116, 129, 177, 216, 273
Chechnya, 136, 139, 187, 200, 206, 223–24, 233, 259–60
Chekhov, Anton, 7–8, 104
chifir, 124–25, 194, 210–11, 220
criminal ideology. *See* A.U.E.

Dagestan, 137, 198, 215–16, 220, 221, 240, 256, 261
dawah, 208, 209, 210, 211, 274
defrost, 20, 134, 138–43, 240
Dostoyevsky, Fyodor, 7–8, 105

fenya, 118–19. *See also* prison slang
freeze, 23, 153–58

Gegechkori, Ruslan, 233, 236, 251
gray prisons, 158–60, 266
green prisons, 185, 211, 230–31, 237, 239, 262
Gulag, 1, 6, 35–36, 38, 40–41, 71, 88, 99, 117–18, 124, 150, 274
Gulag Archipelago, 1, 37, 141

hunger strikes, 21, 62, 141

ISIS, 3, 8, 186, 200, 237, 242, 250, 252, 272, 282, 284
ISIS foreign fighters, 3, 200, 204, 206
Islamist ideology, 5, 25, 189–90, 192
Islamist veterans, 3, 185–86, 200, 204, 206, 243

jamaat, 7, 25, 185, 188, 205, 211, 216, 226, 284
  leadership, 188, 197–98, 213–14, 232, 245, 247, 254–55 (*see also* Islamist veterans)

law enforcement, 31

Mikhail Khodorkovsky, 140
Music, 121, 200, 263
mutual fund, 54, 100, 102, 106, 196, 219, 251

neo-Nazis, 262, 263, 265, 269, 274

obshyak. *See* mutual fund

ponyatiya, 56, 72, 75–76, 87–88, 91, 109, 155, 163, 180, 211
prison authorities, 5, 12, 15, 19, 20, 41, 59–60, 66, 70, 75
prison slang, 3, 43, 116, 119, 198–99, 218, 263
progon, 115, 116, 153, 155–56, 227–28, 236

radicalization, 283–84, 285
red prisons, 127, 130, 145, 150, 152, 179
rioting, 21, 62, 142, 153, 170, 230, 240
roads, 18, 22, 113–14

self-harm, 21, 45, 62, 133, 141, 230
Solzhenitsyn, Alexander, 37, 38, 39, 141
suki, 44, 45–46, 120, 123, 124, 163, 180–81
Suki Wars, 44, 45–46, 120, 123, 124, 163, 180–81

tattoos, 48, 51, 122, 123, 224, 268
terrorism, 3, 8, 142–43, 186, 237, 242, 252, 272, 282, 283–84
Thieves in Law, 1, 31. *See also* vory criminal organization
torture, 19, 22, 23, 75, 128, 145, 171, 220–21

Ukraine, 31, 46, 109, 119, 162–63, 283
Umar al-Shishani, 3

White Swan, 150–51, 170, 203
whites (*see* neo-Nazis)